About the Author

John Gurr was born in Gillingham, Kent in 1906, the elder son of John Henry Gurr, a Ship's Corporal (Police Petty Officer) in the Royal Navy, from whom he inherited his love of the sea and ships.

The year after he was born the family moved to Chatham where his brother and sister were born, and in September 1914 his father went down on his ship, HMS Cressy when she was torpedoed, leaving his widow to bring up her family of three on a five shillings a week pension and what she could earn with dressmaking.

From St Paul's C of E Boys' School Chatham, John Gurr gained a scholarship to Chatham Technical Institute where Isaac Keen, M.A. was Principal.

Having passed the entry examination to the Royal Navy as an Artificer Apprentice, John joined HMS Fisgard, the Navy's Mechanical Training Establishment in Portsmouth Harbour, and in December 1926 after a four-and-a-half year Apprenticeship, he was directed to Devonport Division as a result of the Armaments cut-back which had caused a shortage of Artificers in the West Country.

It was a circumstance that was to affect his whole career, and this story is the result . . .

IN PEACE
AND IN WAR

A Chronicle of experiences
in
THE ROYAL NAVY
(1922 to 1946)

Compiled from notes made at the time

of the Events recorded.

John A. Gurr

John A. Gurr
Oct. 1993

A Square One Publication

First published in 1993 by
Square One Publications
Saga House, Sansome Place, Worcester, WR1 1UA

© John A. Gurr 1993

ISBN: 1 872017 72 X

British Library Cataloguing in Publication Data
is available for this book

Typeset by Avon Dataset, Bidford on Avon, Warwickshire B50 4JH
Printed in Great Britain by
Antony Rowe Ltd, Chippenham, Wiltshire

I would like to thank:-
The Portland (Oregon) News' reporter Robert McGuire for his "Firemen have no luck; British too exclusive." article on p. 70.

The Daily Mail (U.K., Malta, or Egyptian) Special Corresppondent, W. F. Harris, for his "McCarthy of the *AJAX* — (An Appreciation of Captain E.D.B. McCarthy, R. N.)" p. 187.

The American Red Cross Club (Shanghai) for the extract from their pamphlet "The Chinese New Year Holiday, 1946", p. 247.
and

Navy News — for publishing my letter, "What happened to *DRAGON*'s dog, Jack?" in October, 1985, and the replies it engendered in December, 1985, and March, 1986, issues. p. 77 and Appendix (B) on p. 276.

John A. Gurr

Contents

FOREWORD
by
Admiral Sir D. P. Dreyer, G.C.B., C.B.E., D.S.C., R.N.

John Gurr has written a fascinating and detailed account of his life in the Royal Navy from 1922 to 1946 covering service in a wide variety of ships from the coal-burning Battleship *Emperor of India* to one of the latest small cruisers built during the war.

His travels carried him to many different countries world-wide where he made many good friends and he gives clear and lively descriptions of places he visited from Home Waters and the Mediterranean to the West Indies and North and South America, Australia and the Far East. But the most vivid parts of his book are the descriptions of his Wartime experiences in H.M.S. *Ajax* at the beginning of the war including the Battle of the River Plate and the very intense period in the Mediterranean in 1941 and 1942. The pressures on our ships at that time emerge very clearly. Then after a brief interval in less demanding work he joined H.M.S. *Euryalus* and went first to the East Indies Fleet and then to the British Pacific Fleet. Again we are made aware of the pressures on our ships during long periods at sea, particularly on the Engineroom Department amongst whom Mr. Gurr played a very prominent role as the Chief Engine Room Artificer.

At the end of the book he expresses the hope that he served the Navy well. After reading this account of his activities I have not the slightest doubt that he could not have served it better or more effectively.

He has written an absorbing Chronicle of his Naval Career.

Desmond Dreyer

PREFACE

An old adage has it that there is a story in everyone, and this is *my* story, which I hope will convey to the reader how life was during my time in the Royal Navy in the years between two World Wars, and continuing until a year after the end of the second of those wars.

A number of coincidences were significant in my career, and I consider myself to have been fortunate with my ships and stations, and to have visited so many parts of the world before the days of 'Package Holidays', mass travel and modern development; before the creed of 'greed-and-grab' polluted almost everywhere; when people were still friendly and generous with their help, there was space to move in towns, villages and the countryside; and Servicemen wore their uniforms with pride.

I recall pleasant jaunts, and meeting folk from practically every social level in life.

My story is garnered from diaries and notes written between the years 1922 and 1946, with details of incidents — dates, times, places, people (and some great personalities), and with accounts of events such as battles, bombings, bombardments etc, often written up within a few hours of their occurrence, sometimes with the help of gunners, signalmen or messmates. But it is essentially MY story, the story of my hopes and frustrations from the day I joined the Navy direct from school, a few weeks before my sixteenth birthday, until I was discharged to Pension on my fortieth birthday, September 30th, 1946.

John A. Gurr

CHAPTER 1

Joining

"You are hereby informed that, by an Admiralty Order, you have been approved for entry into the Royal Navy as an Artificer Apprentice, and allotted to the Training Establishment at Portsmouth. You should, therefore, join His Majesty's Ship *Fisgard* at Portsmouth before 6 p.m. on the 8th of August 1922. A Railway Pass for your journey is enclosed. A Petty Officer Instructor will be at the Main Gate of the Dockyard to meet you from 4 p.m... etc." (Signed) C. P. Beaty-Pownall, Capt. R.N.

The above is a copy of part of the Notice I received on July 28th 1922, — a letter I had awaited since taking part with some two-thousand other 15- to 16-year-old boys from all over the U.K., in the Civil Service Examination for entry into one of the Royal Dockyards (Portsmouth, Chatham, Devonport or Rosyth), or into the Royal Navy as an Artificer Apprentice. The exam had taken place over two days the previous April, the results being published on June 9th and I was pleased when my Headmaster called me to his study to tell me I had been successful. I had been assisted by Nomination on account of my father, a Petty Officer (Naval Police), who had been killed when his ship, H.M.S. *Cressy* was torpedoed with her sister cruisers, *Hogue* and *Aboukir* on September 22nd 1914.

Of the few boys from Chatham Junior Technical Institute who sat the exam. I was the only one to opt for the Navy; the others had chosen the local Dockyard and early in July I had to report at H.M.S. *Pembroke*, (Chatham Naval Barracks) for a Medical examination and to be interviewed by a Board of three Officers. Having answered all their questions satisfactorily, I then waited for the 'call', and on Tuesday, August 8th duly travelled to Portsmouth and at the Dockyard Gate met up with most of the other 24 boys from various parts of the country who were to form the new "A" Class of Apprentices and with whom I would live, work and play for the next four-and-a-half years.

The Petty Officer Instructor escorted us in to the Yard to the harbour launch and the twenty-minute trip to the *Fisgard* Establishment moored off the tiny village of Hardway where we arrived just before six o'clock.

Lively spirits were well in evidence during the short journey with the Petty Officer being addressed as "Cap'n" and "Admiral" and being asked the name of our 'next port of call' and 'expected time of arrival', and some of the lads celebrated by throwing their redundant school-caps into the water — receiving mild reprimands for littering the harbour.

On board we were mustered at the Regulating Office for all particulars to be taken before we were conducted to the vast dining-deck where supper was ready on a mess-table. When we had finished eating we were taken to our living quarters on the Chest Flat to be issued with our hammocks and bedding and given instructions on how to sling a hammock, how to climb into it and get out again, and how to lash it up for stowage. And, of course, we were introduced to the bathroom deck, and to the heads (toilets) right in the bows of the ship.

As its name implies, the Chest Flat was where the sea-chests of all the apprentices were located, rows upon rows and each chest having a brass plate with the owner's name stamped on it, for up until about that time the sea-chest was the sole property of the individual and remained with him throughout his service career. It was about 2 feet in height by 4 feet long and 2 feet deep, painted black and contained one long drawer at the bottom with two smaller drawers side by side above, all lockable. There was a back-board with some dozen brass screws which could be transferred to cover the front of the chest when its owner had been on the move between ships. All kit and personal belongings were to be stored in our chests, and in small wooden ditty-boxes which were stowed on bulkhead racks.

At 9.30 p.m. we were told to turn-in and that lights-out would be at ten o'clock. We were tired. We were excited, and I think most of us were feeling a little homesick and wondering just what we had let ourselves in for, but there was still jollity and a lot of skylarking that first night as our attempts to clamber into our 'micks' became successful and we swung and deliberately bumped against each other, talking until lights-out and learning more about our new 'family'.

Reveille was at 6.15 and breakfast at seven after which we were given another lesson on How to Lash a Hammock Neatly for Stowing. During the morning we were issued with our kit — two of everything from caps to boots and shoes (except for suits) plus a greatcoat, an oilskin, and a pair of brown canvas shoes for evening-wear on board. Every item of clothing had to be marked with owner's name in black ink or paint, using the wooden block carved with ½″ letters for each individual apprentice. Hammocks and bedding had to be marked in 1″ lettering using separate wooden dies. (One boy earned a life-long nickname when he inadvertently used the "J" for his first initial upside-down — so that it looked to be a 'hook' — and with his second initial being "E" he was immediately called "Hookey", and remained "Hookey" to all his classmates thereafter.)

The tailor arrived that afternoon to take measurements for our uniforms — two serge single-breasted suits with black buttons for wear on board, and one tartan-cloth, double-breasted suit with brass buttons for Number One going-ashore rig.

Also on this, our first full day, all the other apprentices returned from their 3-weeks Summer leave, I suppose about 900 of them, and almost half the number would be just as new to *Fisgard* as were we "A" Class.

For reasons of national economy the sister training establishment *Indus* at Devonport was shut down in July and all her classes would now integrate their respective levels in *Fisgard*, and for those same reasons our Entry of 25 boys was the smallest number so far. The previous Entry in January had been 64 boys and prior to that the average intakes were 100 each August and 70 each January — the January entries being by Nomination from selected Secondary schools and Colleges with an Entry Examination each November.

Our first two weeks were spent exercising — drilling and marching, playing cricket, football and rugby, either on board in the gymnasium or at the Sports Ground about half-a-mile from the ship, and every morning we went swimming in the Tray, a floating wooden-framed 'pool' about 50-feet by 20-feet which was moored to a pontoon midway along the bridge connecting ship to shore at Hardway village about one hundred yards from the ship. We were also instructed in the art of Boat-pulling in heavy gigs and whalers, all very exhausting but keeping us fit and healthy, and at the end of the second week we had to take the Swimming Test by donning a duck suit and swimming three lengths of the Tray and then staying afloat for a further two minutes in the water-logged suit. There were no failures. With those two weeks behind us we then began our real training to become artificers, working at the benches in the Factory ship and learning how to use hammers, cold-chisels and files and working with mild steel and cast iron. Hands soon became hardened and the blisters, cuts and bruises caused through mis-hits soon healed. Our Instructors were pensioner Chief and Engine Room Artificers and to us they appeared as old as the hills!

The *Fisgard* Establishment was a group of four old ships — two of them hulks — numbered Fisgard I, II, III, and IV, moored in pairs off Hardway. 'Fizzy' III was connected to the shore by the 6-feet-wide bridge, and she was the ex-*Terrible*, a heavy cruiser bult in 1895 and was the accommodation-ship for all apprentices and besides our living-quarters she had the Regulating Office, Post Office, Chapel, gymnasium, laundry, N.A.A.F.I. canteen shop, Barber's shop and eight class-rooms — all on the upper deck. The next deck down contained the Port and Starboard dining-rooms with galleys and serveries amidships where our meals were served at table by a host of Naval pensioners termed 'Gobbies' (Origin unknown).

Aft of the dining-room were the "J" Class flat and the Senior Recreation Room with its full-sized billiard table, writing-desks, book-shelves and easy-chairs. There was also a Hobbies Room and a Dark-room for amateur photographers. Below that deck was the Chest Flat Deck where we lived and slept, and there was a Junior Recreation Room with a three-quarter-sized billiard table, a Ping-pong table, a couple of writing-tables and some chairs, and alongside that room was a Music Room with an upright piano. The deck below that — the lowest for apprentices — consisted of bathrooms, salt-water showers and a huge plunge-bath, ideal for use when returning from our sporting activites on shore or in the gymnasium.

'Fizzy' I — lying astern of III and connected to her by a brow — was the ex-*Spartiate*, another heavy cruiser, built in 1898 and accommodating the Captain, Officers and general crew and the Administration Offices. Apprentices were not allowed to board 'Fizzy' I, abreast of which was 'Fizzy' II. She was an old hulk, the ex-*Hindustan* — 4th. rate ship of the Line built in 1844 and now contained several fitting-shops with work-benches, and some general machine-shops and turneries. Ahead of her was the fourth of the group — another hulk — the ex-*Sultan* (vintage 1870's iron-clad) fitted out with the heavier machines of the boilermakers and enginesmiths' shops, pattern-makers and moulder shops, the foundry and the Main Stores. She was of course, 'Fizzy' IV lying abreast of 'III' — all four being connected by brows — and when crossing from ship to ship on our way to work and back all apprentices had to move at the double.

Apprentices were split into four Divisions — Anson, Benbow, Grenville and Rodney, with divisional colours of white, blue, green and red respectively for recognition and sporting activities, and there was keen rivalry in all categories and all events.

Our days were full. We were called at 0630, breakfast was at 0700 and we were at our work-benches or machines by 0745 until 0900 when we returned to the gymnasium to muster by Divisions for Prayers, after which a couple of classes remained in the gym for 15-minutes of Activity Exercises before everyone went back to work again until 1145 when overalls were taken off and we trooped over to Fizzy III to get cleaned for mid-day dinner. At 1 p.m. we were at work again until 4 p.m. and then everybody cleaned and dressed in evening rig of check shirt with collar and tie, serge suit and brown canvas shoes, ready for tea and at 5.30 p.m. on three- or four- evenings a week we attended school until 7.30 p.m. Then it was supper-time and the rest of the day was our own.

I think that most of us had the idea that when we joined the Navy we had finished with school, as such, for good, but we just carried on from where we had left off and had even more subjects in our syllabus, for in addition to maths, science, history, geography and English there were lectures on Engineering Heat and Steam, Electricity, and Machine-drawing, all Masters and Lecturers being drawn from the top schools and colleges of Portsmouth.

Relaxing after school and supper was not difficult. One could sit on one's sea-chest (quite hard) and read or talk to one's neighbours, or go to the gym to romp on the equipment, skylark, or have a sing-song at the piano. If you were lucky you might be able to get a game of billiards in the Rec. room, but even so — that was a strenuous and generally frustrating pastime because a ship does not remain on an even keel for very long. Fuel, water, provisions and stores coming on board altered the trim, as did the consumption of such items and during the course of a game the balls would begin to run 'downhill' of their own volition or take a curving line after being struck with the cue, and then it was a case of a strong back being needed by one of the players to take the weight while another used the spirit-level (which was always kept handy) and adjusted the screwed legs until the table was level again — sometimes not for long!

Juniors — "D" Class and below — had to turn-in at 9.30 p.m. and lights-out was at ten. Seniors need not turn-in until 10.30 p.m. with lights-out for them at eleven.

Each Division had one afternoon for sport and recreation during the week and proceeded to the Playing-fields for organised games or drill, or maybe a route-march or trot around the local country roads and lanes. As regards shore-leave, Juniors were allowed ashore on their one school-free evening from 4.30 until 9 o'clock, and Seniors — having dropped the subjects of History and Geography at school — could now have two evenings ashore, until 10 o'clock.

Factory work finished at noon on Saturdays and leave was given from 1 p.m. until the same 9 p.m. and 10 p.m. limits and again on Sunday, there being no all-night leave — even for those who lived locally, except by extra-special request.

On Sundays we were not called until 0700 and it was always egg and bacon for breakfast. Then we donned our No. 1 uniforms ready for Divisions at nine and Captain's Inspection after which a Junior Class was detailed to rig church in the gymnasium and un-rig after the Service, which was always boisterously sung. At one o'clock we were all at liberty to go ashore if we so wished — either by "Gosport Liner" (ferry boat) direct from the ship to Harbour Station Pier — Fare One Penny, or by walking from Hardway to Gosport and take the ferry from there to Harbour Station — Fare One Half-penny — quite a money-saver.

Our pay was six-shillings per week, paid fortnightly, during our first year, rising to eight-shillings in the second year, twelve in the third and sixteen-shillings in the final year and a half.

Abreast of our four ships and about 500-yards away across the harbour the laid-up light-battlecruiser *Courageous* was moored, a beautiful ship of 19,000-tons, about 800-feet long, with sleek and graceful lines with one broad funnel, a single 18″ gun turret forward and another aft. She was really handsome to look at and we thought she was a permanent fixture until a morning in October when she was towed away down the harbour, leaving a terrific gap in our lives as we wondered where she had gone. It was as though a favourite picture had been stolen; all that was left was a vast expanse of mud-flats stretching miles across to Portsea Island. We were happy to see her back in her berth in December — after her docking period in Portsmouth Dockyard. Our picture had been returned to its place on the wall!

The Entry of 25 apprentices was made up of 16 Engine Room, 6 Ordnance, and 3 Electrical branch (their own preferences on joining), and during the first six-months we all did the same school and factory work, at the end of which period we 16 Engine Room Artificer Apprentices were allotted our Trades. There were four categories — Fitter & Turner, Boilermaker, Enginesmith, and Coppersmith — and we were asked to state our preference in order of choice on our exam paper. After work one December afternoon we mustered in Study 7 in the presence of the Superintendent Engineer and the four Divisional Engineer Officers, and as each of our names was called so our Trade followed. My name was called. — "Enginesmith" — It had been my second choice. Two further names and trades and then a third — but before a Trade could be announced my name was called again and *my* trade was altered to Fitter & Turner and that third name became an Enginesmith. (Many years later I learned from another class-mate that 'Enginesmith' bore a personal grudge against me throughout his Naval career. I did not know!) So we had eleven fitters and turners, two boilermakers, two coppersmiths and just that one enginesmith, and I think that change of trade affected the whole direction of my career in the Navy, as will be seen.

Christmas 1922 came and with it 14-days home leave, a very welcome break and with two other lads who lived in my area I travelled home. (Fare:- £1-0-6d. Portsmouth Harbour to Chatham via London, and back.)

Returning in January, we were no longer "A" boys because another class of New Entries had arrived and we were now "B" Class. The new "A" Class was only 24 strong, but subsequent entries rose again to between 60 and 100. We were off the bottom rung of the ladder.

Our Senior years began in 1924 when we all reached our 18th birthdays and signed 'on the dotted line' to serve for 12 years in the Navy. We worked hard, but what free time we had we used to the full. 1926, and our penultimate term began. In addition to our factory and school work we had several outings, making visits to some of the massive machine-shops in Portsmouth Dockyard, going aboard the battleship *Queen Elizabeth* to see the main engines being opened for inspection and to the battlecruiser *Repulse* when her boilers were being re-tubed. On February 16th. we were part of the official party at the launch of the County Class cruiser *Suffolk*, built in Portsmouth. Then there was a trip to sea for a day in Submarine

L6. The Submarine Service was composed entirely of volunteers and in order to attract more men into the Service these trips were taken to demonstrate how safe the boats are.

At a point some miles south of the Isle of Wight her Captain — a young-ish Lt. Commander — took the boat 40-feet below the surface and gave a short lecture then allowed each of us a view of the Channel shipping through the periscope — and there were quite a few craft about. He then took us in a steep dive as further proof of safety and told us he would have 'looped-the-loop' had there been less traffic about! One of the class was heard to say, "Blimey! L6 — Hell Quick!" It was an exciting experience, but we still had more months of apprenticeship to complete.

When we returned from Summer leave in August *we* were the new "J" Class — the top dogs — and our sea-chests had been moved to the "J" Class flat. We were the elite. Our final term had begun.

Everyone of the Class passed the final exams which were both written tests and a Passing Out Test Job. (Failure in either Exams or the Test Job meant automatic deferment for six months to tackle both again, and a second failure would result in discharge from the Service.)

Every day of our last two weeks before Christmas we were taken ashore to Portsmouth Naval Barracks for rifle and small-arms drill and to attend lectures on the Traditions and Customs of the Royal Navy which included a visit to Nelson's flagship, *Victory,* and culminated in a Passing-Out parade with inspection by the Commodore.

Our Passing-out Dinner on December 21st was a very festive affair with about half the members passing out before the end of the evening, and the following morning we dispersed to our homes for the real Festive Season. The first episode of our naval careers was ended.

CHAPTER 2

Emperor of India Atlantic Fleet

We returned to *Fisgard* on January 5th 1927 to collect kit-bags, hammocks and tool-boxes and supervised their loading onto the Gosport Liner for transport to the Naval Barracks. Another adventure had begun. As we disembarked at North Corner we were in time to watch the battlecruiser *Renown* leaving harbour on her way to Australia with the Duke and Duchess of York on board. They were going to open the new Parliament Buildings in Canberra and it was a splendid sight with the ship manned, moving slowly past and the Royal Marine Band playing on the quarterdeck.

In barracks we waited to learn our next move and spending our time drilling on the Square and a visit to the *Suffolk* which was still fitting-out in the dockyard. Then, on January 14th I was told to be ready at 8.30 next morning to "take passage to join the battleship *Revenge*, 2nd Battle Squadron, Mediterranean Fleet, Malta."

We were all at the Drafting Office at 8.30 on that Saturday morning the 15th, when I and four class-mates had had our drafts changed and were told we were to join the battleship *Emperor of India*, and at six o'clock next morning the Dockyard tug *Sprite* transported us out to the aircraft-carrier *Furious* which sailed at 11 a.m. for Portland, dropping anchor there at 4.15 p.m. We were allowed to spend the rest of the afternoon on the flight-deck watching aircraft being flown aboard from shore bases, which was quite a thrill. Picket-boats and motor-boats from the many ships in the harbour were soon coming alongside to collect the many ratings who had taken passage from Pompey, and our Class was split even further as a chugging old motor-launch from the 'E. of I.' came at 7.30 p.m. to take us to our new home. We were welcomed by the Mess President who arranged a late supper for us and issued our Joining Cards which gave information regarding our various Stations for Daywork, Watchkeeping, Action, Fire, Abandon ship, etc., and number and positions of our clothes and bathroom lockers.

At eight o'clock next morning the whole Fleet weighed anchor and steamed down the channel and into the Bay of Biscay. It was a truly magnificent sight — but we were not sight-seers anymore. The Fleet comprised the two most modern battleships of the Navy, (*Nelson* and *Rodney*), the aircraft carriers *Furious* and *Argus*, the battlecruisers *Hood* (the world's biggest warship) and *Repulse* and *Tiger*; our 3rd Battle Squadron of *Iron Duke*, *Benbow* and *Emperor of India*. The fourth ship of

8

the squadron was the *Marlborough* which had been detached to replace *Revenge* in the Mediterranean Fleet. There were also eight 'C' Class cruisers, 27-destroyers, two mine-sweeping sloops and an ocean-going tug towing a huge target.

My first employment was to work in No. 3 Hydraulic Room under supervision of a senior E.R.A. and it was a rather 'hairy-scary' experience at first, for besides the huge hydraulic pump which supplied water at 1,400-lbs./sq. inch to the five turrets for elevating and training the ten 13.5″ guns there were two air-compressors pumping air at 5,000-lbs./sq. in. for charging torpedoes and for blowing-out the gun-barrels after firing, and the noise and commotion was terrific as the machines raced when turrets and guns were being operated.

Biscay was not rough but the giant Atlantic rollers coming broadside at us made for considerable discomfort and as we steamed line-abreast it was possible at one minute to be able to see just the tops of the masts of the ships on either side, and the next minute their bilge-keels would be visible. Exercises were being carried out day and night and when it was possible to get out on deck for a few minutes it was very exciting to watch the destroyers making dummy attacks on the big ships and to see the vast number of ships spread in all directions as far as the eye could range. Such sea-room enabled the Fleet to split into two sections — the Red and the Blue — parting for many hours and then seeking to find each other in mock battle by day or by night. During these 'games' we were closed up at Action Stations and the look-outs on deck had to keep extremely alert, particularly at night as all ships were darkened. Everything would be so very quiet on the upper deck until, suddenly a star-shell would burst in the pitch-black sky announcing that one side, the Red or the Blue, had spotted the other and then there would be a flurry of Aldis-lamp signals flashing from ship to ship, steaming lights would be switched on and we could all relax again.

Emperor of India and her sister-ships were built in 1914/15 and fought at the Battle of Jutland. Each was of 25,000-tons with four shafts driven by Parsons single-reduction geared turbines of 29,000-Horsepower located two sets in the Centre Engine Room and one set in each of the Port and Starboard Wing Engine Rooms, steam at 220-lbs/sq. in. supplied by eighteen boilers, six in each of three boiler-rooms, three furnaces to each boiler and they were coal-fired.

We five new boys were still under training as Artificers 5th Class for a further year and our pay had risen from 16-shillings a week to six shillings and sixpence a day.

A 3-watch system was kept whereby everyone did 24-hours on watch over a three-day period, starting Day One with the Forenoon Watch (8 a.m. till noon), then the Last Dog Watch (6 p.m. till 8 p.m.). Day Two

The Regatta Trophies won by H.M.S. 'Emperor of India' in the 3rd B.S. Regatta. June 1928 at Lamlach.

began with the morning watch (4 a.m. till 8 a.m.) followed by the First Dog (4 p.m. till 6 p.m.) and Day Three was the long one, beginning with the Middle Watch (midnight till 4 a.m.) then the Afternoon (noon till 4 p.m.) and the First Watch (8 p.m. till midnight — and it would be closer to 1 a.m. by the time we had bathed and got rid of the coal-dust). The night watches were the hardest because it was then that we had to expel all the ashes and clinker cleaned from the furnaces during the day. The ash-expeller was worked up to top speed to build the water pressure necessary to jet the ashes through the bottom of the ship and not allow a flood-back into the boiler-room. With full pressure attained we had to swing the huge lever over smartly while stokers began shovelling the debris through the heavy square-holed hopper, smashing the bigger masses of clinker through the grill using 7-lb. hammers. Occasionally an awkward lump lodged across the water-jet causing a flood-back and the lever, a huge, heavy thing, had to be thrown back quickly to shut the hole in the ship's bottom, and the pump had to shut down, the hopper grill lifted away with the aid of ropes and pulleys and the duty 'muggins' (whoever of our five was on watch) had to hang head-first into the pit to remove the obstruction while the bilge-pumps ran flat-out.

As part of our training — 'Start at the bottom and know the lot!' — (except that we did not have to trim coal from the bunkers) — we did our stint at firing the boilers and cleaning the fires, a process entailing shifting the burning coal across the bars to the adjacent furnace using the 12-feet-long heavy rakes and slices, levering the clinker from the fire-bars and raking it forward onto the plates to be drenched with fire-hoses, spluttering with clouds of steam, and raking ashes from the ash-pit to be shovelled into skids and emptied close to the expeller. The fire was then re-spread and stoked.

Sometimes while steaming a fire-bar would become dislodged and fall into the pit, allowing a great deal of fire to follow so that a replacement had to be fitted as quickly as possible. The firing would be pushed to one side and if the gap was towards the front it was comparatively easy to drop a new bar into place. Should the gap occur at the back of the furnace it was a different matter for it meant using a giant pair of tongs about 12-feet long and muscular arms to manoeuvre the new bar into position, and if there happened to be an obstruction at the point to prevent the bar slotting in then it had to be put in by hand. The Chief Stoker would call for a volunteer stoker who, over the top of his working rig of flannel shirt, fearnaught trousers and wooden clogs would be equipped with dark-glassed goggles, asbestos gloves and a really wet coal-sack, shaped to form a cowl to drape over his head and shoulders. A stout rope was tied about his waist and looped round one ankle so that he could be quickly hauled from the furnace in an emergency, and he would scramble rapidly into Hell's mouth while the rest of the Steaming Watch hoped for success at his first attempt and he would be pulled out to receive a congratulatory "Well done, lad!" from the Chief.

Firing of the furnaces was supposed to be regulated by the Kilroy Indicator controlled and set by the Engineer of the Watch in the engine-room which told the boiler-room by the ringing of a bell and a pointer on its dial how many shovels of coal were to be 'fired' in a numbered furnace each time it rang, but the Chief Stoker usually ignored the 'Kill-joy' — as the stokers called it — and used his own discretion as long as he kept steam at 220-lbs./sq. in. pressure.

'Coaling Ship' was quite an evolution and every man in the ship — except the Captain and the Chiefs and E.R.A.'s — was employed in some capacity in the operation. (*We* carried on with our normal jobs of engine and boiler maintenance). Senior officers wore white overalls, doing the organizing and keeping things moving. Stewards, writers and supply ratings acted as tally-clerks to keep count of the numbers of sacks and baskets coming on board. Chiefs and Petty Officers and Royal Marines manned the ship's winches and derricks used in co-operation with the collier's cranes to hoist the huge nets filled with sacks and baskets of coal inboard. Seamen and stokers worked in the collier's holds filling the nets, while other stokers were in the ship's bunkers trimming the coal down and filling them in their proper order. Catering staff and cooks were busy getting the meals — mainly corned beef — or cheese sandwiches, liberally laced with coal-dust, and mugs of tea or cocoa, which were taken in shifts so as not to interfere with progress, and the Royal Marine Band, perched on top of a turret played lively music intended to keep the workers happy and on the move all day long.

The main idea was to take in as much coal as we needed in the shortest possible time, usually about 2,000-tons at 200-tons per hour, all of it down the chutes and into the bunkers (inner, outers, uppers, lowers, ports and starboards, for'ards and afts) the stokers working as fast as they could. The ships of the squadron competed with one another, the times and quantities being recorded. "Must be bettered next time!"

On the day before coaling all air-vents and fan inlets were closed and sealed; doors of offices and enclosed messes had sheets of newspaper gummed over the louvred upper panels, and on the morning of coaling-day the doors themselves were sealed with gummed paper strips round the edges as they would probably remain shut until coaling was completed. Even so, the dust managed to find its way everywhere despite those measures. And there was no "Dress of the Day". The ship's company could wear whatever rig they chose and took full advantage of the fact by dressing in the most outlandish gear, looking more like a bunch of pirates. It was a happy-go-lucky day but always a number of accidents to keep the doctors and Sick Berth staff busy; someone would fall into the collier's hold and others were hit by the swinging net — empty or fully-laden. Some tripped over the trailing wires and ropes, and hands got caught in the drums of winches. And the band played on!

When the collier moved off the seamen hosed the decks with sea water and the ship's company cleaned themselves, but there was coal-dust about for days and it was always easy to spot a man on shore who was serving in a coal-burner by the ingrained particles, especially around his eyes. Coaling took place about once a month depending on the amount of steaming and sea-time put in, and whether a Full Power Trial had taken place in the interval.

A Full Power Trial was both gruelling and hectic with all boilers and every bit of steam-driven machinery being used to maximum capacity at the one time and for at least one hour's duration, and every member of the Engineering department — whichever previous watch he had kept — was required below to take part. The Engineer Commander, known as 'the Old Man', was the supremo controlling from the Centre Engine-room. His second-in-command, the Senior Engineer, had a roving commission visiting every machinery space and all boiler-rooms and the shaft-tunnels through to the stern tubes, receiving reports at all positions where men were taking temperatures and pressures every half-hour.

The Chief E.R.A. boilermaker looked after all boilers throughout the trial and the other chiefs acted as seconds-in-command to the engineer lieutenants in the three engine-rooms. Senior E.R.A's operated throttles while not-so-senior ones moved about taking readings from, and adjusting bearings of, all moving machinery and noting general behaviour of pumps.

We 'sprogs' were perched on the upper gratings over the boilers in dry, exhausting heat, ready to replace water-level gauges when they shattered. On the plates twenty-or-more feet below us a Warrant Engineer and Chief Stoker supervised as the Kilroy's urgent clanging called for more and more fuel to be fed to the hungry furnaces. Stoker P.O's urged the stoker to more effort and speed in filling the skids with coal to keep the 'firers' supplied. Other junior E.R.A.'s kept constant watch on feed- bilge- and fire-pumps and operated the ash-expellers as required, and white-overalled Sub-lieutenants flitted about the place shining their electric torches at anything and everything (already well-illuminated) that caught their eyes. One actually opened a furnace-door and shone his torch at the gleaming white flames — normally looked at through a hand-held, very dark glass — "Just to see if the firing was level," he said.

As speed was worked up the noise, vibration and commotion increased and was terrific throughout, and it was even worse when, during the Trial there was a "Full-calibre, full-charge" salvo fired from all ten big guns, felt especially in the boiler-rooms as coal- and asbestos-dust showered from tops of boilers and pipes and a couple of gauge-glasses burst with great rushes of steam and boiling water and we 'sprogs' had to fit new glasses as quickly as possible.

At the end of the hour revolutions were reduced, excess machinery shut down and some boilers were disconnected, and life began to return to normal. All records and readings taken from start to finish of the Trial were delivered to the Engineers' Office for assessment and collating and were passed to the Fleet Engineer and thence to the Admiralty, and it was easy to tell that it had all been a success by the wide grins on the faces of everyone from the 'Old Man' down to the 2nd Class stokers. As soon as the boilers were cool enough they were opened to check for any distortion to water-tubes or furnaces. But there was always an aftermath, for the continuous high speed resulted in extra wear-and-tear on all moving parts, and the vibration, especially from the firing of the big guns started leaks in lots of joints and glands. It all meant extra work for our Department.

After our mock battles the Fleet split into several sections to pay Courtesy visits to Spanish north-west ports — our 3rd Battle Squadron with some cruisers and destroyers anchoring off Vigo.

This was my first time out of England, my first foreign port, and I didn't think much of it! The town was small, more a large village, hilly and dirty and a couple of afternoon walks for us was quite enough to see what little there was to see, and sample the Spanish wine.

On January 23rd we fired a 15-gun salute in honour of King Alphonso's birthday, and in the afternoon all the ships were Open to Visitors. In the evening a spectacular Searchlight Display by all ships was much appreciated by the crowds on shore with a really loud cheer. The show began with all searchlight beams focused and froze on a single point in the black sky. Then the weaving and wheeling started, making patterns all over in synchronised moves for what seemed an age. Then the light beams froze again at the starting-point for half-a-minute before they faded as though controlled by a single switch, the perfect timing bringing praise from the Flagship.

Leaving Vigo on the 26th we met the rest of the Fleet and had exercises and mock attacks before anchoring in *Gibraltar Bay* late on the 28th. Ah! This was better. Clean streets — or Street, as there was only the one — Main Street, and the weather was so much better, warm and sunny, after the grey and stormy days in the north Atlantic; *Emperor of India*, *Benbow*, the two aircraft-carriers and a couple of the cruisers had to anchor miles out in the bay which meant a very long boat-trip to get ashore. The flagships were secured alongside the Mole inside the harbour, the other cruisers tied up at buoys also inside and the destroyers safely in their Pens.

My class-mates and I were still employed on watchkeeping duties and so were able to get ashore some afternoons and going to the top of the Rock is a 'must' for every visitor. We made the climb up the long winding road to the 1,467-feet summit on a Sunday afternoon with visibility perfect and the effort was rewarded by the wonderful view, calculating the horizon as being about 15-miles — mostly the sea but also over a very barren-looking bit of Spain, although we could pick out a few tiny villages nestling in the hills. Back down to the town we enjoyed a rest and some tea in the Y.M.C.A. before making the long trip out to the ship.

We went to sea with the Fleet on a couple of occasions but were fortunately back at our anchorage on February 10th when our sister-ship *Marlborough* passed through on her way home from Malta where she had been a replacement for *Revenge* (refitting at home). I say 'fortunately' because my brother was serving in her and I was able to see him before his ship left again. On the 25th the Fleet sailed for more Courtesy-calls — this time to ports on Spain's Mediterranean coast — and *we* anchored more than a mile off-shore at Malaga for a five-day visit. On the second day, when *I* was able to go ashore the motor-launch had broken down so the 'powers-that-be' decided the sailing-pinnace would take libertymen ashore at 4.40 p.m., not a great distance to sail but there was very little wind and it took two-hours. There was little time to see the town but although it was small it was certainly a lot cleaner than Vigo and we enjoyed a walk and a glass of wine and arrived back at the jetty for the 8 p.m. boat back. Alas, by then there was no wind at all: Sails were hoisted and the boat's crew cast her off and we drifted away until a strong current took charge of the boat and — away we went as darkness quickly fell and *Emperor of India* faded into the night. There were some thirty men in the boat and luckily the oars had been left in her, so we 'shipped' them and we all toiled laboriously against a strong tide for more than two-hours to get back 'home'. Such are the pleasues of lying far out, but after that incident sails were not relied on. The motor-launch was used but she was unreliable and frequently had to be rescued by one of our steam picket-boats.

We steamed away on March 2nd to re-join our squadron and the Fleet but instead had to increase speed to 19-knots to rush a sick seaman to hospital at Gibraltar. A launch met us outside the Breakwater at dawn next day to take the patient and we steamed through the Strait out into the Atlantic where we re-joined the Fleet 24-hours later.

We were all well clear of Gib because the Mediterranean Fleet was on its way from Malta and would come looking for us to do battle with them after a game of hide and seek, and at midnight on March 8th we assumed 'Battle Stations', living and sleeping at our posts. 'Enemy' cruisers were sighted on the horizon the following evening. They laid a smoke-screen and disappeared behind it and a night of extreme activity began as speeds were increased and reduced, sometimes stopping altogether then moving off again; telegraph- and Kilroy-bells clanging, and at dawn the 'enemy' ships were in sight. Lights were flashing from every bridge and signal-deck either to simulate gunfire or to pass messages, and that night we were all back in port — more than a hundred ships — so many more had to anchor way out in the bay. E. of I's first order was 'Prepare for Coaling. Collier due alongside at 0700" — more panic to get everything ready and then she was 26-hours late in arriving! Taking in 2,000-tons of coal and the subsequent cleaning-down occupied the whole week-end.

All ships gave shore-leave from 4 p.m. until 10 or 11 p.m. each night and from 1 p.m. on Saturdays and Sundays so the Rock was alive with thousands of mateloes and marines. I met one of my uncles who was serving in *Royal Oak* as Chief Shipwright, spending a pleasant evening with him in the Garrison Sergeants' Mess on the Rock where Chiefs and P.O's had an open invitation to enjoy the amenities. The bars and souvenir shops did record business in that hectic week and then we, the Atlantic Fleet, left for home. Biscay was too rough for our 'Speed and Consumption' trial which had been planned for that part of the voyage. It was quite a relief when, on March 28th, the Devonport-manned ships

15

entered Plymouth Sound and proceeded up harbour for Easter leave to be given.

Returning from leave on April 13th the 2nd Watch went on their leave, leaving us to move the ship to the Coaling Wharf and take in 2,000-tons ready for when we steamed up Channel on May 3rd to the Fleet assembly point at Portland where we spent a week of intensive basic training in Harbour drills and Boat-work for the New Entries — Seamen and Stokers. The Fleet then had three-days steaming up to Cromarty Firth from whence we carried out day-and-night exercises in the North Sea.

There was not a lot to do ashore except play football — ship versus ship and Department versus Department, the matches always keenly competitive and attracting large gatherings of supporters. Of course, the Naval Canteen and Cinema also attracted the crowds and it was quite hectic at the jetty every night when the Canteen closed and all the ships' drifters came to pick up their human cargo. (All capital ships had their own 'attached' tenders — drifters — in Home waters to ferry liberty-men to and from shore and to collect stores and mail. Our's was *Noontide*.)

The Fleet moved north to Scapa Flow, anchoring on June 7th amongst the wrecks of the scuttled German High Seas Fleet and we took in another 2,000-tons of coal before the ships dispersed to visit Scottish holiday resorts. *E. of I.* received a great welcome at Oban and attracted thousands on board on the two 'open' afternoons, proving a godsend to the local boatmen who augmented their earnings considerabley during our stay. Preparations were now under way for the Fleet Regatta and every day, mornings and evenings, boats' crews were out training in the whalers, gigs and cutters, ready for the big event which was to be held at our next port of call, Lamlash on the Isle of Arran.

Two days had been set aside to accommodate the regatta but there was only time to complete three events before the weather deteriorated and all ships had to raise steam to ride out the next 48-hours. I rowed in that third race in the E.R.A.'s gig — placed fourth out of eight boats.

When the gale eased down a party of scientists joined our ship with the notion of studying an eclipse of the sun from the most favourable point in the British Isles to observe the phenomenon — St. Bride's Bay at the south-west corner of Wales. Rain and low cloud made any hope of even a glimpse of the sun an impossibility but we anchored for a few hours just to satisfy our passengers before continuing the voyage to Weymouth Bay and ten days later, back to Plymouth.

Plymouth was the ship's Home Port where most of the crew had their homes and families, and — it was Carnival Week! We were "Open" most afternoons and had even more visitors as the wives, mothers and fathers and children of the entire (almost) ship's company came on board, and on one day we held a Childrens' Party. What a day! They were everywhere and we all had to see that they came to no harm. The capstan was rigged as a roundabout; the barrels of the guns of "A"-turret on the foc's'le were used to support swings; a long slide was rigged from the top of "Y" turret down to the quarterdeck, and the main derrick — normally used for hoisting the steam picket-boats inboard — was used to lift a large 'viewing platform' high into the air to give the children a sea-gull's-eye view of the ship and Plymouth Sound. Tables were brought up from messes and set below the guns of "Q" turret amidships laden with tea, bread and butter, jam and cakes for our young guests, and a wonderful time was had by all; The Week ended with a dance on board and a Search-light Display, and we steamed along to Torbay to entertain thousands of holiday-makers and residents of the towns of Torquay and Paignton all keen to see 'their Navy' as they climbed and clambered everywhere. The civic authorities of both communities made sure that the ship's company was well cared for by granting free entrance to all places of entertainment in the two towns, and the usual 'thank you' in the form of a Search-light Display was given before we left for Devonport on July 25th for the Summer leave period.

On September 15th we sailed with the Fleet to Invergordon where the routine was exactly the same as before — except that on one very black night while exercising in the North Sea we were almost rammed by our sister-ship *Marlborough*. A collision was narrowly averted by prompt action in the engine-rooms when "Full Ahead Port — Full Astern Starboard" was given and we slewed out of her way just as the cry, "Stand by for Collision" was heard, but it was a very close thing.

We prepared to sail south again on October 10th but the Fleet sailed without us as one of our Boy Seamen had acute appendicitis and it was imperitive the doctor operate immediately with no vibration in the ship. We sailed 36-hours later with the patient out of danger and landed him at Portland when we rejoined the Fleet for a six-weeks stay in the storm-bound harbour. *Noontide* was with us to ferry liberty-men to and from the pier at Weymouth. She was a sturdy sea-boat but I boarded her one night in November with about 200 others to return to the ship. As soon as we left the pier we all crowded to the lee side and gave her a heavy list, the wind and waves threatening to capsize her. The Lieutenant-in-command turned her head into the weather and kept it there until the men spread themselves on both sides, saying that 'It is better for everyone to accept a drenching rather than a certain drowning.' We certainly got very wet. (At 6 p.m. on November 11th another drifter capsized as she put her nose through the harbour exit, fortunately with no loss of life.)

The bad weather did not prevent visits by the Squadron Commander — Rear-Admiral Hall Thompson, nor by the C. in C., Vice-Admiral Sir Hubert Brand a few days later, but everyone was a lot happier at the end of November when we steamed round to Devonport. That signalled the end of my — our — year of training afloat and a written examination followed by an oral one at the Fleet Engineer's Office at Base confirmed our up-rating to Acting 4th Class E.R.A.'s, our daily rate of pay rising to ten shillings and sixpence.

Our movements throughout 1928 were destined to be much the same as 1927 though my experiences quite different.

We sailed with the Fleet on January 10th to start the Spring Cruise, and on March 14th we steamed eastward to meet, and do battle with the Mediterranean Fleet coming from Malta. For more than 24-hours the jockeying for position continued, with dummy attacks being made on each other by squadrons of planes from their respective carriers, and flotillas of destroyers weaving criss-cross patterns as they nipped in to launch torpedoes — which they then had to chase and retrieve.

Suddenly the 'battle' was over. Who won? Both Fleets steamed together towards Gibraltar and what a magnificent sight in brilliant sunshine and on a calm, blue sea; the Med. Fleet in their light-grey livery, looking so bright and clean in comparison with the sombre dark grey of Atlantic Fleet ships. And what a host of ships! The Med. Fleet consisted of the 1st Battle Squadron — *Queen Elizabeth* (Flagship), *Warspite*, *Barham*, *Valiant* and *Malaya*, all of 27,500-tons, the 2nd Battle Squadron comprising of *Royal Oak* (Flag), *Revenge*, *Ramillies*, *Royal Sovereign* and *Resolution*, — 25,000-tons each, — the 1st and 3rd Cruiser Squadrons each of four "C" Class cruisers, four flotillas (1st, 2nd, 3rd and 4th) of destroyers, each flotilla being eight boats and a Leader plus an extra cruiser wearing the Flag of Rear-Admiral of Destroyers (R.A.D.), the aircraft-carrier *Eagle* with her two attendant destroyers, two flotillas of 'H' Class submarines (twelve boats) and a couple of mine-sweeping sloops.

In the Atlantic Fleet the Battle-Cruiser Squadron which included the world's largest warship *Hood* (Flagship), 40,000-tons, *Repulse*, 27,000-tons, *Tiger*, 30,000-tons, the Navy's two newest battleships, *Nelson* (Flagship of the C. in C.) and *Rodney* — both 32,000-tons — plus our 3rd Battle Squadron, (Training) as already mentioned of *Iron Duke* (Flagship), *Marlborough*, *Benbow* and *Emperor of India*, each of 25,000-tons, eight "C" Class cruisers and 30 destroyers plus a flotilla of submarines and the aircraft-carriers *Furious* and *Argus* each with two attendent destroyers, so the combination formed an impressive armada.

At Gib. only the senior ships could be accommodated inside the harbour, the rest anchoring in the Bay where every time the wind started to blow a bit hard the routine became — "Split-watch below. Raise steam for slow speed and detail anchor watches," and even in good weather it was a risky business going ashore as our boats were so antiquated and unreliable.

My brother was now serving in *Ramillies* so I tried to meet him as often as possible on shore where we did the usual things, such as walking to the top (again!) and having a decent meal in the Y.M.C.A., a drink in one of the many bars on Main Street, haggle with a souvenir-shop owner over the price of some silken apparel we thought to buy, and get a dozen oranges, but it was always a gamble as to whether I could meet him on time and what time I would arrive back to my ship. One night my launch left the jetty at 11 o'clock laden with libertymen and broke down as soon as we left the harbour. We drifted in the darkness for more than an hour before the engine could be re-started. Then there was the night on the inter-Fleet Boxing tournament in the Naval Canteen. The launch had already broken down so a sailing cutter was sent in to pick up our ship's people, but by the time the last bout had been fought there was no wind to waft us back and again we had to man the oars and pull against a strong current to arrive alongside at 1.30 a.m. Another disastrous night was when my old classmate, Whiting, serving in *Repulse*, invited me to his ship's Concert on the quarterdeck. Halfway through the show the weather rapidly deteriorated and it was abandoned. Other ships' boats soon began to come alongside to collect the guests and luckily there were only a few from my ship so a picket-boat was sent for us. Unluckily though, there was only enough room in the stern-sheets cabin for our Captain and his entourage, the rest of us huddled on the deck as she laboured against the rising sea and were thoroughly soaked by the time we got back and found that "Steam for slow speed" had been raised and "Anchor watches" being kept, and I was required for the Middle Watch below. Just some of the trials and tribulations of life at sea!

All ships left Gibraltar on March 22nd, the Med. Fleet turning east while we went into the Atlantic and 24-hours later came back to attack the Rock, which was being defended by the others and after many hours at Action Stations and plenty of manoeuvrings we quite suddenly broke off and turned for home on the 24th arriving in Portland on the 28th without touching any Spanish ports en route. Nobody knew why we had come direct home until the mystery was apparently solved when, on April 3rd we left harbour and all the ship's company had to line the guardrails to cheer King Amanullah of Afghanistan who had been on a State Visit to Britain and was now returning home. Our ship escorted the liner down the Channel as far as Plymouth and then we went in to Devonport for the Easter period and for leave.

The Summer Cruise began on May 2nd 1928, with a very rough passage up the east coast to Invergordon where the Fleet's exercises were disrupted by persistent fog. The ships would get under way from the anchorage and within an hour the fog would drop again, and so would all anchors. We had to shut down half the boilers but remain on watch below while up top the fog-horns and bells sounded every few minutes until the fog lifted and

Some of "E of I's" ship's Company — proud of winning the Regatta. Lamlash 1928.

there was another opportunity, albeit short, for the Training Schedule of Boys and 2nd Class Stokers to be advanced. Despite all the frustrations our pre-arranged Cruise programme was adhered to and we anchored in Scapa Flow on June 4th with the weather much improved.

Next came a repeat visit to Oban, but this time it was for nine days of non-stop rain so there were very few visitors coming on board — which was just as well because we coaled ship when we arrived and the rain turned the dust into black mud which seemed to linger on the upper deck for ages.

We moved down the west coast to Arran and anchored in Brodick Bay where the Fleet Regatta was to be held the following week. All boats crews had been in training and there was a great enthusiasm, mostly engendered by the popular new Executive Commander, Guy Lydekker, who parodied the words of some of the songs of the day and had them put onto a screen so that the ship's company could sing them at the Community-singing sessions which he himself conducted each evening. One of the songs was, "I'm one of the Nuts from Barcelona", which became "I'm one of the nuts who's always training. I make-a da float, I row-a da boat. I do not-a care if it's fine or raining . . .". (It sure did rain at Oban!)

In the Regatta our ship 'swept the board' by winning seven of the eight Cups competed for, *and* the magnificent solid silver Championship Cock with fourteen "Firsts" out of fifteen races, the only loser was the E.R.A.'s gig which came fourth, as we did last year.

Next morning our Captain, W. F. Sells — who I learned later was a Midshipman survivor from my father's ship, *Cressy*, when she was lost in 1914 — returned from the flagship with the trophies and then all the winning boats' crews boarded *Noontide* and, with the Cock proudly perched on its bridge did a Lap of Honour round the Fleet, cheered by all ships.

Then an Admiralty Fleet Notice came to our Mess stating that volunteers were required for the cruiser *Diomede*, commissioning for service with the New Zealand Division of the Royal Navy. I put my name forward and the Captain allowed it to go through, and a few days later I was passed "Fit" by doctor and dentist — and that was the last I ever heard of that! Still, it was worth a try.

The Fleet moved south again at the beginning of November, a 3½-day trip to Portland where the weather was so bad that we had no communication with the shore for several days — until it was decided to send our drifter in to Weymouth to pick up stores and mail and "You'd better go with her in case there's any trouble." What a trip! She was on her beam-ends there and back, nigh impossible to keep one's feet and all the crew hanging on for dear life.

The Fleet dispersed in mid-December and my first job on our arrival in Devonport was to contact the Boat Construction Department about the warping of the picket boat. The verdict was that she was so old she must be written off and a replacement was supplied.

CHAPTER 3

1929

On January 9th we joined the Fleet and our Squadron at Portland where on arrival I took trips in all boats to check they were O.K. and running well; they were — until 7.30 that evening when an emergency call came, 'Motor boat adrift in the harbour. Boats' E.R.A. required at the gangway.' The picket boat was waiting to take me to locate S.E.O.D's boat which we found by the Breakwater. A flywheel bolt had sheared so she had to be towed back and I worked till midnight fitting a new bolt and giving a test run, and at 8 a.m. I took *Noontide* in to Portland base to put her into a state of preservation for the time we would be away on the Spring Cruise.

S.E.O.D's boat came to pick me up in the evening but the cox'n said he had to take me to Portland Pier where the launch had broken down. I was dumped there — fortunately with my tools — and this time it was a seized clutch. I freed it within half-an-hour and we went back to the ship to find that our mess-men had not saved any supper for me because they thought I was ashore for the night. What a life! But that was not all, for I looked at the Steaming Watch Bill and found that I had the Morning Watch as we were leaving for Arosa Bay at 11.30 a.m! "Keeping Middle Watches — (Morning Watches?) — working all day. O Lord have mercy on a poor E.R.A."

Biscay was fairly calm and again it was a wonderful sight watching a great number a ships steaming majestically forward across the seas, but three days later when we anchored in Arosa Bay the gales were terrific. Steam was kept on main engines and anchor-watches maintained. No leave was given and the boats remained on their chocks where I did odd maintenance work on them ready for our arrival at Gibraltar.

It was still stormy when we left Arosa Bay and that night we narrowly missed ramming *Marlborough* in the darkness. Previously — 1927 I think — it was she who had nearly rammed us, so now we were 'square' and the talk on board was, "Let's hope there won't be a third time!"

All boats were lowered when we anchored in Gibraltar Bay and I did trips in them in turn, taking the Commander ashore and the Captain to *Iron Duke*, then in S.E.O.D's boat for its crew to collect him (Senior Engineer Officer, Destroyers) from his accommodation-ship *Coventry* and in the launch to pick up the mail. All was sweetness and light and the boats were running — until the evening and then the launch's clutch lever snapped off at the bottom.

The clutch had to be dismantled and I took all the bits and pieces inboard to make a new lever but before I could finish we were ordered to sea and once again my off-watch time was spent repairing an engine for the boat to be ready when we anchored four days later.

Several days — and nights — of good running and I was working in the 1st. picket boat tied at the stern boom when a seaplane crashed about a mile away. Luckily we had a full head of steam and the crew were still in the boat so we were off at full speed to rescue two men from the sea and land them in Gibraltar. Back at the ship I had to give corroborative details to the Officer of the Day and as I walked away from him I met the driver of S.E.O.D's boat and was greeted with, "Can you come out, chief? The crank-shaft's bent." I knew it wasn't straight but I found the boat a complete shambles: one of the four connecting-rods had fractured at its gudgeon-end while the engine was at full speed, punching holes through

22

the crank-case before wrapping itself totally round the big-end bearing. S.E.O.(D) followed me out to his boat, saw the mess and told me to strip the engine very carefully so that certain parts could be sent for specialist examination. (I was thankful when the Fleet Engineer's report diagnosed "Metal fatigue. No blame to be attached." — and wondered who they would have liked to have blamed?) There was no spare con-rod anywhere in the Fleet and the boat was wanted urgently so the answer was, "Make one", although a spare ordered from U.K. would arrive in a couple of weeks.

Our enginesmith forged one from a solid lump of metal to be milled and shaped in the machine-shop while I rebuilt the engine and repaired the crankcase. The weight of the new rod could not be brought down to that of the other three for a perfect balance but the engine ran well until the replacement arrived.

The Fleet dispersed on February 22nd for individual ships to visit Spanish Mediterranean ports and *we* anchored off Tarragona on the 26th in atrocious weather which remained with us for the six days of our stay in that small, drab-looking town. I did 'nursing trips' in every boat every day with the few members of the ship who ventured ashore in the launch getting very wet, both going and returning. At the end of the fourth day I had such a cold that I called at the Sick Bay for a drop of Mist. Pect. — the 'normal' cure — but the Steward took my temperature and called the surgeon from the Wardroom. He ordered me into a cot right away and it was so warm and comfortable, but when he came on his morning visit at 9 a.m. he came straight to my bed and with no preamble said, "Duty. You can get up now," and I can only surmise that when he returned to the Wardroom the night before and said he had put an E.R.A. to bed one of the engineer officers had said, 'Which one?', and when told had replied with, "Well, if you want to be certain of being able to get ashore — and back again — you had better get him on his feet again, fast!" Actually all boats were behaving well but we sailed the next day, just six-hours steaming round to Barcelona where we anchored a mile or more outside the harbour with a terrific swell running. It was the aftermath of the storm which had raged for the past week, and it lasted most of the six days we were there. I and the boats' crews had to be very agile when manning the boats for even in good conditions the boats were some 15-feet below the booms, port or starboard, but now — the swell was such that at one instant it would be possible to walk out onto the boom and the bows of the launch or picket boat would come up level to be able to jump (quickly) over, and a second later the boat would have dropped 25 to 30-feet, and the crests of the rollers did not remain uniform.

I went ashore on the second day, to the most beautiful city so far in my travels. A mess-mate and I walked in the wide and clean avenues and parks

23

before resting at a table outside a restaurant in the main Boulevard — Las Ramblas — with a nice meal and a bottle of champagne (12/6 a bottle) and watching the evening strollers.

I was lucky to have got that visit because a couple of mornings later I had risked life and limb going out to the launch at 6.30 a.m. — just to make sure she started all right. Satisfied, and with the boat still heaving twenty or more feet, I sat in the stern sheets and lit my first cigarette of the day. One 'puff' and there was a shout from the upper deck: "That man there! Come inboard at once!" It was the voice of the Officer of the Watch who took me before the Commander and got me "7-days stoppage of leave." Just another thorn in my flesh, but I had seen Barcelona. That was the main thing. A city I would have hated to miss.

My 'Leave stoppage' did not matter because we left for Pollensa, Majorca, where it rained non-stop and from what I saw of the place on my 'nursing' trips it did not appear worth a visit. I contented myself making continuous runs with the launch, picking up stores and ammunition from the store-ship *Perthshire*, really as a form of insurance because she seldom broke down when I was with her. On completion the Fleet went to sea to meet and do battle with the Med. Fleet which had come from Malta and after the usual excitements, thrills of cat-and-mouse manoeuvrings and some hard work both Fleets anchored in Pollensa Bay where I was able to board *Ramillies* and talk with my brother whom I had not seen since we met in Gibraltar a year ago. Two days later the 3rd Battle Squadron was ordered back to England with a brief call at Gib to pick up mail and no other stops until thick fog held us for 24-hours in Plymouth Sound. What was our hurry? E. of I. was to be paid-off and scrapped! At last I would be leaving (I thought). Instead, everybody else went and only a steaming party was retained, enough to get the ship to Portsmouth in May after she had been de-stored. Our party then transferred to our sister-ship *Benbow* which had been designated "Training-battleship, Devonport" and was to be moored there when we steamed her back, and six days later we had her tied up in Devonport Dockyard. Now I *would* be leaving. That was another ridiculous thought, for two days later news came that *Benbow*, too, was to be scrapped and only a Care and Maintenance Party would be required. For our department it meant just one Chief E.R.A. and three E.R.A's would be staying until she was ready to be towed away to the breaker's yard, and *I* was one of the three, (despite having changed to Chatham Division) so once again I found myself 'guilty' of doing a West Country 'chapsie' out of a Home Service job! But every evening I stood 'duty' for the other two — who were 'natives' — and on one occasion I was about the only person left on board. That was the night before the ship was to be taken into Dockyard control and the kits of everyone except mine had been taken into barracks. I 'played along' and let them all go but at 7.30

next morning, June 7th 1929, a van came to collect me and my kit and take me to Devonport barracks for breakfast, and I said 'Goodbye' to *Benbow*. I had been the last to leave the *Emperor* and the very last to leave *Benbow*. Two-and-a-half years! It was over at last. After breakfast I reported to the Regulating Office and was given charge of 23 Leading Stokers, from some Course or other, to take to Chatham where we arrived at 4.30 p.m.

The Naval Patrol Officer told me to march the squad smartly through the town to barracks and they were anxious to get moving because of the danger of missing shore-leave that evening, so we set off at a brisk pace and soon came to the local tram tracks. I hailed the first Dockyard-bound car and — "Pay your own fares, lads," (One penny each) — I got the conductor to stop about 50-yards short of the Barrack Gate so that we would march those final steps and they were able to finish the first part of the Joining Routine and get ashore.

CHAPTER 4

Mediterranean Fleet

As soon as I had completed my Joining Routine I was sent with a Re-fitting Party into the Dockyard to the cruiser *Curlew*, 4,190-tons, laid-up in a basin as part of the Reserve Fleet and now to be brought forward because of some possible flare-up in the Middle East. It took four weeks to get her ready for sea and work her up to 28-knots in the North Sea, then the crisis passed and we took the ship back to the basin and back into a state of preservation — until the next emergency. On August 8th the Party returned to barracks where I found myself detailed for Commissioning Party of the new County Class cruiser *Shropshire*, completely upsetting my (our) plans to marry at the end of August during the normal Summer Leave period.

Our Day was brought forward and we wed on August 12th 1929 as I began my Foreign Service Draft Leave and a honeymoon in Jersey.

Shropshire, 9,830-tons, being built on the Clyde at Dalmuir, was almost ready to be handed over to the Navy and the Commissioning Party had to sleep in barracks on the night of September 9th, ready to be called at 0430 and entrain in the Dockyard at 0600. There were about 200-officers and men aboard the train as we moved off at 0645, each being handed a packed

H.M.S. "Shropshire" at Gibraltar, Nov. 1929.

lunch and tea in the form of cheese- and corned-beef-sandwiches, a Rock cake and an apple and orange. Liquid refreshment was supplied at two stops on the journey north. Most of the tea-time sandwiches were thrown from the train to children as we passed through the Gorbals suburb of Glasgow, and after twelve very long hours we de-trained at 7 p.m. and marched in to Beardmore's Yard to board our new home.

On the morrow we raised steam and got the 'feel' of the throttles and on the 12th moved down the river to run Acceptance Trials in the open sea. A speed of 34-knots was easily reached and late in the day we anchored off Greenock where a tender came alongside to take off the civilian workers as we, under the guidance of the small crew which had stood by the ship during her building proceeded to shut down in the boiler- and engine-rooms. The tender was only fifty yards from the ship when we were plunged into darkness as an engineer — who should have known better — ordered an isolating valve to be shut and cut off the supply of steam to the dynamos. The cheer which rose from the departing builders echoed round the estuary, but things were soon put right and next morning we began our journey south with lots of manoeuvrings on the way and arrived in Chatham three days later. Everybody was busy during the next three weeks finding their way about the ship and modifying, re-positioning and improving various items such as gauges and indicators for our future convenience, and the seamen completed storing the ship. Finally the remainder of the crew, to bring us up to full complement marched out from the barracks and on October 7th 1929, the ship moved down river to oil at Sheerness (how different an exercise from 'Coaling' the E. of I!) and steamed round to Portland for a month's Working-up period — to turn the crew and the ship into a fighting unit, four weeks of day and night manoeuvres in the Channel; gunnery and torpedo-running; high-speed steaming with emergency stops and starts; Action Stations, collision and Abandon ship, and exercising with submarines and destroyers.

On November 9th we left Portland to join the 1st Cruiser Squadron in the Mediterranean for a two-and-a-half years commission and arrived at Gibraltar on the 13th How peaceful and quiet it was with only the two Local Defence destroyers, a minesweeper and a couple of submarines in port instead of two colossal fleets. The ship was still in a Working-up situation spending another four weeks exercising out of Gibraltar but when we did go into harbour it was to go right inside, making it possible for us to walk ashore. *Shropshire* was new; she was clean and comfortable with lots of space and a high deck-head, more on the lines of a passenger liner. It was also comfortable on shore during our short spells in harbour and we enjoyed the week-ends with some inter-departmental football matches or walking half-way up the Rock to watch the Barbary apes at play, and of course there was plenty of room in the bars and cafes to have a really *quiet* drink. By December 12th we were deemed fit and ready to join our Squadron and steamed in to Grand Harbour, Valetta, on the 16th, nicely in time for Christmas.

Unfortunately, after suffering stomach pains on the 19th and reporting 'sick', I was taken ashore to the Naval hospital at Bighi for an operation which immobilized me until after the Fleet left for the first part of its Spring Cruise although I was fit enough to watch from a balcony as the 1st and 3rd Cruiser Squadrons and 1st Battle Squadron steamed out. I felt a trifle sorry that I was not with my ship.

While sitting on the balcony the following afternoon, January 15th 1930, I watched the battleship *Ramillies* entering harbour, back from England after re-commissioning, and saw her run aground on the sandstone rocks of Egmont Point where she stuck hard and fast. Two Dockyard tugs failed to move her but I had a splendid view from my vantage point as the whole crew mustered on her quarterdeck and jumped in unison to the tunes "Keel Row" and "Pop goes the Weasel" being played by her R.M. Band until the vibration eventually did the trick and she slid quietly back into deeper water, the tugs still in control. A massive cheer rose from people gathered all around the harbour, attracted by the music.

By the 23rd I was fit enough to be allowed out for walks so I crossed the harbour in a dhaighsa to Valetta for shopping and back again by ferry-boat to Senglea, from whence I could walk to the hospital.

On the last day of January I watched the Fleet steam into harbour and could rejoin my ship. They had been to Greece and the Aegean islands, and Athens.

We were soon at sea again although not without a slight contretemps when the steering-engine failed as we were leaving harbour and despite an emergency "Stop! Full Astern both!" the ship ran aground on Fort St. Elmo. Tugs pulled us clear within twenty-minutes and we were able to complete our first exercise, firing salvoes from our eight 8″ guns at the radio-controlled obsolete battleship *Centurion* before anchoring in St. Paul's Bay for our Diver to check for any damage. There was none.

The second part of the Spring Cruise began on March 8th when we left Malta to find and do battle with the Atlantic Fleet. Our Fleet, under Admiral Sir Frederick Field in *Warspite* comprised the 1st. Battle Squadron — *Revenge, Ramillies, Royal Oak, Royal Sovereign* and *Resolution,* — the carrier *Eagle* with her two destroyers, the 1st. Cruiser Squadron — *London, Devonshire, Sussex* and *Shropshire,* the 3rd Cruiser Squadron — *Curacoa, Caledon, Calypso* and *Curlew* (out of Reserve now), plus four flotillas of destroyers (nine boats in each) led by Rear-Admiral (D) in the cruiser *Cairo,* and twelve submarines. Quite an impressive force. The opposing Fleet was in two sections one of which was in Gibraltar, the other at Barcelona. Combined they would be far superior so our purpose was to defeat either portion before they could unite. That was apparently achieved during the night of 10th/11th, for later on the 11th we met the other section and were all steaming towards Pollensa when there was a dramatic change in the weather with a full north-westerly gale blowing making a change of course necessary and all ships anchored in Palma Bay. The storm blew for the whole week and even in that comparatively sheltered position everyone had to keep steam on main engines.

The Atlantic Fleet was commanded by Vice-Admiral Sir Ernle Chatfield in *Nelson,* with *Rodney, Barham* and *Malaya* of the 2nd Battle Squadron, the Battle-Cruiser Squadron of *Renown, Repulse* and *Tiger,* two carriers — *Argus* and *Furious* with four attendant destroyers, the 2nd Cruiser Squadron of *Hawkins, Frobisher, Comus* and *Canterbury,* two flotillas of destroyers led by R.A.(D) in *Centaur,* and ten submarines. Imagine the scene as more than a hundred ships of all sizes steamed in long lines over that calm blue sea towards Gibraltar where we arrived on March 19th, and once again the town became a hive of activity. There were competitions between ships and Fleets on the soccer fields and in the Boxing-rings; bars and restaurants filled, and men shouting across rooms and streets as old friends were glimpsed on the far side, giving an excuse — if one were needed — for yet another drink, and a talk about 'old times'. I met some of my class-mates again and had news of others before the Atlantic Fleet sailed for home, March 25th, leaving a quieter Gibraltar behind.

At 0730 on April 1st the Fleet started to leave harbour. We were the first ship to cast off from the Mole and the mooring-wire promptly wrapped itself round our port outer propeller so we just had to anchor and watch all the others leave before our diver could get down and cut us free, and we were able to move at 10.30 p.m. Catching up 36-hours later we were just in time for the Fleet to disperse and visit various French and Italian ports before returning to Malta. *Shropshire* and the 1st Flotilla dropped anchor off the little fishing port of St. Tropez while *Royal Oak* and another flotilla were at Ste Maxime, a few miles further east.

We could go ashore from 4.30 p.m. so I had a walk in the quaint old streets of the port — just a tiny place — before hiking out through the most beautiful country-side to the village of Ramatuille, six miles as the crow flies but much longer by the road winding through the lovely woodlands — so quiet and so pretty. I had a glass of cognac with 'mine host' at the local inn, M'sieur Plai, who said he was very happy to be living in such peace and tranquillity in 'his' village. I walked on and through another tiny hamlet of cobbled streets and similar quaint beauty. It was Le Feux and it seemed the sort of place where one could live in peace for ever — but I went down the hill and by the lower road back to the ship.

It was a rough 24-hours passage to our next port, Genoa, where we berthed in the inner harbour and were the only British ship present, making a picturesque addition to the scene with the graceful lines and light-grey livery contrasting with the black and buff and reds and blues of liners and cargo-liners, tramps and tugs and fishing-craft crowding the port where all was movement and bustle. The weather was good and shore-leave was given to non-duty watches every night from 4.30 p.m. until 7 a.m., and most took due advantage to see something of the greatest sea-port in the Mediterranean, a city of piazzas, palaces and terraces, hinting at the past influence and wealth, while within the ancient walls were dark and narrow cobbled streets and lanes dating from Roman times.

We left Genoa on April 22nd to rendezvous with the Fleet for exercises on our way back to Malta where we arrived on the 26th and *Shropshire* de-ammunitioned and entered the graving dock to have her bottom scraped and painted with anti-fouling, the four propellers cleaned, smoothed and polished by the seamen and dockyard workmen while we of the Engine-room staff refitted all underwater valves during the eight-day docking period.

There were plenty of opportunities for shore-going and lots of interesting places to visit and things to do, in addition to which I had invitations to Soapy's relatives' flat — his uncle was an Inspector in the 'Yard — and to join the week-end picnics with their friends, picnics on the lovely, sandy beaches at Mellieha and St. Paul's Bay where St. Paul was shipwrecked in A.D. 60 and legend has it that to obtain drinking-water he

Grand Harbour Malta, 1930.

pushed his finger into the sandstone rock and lo! the water flows to this day!

Shropshire's normal berth was in Bighi Bay just inside the harbour and it was very refreshing on some evenings to hail a dhaighsa to row a crowd of us across to the Breakwater to swim and play water-polo.

With the Fleet in port there were thousands of men ashore every night and scores of bars to satisfy their needs. Strada Stretta, the straight street of steps and universally known to sailors as "The Gut", was virtually ALL bars — most named after ships, past and present, of the Navy. A few were quiet, sedate drinking places; most were very noisy and had their own Cabarets, — always billed "Exclusive". One such — I think it was the "Morning Glory" — had a poster proclaiming, "Direct from her Great Success in London. Miss La Verne. See her Final Appearance HERE tomorrow night. Your last chance." A senior member of the Mess told us that that notice was there when he first served in the Med. five years ago, and reckoned it was either the bar-owner's wife or the bar owner.

There was plenty of entertainment on board, too, with Deck Hockey for the energetic, and the sailors' National Game of Uckers for the strong. (One had to be strong to wield the big scrub-bucket with its 6"-cubed dice to cast on the deck!) The Royal Marine Band Orchestra gave concerts of classical music on the upper deck in the early evenings.

Out of the ships there was keen competition in all sports and there were two attractive Naval Clubs with lounges, reading and writing rooms, bars and restaurants, and comfortable beds for those wishing to sleep ashore, and there were two or three sessions of Tombola played in both clubs each week. The number of 'houses' per session was usually eight with the price of tickets for the first three being 3d., the fourth game was 6d., then three more at 3d. and the final 'house' — the BIG one — the tickets were a shilling each. The pay-out on the earlier games would be about £5 for a 'line' and £15 for the 'full house' and gradually build up through the evening as more punters came in. But, the one to win was the BIG one — especially on a Saturday night after the monthly Pay Day of the Fleet — when the pay-out could be in excess of £100 (almost equal to an A.B. or Stoker's annual earnings.) But those big prizes were eventually banned by the wife of a Commander-in-Chief who thought it was too large a sum for a sailor to be carrying back to his ship on a Saturday night — probably with unsteady gait. Maybe she was right!

Our Commission continued with Fleet exercises, using *Centurion* for gunnery practice by day and by night and embarking troops at one point on the island in daylight and landing them at another after dark and, of course, the periodical Full Power Trial — a much cleaner, quieter, and certainly a lot easier than it ever was in the *E. of I.*

On July 2nd 1930, the Fleet sailed for the Summer Cruise to the eastern Med. with all ships darkened for mock attacks by the destroyers, and on the 4th the 1st Cruiser Squadron anchored off the small, very small, town of Nauplia, a few miles south-west of Athens. We were there for 12-days with absolutely nothing to do or see on shore — except for one afternoon when a small party of us from the Mess climbed a hill overlooking the town and walked amongst the ruins of the ancient city of Arg, trying to imagine what life was like there centuries before, when it was alive! — our main pastime was to land and sport on the white sandy beach. It was hot and sunny and we worked a 'Hot Weather' routine of starting work at 0700 and finishing at 1300, then many parties from all the ships would row themselves ashore to picnic and play games on the sands and in the water. Back on board there would always be a queue to the Sick Bay to have the needles of sea-urchins removed from the soles of our feet.

On the 16th we received orders for one hour's notice to leave Nauplia owing to unrest in Egypt and remained at short notice when we moved into the Aegean Sea to our next programmed call — the small island and town of Skiathos. Like most of the island towns and villages it was much better viewed from a distance and its inhabitants were mainly refugees from Greece, Turkey and Armenia, and there was little interest to attract anyone to land but we were thankful for the plentiful supply of fruit and vegetables. We actually spent more time at sea exercising than at anchor and each ship in its turn had the Squadron Engineer and Rear-Admiral

J. C. Henley on board for a day or more checking on procedures and efficiency.

The most important event though was on July 26th when I received a Cable from my wife telling me of the birth that morning of our son. How I wished I could have been home within a few hours to see them, but I knew it would be almost two more years before I had that inestimable pleasure.

Our cruise continued when we left Skiathos on the 30th but was interrupted that same day when a destroyer suffered a mishap in her engine-room and we, *Shropshire*, were detailed to escort her to the nearest shelter and assist with any repairs. The boat was the *Arrow* (*H42*) of the 3rd Flotilla and a steam joint had blown on a manoeuvring valve and allowed superheated steam at 650-degrees and at 500-lbs./sq.in. pressure to escape into the engine-room, making it impossible for anyone to remain below for more than a few minutes. We took her into Problaka Bay and I was one of the four fitters detailed to assist. She, too, was on her first commission since leaving her builders, and they had failed to follow Admiralty specifications by using a jointing material instead of 'metal to metal' joining and the steam had cut its way through the material and gouged deep furrows across the faces of the cast-steel flanges, of which there were seven, each being two-feet in diameter with an 18″ orifice and all had to be filed and scraped to a true and smooth finish without the aid of a surface-plate.

Arrow, like all destroyers, carried one Chief E.R.A. and three E.R.A's — 2-fitters and a boiler-maker — and we four could not be accommodated for sleeping, so the arrangement was — we four would work through the day from 8 a.m. till 8 p.m. and return to our ship while *Arrow*'s fitters worked through the night. The job took four days and nights of non-stop working and everyone was happy when, on the fifth day all our metal-to-metal joints withstood pressure and temperature and *Arrow* was fit for service. We returned to our own ship but an hour later were recalled to *Arrow* to be entertained and thanked by her Captain and the Engineer — Lt. Comm. F. Secretan — in the Wardroom and thanked for "A good job well done".

It had been extremely hot during our enforced stay at Problaka with frequent heavy rain-storms and the only contact with shore was through the Supply Officer who landed to negotiate the purchase of fresh vegetables, and the Petty Officer who accompanied him told us that the town was the village of Erissos, which consisted of two houses, a church, a pub, two goats, a cow and about five people, nestling at the foot of Mt. Athos (6,000-feet), its summit reputed to be of solid marble and surrounded by Greek and Russian monasteries. It was also boasted that there was no female life of any description in the area — which was a rather odd boast when one considered the plentiful supply of eggs and milk the Supply Officer was able to purchase. The Fleet meanwhile had rendezvoused at Argostoli on the island of Cephelonia for its annual regatta and we arrived in time to take part in the 2-day event — not very successfully — and finishing 9th of a total of eleven cruisers. Our flagship, *London*, was the over-all winner, also winning the All-comers race for the Fiume Trophy with *Curlew* second and *Shropshire* third. On August 20th we were all back in Malta.

CHAPTER 5

Three "A's"

August 28th 1930, Mr. A. V. Alexander, First Lord of the Admiralty, visited the ship to tell us that we were to be sent to Australia for one year in exchange for their cruiser, *Canberra*, which would come to the Med. for Fleet Training. The majority of the ship's company were thrilled with the news. It would be a wonderful experience and would speed the Commission. The Rear-Admiral of the Squadron came on board to say "Goodbye" and to wish us a very happy time out there, and on September 2nd we sailed with the Fleet — which was starting its Autumn Cruise then turned and steamed through the columns of ships, each and every one giving us a cheer and signalling messages of "God-speed" and "Good Luck" as we returned to Malta for docking and general titivation for the voyage.

Between the time of being told our 'news' and the departure of the Fleet there had been a great upheaval in the ship's company because some men were approaching Pension date or nearing the completion of their 12-year engagement period; some officers and men had their wives on the island and did not want to leave them, and there were actually men who did not *want* to see Australia!

Volunteers were called for from the rest of the Fleet and provided they had similar qualification as those they were to replace, they were accepted and many new and enthusiastic people and faces appeared amongst us. It was a very busy time in dock with all the 'spit and polish' of our 'wash and brush up', and then the storing, ammunitioning and fuelling.

The Dominion would still have a cruiser and some destroyers in her Home waters with which we would be working, and there would certainly be sporting rivalry 'twixt them and us, so preparations began in earnest to build teams for every likely activity. One newcomer was the Fleet Heavyweight Boxing champion, Physical Training Instructor Petty Officer 'Hoot' Gibson who lost no time in forming a team of fighters of all weights and to set up a 'ring' on "B" gun deck. The upper deck was like a circus arena during the afternoon and evening sessions with shadow-boxers, sparrers, men skipping, running and jumping, and whenever possible the crews of whalers, gigs, galleys and cutters were out rowing or sailing in the harbour. Excitement grew every day as all looked forward to the next eighteen months away from Fleet working and towards independent cruising; it would certainly help by being more interesting and in any case we were not due to return to U.K. until Spring 1932.

The itinerary for the voyage was promulgated and was a very exciting prospect. Leaving Malta on October 15th we would arrive at Port Said on the 18th and pass through the Suez Canal during the night of the 20th to Suez. Then through the Red Sea to Aden and across the Indian Ocean to Colombo, on to Port Swettenham and Singapore. We were to cross the Equator and call at Batavia and Sourabaya in the Dutch East Indies, then Timor and via the Torres Strait to Thursday Island and have Christmas in Brisbane, eventually arriving in Sydney on December 29th. There was even a tentative programme planned for 1931 including visits to Tasmania and New Zealand, and in May we would be in Jervis Bay followed by spending the next two months in Sydney before going north for another visit to Brisbane and then cruise the South Sea Islands of Fiji, Tonga and Samoa. In October Adelaide would receive a visit, and that would bring us handily to November and Melbourne for Cup Week. In December we were to be in Sydney to prepare to rejoin our Squadron and then — Home! — after a Commission of a Lifetime.

The ship undocked on October 3rd and we received a 'bolt from the blue' — The whole scheme had been cancelled: The reason given was that the Australian Government could not afford the cost. What a let-down! Everyone was shocked and disappointed, but I think the hard work and the training had benefited us all, and now we had to get back to the things we thought we had left — or were on the point of leaving.

We were ready for sea on the 15th — the day our great adventure should have begun but instead of which we sailed from Malta in company with the *Revenge* (newly arrived from U.K.) and exercised with her on the way to Piraeus and to meet the Fleet which was nearing the end of the cruise. I was able to get ashore on one of the two days in port and travelled up to Athens to vist the Acropolis, the Parthenon and the Temples of Diana and the Winds, and was very lucky to be in the Modern Olympic Stadium while a platoon of Evzones (skirted Greek troops) were rehearsing a National dance in preparation for some festival. It was fascinating, graceful and melodic. Planes from the carrier *Eagle* gave a thrilling display for the people, looping and diving over and down to the ships as we sailed off on our way to Corfu. What a rough trip that was with terrific winds and battering rain and incessant lightning illuminating the darkened ships throughout the nightly exercises. And for the five of the seven days of our stay we had to keep steam on main engines.

On October 29th all ships left for Malta and on the 31st the Fleet entered Grand Harbour while *Shropshire* continued steaming westward towards Gibraltar. It was reckoned we had spent quite enough time in Malta so would go to Gib for a week and then pay a Courtesy visit to Algiers. It was quiet and peaceful at Gibraltar and the week passed pleasantly, with our Royal Marine Band "Beating the Retreat" in Main Square on one evening and leading the ship's company to church at the English Cathedral on Sunday morning, both events much appreciated by the local populace.

At 4 a.m. on November 13th we went below to raise steam for our 8 a.m. departure for Algiers. The ropes were being cast off when the order came for the visit to be cancelled. There was Plague in Algeria! Another anti-climax. We had said "Goodbye" to our Army friends in the Sergeants' Mess the previous night and felt uncomfortable about wandering up to the Mess again but two evenings later the ship's Concert Party put on a Show in the old Coal Shed with an invitation to the Army to attend. It was in appreciation of their hospitality but half-way through the performance came a Signal — "*Shropshire* to raise steam and proceed with all despatch to Antigua." There was some sort of insurrection on that West Indian island; the show was stopped and everything had be packed up and all props hurried back on board as the disappointed soldiers drifted away. The Steaming Watch was below and within the hour the ship was ready to cast off. Sirens, telegraphs, steering-engine, capstan and main engines, all 'tested and correct, Sir' — when the order came — yet again! "Shut down!" It transpired that *London*, flagship of the squadron, had been home to refit and re-commission and was on her way out again when the Admiralty realised she was much better placed to reach Antigua earlier than us. So — Australia — Algiers — Antigua — three "A's", and the men began to say that we were 'jinxed' and destined to flounder about on our own and away from the squadron for the remainder of the commission. Then, on November 20th we left Gib for a Night Exercise with the local Defence Destroyer *Tourmaline* for our mutual benefit, and on completion continued along to Malta, back to our place in the Fleet, and it was as though we had never been away.

The main sporting activity now was the Fleet Football competition – which *Shropshire* easily won due to the influx of so much talent for the trip to Australia. The Admiral came on board to present the coveted Fleet Shield.

Christmas 1930. We were roughly half-way through our commission. During the past year I had been employed in the Machine-shop for daywork and watchkeeping in the engine-room when at sea and on January 9th 1931, I had just finished a machining job when Bill Gabitas, the senior E.R.A. in the shop asked me to keep an eye on his Milling-machine while he kept a dental appointment. As he made the request he was flicking the swarf away from the cutting-edge of the tool and saying, "Don't *you* ever do this!" — promptly losing the top of his right-hand index finger. He went to the Sick Bay just as the Full Watch was ordered below to raise steam because of the gale which had sprung up, so I carried on with his work to finish it before I went below. I was the only one left in the shop when Lt. Comm. Shaw came in and after watching the job for a while he suddenly asked, "Have you ever served in destroyers?" I had not. "Well," said he, "it's the greatest experience — and you have the chance. An E.R.A. in a destroyer has reported sick and a replacement is required urgently. Pack your bags and get round there tomorrow morning."

It was 'Goodbye' to *Shropshire*.

I was landed at Custom House Jetty at nine o'clock next morning with my kit, hammock and tool-box and met by a Navy van to run me round to the Depot Ship *Sandhurst* lying in Lazaretto Creek where a boat from the *Wren* came for me.

CHAPTER 6

H.M.S. Wren

Wren was one of the famous "V" and "W" Class destroyers built in 1917 – 18 of just over 1,100-tons and reputed to be very good sea-boats — but what a change after the roominess of a 10,000-ton cruiser! I climbed aboard — it was only about six-feet free-board — and walked along the steel deck to the break of the fo'c'sle where, just inside the screen was a 2' 6" diameter hatch with a vertical steel ladder leading down to the E.R.A's Mess, a compartment 16' long by 8' wide and 7' high, and a home for four — the Chief and three E.R.A's. Our kit was stowed in the seat-lockers along the ship's side where we sat at table for meals. Suitcases were kept in overhead racks and hammocks in a bin in the corner while in another corner a rack and cupboard was provided for the crockery, cutlery, condiments, bread and other provisions. There was also a folding wash-basin stand, and one stoker had the task of looking after us and the Mess.

I soon acquainted myself of the lay-out of the engine-room and the two boiler-rooms and discovered that she was a Devonport (Owing to the shortage of E.R.A. fitters and turners) manned ship!

On Monday, 12th we steamed round to the Dockyard in Grand Harbour to go alongside the 4th Flotilla Leader, *Broke*, and pick up Captain (D) and his staff as *Wren* was to take over as Leader while his ship refitted. Then, on Tuesday we went to sea with the Fleet — except that the Fleet did not sail because the weather was atrocious. The destroyers were the first to leave harbour and as we passed through the breakwater we almost stood on our tail-end. The cruisers were to follow but only the 3rd Squadron of four "C" Class boats managed to get out and two of them each lost a man overboard and all four returned to harbour. The destroyers could not risk turning in such mountainous seas; they just had to keep their noses head-on into the waves. It was fascinating to watch the boats of the other flotillas abeam of us, their hulls as far back as the bridge being out of the water and then plunging into the trough to leave the stern-half high in the air with propellers threshing at nothing. When our bows crashed down like that it felt as though the ship had hit rock bottom. Life-lines had been rigged on both sides of the upper deck and when the watches changed it was a case of getting to the top of the ladder from engine- or boiler-room, carefully open the hatch to step out at an opportune moment and quickly close it, grab the 'runner' on the life-line and when the next wave had passed — run like hell!

I picked up the Afternoon Watch in charge of the engine-room and was terribly sick, but managed to perform my duties with thankfulness that we were Leader and did not have to keep 'station' on a boat ahead of us — as it was well-nigh impossible to maintain steady revolutions with propellers racing in the empty air and almost stopping when the stern crashed back into the sea. When my relief came down at 4 p.m. I grabbed a bundle of cotton-waste as a pillow and flopped down on the gratings between the main engines to wait for my next watch — 8 p.m.

The Chief came down at midnight to keep the Middle Watch and I was quite happy to flop between the turbines again but he said I would be better off in the Mess — and that my hammock was slung and my supper waiting (could I even look at food?) I plucked up the courage and made my dash along the deck to the fo'c'sle break and past the crowd of watchkeeping sea-boats' crews, and through the vomit to arrive water-logged in the Mess.

I managed to eat supper and enjoyed the comfort of my hammock. By morning I had regained my 'sea-legs' and found that in spite of the fact that the ships had maintained 94 r.p.m. all night we were still within sight of Sliema and the weather was still bad.

The main Fleet managed to clear the harbour that evening and when the cruiser *Coventry* (Rear-Admiral "D") caught up with us we got to leeward of her in order to lower a whaler and transfer four men with broken bones for treatment in her Sick Bay. All boats then took part in a mass torpedo attack on the Fleet with each destroyer firing two 'fish' and having the task of chasing and retrieving them when they had finished their 'run'. The big ships carried on as the boats stayed and searched. Torpedoes are very expensive toys so, when their 'run' finishes they stand on end with their dummy head out of the water, indicating its position by a calcium flare. Each boat knows its own 'fish' and when located a whaler is lowered and the crew bring it back home to be hoisted inboard. It was dark when all had been accounted for and we went on at 18-knots through heavy seas to catch up with the Fleet, many units being anchored among the Greek Islands repairing storm-damage; those not damaged remained on patrol outside to guard against surprise attack by the Blue section of the Fleet.

With repairs completed our flotilla had the task of screening the *Eagle* while her planes flew off to attack the Blues entailing a deal of high-speed steaming, and a couple of days later we put in to Suda Bay, Crete, where we stayed for ten days. The weather was still bad but I went ashore twice, both times by the 1.30 p.m. boat, the first occasion by myself and walked in an easterly direction, meeting another stroller who was the Governor of Prison K222 at Camela. It was a new construction and as we walked he told me a lot about its building and of the men — prisoners — who laboured to build it with the massive blocks of sandstone hewn from the hills, and when we arrived at its gates he invited me to inspect it. I spent an interesting hour touring the various 'shops' and departments with him and meeting some of his 'guests' — one of them presented me with a necklace he had carved from bones, and I was allowed to give him a few drachmas. My tour included a visit to the central tower where the guards could keep watch over all that went on in the jail and I had a panoramic view of the bay and ships. After having coffee with him in his office the Governor had one of his staff who was going off duty drive me down to Suda in time for the 7 p.m. boat.

Leaving Suda on January 28th we ran into heavy seas on our way to rendezvous with the Fleet 100-miles east of Malta for more exercises before entering harbour where *Wren* went alongside *Broke* to disembark Capt. (D) before proceeding to our proper berth at Sliema, and he came on board the next day to thank us for looking after him and carrying out Leader's duties so efficiently.

February 3rd found us at sea again, this time with all four flotillas under direct control of Read-Admiral (D) in *Coventry*, all movements being at 27-knots and a night-attack on the Fleet at 24-knots with all ships darkened.

While off watch during the night I spent time on the upper deck getting the thrill of the speed and the chase, of boats suddenly appearing out of the darkness — a phosphorescent glow of bow-wave or wake — and just as quickly gone.

Back in harbour the weather became even worse with gales, rain and hail and very, very cold, and remaining so for several days. Our three boilers had to be cleaned one at a time because two had to keep steam in case it got worse — although that seemed impossible — and we would have to move out of the Creek. As soon as all three were clean we were ordered to sea to chase and pick up torpedoes fired by *Ramillies* and then act as tender for the aircraft-carrier *Glorious*, newly arrived on the station, while she worked her planes. It seemed that we had become a general dog's body, in demand for any odd job that wanted doing — and the weather continued bad. The "Times of Malta" pronounced it as the longest continuous spell of cold and rough conditions the Islands had known.

On Sunday, March 1st all boats of our flotilla were flying paying-off pennants, they having been in commission for nearly 2½-years and not returning to Malta after the Spring Cruise — and I would be going home with *Wren*.

I had my final walks ashore to say 'Goodbye' to my Dockyard friends and enjoy the envy of my old *Shropshire* pals when they knew I would soon be on my way home and they had another year to do.

All four flotillas, with two flotillas of submarines and the 3rd Cruiser Squadron sailed in advance of the Fleet from Malta on March 7th in order to replenish with fuel at Gibraltar before their arrival. The Atlantic Fleet was already there when we arrived on the 11th but left next morning to hide itself out in the Atlantic as the Red Fleet of the coming manoeuvres — (the Med. Fleet would be the Blue Fleet and go searching for it) — and the destroyers were to screen the battleships in the ensuing action. Weather conditions were terrible with gale-force winds and heavy rain and all ships darkened when 'battle' was finally joined in the early hours of Monday, March 16th *Wren* became one of the first 'casualties' — I do not know if we had been 'sunk' or only 'damaged' but we were lying with engines stopped, broadside on to the heavy Atlantic swell off Cape St. Vincent all that Monday afternoon until at exactly 3.30 the ship rolled 37-degrees both ways just as First Dog watchmen were piped to tea. The noise of crashes went on for some time as tea-urns fell from tables, crockery and glass-ware smashed and a number of limbs were broken, the sound of the latter breakages probably heard only by the victims. Shortly after that incident "Half Ahead" was ordered on main engines and we headed back to Gib. to land the injured men and to re-fuel, and then be told that our part in the battle was over. We proceeded into the Pens.

The Combined Fleets steamed into the bay and harbour next day, a magnificent sight, and as soon as they had anchored or secured to the moles and jetties the whole area became a mass of movement as motor-boats, launches and picket-boats dashed between ship and ship and ship and shore and back again. And what crowds of men were ashore that first night. The place was teeming with 'old ships' meeting and making merry. From our berth in the Pens we could watch the comings and goings, but the most hectic and amusing times were at 11 and 11.30 p.m. when their boats were loading to take the men back to their ships at the detached Mole or out in the bay. The noise! the songs! The shouted "Good-nights" and "Cheerio's"! The 'See yer, Harry, — or Bill, — or whatever"! Everyone happy and 'three sheets in the wind', singing their hearts out as the boats pulled away from the jetty, but their voices dwindling as they approached their ships.

The Atlantic Fleet sailed for home on March 26th and Gib. became relatively quiet with just the Med. Fleet left in port, and when I walked ashore at 1 o'clock two-days later I chanced to meet one of my *Shropshire* messmates with whom I visited the Acropolis and suggested we crossed into Spain. We travelled by bus to a quaint little town or village called San Roque. The tiny houses and shops appeared to be centuries old and it felt as though time had passed it by. We walked on into the hills until suddenly finding ourselves in what we both reckoned was the healthiest village in the world. It had clean, narrow, cobbled streets. It had bright white houses with red-tiled roofs; there were no bad smells, but just clean, clear and sweet air and a fine view of Gibraltar in the far distance. The village was Jimela and it had been really worth the walk simply to see it.

On March 31st the ships' companies of all the 4th Flotilla landed to march past Rear-Admiral (D) — Sir Charles Forbes — as a Farewell Inspection, and on April 1st we sailed with the Fleet for our final exercise before leaving for home. Warm sunshine and clear blue skies blessed the manoeuvres as we moved at speed (25-knots) twisting and turning, and our Engineer standing on the upper deck by the engine-room hatch, facing outboard by the guard-rail with his hands plunged deep into his trouser-pockets and admiring the spectacle. *Wren* made a sharp turn to port and so listed heavily to starboard and he, in order to maintain his vertical stance swayed back on his heels which unfortunately were equipped with rubbers and — Whoosh! The combination of steel deck, rubber and water proved near fatal as his feet and legs slid under the bottom wire and it was only his girth and the speed with which his hands left his pockets to grab the wire that saved him from going over the side and under the starboard propeller. The Chief E.R.A. happened to be standing by the fo'c'sle screen and spotted the "Old Man's" predicament, ran along the deck and supported him until the ship righted herself on completion of the 180-degree turn when a wet-footed and badly shaken "Old Man" was assisted to his cabin and into his bunk where he remained until next morning.

Glorious meanwhile was flying-off her planes for an attack on the battle-ships and cruisers which all four flotillas were screening and protecting when a French liner, the *Florida*, 9,500-tons, entered the arena and tended to hang about too long and too close for comfort. Maybe she wanted to give her passengers a grandstand view. Maybe she was spying, but for whatever reason she was told, for her own safety to keep clear of the area and continue her voyage. She ignored the polite warning and remained 'hovering' in the vicinity.

I had been on watch in the engine-room during the Forenoon — when the Old Man got wet — so after dinner I took myself and a book along to the "Band-stand" — a circular gun-platform abaft the after funnel — for a quiet read and some fresh air. The platform had a two-feet-high canvas screen to protect me from the wind and I had been reading for about half-an-hour when I was startled by the 'whoop-whoop' of the ship's sirens. I glanced out over the screen to find we were enveloped in a thick, but patchy white fog. All boats had been dashing about picking up the aerial torpedoes which had been aimed at the Fleet, but now the planes were running short of fuel and unable to find their floating hangar. News came through that four planes had ditched and everyone on deck was told to keep their eyes peeled for any signs of the airmen as we steamed slowly with sirens 'whooping' every minute or so. Fortunately all four air-crews were rescued — by *Broke* (our Leader), *Witch*, *Volunteer* and *Whitehall*. We only managed to find a missing torpedo.

Glorious too had been stopped in the fog but, possibly having received a radio message from another ship indicating a fog-free area where she might fly-on some of her brood, she began to move forward and within a couple of minutes collided with the Frenchman. Had she been going a bit faster she would have cut through the liner and caused a major disaster. As it was, both ships locked together with the carrier's bows buried half-way through *Florida* just forward of her bridge on the port side and remained like that as the fog gradually thinned and until it was certain that neither was in danger of sinking.

Planes in the air had watched the collision and realised there was no hope of their being able to return 'home' so rather than ditch and risk being picked up they landed safely on Spanish soil near Malaga — seventeen machines and their crews.

There were casualties in both ships, the 'Fog look-out' man in the bows of *Glorious* had been killed instantly, and more than thirty passengers and crew died in the liner. The fog cleared at 3 p.m. and we saw the full extent of the damage to both vessels — the carrier's bows buckled with the front of the flight-deck pulled down towards the water, and the liner with a gaping hole, thirty-feet wide in her side forward of her bridge and

H.M.S. 'Glorious' off Malaga, April 2nd 1931.
After Colliding with French Liner 'Florida'.

S.S. 'Florida' (Marseilles) after being rammed by H.M. Aircraft Carrier 'Glorious', April
1st 1931. (Note gaping hole in port side).

stretching to below water-level. All destroyers were employed in a search for any further casualties and to pick up debris from the collision or wreckage of planes, and at 4 o'clock the fog came down again and we spent the night with engines stopped and sirens sounding until 4 a.m. when the fog lifted and we went at 20-knots to meet *Glorious* off Malaga. Rescued airmen and the collected bits and pieces were returned to the carrier and we had a close-up view of her damage, the twisted steel had gathered relics such as panelling and what had appeared to be bundles of straw as a result of the impact. *Florida* lay closer inshore and well down by the bows. Our 4th Flotilla returned to Gibraltar; the Fleet resumed its Spring Cruise and next day, Good Friday, the carrier limped to anchor in the bay.

It was a beautifully sunny and warm day and leave had been granted until 7 o'clock next morning and I think that everybody who was not 'duty' went ashore as it was so quiet in the town now. I was the Duty E.R.A. and the most senior engine-room rating left on board to enjoy a most pleasant and peaceful afternoon and evening until — 10 p.m. The Signalman came to the Mess with a signal from "Commodore — Gibraltar. *Wren* to be ready to leave harbour at 0700 with Funeral Party from *Glorious* and proceed to Malaga."

I made out a Steaming Watch for the Stoker Petty Officer and stokers to go below at 0400 and flash No. 2 boiler, and No. 3 boiler to be lit at 0500 and be connected up at 0630. I sent for the S.P.O. and told him that I would be in the engine-room to get things ready there and went to the Engineer's cabin to leave a copy of the Commodore's signal and of my Steaming Orders on his desk and returned to the Mess.

The Engineer came back to the ship after 11 p.m. — half-drunk (maybe more) and as he came over the gangway the Quartermaster, a Leading Seaman, showed him the signal and the "Old Man's" reaction was to send the Sidesman, an Able Seaman, to "Fetch the Duty E.R.A. to me!" I went to his cabin and was greeted with, "What's this about going to sea in the morning? Why wasn't *I* told?" I replied, "You were not on board to be told, sir, and there are my notes on your desk."

"Well — you should have met me at the gangway. I don't want a Leading Seaman telling *me* what we are going to do!" I said I would have met him had I known what time he was coming back. "Well — what have you done about it?" I pointed to my copy of the Steaming Orders on his desk and he began reading them but dropped the paper and said, "Why not No. 1 boiler?" I reminded him that No. 1 was open for cleaning. 'Well — you can get the hands down below and have it closed up right away!'

"That is not necessary, sir. Two boilers will be quite sufficient for our needs." "Don't tell *me* what is necessary and what isn't! Where's the Duty Stoker Petty Officer? (Shout) Messenger! Get the Duty Stoker P.O. along here at once!" When Nick Carter arrived the Engineer said to him, "This damn fool tells me we can't light up No. 1 boiler." S.P.O.: "Well, we can't sir. It's open for cleaning, and numbers two and three are both ready for steaming." Engineer: "You're as much bloody use as he is. Get the Watch down below right away, and get out of here. Get out. Both of you. Get out!" We got out with Carter asking me, "What are you going to do about it?" I said, "Nothing. The old fool's drunk. I'll wait for the Chief to come aboard." I knew *he* would not be staying ashore all night, but as it happened Shore Patrols had visited the Canteen and all Bars telling all *Wrens* to report back to the ship by midnight, and the message had been flashed on the screens at cinemas, theatre and Salvation Army Home.

The Chief and the other two E.R.A's came aboard before midnight and the Chief went to see the "Old Man" — fast asleep (drunken stupor?) on his bunk — who, when roused professed no recollection of any of the events I had mentioned. So the orders stood and we sailed at 0700, arrived in Malaga at noon and were informed that the funeral was postponed until Sunday morning and we had unexpectedly to victual an extra thirty people and accommodate them overnight.

When we got back to Gib. on Sunday evening I made out a request, "To see the Captain in order to state a complaint," and gave it to the Chief. As with all requests it had to go through the normal channels — which meant via my Departmental Head, the very man against whom I was complaining after Friday's fiasco when he had questioned my ability to take charge and had done so in the presence of a rating junior to me — the Stoker P.O. — who incidently and unbeknown to me had also requested to see the Captain with a similar complaint.

The Chief outlined the grievances to the Engineer who said his mind was a complete blank about any of the things we said had occurred that night, but I had some documentary proof in the form of half-a-dozen sheets of Naval Signal-pad he had spoilt while trying to pen an 'official order' to me, for after telling us to get out of his cabin that night he shouted for me to go back and began writing on his signal-pad. In the box marked "To:-" he wrote "Eng Offi". That was wrong. He tore that top sheet from the pad and threw it to the floor. Second sheet — "To:- Duty boiler" — wrong again, and that suffered the same fate. It was about his seventh attempt that he managed to hand one which read, "Get stokers below at once now and light up No. 2 and 3 boilers and close No. 1." I salvaged the lot as 'evidence' but the Chief, who had been in *Wren* with the Engineer for the past two years said, "It's his last ship before his retirement when we get home and forcing the issue now won't do either of you any good, and you and Carter will have to live on with it in other ships."

The upshot was that the "Old Man" had Carter and me — and the Chief — along to his cabin to apologize with a limp handshake and 'No hard feelings?', and the incident was closed, with the thankfulness that we would soon be Paying Off. The 4th Flotilla sailed on April 10th and *Wren, Witch* and *Volunteer* arrived in Devonport on the 14th. I remained with the ship preparing her to be handed over to Dockyard control on April 23rd when I was discharged to my Home Port of Chatham and 20-days Foreign Service Leave.

CHAPTER 7

Where Now?

It was good to be home — to see my wife again and to see my son for the first time, now nine-months old and beginning to walk. But when my leave ended and I returned to barracks at Chatham it was to wonder "What will be my next move?" I just had to wait and see.

For four weeks I had different Courses to attend: Gas Mask Repair; Disciplinary Drill on Parade (training for the King's Birthday March-Past) and a Revolver Shooting Course at the Barracks Range, and able to get ashore most nights and week-ends; not knowing how long it was going to last; always wondering When? Where? and What? The answer came at the end of June when my name appeared on the Drafting Office Notice Board — Detailed *Malcolm*. (And very welcome!)

She was the Leader of the Nore Reserve Flotilla, lying in the Dockyard but with her 'brood' moored outside in the River Medway at Short Reach, which was known as "The Trot".

The flotilla consisted of about a dozen boats of the "V" and "W" Classes, moored to buoys, two or three abreast and head to stern, each boat having one E.R.A., two stokers, a Seaman Petty Officer and two A.B.s as complement, but my charge was the *Abdiel*, a four-funnelled mine-laying Leader, 1,300-tons, built in 1917 and the fastest ship in the Fleet in her day. Our work was purely 'Care and Maintenance' and certainly enough to keep everyone busy each day with the satisfaction of knowing that almost every evening I could go ashore by the 4 p.m. Trot boat and return at 7.30 next morning.

One boat — *Vansittart* — was designated 'Accommodation vessel' in which we had our meals and where one Boat's crew had to sleep each night as "Duty Watch". Lighting, for *Vansittart* only, was supplied by a wartime Boom Defence Vessel (B.D.V.) moored alongside containing a paraffin-fueled motor generator which had to be started by the Duty E.R.A. before sunset each evening and shut down again at 11 p.m. — when oil-lamps took over as Navigational and Emergency lighting.

Yes, it was very nice but there was always the doubt — the feeling that it is too good to last; that any morning there could be a 'Re-call' — a 'Required for Draft' notice waiting on board. But the year wore on. In November *Abdiel* was towed into the Dockyard for dry-docking and I was given three E.R.A. apprentices from the Training Establishment at Chatham to refit, under my supervision, all the underwater valves.

I watched every aspect of their work for the first few days before letting them get on with the job and then waiting for me to inspect prior to allowing them to close the job up.

My two stokers were cleaning each of the four boilers in turn with me keeping checks on them at every stage and entering the boiler to 'sight' the tubes for obstructions as they finished each one. I was in the middle of 'sighting' the last boiler when one of the boys came to tell me that his valve was ready for my inspection. I asked if *he* was satisfied that it was all right. He was, he said and I trusted him. "O.K. Box it up!" The apprentices left; dockyardmen began flooding the dock and, true to form, the only valve-cover to leak was that one. I was checking every valve in the ship's bottom and it was 'panic-stations' for me as I frantically worked to remove and re-joint that cover without having to ask the Yard to stop the flooding operation. That would have heralded an Inquiry which would have been catastrophic for me — but — "All's well . . ." and *Abdiel* floated.

Life resumed its pleasant course — until December 10th. "Report to Drafting Office for draft." I did — and was told I would be joining the battleship *Valiant* on December 29th 1931.

(On September 15th 1931, there had been a strike — a mini-mutiny in the Home Fleet, previously called the Atlantic Fleet, while lying at Invergordon during the Autumn Cruise. The trouble was caused by the Admiralty's intention to reduce the pay of the Lower Deck and following a mass-meeting in the Naval Canteen on shore the ratings' Committee decided to refuse to take the Fleet to sea the next day. Men from *Valiant* had been amongst the ring-leaders and when the Admiralty agreed to waive the cut and conditions had returned to near-normality it resolved to dilute the crews of those ships which had been most actively involved by moving certain individuals to other parts of the world, or out of the Navy! Hence — my Draft.)

I joined her at Sheerness on the 29th 27,500-tons, eight 15″ guns and port and starboard batteries of 6″ guns, 24-boilers in four boiler-rooms and four shafts of 27,000 horse-power, and much cleaner than *Emperor of India*

The Mess consisted of 5-Chiefs and 35-E.R.A.'s and for me it was the start of another period of uncertainty as there was a rumour that she was going to Pay Off and re-commission on January, 12th 1932, so my name was not put on the Ship's Books and therefore I could not be paid. There was the doubt whether "Paying Off" meant that everyone, including me, would be leaving, or not. No one knew.

On 5th January all other ships of the Home Fleet sailed for the Spring Cruise to Gibraltar leaving us swinging round the buoy at Sheerness. A skeleton Advance Party arrived on the 8th and all the old crew left by the same Medway ferry *Harlequin*, leaving me as sole survivor, and on the 12th the new people arrived to bring the ship up to full complement. The first thing to happen was that 'parts of ship' were re-allocated and I was moved from my job in the engine-rooms and given charge of all power-boats. Memories of *E. of I.*! There were two steam picket-boats, a motor-cutter, a skimming-dish and even the extra motor-boat for Capt. (D) of the 5th Flotilla of Destroyers. It was a duplicate performance and I was also 'extra man' in the engine-room when leaving or entering harbour.

We sailed for Spithead on the 15th to carry out trials on launching a radio-controlled sea-plane from a newly installed catapult fitted to the top of "A" turret, but for days the weather was unsuitable. It was either too foggy or blowing a gale; the boats could not be lowered and our only contact with shore was by our old work-horse, the drifter *Horizon*, for the hour-long trip. Then, one afternoon the Captain (W. Maxwell) was summoned to a meeting in Portsmouth and had his picket-boat lowered for the journey. To show some interest I made the long trip in heavy weather and noticed the same symptoms of 'labouring' as had occurred in *E. of I's* boat and came to the same conclusion — There was a 'twist' — so when she was hoisted back inboard I had the propeller-shaft withdrawn and was just lowering it onto the deck with the help of a couple of stokers when "Hands to tea" was piped and they let the thing fall, crushing three fingers of my left hand and putting me on the Sick List.

The weather remained bad and the launch project was about to be abandoned — the ship being under orders to rejoin the Fleet at Gibraltar — when the next morning dawned bright and sunny and ideal for the launch. We steamed up-channel into the wind and worked up to 21-knots and as I had my arm in a sling as well as having been inoculated ready for the Mediterranean — I was able to be on deck to watch the sea-plane fired from the catapult at 1.45 p.m. and crash into the sea at 1.47 p.m. before the boffins could take control of it. We did an emergency 'stop' and salvaged the wreck and were anchored again at Spithead by 2.15 p.m. Two days later our Gib visit was cancelled; we were to proceed to Portland. We were still in a 'Working up' state, trying to attain fighting efficiency with plenty of drills in harbour and lots of sea-time with day and night firing of our 15″ guns — possibly disturbing the sleep of some south-coast residents.

On January 26th the submarine M2 was lost with all hands while exercising off Portland, and on the 16th of February a party of 16 from our Mess and another 16 E.R.A's from the Submarine Base were invited to a Fund-raising Dinner and Dance given by the Mayor of Bridport, Councillor Knight, and resulting in a considerable sum for the dependants.

Until my hand regained its full movement I was employed as a turner in the Machine-shop. Late one afternoon a serious emergency arose when an air-inlet valve on the giant Mirrlees diesel-generator fractured and I was given the task of making a new one from 'scratch' — from a block of steel. It was a very intricate operation involving different machines — lathe, drilling, boring, milling, and some filing — all to fine tolerances, and working through the evening I finished the job in what the Senior Engineer considered a record time and the generator running again by early morning. That episode was to benefit me later.

Valiant pottered about in the Channel around Portland as though she did not know where to go or what to do, until on March 1st we increased to Full Power and the old girl knew she wanted to get back to Sheerness. We were not told why, but Capt. Maxwell was so impressed by the ship's speed and performance that he asked for the entire Engine-room Department to be mustered on the quarterdeck in order to congratulate and thank us. For six weeks we lay at anchor, the crew able to have three nights ashore out of every four, travelling up the Medway in the tender *Harlequin* which normally took about an hour, but three hours in fog.

My wife gave birth to our daughter on March 9th and I saw her when she was just a few hours old.

On April 13th the ship reduced complement and I was returned to barracks again wondering "Where next?" I started a 5-day Drill Course on the second day of which I was hauled in for a March Past when the First Lord of the Admiralty, Sir Bolton Eyres-Monsell, inspected the Parade, and on the third day my name appeared on the 'Report for Draft' Notice Board. Now I would know 'where next?' I was to join *Scout* 'tomorrow'.

Scout — a destroyer of about 900-tons, one of the many "S" and "T" Class boats built in 1915 – 16 and predecessors of the "V's" and "W's" — and undergoing a minor refit in Chatham Dockyard when I joined her, with plenty more work to be done before she was ready to re-commission for duty with the Emergency Flotilla on May 2nd when we raised steam. On the 3rd we went down river to Sheerness to oil and take in ammunition, returning to the Emergency berth in Short Reach and just to sea-ward of the Reserve boats in the Trot.

There were three boats in the flotilla, the other two being *Scimitar* and *Tempest*, each taking its turn as Duty Emergency Destroyer for one week — Monday to Monday. The Duty boat had to be ready to go to sea at one-hour's notice; the Stand-by boat at four-hours', and the third boat was 'free'. This seemed quite a pleasant interlude despite the fact that there were only two E.R.A's and a Chief to each boat, which meant that we two had to work a "2-watch" system — one watch on and one off — both for shore-leave and for steaming when a boat was either Duty or Stand-by, and no all-night leave for the Duty boat's crew.

Life rolled quietly along until at 6.20 on the morning of May 31st we received a signal to "Proceed with all despatch" and at 7.30 were doing 15-knots between the mud-flats of the banks of the Medway into the Thames estuary and out into the North Sea and thick fog. Our mission was to locate the destroyer-leader *Stuart* which had been holed in collision with a merchant-ship during the night. We found her at 2.30 in the afternoon lying stopped some miles off Great Yarmouth and sent a 'help' party to her, then escorted her to Sheerness Dockyard dry-dock.

Arriving back at our berth at 11 p.m. we two E.R.A's had to start work at once to strip down the starboard Ahead main throttle valve which for some inexplicable reason had refused to shut when we wanted to 'lay stopped' in company with *Stuart*. In order to stop the starboard engines the Astern throttle had to be kept open and then our forward speed regulated by that. Everything was very hot but we finished at 3 a.m. — ready for any further emergency, which fortunately there wasn't.

For a week from 8th July we were Guardship for the Royal Thames Yacht Club Regatta at Southend. Every evening the ship was illuminated over-all with light-bulbs outlining the shape of the hull and funnels, and with a string of lights from jack-staff to foremast-head and mainmast-head to ensign-staff which all made for a perfect holiday-picture for the cameras. A Searchlight Display was also given on one evening but on July 13th the weather deteriorated, putting an end to the racing and by evening a full gale was blowing. A motor-boat tender from one of the bigger yachts had broken down and was drifting rapidly towards the open sea and just after passing us she fired a Distress Flare. The Quartermaster piped "Away life-boat's crew" — a call which means that anyone nearby should man the boat. I happened to be on deck and as it was our tiny motor-boat which was going away I jumped into it with two seamen and a Leading-seaman cox'n and away we went, our 'brief' — shouted by the Officer of the Watch — was to "Take off any women and bring them back here". What an outing that was! We careered towards the open sea in the dusk helped by the wind, wave and tide for about five miles and then were too late to effect a rescue because the Shoeburyness Lifeboat had also been alerted and reached the tender ahead of us. She fired a line over the distressed boat and

49

took it in tow, leaving us to battle our way back against storm and tide. We really needed assistance ourselves for it took us more than an hour to reach our ship with our boat half-filled with water and our four-man crew drenched. Next day, the Regatta over, we returned to Short Reach and a week later we steamed up the Thames to moor between two buoys in the river at the small town of Erith (between Gravesend and Woolwich — on the Kent side) where we were guests for their Civic Week and the main attraction for the August Bank Holiday week-end. Hundreds of visitors came on board every afternoon and the townspeople opened their Clubs and arranged dances; the Mayor gave a Party for the non-duty Watch of the ship's company and the cinemas gave free admission. Monday was Regatta Day with our two whalers being manned by seamen and stokers who were dressed as pirates, thus giving a touch of gaiety and comedy. The evening and the festivities ended with a Searchlight Display by *Scout* — and a tremendous cheer from Erith's people. The ship returned to Base next morning and as we passed the holiday resort of Canvey Island at the mouth of the Thames a couple of 'Speed-boats' (Two-shillings to see the warship pass!) vainly tried to keep pace with us. We were doing 18-knots with scarcely a ripple at our bows while the so-called 'Speed-boats' doing about 15-knots with their bows in the air had a bow wave giving the impression of about 35-knots, but we walked away from them.

My time with *Scout* ended two days later with a signal, "Return to Depot for Draft — on relief." and he arrived that afternoon. He thought he had seen my name on the list for the *Cumberland*, serving on the China Station — "or perhaps it was for one of the River Gun-boats. But it was definitely China!"

I scanned the Draft Lists when I arrived and could not see my name on any list but I did see — on *Cumberland*'s Advance Party List — the name of my old class mate, 'Tich' Whiting, who told me that our mutual chum and class-mate 'Soapy' Hudson, Ordnance Artificer, was also detailed. He asked "Why don't you volunteer and come with us?" (The Advance Party were to take passage out to meet her at Colombo and help steam her home to Chatham where she would be refitting for a month or two and then re-commission for further service in China.) I told him that I had done all the volunteering I was likely to do — Diver, Submarines, New Zealand — and henceforth would take whatever came my way, but hoped it would be something good.

As I was not detailed I made enquiries about other possibilities — which ships were due for re-commissioning or perhaps one being built somewhere — and was told there were also half-crews required for destroyers of the 8th Flotilla (China) and for the Submarine Depot Ship *Medway* (China) who would be taking passage out. My informant also thought that a flotilla of new destroyers was getting ready for the

Mediterranean and, "Of course, there's the *Dragon* coming in shortly and will re-commission for the West Indies, but you won't get *her*! There are enough volunteers to man her twice over!" But he had been unaware of the recent appointment of a new Drafting Commander who realised that some men 'in the know' obtained pre-knowledge of re-commissioning dates and destinations and, knowing themselves to be almost due for Foreign Service volunteered for one of the Stations regarded as a 'plum' job, such as the Africa or the America and West Indies Stations where only a small squadron operated, while others accepted, or had to accept, repeated stints in the Med or on the China Station working with big fleets, or maybe have to spend a couple of years on a sloop in the tropical heat of the Red Sea and Persian Gulf.

I knew nothing of it either and awaited my 'definitely China' draft. Two days later I was detailed "Advance Party — *Dragon*".

CHAPTER 8

West Indies

I was one of the twenty Engine-room ratings to join the *Dragon* on September 5th 1932 as she entered Chatham Dockyard on her return from two-and-a-half years on the American & West Indies Station and we took over from her home-coming crew. On the 8th the new crew marched out from the Depot and we re-commissioned for further service in the 8th Cruiser Squadron. She was one of quite a number of "C" and "D" Classes built in 1917 – 18 — handsome and rakish ships of about 4,800-tons with six 6"-guns — and I was working in the engine-room when the new Commander (E) walked through on his first day aboard. He was D. H. Tollemache who had been Senior Engineer in *Valiant* during my short time there and remembered me. He asked, 'Why aren't you in the Machine Shop?" and I said I was quite happy where I was, but half-an-hour later I was called to the Engineers' Office to be told, "I'm putting you in charge of the Machine Shop. It's a chance to make a name for yourself." (Whatever did that mean? To me it was just a job — my 'part of ship'.)

On September 21st 1932 we said our Goodbyes to wives and families as the ship sailed to rejoin the 8th Cruiser Squadron in Bermuda, and on our fourth day out into the Atlantic we received a signal that the Survey Vessel *Challenger* was aground on the coast of Labrador and we were to 'render assistance'. Speed was increased to 20-knots in worsening seas and everything was battened down with the decks awash, and it became very hot and clammy below decks and continued so even after the emergency ended 12-hours later when the "*Challenger* re-floated" signal came and we reverted to our proper course and our economical speed of 12-knots. On the eighth day one of our engine-room watchkeepers was taken ill and I had to leave my workshop job and pick up his watches until we reached Bermuda on October 2nd.

The Squadron comprised of five cruisers and two sloops, with the Commander-in-Chief of the Station wearing his flag in the County Class cruiser, *Norfolk*; he was Vice-Admiral Sir R.A.R. Plunkett-Ernle-Erle-Drax.

The other cruisers were *Danae*, *Dauntless* and *Durban*; the sloops were the Flower Class (1918 vintage) Heliotrope and the modern Town Class *Scarborough*. We and *Danae* were North American Division; *Durban* and *Dauntless* South American Division, and the Flagship's duties carried her wherever Diplomatic or Strategic circumstances demanded.

Our Captain was W. F. Wake-Walker; the Executive Commander — the Rt. Hon. R. O. Fitzroy (son of the Speaker of the House of Commons).

Bermuda — a group of islands (about 365 of them) lying about 500-miles south-east from New York, and our Base and Depot *Malabar* was on Ireland Island with the Dockyard at one end of the horse-shoe-shaped group. Hamilton, the capital, was about 15-miles by road from the Base, and the other main town, St. George's, some seven miles further on at the extreme end of the other 'arm' of the horse-shoe from the Base.

The only means of transport on the islands was by bicycle or horse and buggy and it was a resort for American tourists, very expensive and beyond the pockets of the Lower Deck, but there was a nice Naval Canteen and a Chief & Petty Officers Club on Boaz Island within pleasant walking distance of the Dockyard gate, where we could have a glass of tepid beer and play billiards, snooker, cards or table-tennis, or enjoy the periodic concert. There was a cinema in the 'Yard, created by the transformation of the Sail Loft — draping its windows with canvas and using planks of timber for seating (Bring your own cushions from your Mess) and the films mainly recent releases from the States.

But the first priority for most of the crew was a walk to the Cycle Shed to purchase a second-hand bicycle (£2) from the huge stock and have it registered with an enamel disc at a cost of two-shillings for one year. We put in plenty of sea-time — "Working-up" period — to attain Fleet efficiency with day and night gunnery and torpedo-running — and having to recover our own 'fish' after every firing. There were two hurricane-warnings in the first few weeks which, after making all preparations to meet them turned to just very strong winds, but the third warning — which came at 6 a.m. on November 10th was somewhat different. *Dragon* was Emergency Cruiser and ready at short notice for any exigency as we waited for the hurricane to strike. Apparently we only caught the tail-end in Bermuda but even that was terrific with winds of more than 100 m.p.h. when it hit us on the 12th at seven o'clock in the morning. There was six-hours of the heaviest rain darkening the sky and blotting out the entire land- and sea-scape and then, as suddenly as it had started it ceased and the sea became flat-calm, the sun shone and it was a glorious summer day! Then came news that some of the Caribbean Islands had suffered the full blast and we were ordered to proceed south, reaching Acklin Island in the Bahamas early on the 16th and landing some stores in our motor-cutter. We did not anchor but were too far off-shore to be able to see what — if any — damage had been caused. We moved off again at noon, passed Cuba that evening and arrived off the small island of Cayman Brac at 10.30 next morning. We were fairly close in-shore but it was too deep for the ship to anchor so we steamed slowly to and fro as stores and water were loaded into the cutter and the two whalers and ferried ashore — the water being carried in a huge canvas container rigged in the cutter. (The 'container' was actually a plunge-bath or swimming-pool which could be rigged on the upper deck when the ship was in shark-infested waters so that the hands could splash about in the Dog-Watches).

As we steamed slowly back and forth we were continually distilling fresh water into the 'carrier', consequently being very short of water for our own consumption, but realising that the islanders' needs were far greater than ours. Sixty-seven people had been lost in the hurricane and more than 300 injured. Houses had been flattened and large fishing boats carried a hundred yards or more from the beaches to lie, high and dry where houses had previously stood. A Burial Party of marines landed to help in the clear-up operation and when they returned at 8 p.m. on the 18th it was quite a relief for everyone when the ship got moving at a reasonable speed as we headed for the adjacent island of Little Cayman to land more stores and water, for the temperature below decks had risen to an almost unbearable degree.

On completing our mission of mercy we steamed on to Kingston, Jamaica, where, although it was extremely hot it was a pleasant change from Bermuda. As we were only to remain in port for 24-hours I, with two mess-mates — "Sandy" Saunders and "Fender" Friend — went ashore, hired a car and asked the Jamaican driver to show us something of the urban district around the town. The car was an open-tourer and it was wonderfully cool as we drove in the hills and through groves of bananas and oranges and in the beautiful Hope Gardens Botanical Park and the hamlets of Constant Springs and Stony Hill, stopping at Assi's Club for a refreshing drink of rum and lemonade while we watched part of a Baseball match between Kingston Club and Cuban Stars. We met some sergeants of the 1st Battalion, 5th Northumberland Fusiliers who were garrisoned in the island and were invited to their Mess at Up Park Camp where a number of Chiefs and P.O's were already being entertained. They were a splendid crowd and after a convivial evening we were back at the ship by 11 p.m. Next morning we oiled and started a very rough passage back to a cold, dull and wet Bermuda where we arrived on November 25th.

Dragon — so young in commission — had already assembled a good football team and in the course of the next four weeks had beaten *Danae* (6 – 0) in the quarter-final of the Governor's Cup, *Norfolk* (2 – 1) in Bermuda League followed by a 7 – 1 win over the Army Staff and an 'away' victory against *Norfolk* (2 – 1) to become League Champions.

But the "Best match ever seen in Bermuda" — according to the local Press — was the semi-final for the Governor's Cup, *Norfolk* versus the 2nd Battalion, 5th Northumberland Fusiliers (the other half of the Jamaican bunch) which resulted in a 3 – 2 win for the Navy. Then on Christmas Eve on the Army's ground at Prospect Camp outside Hamilton our team beat *Norfolk* by three goals to one and added the Governor's Cup to the ship's Trophy Case.

Meanwhile, *Danae* was coming to the end of her 2½-years on the Station and would be at home for Christmas, and on December 4th her Concert Party gave a great Farewell Show in the Canteen, attended by most of the men from every ship on the Station. It was a most pleasant evening as anyone can imagine and I *had* to be present as Chief of the Canteen Patrol. It was a duty which fell to the C.P.O's of the Duty Cruiser by rota, and I am happy to say that everyone was well-behaved, but I was quite relieved when the Canteen had been cleared by 10.30 p.m. and no 'reporting' to be done and I and my Patrolmen could repair to the Club and our beds.

Danae was 'cheered' out a couple of days later followed by the thoughts and good wishes of everybody left behind.

December 23rd — *Dragon* steamed from the Dockyard over to anchor in the bay at Hamilton. We could not go alongside the jetty because the main berth there was occupied by the Furness-Withey liner *Monarch of Bermuda* laden with Christmas Cruise passengers from the U.S.A.

On the 24th practically everyone not actually required for duty on board landed to cheer the ship's team to victory in the Governor's Cup and afterwards the Chiefs and P.O's were entertained to tea in the Sergeants' Mess. Then someone issued a challenge to a snooker match — 'Losers to pay for the beer'. We won, and a jolly, musical evening ended with the Army giving us a rousing send-off as we departed in our several horse-drawn buggies to catch the midnight boat back and be in time for Father Christmas!

Christmas Day, 1932 — Divisions (in white uniforms). Captain's Inspection and Church on the quarterdeck with lusty singing of carols. A splendid dinner (lunch) of roast turkey, during which I, being the Duty E.R.A., was called away to the engine-room to adjust one of the pumps. The afternoon was quiet; the evening was hilarious — with a lot of silly, childish party games and everyone happy.

Next morning the *Monarch* sailed for New York and we moved in to the empty berth. A huge crowd flocked aboard when we were 'Open to visitors' that afternoon — mostly vacationing Americans — and Sandy and I showed a middle-aged couple over the ship and were then invited ashore to spend the evening with them in their prestigious Royal Prince Hotel while we, in our turn invited them to *Dragon*'s Dance in No. 1 Shed the following evening. It was an enjoyable 'break' and on the 28th we steamed back across Great Sound to the Dockyard basin and 'reality', and into 1933.

Early in January we left for a cruise in the Caribbean and again it soon got very hot below decks as the sea became a little 'lumpy' and the hatches battened down, and it was really quite rough as we approached our first 'call' — San Juan, Porto Rico.

My work was still 'in charge of the Machine Shop' but always to assist on the throttles when entering or leaving harbour. (I also kept an occasional full Watch below at sea in order to qualify for Tropical pay — an extra shilling per day while the ship was in the Tropical Zone.) On this day, January 9th, the Joiner was rigging the gangway ready for the Captain to leave the ship on arrival and make his customary Courtesy Call on the Port Captain when a freak wave washed him — the Joiner — into the shark-infested waters. "Man Overboard" and "Emergency Stop — Full Astern" were regular features of Dog Watch Evolutions so we were well prepared and alert, and as soon as the alarm was raised a life-belt was thrown and the ship stopped in the shortest possible distance. 'Chippie' was plucked from the sea, a bit shaken but none the worse for his dip.

An invitation was received for "60-men to visit Treasure Island Plantation. They need only bring swimming gear with them!" I went with six others from our Mess and we quite naturally thought our destination was an island, but when we got ashore our hosts were waiting with two single-decker buses in which we were taken about 40-miles into the hills beyond the city — a beautiful scenic drive — to a big pineapple plantation. We had landed at 10 a.m. and arrived at Treasure Island at 2 p.m. to find tables set out in the open and the luscious smell of suckling-pig spit-roasting over pineapple-leaf fires intimating that lunch was almost ready — a delicious meal even though it was 'all pineapple'. Aperitif: pineapple juice. Main course: meat cooked *over* pineapple fire with yams boiled *in* pineapple juice. Dessert: pineapple with ice-cream and all washed down with a sweet, black coffee: which *tasted* like coffee!

Then came a three-day voyage to Georgetown, British Guiana, below-decks resembling a Turkish-bath and everyone trying to find a place to sleep on the upper deck each night — and before entering the Demerara River for the run up to the capital we had to anchor on the seaward side of the Bar (a submerged bank of silt brought down by the river water) while the starboard engines were shut down together with the associated underwater valves. We then crossed the Bar using the port engines only, thus avoiding the risk of both the condensers becoming clogged, but once we were over we used both sets to take us up the fast-flowing, yellow-brown muddy river to anchor head and stern, and then the port condenser was opened and its tubes cleared — a task which we had to perform several times during our eight-day stay.

Georgetown lies only six degrees north of the Equator and was very hot by day and by night. Its people — the Coloured, the Portuguese and the Chinese — all made us welcome and we accepted a challenge issued by their Tennis Club to play a match against them. We were hopelessly outclassed and did not win one set, but the supper laid on by the Club was well worth the energy expended. I also played in the Billiards match against the Demerara Union Club. We lost that, too. Our only success was by the Football team beating the Colony X1 by two goals to one.

From Georgetown we sailed to Port of Spain, Trinidad, leaving there on February 7th with an old hulk — *Ravenswood* — in tow, ready to be used as a target by our flagship and two Canadian destroyers — *Saguenay* and *Champlain* — whom we were to meet later in the day. On sighting them we released our tow and 'stood off' to watch the accurate fire of the other three ships and the demise of the hulk as she sank beneath the waves. Then, for us it was almost like being in a Fleet again as we kept station behind *Norfolk* and had the two destroyers tagging astern. It was quite different from the independent cruising we had expected as we carried out a night-action attack on each other at 25-knots. At dawn *Dragon* attempted to take the "damaged" *Norfolk* in tow but worsening weather frustrated all efforts and all ships steamed into Kingston harbour on Feb. 11th.

During our stay we worked a Tropical routine, starting work at 7 a.m. and finishing at 1 p.m., the remainder of the day being free unless one was in the Duty Watch, thus giving us a bit more time to explore the town than on our previous visit. Like Port of Spain, it was a busy place, lots of trams and buses and thousands of cars — mostly taxi-cabs — and crowds of people abroad in the only two really 'main' streets.

We renewed our friendship with the Army at Up Park Camp and had pleasant times at the big and welcoming Y.M.C.A. where the Net-ball

H.M.S. 'Dragon'
at Trinidad, January 28th
1933.
Shark 11 ft. 7 ins.

Trinidad Street in Port of Spain. 'Dragon' 1933.

57

teams from the Canadian boats played each other and against the "Y" team.

The destroyers were lying alongside us and took advantage of the fact by sending a ton of work — valves and valve-boxes to be machined — to our machine-shop for me and my staff to do, as well as keeping pace with our own maintenance jobs.

On Feb. 22nd *Dragon* steamed along the coast to the small resort of Montego Bay with its beautiful beaches, backed by palm trees. There was nothing for us ashore except to picnic on the beach and swim in the warm, clear water most afternoons, but on the 28th we embarked the Commissioner of Cayman Brac and landed him that same evening at his island together with a few thousands of gallons of fresh water before continuing with our programmed cruise which took us to Belize, the capital town of British Honduras, where we anchored on March 2nd.

My one trip ashore there was on Sunday morning when a fair number of the ship's company attended a service in the Cathedral and then paraded before the colony's Governor with our Royal Marine Band at our head. It was a bit of pageantry much appreciated by the populace who were recovering fom the devastating effects of the recent hurricane and were in the midst of re-building.

On March 6th we moved about 50-miles down the coast of Honduras to the tiny town of Stann Creek where the Captain was the only man to go ashore, and that was only for one hour, but during that time — and for a few more hours — we did have the two whalers and the gig lowered into the water for the crews to get more training. (The Squadron regatta was being held on our return to Bermuda and for the past few weeks — when possible — we trained morning and evening. I was in the E.R.A's gig's crew and our times for having the boat were 0630 and 1600 normally.)

We steamed north next morning into the Gulf of Mexico with the temperature dropping dramatically every hour — from tropical to almost Arctic — until we picked up the pilot who was to take us the 40-odd miles up Mobile River to the city of Mobile, Alabama, on March 10th *Dragon* secured at a jetty adjacent to others at which enormous bales of raw cotton were being loaded onto cargo vessels for export; we were also close to the Dock Gates. The hospitality of the people amazed us, for as soon as any member of the crew stepped outside the gate he, or they, would be picked up by an American family in a car with an offer to be shown their fair city and all its landmarks, an offer which, if accepted was invariably followed by an invitation, "Come on home for supper".

Vic, my Fisgard class-mate, and I were invited by a Mr. and Mrs. Sherman to "Follow the Azalea Trail" with them in their open tourer. It was indeed a wonderful sight and we showed appropriate and enthusiastic appreciation and thanked our hosts for their kindness in showing us the beauty of their fair city. The 'Trail' ended at 4.30 with an invitation to continue with them to their home for supper but we suggested they take us to the ship so that we could freshen-up and show them over *our* home. Then, after a short tour of the ship I entertained them and Vic to Sunday tea in the E.R.A's Mess, the American couple being 'thrilled' (they said) at having 'English tea' with 'English boys' on an 'English ship'. Arriving at their home they began phoning friends, saying "Come on over and meet some boys from the English ship" with the result that a dozen people sat at their table for supper. The evening was a success which culminated with invitations to more parties to attend during our short stay, and I am sure our experience was common to most members of the crew judging by the number of people on the jetty when the ship cast off at 3 p.m. on March 15th. It was more like the departure of a liner except there were no 'streamers' linking ship to shore.

It was a short trip — 387-miles — to Tampa, Florida, a holiday resort in Tampa Bay and a big, bright and clean city where my adventures were somewhat different.

As usual we berthed alongside so did not have to rely on boats to take us ashore; we could take our time getting ready after a hard day's work and saunter ashore at any time during the evening. Sandy and I walked off at 8.30 p.m. to 'stretch our legs', have a coffee and a toasted sandwich — (Prohibition was still in force in the U.S.A.) — see a bit of the city and return aboard. We had not travelled far when a car drew up beside us and two young 'ladies' — one driving, the other beside her — asked us if we would like a ride out to Seminole Heights and Sulphur Springs. We could not forget the friendliness and hospitality of recent days so accepted. Phew! Our driver was either mad or imagined she was at Brooklands. Maybe she wanted to show off her driving skills, or perhaps wanted to scare the living daylights out of us — which she certainly did, especially when we left the city limits. It was a very dark night. Sandy and I were sitting in the rear passenger seats with the car roaring along at a terrific speed as it took a bend at a 'Y' junction on the rims of two wheels. We clung to the door-grips as we thought the car would roll over but were thankful that it stayed upright although there was no reduction in its speed. Bright head-lights began flashing behind us and one of the 'ladies' yelled, "It's the cops!" The driver doused the car's lights and pressed even harder on the accelerator so that we leapt forward at what must have been about a hundred miles per hour along that dark road with the following car keeping us in the beams of its head-lights — until we rounded a right-hand bend and out of the gleam the brakes were slammed on, catapulting Sandy and me almost through the windscreen. She banged the gears into reverse and roared the car back into the roadside scrub as the police car followed round the bend and disappeared into the night. Sandy and I had had

59

enough and discretion being the better part of valour we decided to leave the 'ladies' and walked away. This was new country to us — both literally and metaphorically — and we dare not, as Chief Petty Officers, get into any sort of trouble on shore. They drove off without a word, but probably with thoughts! and we made our way back towards Tampa with no idea how far we had come. The road was deserted but eventually a car travelling in our direction pulled up and an elderly couple asked if we would like a lift into town? In conversation in the car we explained what had happened and their response was, "Oh, a lot of that goes on here. Boys — and girls — take an automobile and go joy-riding at night and they don't mind what they do to the vehicle, or where they leave it."

When our Samaritans knew we had been in Mobile they said, "We have friends there, name of Sherman." They were the same Shermans who had entertained Vic Evans and me! A remarkable coincidence.

A big crowd were on the jetty to see the ship move away at two o'clock next afternoon for our five-day voyage back to Bermuda and meet up with the Squadron again. Day and night exercises shook us back to reality and the weather became very cold and rough. *Dragon* was due to enter Floating Dock on April 26th and our boilers were shut down when, as we sat at breakfast that morning Commander Fitzroy came to the Mess to ask the senior Chief E.R.A., "How long will it take to raise steam?" "About six-hours, sir!" The Commander said that a hurricane to the south had changed course and was now heading for Bermuda. He hurried away — possibly to have additional hawsers rigged for security — and within half-an-hour the wind-speed had reached 132 m.p.h. taking control of a string of railway wagons on the dockside and crashing them into the buffers at the end of the line. *Danae* was tied up ahead of us with her bows projecting beyond the end of the wall; she too had rigged extra wires but the wind was so strong it carried her away, dragging the massive iron bollards together with the concrete in which they were embedded to fall into the harbour. Her stern hawsers were still holding her so she dropped her two bower anchors to keep her steady. The sky was leaden and the roar of the wind terrific, but yet again it was the tail-end of the hurricane which hit the islands and by 10 a.m. the harbour and Grassy Bay outside it were flat calm and the sun shone brilliantly.

We entered the Floating Dock that afternoon and remained there until May 16th during which time every underwater valve and fitting was brought to the workshop to be machined and refitted by me and my staff. It was a very busy time during which the Squadron Regatta was held at Port Royal. The other ships went to anchor there while our boats and crews had to be towed out to the Course on both days of racing. I, and the rest of our gig's crew managed time off to go out and win our race, happy to know that our sacrifice (rowing on those tropic mornings and evenings) had paid off. But at the end of the day *Dragon* was 4th on aggregate.

An Annual event was the E.R.A's Challenge Relay Race round the Yard and harbour. Five E.R.A's from each of the five cruisers formed the teams; the 'baton' was a bicycle clip and the Trophy competed for was a rough-turned brass cup about 3″ tall and 1½″ diameter screwed to a very rough wooden plinth. There were no shields or inscriptions to indicate previous winners (no space for anything like that!) Actually, we were the current holders, it having been won by our predecesors, but I regret to say that we lost it to *Danae* in May, 1933.

The first 'leg' was a run from the head of the Slipway (where *Danae* had dislodged the bollards) along the Dockyard wall and short breakwater to the harbour entrance, a distance of about 400-yards, where No. 2 slid the clip over his wrist and dived off to swim the 50-yard gap to the detached breakwater. No. 3 waited at the bottom of the steps for the clip, climbed and ran the 100-yards to the steps at the other end where No. 4 waited in his ship's dinghy to collect the clip and row the boat some 200-yards to a point level with the Floating Dock, and the No. 5's took the final 'leg' — 600-yards to the Slipway starting point — on their bicycles. Supporters from all departments of all ships lined the Course to cheer the Tiffies along, and on this occasion I was our cyclist, but in spite of my frantic pedalling I could only come second.

The transfer of the Cup to its new owners took place at the Club that evening when it was "E.R.A's Night" and an excuse for everyone to 'celebrate'.

Our ship also boasted a super Water-polo team which, in the knock-out competition for the Fleet Polo Cup won it by beating *Norfolk* 5−1, *Dauntless* 5−0, *Durban* 9−0, *Danae* 5−0, *Malabar* (the Base) 5−0, and a team from St. George by 3-goals to 1. Then, in a challenge they beat a "Pick of the Fleet" team by that same score — 3−1. Yes, it was a great team!

It was at this time that I passed my examination for Chief — a written paper in the Engineer-in-Chief's office ashore followed by an Oral 'face-to-face' — me versus the E-in C. and the Fleet Engineer — quick-fire questions and answers, and gained my Certificate of Competence — "To take full charge of the Engine-room of a small ship" — which of course I had already done (*Wren* and *Scout*).

CHAPTER 9

California — (Here we come)

May 30th 1933 we put our bicycles into store and the ship sailed at 3 p.m. for Panama. Two days later everyone was inoculated against Yellow fever and as a result of the jab I almost 'blacked out' during my Middle Watch in the engine-room that night and was told to see the doctor in the morning. I had lost some weight, too, so Doc put me on a diet which included a bottle of Guinness every evening, plenty of fresh air, and excused me all duties — "until further orders".

My favourite parking place when conditions allowed was No. 2 Gun deck just for'ard of the bridge where I would hide myself with a book or writing materials and a cushion from the Mess. I settled in the warm sunshine, a nice breeze being created by our movement when presently someone came and put a deckchair beside me, sat and began speaking. My companion was Noel Coward, actor and playwright, who had come aboard just prior to our leaving Bermuda by arrangement with Admiralty, and with permission from Capt. W. F. Wake-Walker.

Our initial conversation revolved mainly around my duties as an artificer in *Dragon*, which had been varied although mostly in the Machine shop. He then wanted to know what other ships I had served in, and where, and also asked about my wife and children.

Next morning he brought two deck-chairs from the Captain's cabin 'so that he wasn't talking-down to me', and on that and subsequent days he did most of the talking. He spoke of wanting to rest and drop out of the public gaze for a while; of meeting the Captain and Commander Fitzroy and of their help; of his deep love and affection for Gertrude Lawrence (Dearest Gertie, he called her) and told me that he would like to marry her. It was a very confidential admission, slightly embarrassing for me and I could only wish him the best of luck. He said that he would be leaving us at Panama and probably get a ship on to New Zealand and Australia.

As we neared the Canal Zone rain-storms became frequent and on the night of June 4th/5th the rain was so thick as to be almost solid. Our sirens sounded throughout the night as we crept ahead to arrive at Cristobal Colon on the 5th where I was sent ashore to Colon Hospital for a chest X-ray (and a brief walk in the town!)

That evening the Ward-room piano was brought up to the quarter deck and Noel Coward sang and generally entertained the officers and ship's company from 8.30 until 10 o'clock, dedicating his final number —

Noel Coward on Board H.M.S. Dragon, May 30th. 1933 – June 5th.
Bermuda to Balboa, Panama.

"Someday I'll find you" to his 'Dear Gertie'. It was a happy show and much appreciated by all.

We passed through the Canal on June 7th. My X-ray had proved 'clear' and I resumed my duties by picking up the Afternoon Watch in the engine-room. Dayworkers would come down at intervals to relieve the watchkeepers and let them go to the upper deck for a few minutes to see the scenery and our progress through. It was very interesting to see how the electric 'mules' took charge of the ship to move us through the three sets of locks at Gatun, raising us 85-feet to Gatun Lake, and to be able to look down into the water of the lake and see tops of trees still standing since the land was flooded years before. It was hot and sticky all the way and we spoke of what it must have been like for those building the Canal. At Balboa we dropped the Pilot and Noel Coward and proceeded directly into the Pacific and our voyage to San Diego, California.

It would take ten days so we went to a 4-watch routine and I remained on the watch-bill to qualify for Tropical Pay. It was indeed 'pacific' — steaming sedately in the long swell, seeing many sharks, having lots of rain, and plenty of exercises, Action Stations and Dog Watch evolutions, and arriving in San Diego at 0730 on June 19th.

This was a fine big city with U.S. Army, Navy and Air Force bases and quite a contrast to the wooden-shacked Island towns, the sleepy southern-States town of Mobile and the flashy resort of Tampa, but the hospitality was as great. We had our first introduction to dirt-track motor-cycle racing under flood-lights, a thrilling couple of hours watching two riders, the world's most famous — Wilbur Lameroux and 'Sprouts' Elder — racing for the title. It was rather too noisy.

The Canadian Legion invited the ship's company to "A Concert at the Hall with Free Food and Drink". A big crowd attended; the food was hamburgers and hot-dogs, and the drinks were coffee and Cola; the concert? it somehow failed to materialise. Everybody stood or sat around talking and enjoying the company and at the end of the evening I received an invitation to visit the home of my 'hosts' for dinner at a later date.

Two seamen and the Supply Chief Petty Officer failed to return to the ship before we sailed and were classed as deserters. It came to light that the Supply C.P.O. had been playing the gaming-tables in Tia Juana over the Mexican border and to make good his losses had sold items from the ship's Clothing Store and pocketed the proceeds. More than £200 had been taken and it was assumed he could not face the disgrace of returning to the ship. Regarding the two seamen it was thought they had been overcome by the hospitality and did not fancy coming back to the rigours of life at sea. We steamed northwards and carried out a 'rattling' good Full Power Trial in fairly rough weather before arriving at Esquimalt, the Canadian Navy base on Vancouver Island — and 'rattling' is the operative word for that Trial because it generated a surfeit of work for the Machine-shop.

Esquimalt was our first Canadian port — a sort of 'front door' and we stopped just long enough for the Captain to make his Courtesy Call and announce our arrival and then steamed across the Strait of Georgia to Vancouver and secured at C.P.R. jetty at 0900 on July 1st — Dominion Day. A Sunday. A Public Holiday, and rain teeming down! What a welcome!

Our first impressions were not at all good, but during our week-long stay our opinions changed and we discovered an interesting and beautiful city of fine streets and buildings, and the lovely Stanley Park where the populace could escape the noise of traffic, and the magnificent Marine Drive on the banks of the Fraser River. (I think every member of the ship's company must have been taken along it — and through the well-laid-out suburbs — during our stay.)

Sandy and I were taken on this scenic drive and various others on successive evenings, including a visit to New Westminister from where we could clearly see the snow-capped Mount Baker more than 80-miles distant in the U.S.A., and a drive through North Vancouver and out to Capilano Canyon about 50-miles further along the road. We left the car in order to cross the deep, tree-lined ravine via a rope bridge simply for the experience. Our legs turned to jelly before we reached the far side, and then we had to wobble our way back again.

On July 6th the ship steamed back to Esquimalt which is on the outskirts of Victoria, the capital city of British Columbia, where we were to remain for nine days, and on arrival I was sent to the Jubilee Hospital for a further check following an X-ray taken at the U.S. Naval Hospital at San Diego. I was pronounced 'fit' and took a walk in this so-English-like city — not a regimented square grid of criss-cross streets and avenues — more like London's crescents or a seaside retirement town.

On our final evening there I had a walk as far as the Gorge — a close-by local beauty spot similar to a Village Green in England where people go for their evening stroll and a pint — except that there were no pints to be had there, only the usual tea, coffee or 'coke'. I was with another Messmate, Les Walley, and we could not sit drinking that sort of refreshment all evening so arrived back at the Base gates at 8.30 and then spent three hours drinking coffee with the Canadian Mounties in their office, talking with them and listening to tales of their experiences. Three hours passed in a flash.

From 'Squimo to Seattle, Washington State, was only a 7-hours trip and we anchored amidst an American Fleet comprised of the battleships *Texas, Tennessee, Maryland, Pennsylvania, Detroit, Arizona, West Virginia, New York*, and *California*. I do not know why so many had congregated nor the significance of the date (July 17th) but that evening our ship joined with them in giving a most wonderful Searchlight Display.

Dragon was quite happy to accept *Tennessee*'s offer to carry our libertymen ashore in their boats as they were more reliable than ours. (Our biggest boat, the motor-cutter, had a six-cylinder two-stroke engine — an odd feature — and a constant source of trouble).

At *Tennessee*'s invitation a large number of us were taken in her launch to follow the race for the Seattle Times Cup on Lake Washington. It was a race for cutters — 20 oarsmen in each boat from all the U.S. ships — over a three-mile course, a thrilling battle with each ship's power-boats jockeying for position behind its crew to cheer it on. Our host ship won the race and Cup and then landed us at a lake-side pier where we boarded a street-car for the return to the city.

On Sunday the C.P.O's of *Dragon* were invited to lunch with the C.P.O's of *Tennessee* aboard their ship. She was vast, and spotlessly clean and we were treated to an excellent meal of roast beef and apple pie with lashings of ice cream and a tour of the ship which was most interesting to us of the engine-room department to be able to inspect the machinery of a turbo-electric vessel. How we noticed the difference when we returned to the cramped quarters of our own little ship!

65

The Stockade camp at Comox. B.C. August 1933. Dragon in Background.

We sailed next morning, calling at Esquimalt to pick up "Stores for Camp" and a couple of days later dropped anchor off Comox on the eastern shores of Vancouver Island, and what a quiet, peaceful little village it was, surrounded by beautiful scenery of snow-capped mountains behind and white-sand beaches in front, and on the morning after our arrival one third of the crew landed and went into camp at Goose Spit a mile or so north of the village, leaving the ship more peaceful.

I was not keen on living under canvas and thought of pleading 'pressure of work' when my turn came for going ashore. (My plea might easily have been accepted because since we left Bermuda most of my spare time had been spent helping to fit out a motor-boat being built for the Captain. On our 'hurricane relief' visit to Belize he had been given some mahogany boles which Bermuda dockyard shipwrights had planked for him and our own shipwrights had fashioned to build the hull of a 15-ft. boat. At Tampa the Captain had bought a second-hand car-engine and from then on it had been my task to fit the engine into the boat and 'manufacture' all the bits and pieces — fixtures and fittings — from any scrap material I could find, and they included the propeller and shaft, the couplings, rudder-post, bushes, bilge-pump, deck fittings and tank filler-cap, — everything, and enjoying the challenge.)

Anyway I thought there must be a reason for sending everyone to camp for a week so I did not ask to be excused. If I had I would have missed one of the happiest and most care-free weeks of my Navy life away from home!

On Wednesday, August 2nd the 1st Camp Party returned and I went ashore with the 2nd to live in a Bell tent, two men to each and a camp-bed to sleep on and it was like the first day of school holidays as we kicked a football about on the green sward by the beach.

The routine was easy-going with Reveille at 0600, breakfast in the communal hut followed by Divisions at 0730 after which we collected rifles and went to the Firing Range until noon. The rest of the day was free. Dinner in the hut at one o'clock with a plentiful supply of Silver Springs beer from the Camp Canteen, then soccer and baseball — barefoot on the sand which was littered with driftwood from the logging rafts being towed from the northern forests to the saw-mills further south. We had permission to burn as much of the sun-bleached timber as we liked — and we certainly 'liked' and built beacons ten-feet high every night, dancing and 'whooping' and singing round the flames. On two evenings four of us from the Mess 'borrowed' a rowing-boat from the beach near the village and pulled out over the dark, placid water to look back at the glowing flames and to listen to the voices echoing over the bay.

Shooting on the Range varied each morning between firing at targets at 200-yards Deliberate Aim, "Rapid Shot" or "Snap Shoot", and "Deliberate" at 500-yards range, five or ten shots for 'self' and the same number for 'ship' — aggregated at the end of the whole period to qualify for medals. I think one ship from the Squadron visited the Camp every year and that a Cup or Trophy was held by the one with the highest "Ship" points. Sunday was a 'Rest Day' — (in a week of 'Rest Days'!) — and after Divisions and a brief Service some of us dug cockles and had the Cook prepare them for our tea. Some hardy chaps tried swimming but found the water too cold, and in the evening a few of us took a walk out to Point Home whence we could see the shimmering light of the giant paper-mill across on the mainland at Powell River. The night was so dark and the air so clean and clear that it was fascinating — hypnotic — just to stand and watch the glittering, distant sky.

Monday was our last day on the Firing Range and on Tuesday the whole company did an eight-mile march through the countryside to shake off the sloth and finished the evening with an impromptu concert. I think everyone was sorry that our lazy week was ending. We returned to the ship on Wednesday morning and the final Party, — Daymen — marines, writers, stewards, etc., went ashore.

Back on board I had plenty of work catching up with all the jobs which had accumulated in my absence, and making a set of six croquet mallets for Commander Fitzroy to present to the local Club.

All hands were back on board by Tuesday evening and we sailed from Comox early next morning, northwards through Queen Charlotte Strait on our way to Prince Rupert, at dusk anchoring in Alert Bay and opposite an Indian Reservation village. How peaceful and serene, the mirror-like surface of the water perfectly reflecting the forest-clad moutains on either side of the two-mile wide channel which, in the cool clear air seemed to narrow down so much that I felt I could have stretched out my arms and touched both sides at the same time.

We weighed anchor at 4 a.m. and as usual I had to be in the engine-room during the manoeuvring, but instead of returning to my hammock when the ship was clear of the bay I went to the upper deck and remained there until breakfast-time as we passed innumerable small islands floating like rafts on that mirror surface and feasting my eyes on the magnificent scenery of mountains, trees, and waterfalls cascading white water through the forests and from great heights. I was rivetted to the deck by the sheer beauty until it was time to get on with my day's work.

Again we anchored at dusk in another tiny bay but this time there was no sign of habitation,and when I was called at 4 a.m. the heavy rain and dense fog prevented us from moving out of the bay for more than an hour but we eventually arrived at the small fishing-town of Prince Rupert, which stands on an island off the coast of northern British Columbia, and secured at a wooden jetty at 3.30 p.m. This was another 'outpost of the Empire', with no sign of any public transport. Apparently none was needed in a such 'cut-off' place, the population of which seemed to be mainly Indians, Chinese, Japanese, and Norwegians. The ship's Church Parade on August 20th. with the Royal Marine Band leading attracted what must have been the whole population onto the streets to watch and to listen to the music. Sandy and I were invited to the home of the local manager of the Canadian Northern Railway — an extension of the National line — for tea and supper, and for an afternoon of tennis with his assistant, at the C.N.R. Club. The court was of timber planks, so it was wise to not fall and risk the splinters. As we returned aboard at 7 p.m. we walked with John Barrymore, the film actor, and his actress wife, Dolores Costello, who had arrived in their yacht, *Dolores*, that afternoon and were to be the Captain's guests at dinner on board.

We sailed at 7.30 next morning and steamed at 15-knots southwards until 7.30 p.m. when we dropped anchor off some tiny hamlet where we could see a few flickering lamps on shore. It must have been a very small community and I wondered whether any of them ever realised that we had anchored there, because we were away again at 4 a.m. — another early call for me! We do not realise the isolation some people have to bear.

Anyway, we had to wake up that day as all hands were called to Action Stations. It was probably felt that we needed a shake-up after our long period of relaxation and to remind us we were still in the Navy.

At dusk we anchored close to a huge Lumber & Logging Camp on the mainland side of Queen Charlotte Strait but made no contact with the shore and were on the move again at dawn to arrive at the paper-mill town of Powell River, the lights of which we had seen from Comox, at mid-day.

The Mill and the Town were built and owned by the P.R. Paper Company and were about 70-miles north of Vancouver but accessible only by sea, and during our four-day stay a party from the ship were invited to follow the whole process of paper-making, from the arrival of the timber rafts to the finished rolls of high-class paper. It was most interesting to see the massive tree-boles dragged from the water and hauled to the top of the building where they were dragged, flung about, sawn and shredded, reduced by the addition of liquid size and then passed over steam-heated rollers to emerge, miraculously, on a lower floor as miles and miles of high quality paper, 12-feet wide, on massive bobbins, and it was a continuous day-and-night operation.

The community were like one big happy family and Dragons were invited to their Sports Day as spectators, and at a concert organized by their ex-Servicemen our R.M. Band Orchestra also entertained — a gesture much appreciated by all. We said "Goodbye" to Powell River at 0830 on August 30th having given as much pleasure to them in their isolation as they had given us. Two mornings later we picked up a Pilot to con the ship a hundred miles up the Columbia River and its tributary, the Williamette, to Portland, Oregon, where we berthed at Stark Street Dock at 3.30 p.m. This was a fine big city, spread on both sides of the river which was spanned by several bridges each of different design and on our passage to the dock we passed through, or under — Fixed Span — Swing — Centre-span 'Lift' — Suspension — and Cantilever. A great variety.

Hospitality was almost overpowering and it was difficult to convince the kind people that sometimes we would prefer to walk and get some real exercise, but of course, if we wanted to see as much as possible it was essential to have transport, and a guide.

One evening Sandy and I stood looking down through basement windows, fascinated by the workings of the huge presses of "The Oregonian" newspaper when a gentleman who looked as though he was on his way home, stopped and asked if "two boys from the Old Country" would care to look over the works? He gave us a complete tour during the printing of the late edition, starting at the point where news came into the building, through the editorial offices to the compositors and the etching process for photographs and adverts, the formation of the platens from molten-metal, the actual printing and finally the bundling for distribution. He then took us to the Broadcasting Station KEX at the top of the very tall building to watch transmission of a drama programme — when he suddenly remembered that he had a wife and children to get home to and asked us to supper with the family "tomorrow". Unfortunately I would be Duty, but Sandy accepted.

That "tomorrow" was Sunday and, having shown some visitors over the ship in the afternoon I had to decline their invitation to go ashore with them so they extended the offer to "Dinner on Wednesday — and bring a friend. We'll pick you up at 5.30." Well, what could I do!

Sandy was Duty that night so I asked Walley and the lady duly arrived (in a chauffeur-driven limousine) to whisk us out to the suburban family house which stood in an avenue of trees fully laden with apples, pears, plums and damsons. There were six at table for dinner and after a very pleasant evening we returned aboard with four huge bags of fruit for the Mess.

Earlier that day there had been a minor incident on board when a small electrical fire occurred in the W/T Office on the upper deck. It was quickly dealt with by the duty Fire Party but not before a member of the public on the dockside called the City Fire Brigade and here is the local newspaper's report of the event:-

FIREMEN HAVE NO LUCK: BRITISH TOO EXCLUSIVE
By Roger McGuire

Firemen, the silly asses, tried to board his majesty's ship *Dragon* at the Stark St. dock Wednesday. Oh, to be sure, there was a jolly old fire burning on the bloody old craft. "You cawn't come aboard 'er," said the royal guard of his majesty's warship. "There's a fire, isn't there?" the firemen countered. "Cawn't help it, me lads. I've got me orders, donchaknow, so it isn't being done," the guard replied firmly. "Blow me down," chorused the fire-eaters. "Blye me, too," sympathized the guard. Firemen, some on land and others on water — sulked. It was the first time they had ever been barred from a fire. (They had their nice axes along, too. The ones they break windows with.) Pretty soon they realised it wasn't being done, so the east side laddies took their hook-and-ladder, and the river men took their fireboat, and all pulled stakes just like world powers at an international conference. The crew of the British ship controlled the fire, which was said to have damaged the ship's radio room.

Although it was 8 o'clock on a Saturday morning when we sailed there were hundreds of people on the dockside to watch our departure and lots more on the bridges as the ship made for the ocean and a rolling voyage down to Santa Barbara where we arrived three days later to anchor in the bay. On shore we were met by the same hospitality, for as soon as Reg Kirby — a messmate who had been in *Shropshire* with me — and I stepped ashore we were picked up and taken for a drive round the city (actually a small town but the folk called it a city) and taken to the residents' "pride" — the newly-built Fox-Arlington Theatre — to see one of latest films out of Hollywood. Our hosts left us at the pier with an invitation to dinner at their home 'tomorrow evening'. The kindness shown everywhere was embarrassing as there was so little for us to offer, except our gratitude, in return, but it was certainly a nice feeling for the whole ship's company to know that we were welcome and popular on shore.

The next day was "Dragon's Day" — the day when the new Dwight-Murphy Recreation Field was to be Dedicated with an Opening match between our football team and Santa Barbara, so as a small return for their kindness we invited our hosts to the cermony. Our Royal Marines and the Band gave a Marching Display, thrilling the big crowd with their smartness, and then the ship's team gave an equally thrilling display of its genius by winning by five goals to nil.

We had tea at home with our hosts and then the husband — an official at the Court House — took us for a walk inside the County Jail, along the rows of cells. In one open-grilled cell half-a-dozen men sat playing a card game and Mr. Garland told us they were all murderers by shootings and were on Death Row awaiting the ultimate penalty. Reg and I were happy to be going back to our ship.

Thick fog engulfed us next day as we steamed slowly down the coast to Long Beach, the port of Los Angeles, where we anchored that evening, Sept. 19th. It was a U.S. Navy Base and their ships made us very welcome. One of our first priorities of the Mess was to organize a small coach-party to visit Hollywood, about 20-miles along the road in L.A. Our choice was the Paramount Studios where a Guide took us on a tour of the sets and settings, one of which was a steamy jungle with a pool for the film, "White Lady".

The comedian, W. C. Fields, who was making a publicity film came over to ask if "Any of you boys like the telephone numbers of these be-yutiful gals I'm filming with?" Charles Laughton, Chico Marx, and Carole Lombard passed us separately on the studio road and Mae West gave a wave as she left her dressing-room for the set. We were given lunch and as we came out I bumped into Edward Everett Horton quite accidentally. He was quite nice as I apologized and asked how he enjoyed working with Maurice Chevalier on the film, "Bringing up Baby" (Our Guide had previously taken us to the studio but filming was in progress so we could not enter). Mr. Horton's reply was, "Oh, it is great fun." (My moments of 'greatness!')

Back in Long Beach that evening *Dragons* were the guests of the heavy cruiser, *U.S.S. Louisville*, flagship of the American fleet in port, at a reception in the huge auditorium followed by a dance and cabaret with music by the *Louisville*'s orchestra. It was a splendid and hilarious evening until some nefarious individual(s) 'spiked' the fruit Punch-bowl with a flagon of neat alcohol which soon began to take effect and men from both ships, and even female guests, became obstreperous, spoiling for fights. The American Shore Patrols soon appeared with the Night-sticks at the ready to quieten the scene and disperse trouble-makers.

In Seattle we had been Sunday lunch guests of *Tennessee*'s chiefs; here we were guests of the *Louisville* Chiefs for a dinner on board their almost new 10,000-ton ship which, compared with ours, was a palace — spacious, light and airy — and after a splendid meal the general trend was towards their Recreation Space for a Smoking Concert — but — Sandy and I had come together with another ship-board chum, our R.M. Bandmaster ('Polly' Perkins) the guest of *Louisville*'s Bandmaster Lawrence, and it was the latter's suggestion that we "get away from the fug and let's have a run up to L.A." He had a signal sent ahead to the Shore Base for his car to be ready at the pier at 7 p.m. and then had a boat called away to take the four of us ashore.

His car was a Chrysler 'Straight Eight with Overdrive' and he showed us what speed it could attain on the 20-miles of 8-lane Highway to the city, touching 80 m.p.h. at times. He gave us a royal tour of the city's Night Spots — without going inside any of them — but on the way back we pulled in at a Road-house for a coffee. A 5-piece band was playing and some of the clients were dancing on a postage-stamp-size floor. Sandy, a keen Terpsichorean, approached a young lady at a nearby table and was soon guiding and gliding over the floor with her. The number finished and he came back to our table to sip his coffee. The music started again and so did Sandy — straight to ask for another dance with the same partner except this time there was another guy at her table, but she accepted Sandy's arm and was leaving the table with him when the other chap rose and made some derogatory remark about "bloody limeys" and pushed Sandy out of the way. Normally a placid fellow, Sandy resented being shoved and drew back his right arm and jabbed the chap squarely on the point of his jaw knocking him over the table and chairs. (Sandy was our Engine-Smith — used to wielding a 7-lb. hammer). There was uproar but before it could develop into a riot, Lawrence said, "Come on. Get away from here — fast!" — and we did! His car was an open tourer and we were out on the Highway in double-quick time with his warning words, "Don't go anywhere near that place again during your stay!"

We sailed from Long Beach on Sept. 25th on the ten-day voyage to Balboa during which period we tried to recover the fighting-efficiency of ourselves and the ship with exercises and evolutions, and being called to

Action Stations at any time of day or night.

Dragon was old! Launched in 1917, her main and auxiliary machinery had been refitted many times over the years but I doubt if the Workshop machinery had ever been inspected, let alone refitted, since the day it was installed, so in between doing the maintenance work for the running of the ship I managed — over a period of time — to take down and refit or renew all bearings, shafting and counter-shafting.

Another of my duties was the training of suitable stokers in the use of the various machines in order to enhance their prospects of becoming Mechanicians when they returned to England.

My work on the building up of the Captain's motor-boat continued with help from our coppersmith and enginesmith, but one of the trickiest tasks was the shaping and balancing of the blades of its propeller. Our efforts were successful; the Captain had his own personal boat. While the ship was in British Guiana a quantity of lignum-vitae had been acquired and it was suddenly produced by Commander (E) Tollemache with a request that I make items such as fruit-stands and dishes, napkin-rings, trinket-boxes and ash-trays, and from teak I made and polished mounts for brass Ship's Crests for presentation to the Mayors or other representatives and dignitaries at most of the ports visited.

At 6 a.m. on Oct. 9th we entered Miraflores Locks for passage through the canal and at 1.30 p.m. passed Colon without stopping and arrived at Kingston on the 11th. We were due to leave for Bermuda on the 14th but departure was delayed by rumours of revolution in Cuba and the possibility of our being needed for the protection of British nationals and interests. We renewed our friendship with the Fusiliers at Up Park Camp and drank a lot of their excellent ale, and our Bandmaster arranged for his orchestra to play for all ranks on one Gala Evening.

The Cuban crisis eased and we were able to leave on November 8th, and rejoin the other ships — all returned from their respective cruises — in Bermuda on Nov. 12th when the whole squadron went to sea for two weeks of exercises.

Back in harbour the main shore interests were our visits to the Club and the Canteen — and the hard-seated Dockyard cinema where the first film to be shown on our return was, "White Woman" (the film being made as "White Lady" when we visited the studio, and we recognized the 'set' of the jungle pool). There was plenty of sporting activity with the football season in full swing. Our team was out of the Governor's Cup in the first round but fared better in the League by winning the Shield. The Squadron Road Race — from the Dockyard to Gibbs Lighthouse and back — was won by *Dragon* on December 21st, more than 300 runners taking part and I finished in 27th place and the C. in C. came to present the Running Shield on Christmas Eve.

73

One of the greater pleasures was the sighting of the mail boat and the word soon spread when someone spotted the "Monarch" (*Monarch of Bermuda*) or the "Queen" (*Queen of Bermuda*) crossing Great Sound towards Hamilton. The two Furness-Withy liners ran a weekly 36-hour shuttle between New York and Bermuda. The other mail-carriers were the "Lady" boats, smaller cargo boats which traded between Halifax, Nova Scotia, and Georgetown, Br. Guiana, via Bermuda and most of the Caribbean islands and Belize, Br. Honduras. There were five of them — *Lady Nelson*, *Lady Drake*, *L-Hawkins*, *L-Rodney*, and *L-Somers* — all most welcome sights wherever they were met.

Christmas Day 1933 was fine and warm as contingents from all ships marched to the Dockyard Church to swell the congregation of Yard personnel, their families and the C. in C. with Lady Plunkett and their four daughters and seven-year-old sailor-suited son.

Our cooks surpassed themselves with the Yuletide fare — plenty of it and everyone of good humour. And we were almost half-way through our commission! The year ended with a very cold spell which continued into 1934 and became worse when we sailed on January 3rd for our Spring Cruise to the islands. Seas were breaking over the bridge, causing us to heave-to and turn and run while all boats and deck-gear was double-lashed and made secure — or more secure — for the voyage.

Our first call was Charleston, South Carolina, where we docked on the 6th and remained for a week. It was a long, long walk to the town, plodding over masses of railway tracks past ramshackle and dirty old buildings, in bleak'n cold rainy weather to eventually reach a dull and dreary red-bricked old houses city (any place with more than 2,000 inhabitants is a "City" in America) and the majority of the population were black. Very little interest was shown in the ship, but that could possibly be explained by the inaccessibility and the inclement weather. The most popular venue for the crew was the Seamen's Mission, which was clean and comfortable and served excellent food.

On one evening a party of Chiefs was invited to "Supper and a Movie" at the Sergeants' Mess of the U.S. Infantry stationed at Fort Moultrie way across the harbour. It was a long, cold and dark boat-trip but the ensuing meal, movie and socializing were ample compensation.

Four days after leaving Charleston we docked at San Juan, Porto Rico, for a week's visit, a repeat of last year, so I did not venture far and two days out from San Juan we were diverted to Kingston, Jamaica, to discharge an injured seaman to hospital before we steamed on to Montego Bay. It was hot now and we worked a Tropical Routine whereby anyone could go ashore to the beaches after 1 p.m., — and that was about the best thing to do.

While at Montego we learned that the bones of an old Navy Gunner who had died about a hundred years ago had been uncovered about two miles along the coast, so an officer and whaler's crew were sent to collect them for a proper Christian burial at sea on our way to Kingston. He was finally laid to rest in a coffin made by our shipwrights, in the evening of February 2nd 1934, and later that night we met *Danae* and *Scarborough* for some night gunnery exercises before arriving at Kingston on the 3rd.

Scarborough had developed some serious defects since leaving Bermuda and lacked facilities and staff to rectify them so two of our E.R.A's were sent to assist and to send all items for machining back to me — entailing some evening working in order get her ready for sea.

Luckily no work arrived on that first day so I was able to join the crowd from the Mess for a 'run' to Up Park Camp, only to find our old friends, the 5th Northumberland Fusiliers, were packed and ready to leave. Their two-year tour of duty in the West Indies was over and they were now embarking on the troopship S.S.; *Dorsetshire* to sail to India on the 9th. It seemed that we had known them all our lives, but now it was "Goodbye" and unlikely that we would ever meet again.

We and *Scarborough* escorted the troopship out of harbour and then went on our way to Grenada where we anchored on the 13th and were surprised to find the Home Fleet battleship *Rodney* anchored at St. George's. I do not know why she was so far off course but our Captain went over and returned with an open invitation to both new arrivals to attend *Rodney*'s cinema show before she left for home on the 16th.

Grenada was very mountainous — and very wet — and green. So green!

The island's football team challenged us to a game and I took the afternoon off work to watch the match (a win for the ship by two goals to nil) and then took a walk up the valley, through groves of coconuts and bananas to the fort at the top and a fine view over that lovely green landscape and our ships in the bay.

On Feb. 20th we parted company with *Scarborough* to proceed with our programmed cruise and were in Georgetown, Br. Guiana, on the 22nd — after crossing the Bar with the same rigmarole as last year's visit.

Sandy and I gave the tennis-court a wide berth remembering our drubbing, but were able to take advantage of an invitation to Blairmont Sugar Plantation, a trip that pressure of work kept us from making last year. We landed with the party for the 8 a.m. train from Georgetown travelling eastwards on a 3½-hours ride to Rosignol, through country bearing evidence of recent flooding with dead cattle still lying in the fields; through some desolate jungle patches and through estates of bananas, coconuts and mangoes. Leaving the train we boarded a motor launch for the short trip up the Berbice River to Blairmont Estate where we were taken on a tour of the fields to watch Guianese workers cutting the cane — and certainly chewing a lot of it — and those I spoke to told me that they often had trouble with alligators. In the Factory we were given a taste — a thimbleful — of the strongest and fiercest rum and then a splendid lunch in the Club-house hosted by some of the nicest people (ex-patriots) it was possible to meet. We left the estate at 2.30 p.m. to return to Rosignol and our train, and the following day, March 1st we crossed the Bar again and were on our way to Trinidad for oil. On March 9th we moved on to the island of St. Vincent and with a Full Power Trial on the way it only took ten hours. This was another small island, devoted to sugar-cane and rain. Two hours on shore was quite long enough, and I think the Captain also tired of shore-going because he took up a hobby — leather-etching. He sent for me and asked if I could design and make a 'press' which would enable him to iron out *his* designs. He had a rough idea of what he wanted and I eventually produced a gadget similar to a domestic mangle with twin steel rollers 1½″ diameter, the pressure to be applied by calibrated fine-thread screwing devices at each end of the top roller, the leather being carried through on a machined 1/4″ thick steel plate. Comm. (E) presented it to the Captain who later came to the 'shop' to personally thank me. (His boat had been completed earlier and was a great success, but it was a joint effort and on that occasion he had thanked us collectively.)

The Surgeon Lieutenant had acquired some cinchona-wood from which I turned four goblets. The wood is the basis of quinine and by filling a goblet with water and letting it stand for an hour — and — hey presto! some real quinine to quaff.

March 14th and we moved on to Barbados, anchoring off Bridgetown where one short trip ashore was quite enough for Sandy and me. It was smelly and grubby in the town so we walked into the surrounding quiet and unspoilt countryside for exercise. We found Randall's Club, which was very pleasant and welcoming and had a game of billiards while sipping our rum. On the 22nd we were island-hopping again, this time to Montserrat. As the ship approached the island there was a very peculiar smell which turned out to be sulphurous fumes from the island's volcano. The bay at Plymouth, the capital, was most beautiful, a wonderful setting, but the permeating odour was overbearing and I think the very thought of getting closer to its source kept most of the crew from going ashore.

Norfolk — our 'flag' — steamed into the bay on Sunday, the 25th and anchored for a couple of hours, then left again! No one knew 'Why?' such a short stay, but we moved on on the 27th — another 'hop' of 3-hours steaming — to anchor in English Harbour at St. John's, the quaint little capital town of Antigua. A walk ashore was like turning back the pages of history, and it was easy to imagine what life was like when Nelson had his ships and Dockyard there. The place was full of relics including the old Mast Yard and Sail Store, and I wouldn't have been too surprised if one of his matloes had come round the corner. But my main memory of Antigua

'Jack' and the Milestone'. H.M.S. Dragon, 1933.

concerns a dog, a mongrel black Labrador cross by the name of 'Jack' who lived on our Stokers Mess Deck and had been in the ship since the start of the commission. He was cared for by the stokers; he went ashore with the stokers, and he drank with the stokers. There was always a pint for Jack.

While we were at anchor one of the sirens was taken down from the funnel to be refitted, and when replaced it had to be tested with a few short 'toots' — the same as are given when the ship is preparing to leave harbour (the Steaming Orders state, "Try main engines, test sirens and steering gear.") and that afternoon Jack was ashore with some of the off-watch stokers.

They said they were not far from the jetty when the test was carried out and Jack immediately trotted away across the road to plunge into the harbour and paddle out to the ship which was about a mile off shore. If dogs can think, he must have thought the ship was going without him. The Corporal of the Gangway and the Quartermaster were amazed to see him at the foot of the gangway and had a difficult, and wet task lifting him from the water onto the bottom platform where he had a good shake before struggling to the top and then trotting along the upper deck to his home. He was quite a hero, and even more fuss was made of him.

We left Antigua on April 2nd and four days later we were back with our

77

squadron in chilly Bermuda, but were soon at sea again with all ships exercising at gunnery practice and torpedo-running, depth-charge dropping and high-speed manoeuvring, — a good shake-up for everyone.

On our return to harbour our new Senior Engineer — Lt. (E) Briggs — who had recently joined the ship — bought a speed-boat in Hamilton and asked if I would care to look after it for him in my spare time. There was no compulsion but I thought it could be interesting and agreed. I went over on the School Ferry to collect *Estrellita* from the Pound, and it was quite a thrill speeding back across Great Sound, and cruising nonchalantly into harbour beneath the gaze of many curious eyes aboard the ship as I made fast at the slipway. She was a trim craft capable of 20-knots and the first thing he wanted was for me to alter the position of the controls to make driving more comfortable. The weather had improved so it was very pleasant to potter about after tea and give it a test run should he want to take some of his fellows socialising after dinner, and I had his permission to use the boat at any time if he did not require it for his own use. I certainly took advantage — especially on Saturday or Sunday afternoons — to run messmates across to Hamilton either for a shopping trip or for an evening at Prospect Camp with the sergeants of the Manchester Regiment which had replaced our old friends the Fusiliers.

The Senior had only been in the ship a very short time when he acquired a nick-name — "Pongo" — and fortunately there was a simple explanation for it. He had overheard one of the stokers referring to him by that sobriquet and later, while talking to me in the machine ship asked, "Why?" I was thankful that I could tell him it was nothing derogatory or insulting and took one of his signed notices from the Board to point to his signature — C. D. H. 'Briggs' — how his 'B' was formed to look more like 'Po', and the 'ri' appeared as 'n' while the two 'g's overlapped into almost one letter, and the final 's' became an 'o'. Hence — 'Pongo'. He was quite intrigued but also pleased that nothing sinister was intended.

At the end of April the ship went into the Floating Dock for our self-refit and as last year, it was at the same time as the Fleet regatta and the other ships went to anchor in Great Sound.

Last year the people of our department who wanted to follow any particular race had to pile into the unreliable motor-cutter and hope for the best; this year my first job on each of the three race-days was at 9 a.m. take the Senior and any of his 'cronies' out to the flagship, *Norfolk*, for a 'Grandstand view' and where they could sip their gins and tonics, and then return to the Dock to pick up a limited number of Engine-room staff (on a basis of 'first come, first served') and follow events such as the Stokers' Cutter race, E.R.A's gig, and the Medley race. We could not afford the time to follow races other than our own Department's.

Dragon was more successful this year and the C. in C. came to the Dock to present the Championship Cock.

The cricket season started and I picked up my scorer's job again for the E.R.A's of the North division when we played those of the South division, and again when the Combined E.R.A's played against the Officers of the Fleet, in which we were the winners of both matches.

Our Water-polo team carried on where they had left off last year by beating *Malabar* by 7-goals to nil, followed by an 8 – 1 victory over *York* — (which had relieved *Dauntless*), a 3-nil win against *Norfolk*, and beating *Exeter* (which had relieved *Durban*) by 3-goals to one and retaining the Polo Cup. Our Mess regained possession of the E.R.A's "Round the Harbour" Relay Race Cup, my team-mates giving me a good lead for the final-leg bike-ride to the winning-post — and Walley admitted responsibility for its loss last year because (he said) he was about to dive to swim the harbour-entrance gap when he realised he was still wearing his 'dust-proof, water-proof and shock-proof' Rotary wrist watch and had tried to hold his left arm clear of the water!

Sandy spent most of the month of May in hospital but was discharged in time to rejoin us before we left for our Summer Cruise. This year we would be doing the Atlantic coast cruise while *Danae* left harbour on June 7th on her way to the Panama Canal and the Pacific coast.

CHAPTER 10

The America's Cup 1934

Dragon steamed northward from Bermuda on June 15th with every day being much colder than its predecessor until on the 19th we passed two enormous icebergs outside the harbour at St. John's, Newfoundland, and the coldness permeated the whole town.

It was a fair-sized place but seemed to be very poor, maybe because we were prone to compare it with the brighter (warmer?) and more glamorous (wealthier?) towns and cities of the U.S.A. During our four-day stay in port I met the local Fire Chief and after showing him over the ship he invited me to his domain — the Central Fire Hall — and it was interesting to see the fire-appliances without wheels (they had runners) and the beautiful horses in the stables. Little imagination was needed to envisage the whole outfits galloping through a dark and snowy night to a blazing building. I then sat down at tea with the Duty Fire Crew.

Our next call was just 36-hours steaming-time west to St George's Bay on the south-west corner of the island, anchoring at 7 p.m. on Sunday, 24th. It was a small, isolated fishing community with many children — proved when we held a party for them on board. They overran us. There were children on all decks and in all compartments beside the hordes having a grand time on the slides, swings and roundabouts rigged on the upper deck, and when they tired they were entertained by all messes with tea and cakes. I am sure the ship's company were more exhausted than any of our guests at the end of the afternoon.

In conversation with one of the parents, a fisherman (what else?) he let slip the fact that his boat was out of action with a broken propeller-shaft and no hope of getting a replacement for months. Feeling sorry for the poor old chap I suggested to the Senior that we provide him with a new one, pointing out that it would only entail the expenditure of six-feet of 1½″ H.T. brass boltstave and a couple of hours of my time to fit the coupling flange, the propeller and securing nut. He readily agreed and the boat was towed out and hoisted at 6 p.m. Three hours later it was ready for the water again and the old man almost in tears of happiness and gratitude when he chugged towards the shore. Next morning a message came asking me to visit him at his home but unfortunately the weather deteriorated and we had no further contact with shore before the ship sailed at 7.30 on Sunday morning, July 1st. Twelve hours later we anchored in Bonne Bay, a tiny fishing village on the west coast of the island where we remained for just a few hours, during which time almost every member of the crew was catching fish. It was remarkable. The water was not deep and you simply dropped an unbaited line over the side and pulled up a dab. Hundreds were caught and handed in to the galley and were sufficient to provide suppers for two successive evenings for the whole company. Then we moved on to Charlottetown, Prince Edward Island, arriving there on July 4th. This was another small town in a fruit-growing area, quiet, clean, and 'dry' — no bars and no booze — and the townsfolk not very partial to having the Royal Navy parked on their doorstep. (We learned that this was because there had been a near-riot a few weeks earlier when two Canadian destroyers had called at the town: the two which had been with us in the islands?) "Dragons" behaved impeccably during our eight days' visit with the ship being 'Open' on four afternoons and the rarity of the ship's company being allowed to give a Farewell Dance on the quarterdeck the night before we sailed. Although the town itself had been dull and lifeless it was a nice place for walking in and around.

Twenty-four hours steaming took us to Dalhousie, New Brunswick, smaller than Charlottetown and not as clean. The main industry, its reason for so being, was the Imperial Paper Company's giant plant with its odour redolent of Powell River, and there was really only one street and one cinema. The cinema was a timber building which boasted the title "The Opera House". One morning the ship's motor-boat ran astern onto rocks near the landing-stage and suffered a broken propellor, damaged rudder-post and a bent shaft. She was towed back to the ship and it was an emergency job to get her back into service again as there were no spares. Our only other powerboat besides the Captain's 'now personal' boat was the unreliable motorcutter (*Estrellita* had to be left in Bermuda) so Sandy (engine-smith), the coppersmith, the boats' E.R.A. and his two stoker drivers and I worked non-stop for twenty hours to get the boat back into the water.

On July 20th another 24-hours steaming took us to Sydney, Cape Breton Island, a big, well-spread-out and busy city of coal and steel industries, and one of the highlights of our five-days stay was a conducted tour of the Dominion Steel and Iron Works when a party from the Mess landed at 1.30 p.m. and were able to follow the whole process from the arrival of the ore-carriers from Newfoundland to the finished products.

We were welcomed aboard the *Daghild* by her Captain with glasses of refreshing beer in his cabin and then watched dock-side grabs hoisting the ore from the holds, dump it into railway wagons which later tipped their contents into the huge hoppers above the blast furnaces. Down in the factory workshop the molten metal formed huge ingots which, while still in white-hot state were moved about at speed on steel rollers by hydraulic rams and within a very short time became lengths of railway-track line. Other operations turned out miles of iron wire and hundreds of thousands of nails.

There was very little else of interest to us in the city — as was indicated by the fact that when our R.M. Band gave an orchestral concert in Wentworth Park one evening it attracted a very large and appreciative audience and practically the whole of the ship's company turned out to listen. (They were proud of the Band and the ship.)

Twenty Royal Canadian Reservists joined us as we sailed on July 26th for the next part of our cruise so we had more activity than usual as we exercised them with all kinds of drills as the ship crawled slowly through thick fog along the rocky coast of Maine and then lay fog-bound outside Bar Harbour for 12-hours. We eventually anchored inside the harbour late on the 28th.

The *U.S.S. Louisville* came into harbour followed two days later by *U.S.S. Indianapolis*, both ships inviting our crew to attend their Baseball games and a Boxing tournament, and our Bandmaster (Polly Perkins) tried to contact Bandmaster Lawrence and was told that he had been drafted ashore at Long Beach.

Prime Minister Hon. J. Ramsay Macdonald, and Ishbel, aboard 'Dragon',
August 8th 1934. Sydney, C.B.I. to St. John's, N.F.

Dragon sailed on August 6th and called in at Halifax, Nova Scotia, on
the 7th to disembark the Canadian Reservists and left immediately for
Sydney, C.B.I., arriving there at 8.30 a.m. on the 8th to embark our Prime
Minister, the Rt. Hon. Ramsay Macdoald, M.P., and his daughter Ishbel,
and within the hour we were on our way to land them at St. John's,
Newfoundland, at 5.30 p.m. on the 9th. Then we were away again. It was
like some 'cloak-and-dagger' operation, but it could have been just a matter
of 'convenience'.

Now we were back to our scheduled cruise programme, ploughing
through rough and cold seas towards the estuary of the St. Lawrence
where it seemed Canada's winter had arrived early. We passed Quebec on
Sunday evening, August 12th and went alongside in Montreal at 9 o'clock
next morning after being involved in a serious accident.

A pilot was on board to conduct us up-river and as the ship approached
her berth she had to turn to starboard to enter the Basin. I was at my
normal station for entering and leaving harbour when — "Full Astern"
was ordered at the same time as severe jolting was felt on the starboard
shaft and the ship's side.

As we had turned to enter the Basin the strong ebb tide carried our stern

82

towards the port side of the 600-ton tanker, *Maplebranch*, berthed at the entrance to the Basin, and our starboard propeller-blades cut a huge hole in her bottom, causing her to sink and rest on the bed of the river. Fortunately there were no casualties although damage was considerable. Divers found that one blade of our starboard propeller was completely missing; a second blade had lost two-thirds of its surface area and the third blade had folded over on itself. Our own diver smoothed the ragged edges and the best was hoped for in the knowledge that there was a spare kept in Bermuda Dockyard.

Montreal was a fine, big and clean city but I did not see much of it because I had obtained six-days leave to travel to Toronto to visit my brother who had left the Navy in 1931 to marry and emigrate with his new wife, so as soon as our damage had been assessed and main engines were finished with I went ashore to catch the 3.45 p.m. train to Toronto. It was quite an interesting journey as the train travelled along the river bank to Kingston and then the lake shore as darkness fell.

Toronto at 10.15 p.m. — my brother waiting, and a hectic five days of sight-seeing ensued. His home was at Scarboro' Bluffs, the house standing in three acres of market-garden on the shores of the lake where, with his wife and 3-year-old son we had pleasant picnics on the beach.

They saw me onto the 5 p.m. train to Montreal on Sunday, August 19th and at nine o'clock next morning the ship moved off down the river on the eleven-hours trip to Quebec, and it was then that the vibration of the starboard shaft was felt. We spent all the time taking readings and measurements along the shaft and found it was bent and giving movements of more than a quarter-of-an-inch and could only get worse because of the imbalance of that propeller. It must have been a very worrying time for both the Captain and the Commander (E) with regard to the fighting-efficiency of the ship (and the Captain's apportionment of blame or responsibility for the collision) and the wear-and-tear and damage to other parts of the main engines which might be affected. The vibration was such that the golden ball at the peak of our foremast was in danger of being shaken off, so a seaman had to go aloft to remove it.

Our stay in Quebec was for only two days but I managed to get ashore on both evenings and found it not as nice as either Montreal or Toronto — maybe because it was much older — or perhaps it was the French element adding to my 'anti' feelings, but all was compensated for by the fine views over river and city from the Promenade in front of the Chateau Frontenac (now a Canadian National Railway hotel — which I entered and found most opulent, with dinner-prices far beyond my pockct.)

We sailed from Quebec at 6.30 p.m. on August 23rd — a very cold trip to Gaspé, a very small town in the part of Quebec Province to the south of the river, anchoring at 1.30 in the morning of the 25th. We were there to take a very small part in the Jacques Cartier Quatercentenary celebrations (he had landed at that point in 1534) and a Royal Marine Guard of Honour landed for the ceremony. No other leave was given — probably because it was a predominantly French anniversary — but the following morning (Sunday) Admiral of the Fleet Sir Roger Keyes, who incidentally was an Honorary Colonel Commandant of Royal Marines, came on board to attend our Church Service. We sailed that afternoon and at 6.30 on the morning of August 28th berthed at the Jetty in Halifax, Nova Scotia. Our first impression of this busy port and Canadian Navy Base was that it was small, dull (the dingy and chill weather accounting for that), and dirty, and to reach any semblance of light and life we had to tramp through a mile of slum-land. And — we were there for two whole weeks! My few jaunts were mainly for walks, and most of what I saw did nothing to dispel my opinions of the place. The most memorable sight was of two ship's ventilators and a massive anchor lying on a path of grass some two miles inland from the dock area. The items were fenced in and a plaque stated that they had been left where they had landed after a ship had blown up in the harbour in 1918 and were a permanent monument. It must have been some explosion!

Early in September the French destroyer *Vauquiline* came into harbour and secured astern of *Dragon*. She was brand new and on a 'shake down' cruise and on the afternoon when she was "Open" I was too busy to visit her, but after tea our Chief Mechanician (Fred May) and I decided to go along even though it was after hours and when we arrived alongside her we could see no sign of life — not even a Gangway sentry. Her whole crew were at their evening meal. We strolled on board, wandered along the upper deck until we found a door leading to the engine-room, opened it and went below. Nobody there although some auxiliary machinery was in use and all lights were on. (Shades of the *Marie Celeste*!)

We made a thorough inspection as we discussed points about the lay-out and the types and makes of all the plant and then passed through to the steaming boiler-room. There was actually a man on duty there but he took no notice of us — nor we of him — as we wandered hither and thither, examining everything before returning to our own ship where, as we went on board we met the Duty Engineer Officer and mentioned our exploratory trip to him. He was amazed when he learned we had been able to visit her machinery spaces, telling us that he and the Commander (E) had been refused permission to go below when they had visited the Frenchman earlier. I had been in my Mess for only a few minutes when a messenger came to say that Tollemache wanted to see me at once, and when I arrived at his cabin he asked lots of questions and asked me to write it all down while he interviewed the Chief Mech and then had him write a corrobative report. Although I heard nothing further of the matter the

84

Senior Engineer of a later ship in which I was serving remarked that I "must have made a good impression in *Dragon* — judging by the 'Confidential Report' of her Commander."

We sailed from Halifax on September 11th and arrived at Newport Rhode Island, on the 13th to take up our duty as British Guard-ship during the series of races for the America's Cup, the two competing "J"-Class yachts being *Rainbow*, the defender, owned by Cornelius Vanderbilt, and the challenger, *Endeavour*, owned by Tommy Sopwith of England. Newport was on a par with Bar Harbour but there was certainly more activity in this yachting centre, summer resort and home of millionaires, — especially at the time of this prestigious event.

The first race — on the 15th was void because it failed to finish within the specified 5½-hours. On the Monday, 17th, the race was won by *Endeavour* and there was great excitement on her return to harbour, and plenty of high jinks on shore that night.

On the 18th I followed the race aboard the U.S. Coastguard cutter *Cayuga* over a triangular course of 15-miles each leg. *Rainbow* crossed the starting line first but *Endeavour* soon picked up and then led all the way — to even greater jubilation with the British boat holding a two–nil advantage, and I had thoroughly enjoyed the chase.

The race on the 20th was a 'straight out and back' 15-miles each way with *Endeavour* leading by 550-yards at the turn — and then losing by three minutes: it was so strange — almost suspicious — and *Rainbow* won again on the 22nd so it was now 'two–all'. She then won the fifth and as the challenge was for 'the best of seven' it began to look as Britain would be runners-up yet again — a position which was confirmed when *Rainbow* won the final race over the triangular course on the 25th and the America's Cup remained in America.

Amongst the many luxury powered yachts present were *Colleen*, *Corsair*, and *Lone Star*, owned by such wealthy men as Andrew Melon, J. Pierpont Morgan, and John D. Rockefeller, and after attending an Invitation Supper at the Yacht Club one evening I went in *Lone Star*'s tender with the designer and builder of *Rainbow* to visit *Endeavour* and her splendid crew. She was a lovely, sleek craft, bereft of many niceties because of her racing status, but her bar was adequately stocked that night.

Another experience was to attend the service in Trinity Church — the oldest Anglican church in the United States (It has the Union Jack built into its structure). A large number of us landed and marched there with our R.M. Band to the applause of the crowds lining the streets — Always a crowd-puller, the Royal Marine Band! — and entered this quaint, old building. It had a tall, three-tier pulpit, and all the pews were individual boxes, so that when you were in one you could not see anyone else. It was more "segregation" than "congregation".

On the day of the last "Cup" race — September 25th — we embarked a number of private guests, Consular officials, etc., and followed the yachts on their triangular course. It seemed as though it was a foregone conclusion that *Rainbow* would win because as *she* crossed the finishing-line *we* entered the harbour, landed our passengers and steamed out on our way to Boston, Massachusetts, going alongside the jetty there at 4 p.m. the next day.

Boston was quite a big city much like London in the way it was laid out — or *not* laid out, with terraces, crescents, squares, circles, etc., and the buildings, both in design and materials — red and yellow brick — were typically London.

It was quite a distance, too, from ship to 'bright lights', entailing a journey by 'Elevated' and 'Subway' but well worth the hassle although I did have a rather unnerving experience early one evening while walking in one of the main streets. A vagrant type suddenly attached himself on my right and said, "Give us a nickel." I said I did not have one and carried on walking. He then demanded a dime. I ignored him and continued my stride only to find another 'bum' had attached himself on my left side with both in unison menacingly saying, "Give us a dollar!" I simply said, "Look! If I'm not prepared to give a nickel or a dime, I am certainly not passing over a dollar. Get going." And then I must have had a presentiment, for just as we drew level with a narrow alley — a gap between buildings to our left — I stopped dead in my tracks as the one on my right lunged to shoulder and bundle me into the alley with a lurid curse and collided with his partner. I increased my pace to bound up the few steps into the Shubert Theatre right next to the alley. I strode through the foyer without purchasing a ticket and into the darkened auditorium where Ethel Waters was performing in a show entitled, "As Thousands Cheer" — a skit on our Royal Family with impersonations of King George V, Queen Mary, and the Prince of Wales and the British Empire. When the show ended I mingled with the crowd boarding a street-car going in the direction of the docks. It was the first time I had felt in danger on shore anywhere — my first encounter with a mugging despite the fact that after walking back to the ship one night in Halifax, through those slum areas, I had been told that I had taken a grave risk as it was dangerous for anyone to be alone in that area after dark. But — ignorance is bliss — and I had survived.

Two days after leaving Boston, *Dragon* arrived in Philadelphia on Oct. 5th and secured alongside a roadway and almost immediately beneath the high suspension bridge which crosses the Delaware River at that point. This was another vast, sprawling city where the hospitality was again overwhelming and when the ship was "Open" we had approximately 15,000-visitors (about fifty-times the number of our entire complement) on

86

board during the three hours. It was really uncomfortable with all those people milling about like crowds leaving a theatre or football match. Sandy, having been in hospital at Montreal, had rejoined us before we left Halifax and was now practically back to full health and able to accept a few of the many invitations to dinners, suppers and parties which flooded in.

The British War Veterans Association of Pennsylvania gave a Dinner and Reception at the Turners Hall for as many of the crew as could attend and that was a real festive 'do' — as might be expected!

As we were only 90-miles from New York I thought it a good opportunity to visit the world's second-largest city. I might never get another chance. I asked around the Mess if anyone else had thought of having a day there (Sandy did not feel fit enough) but some had local commitments and others were just not interested — so I would go it alone.

My request for time off was granted and I travelled by the 9 a.m. train to arrive at Penn Station on 34th Street in New York at 10.30 intent on seeing all that should be seen in such a brief visit. I walked down 34th to Fifth Avenue, passing the Empire State Building without even noticing it until I happened to glance back when I was some distance away.

I walked to 42nd Street and up Broadway to have lunch in a Times Square restaurant, boarded a bus to Riverside Drive and the George Washington Bridge over the Hudson River and returned via Central Park to Radio City and the Rockefeller Centre Building — then, at 70-storeys, the second-tallest in the world. The Empire State was taller and had been open just three years but according to a New Yorker I spoke to, it was a "White Elephant" and still three-parts empty and "The R.C.A. is the better to visit". So the R.C.A. it was!

The ascent was made in two stages, the first elevator taking me from Ground to (I think) the 55th floor in less than one minute, the second lift was to the 70th floor and then it was just a few steps up to the Observation Platform for the most wonderful all-round view over New York City.

Another walk and I was at Union Square — where Broadway crosses 5th Ave. — and took the Express Subway to Times Square with the intention of seeing a theatre-show before returning to Philadelphia, but prices were exorbitant and far beyond by slender means. Disappointing — but it was now dark and a cold wind whistled through the canyon streets. I had had a satisfying but tiring day, doing just what I wanted to do in my own time. The 8 p.m. train had me back to the warmth of *Dragon* by 10.30.

Admiralty Constructors from England and Dockyard officials from Bermuda joined the ship for the voyage back to Bermuda in order to study the effects of our damaged propeller and shaft on the ship's performance. We sailed at 10 a.m. on Oct. 16th and almost immediately developed 'condenseritis' and I had to leave the machine-shop and join the small team sent below to rectify the situation, a task we completed at midnight. (Sea-water was finding its way into the boiler feed-water).

The ship went into the Floating Dock as soon as we arrived on the 18th and the spare propeller was fitted but it had already been decided that a new shaft was essential and that could only be done at a ship-building yard. Rumours abounded as to where the work would be carried out; Norfolk, Virginia, being the nearest such yard was the top-of-the-list of the 'spreaders' with Halifax a close second. The Clyde was also strongly favoured, but everybody was happy when it became known that Chatham, our Home Port dockyard was to do the job.

Bad weather delayed our departure until November 9th when it became perfect and remained a flat calm for the whole of the voyage. To minimise further damage through vibration the starboard shaft was run at a constant 95 r.p.m. and a round-the-clock check on the shaft bearings and stern tube was maintained during the 11-day voyage. De-ammunitioning took place at Sheerness on the 20th and we proceeded up-river next morning and into No. 5 Dry-dock in Chatham Yard. We were Home!

Dragon had been away for two years and two months. My son had been just 2-years old and my daughter only six-months when I last saw them so I had a lot of catching-up to do to get to know them again. Twelve-days leave to each Watch was very welcome.

The new shaft and propeller were in place and we had refitted all underwater valves by January 9th 1935 when the ship was re-floated and steam was raised for the main engines to be run for many hours with the ship secured to the bollards in the Basin and constant checks kept on oil temperatures and pressures.

On the 18th we embarked some Admiralty and Dockyard Inspectors to supervise a Full Power Trial through the English Channel. That was satisfactory — the Inspectors left us at Spithead at 5.30 p.m. and we were on our way back to Bermuda to finish our commission.

It was quite a rough passage and as there had been a number of changes in the complement we were treating it as a 'Working up' period. On the sixth day out a seaman became very ill and needed hospital treatment urgently, so speed was increased and we were doing 22-knots through rising seas when a tremendous wave crashed down and almost swamped us, causing us to reduce to 16-knots. Even so, we had managed to knock 48-hours from our passage time and the man was in the Naval Hospital, Bermuda, on Jan. 27th — and *Dragon* was quarantined for suspected mumps. We were isolated at the detached Mole; no-one could leave the ship or make contact with anybody coming alongside with stores or mail — and we had been looking forward to a pint at the Club after our battering!

Two days passed and then orders were received for *Dragon* to proceed to St. Kitts in the Leeward Islands to relieve the Home Fleet cruiser *Leander*. Two hours later some-one must have realised we were quarantined and the order was rescinded and another of the squadron was despatched. It was not until February 4th that we were deemed free from contagion and that was on the day we were leaving for our Spring Cruise to the Islands.

Once again we ran into heavy weather and on the second evening I was having a breath of air just before sunset and standing close by the Lamp Room door when the order "Place oil Navigation lights" was piped. (That was piped every night just before sunset when at sea, and I had always thought it was "*All* Navigation lights" and wondered 'Why?' as the lamps are permanent fittings.) Anyway, "Tanky" came along, opened the Lamp Room and brought out a number of lit oil lamps — a red and a green and two or three whites — stood them on the deck while he re-locked the door. I asked him, "Why so many?" and he said the red and green were for use if the electric Navigation lights failed, and the white ones were needed if all power should be lost and the ship would be "Out of control". Fair enough I suppose, but neither he nor I had ever known it happen, and as far as he was concerned it was routine and a necessary chore. Action Stations sounded when it became really dark and everyone closed to his station. The exercise lasted an hour or so. "Secure" was sounded and we were busy replacing fire-hoses, tools, etc., when the ship was plunged into darkness! The main engines slowed, then stopped and there was a momentary silence until the ship began to roll almost onto her beam-ends and anything that was the least bit loose went crashing. Crockery was smashed and personal effects flung from shelves, racks and cupboards throughout the ship, and it was extremely difficult to keep ones feet in the violent movement. "Close all water-tight doors and hatches" was piped and it was an alarming situation in the blackness. The reason for the contretemps? After our Exercise, and conditions were returning to normal the Double-bottom Party switched the fuel tanks for the steaming boilers, from the near-empty ones to full ones, but unfortunately the pipes between the full tanks and the boiler furnaces were full of salt water inadvertently left in them when the tanks had been cleaned in Bermuda. The water extinguished the flames of the furnace-sprayers and as we were steaming on just two boilers (of six) the steam rapidly drained from them through the main engines and auxiliaries *and* the two dynamos. One of the boilers was then shut down as the D.B. Party tried switching back to the near-empty tank in an effort to clear the salt water, but the feed-water level in the boiler which was still connected fell too low and all its tubes became distorted and leaking. A most uncomfortable hour passed before there was sufficient steam to re-start one dynamo and get main engines turning slowly, and the ship began to steady herself. When full lighting was restored there were some forty sharks swimming close by, waiting for 'perks'.

An Inquiry was held and several heads rolled — with Severe Reprimands for the Chief Stoker (for failing to ensure that all sea-water was mopped from the tanks after cleaning), the Duty Stoker Petty Officer (for not testing the pipes before switching tanks), the E.R.A. Boilermaker (for having too many — two of our six — boilers open for cleaning at one time), and even old "Tanky" because his lamps were not properly trimmed and had insufficient oil to survive the crisis.

On our arrival at San Juan, Porto Rico, on Feb. 7th both boilers which had been in use had to be completely re-tubed by our own staff and it was certainly very hot work, but as it was our third visit to the port — for most of us anyway — it did not really matter about getting ashore. The Duke and Duchess of Kent arrived on the island by aeroplane on the 13th and came on board to sail with us on the 14th — to be landed at some isolated spot on the Jamaican coast two days later. We did not stop, the motor-boat was lowered, they were taken to the beach, the boat returned and we steamed away. That evening we met the cruiser *York* for a Night Action exercise followed by a day of high-speed manoeuvres and were not sorry to leave her on the 21st as this was becoming a very tough 'Working-up' period for, besides some changes on the Lower Deck there were also a number of changes in the higher echelons (*Tollemache* had been relieved by Comm. "E" P. D. Oliver) and we were being called to Action Stations at any odd hour of day or night; ventilation of engine-rooms and other machinery spaces and messes would be suddenly cut off and it was to be assumed that gun-fire or torpedo had made parts of the ship inaccessible. It was all very tiring but it was necessary as part of the 'working-up' process.

When we parted company with *York* the temperature of the sea-water was 84° but as we moved into the Gulf of Mexico it soon began to cool down and by the time we reached Galveston, Texas, it was down to 48° and the air was really cold.

This was a relatively small town with lots of wooden buildings as one sees in the Wild West on cinema screens and it had its fair share of cowboys and horses and hitching-rails. All was quiet when Sandy and I went ashore for a walk and later in the evening — about 9 o'clock — went into an hotel for a traditional Texas steak. The owner or receptionist, seeing we were British asked if we would like a drink with our meal and led us to a very large room furnished with tables and chairs, the former being covered with blue-and-white-check cloths, somewhat like an English country tea-room except that about twelve-feet of the wall at one end was taken up by a Bar — the counter of which was semi-circular, the mirrored wall behind it accommodated bottles of spirits and racks of glasses. Practically all places were occupied when we sat to enjoy massive inch-thick steaks and glasses of beer then, suddenly there was a call from the door — "The Troopers are coming!" The staff reacted with speed by scooping all glasses from the tables and depositing them on the bar counter as the whole section of the wall revolved to be replaced by its reverse side — a similar counter but with a tea-urn and trays of cups and saucers and bottles of coca-cola which were hastily distributed to most of the customers. The back wall was not mirrored but bore sedate Temperance notices and we all stayed calm and continued eating.

Galveston is an island connected to the mainland of Texas by just one bridge and it was the duty of the Texas State Troopers to uphold the Prohibition Laws, so the saloons each had look-out men posted near the bridge with horses and at the first sight of Troopers would gallop to warn of impending danger. Whether the Troopers were aware of the set-up and the sale of liquor I do not know, but it was more than half-an-hour before the Bar swung back into view. (It might even have been a 'theatrical show-piece' rigged specially for clients!).

Leaving Galveston on March 4th we ran into thick fog on the way along to Mobile and had to wait at the mouth of the river until the evening of the 6th before we could proceed to that charming little city. News spread of *Dragon*'s arrival and the friends we had made on our previous visit remembered us and invitations flooded in from everyone during the next five days.

Sailing on March 11th we ran into more severe weather and anchored in the harbour at Havana, Cuba, on the 13th to find the city under Martial Law at the start of a Revolution. The new man in control, Sergeant Batista, came on board as soon as we arrived but the Captain was 'too busy' to greet him; that honour was left to Commander Fitzroy. Our next visitors a little later that day were Douglas Fairbanks, Snr., and his lover, Lady Sylvia Ashley, who were holidaying on the island and were welcomed at the gangway by the Captain as dinner-guests.

There was sporadic sniping from rooftops during the evening and after dark we could actually see as well as hear, longer bursts of machine-gunfire, so no shore-leave was given — at least not until the Saturday (16th) when things had quietened a bit and a few Chiefs and Petty Officers were allowed ashore from 1.30 p.m. until sunset — 7 p.m. — and I took the opportunity to see something of the city.

Although the curfew did not come into force until dusk there were very few pedestrians about but there seemed to be thousands of taxis, speeding and weaving through the wide streets (probably occupied by wary and nervous citizens getting their week-end shopping). The most beautiful of many beautiful buildings was the Capitol with its gold dome, but it was a great disappointment to us that we were unable to get ashore again to see more. The ship was 'Open' for two hours on the Sunday afternoon, but for

British nationals only and it was surprising the numbers there were — all re-assured by our presence in the harbour.

The ship's company's frustration at being 'shore-less' was somewhat mitigated by the thoughts that we would soon be on our way home again. Our programme until the end of March was known and it was generally assumed we would be home by June. I suppose the mens' hopes percolated through to the Captain for, to put minds at rest it was announced that "The ship will not be going home until August 'at the earliest'." (Probably to make up for those two months we were away from the Station.)

It was eventually quiet enough for us to leave Havana on March 20th and on the next day we secured at a jetty in Miami, Florida, a bright summer-resort for wealthy people and consequently expensive. Sandy and I went ashore for an exercise walk, a hamburger and a coffee (couldn't afford a meal at the prices being charged) and met a chap who introduced himself as Mr. Dyble — born in Clapham, London, and had been in Miami for a number of years. He arranged to meet us the following evening, saying he might be a bit late but when we arrived at the meeting place his chauffeur was there in a large Cadillac to apologise for Dyble's non-appearance and to take us for a drive around the brightly-lit city, pointing out the palatial homes of the wealthy and the outside of the newly-opened Biscayne Hotel where the prices of rooms were upwards of $35 a day. We also drove along the Causeway to Ocean Beach and Deauville, making us feel as though *we* were rich holiday-makers.

When we left Miami on March 28th we met *York* and were exercising with her at day- and night-action until we arrived back in Bermuda on the 31st — back to the quietude of the Base but certainly respite from the adventures of being in a different place every other week or so, and being entertained by welcoming people anxious and proud to show the delights of their home-towns. Yes, it was pleasant after a day's work to walk or cycle to the Club or Canteen for a glass (or two) of tepid beer and a game of snooker, or maybe there would be a Sods Opera in progress. Longer rides could be taken at week-ends, the weather not being suitable for picnics in Estrellita.

A new C. in C., Vice-Admiral Sir Matthew Best, had arrived on the Station and was visiting each ship in his command. He would come to inspect and to make himself known to ships' companies, usually on a Sunday when he took the Salute at a March past on the quarterdeck and attended the Church Service which followed. Then there would be a second visit to take the ship to sea where there was plenty of room for all the drills and exercises and evolutions — "Emergency Stop" (to avoid collision, dodge torpedoes or for 'Man Overboard'), "Away Sea-boat's Crew" (for rescue, or taking a Boarding Party), "Lower and raise anchors by hand" (a reversion to days of old, using capstan-bars and actually having a fiddler sitting on the capstan-head 'scraping' Sea-shanties), — and stations for "Action", "Collision", "Abandon Ship", "Flood and Counter-flood", "Fire on board", etc., and it was during that drill he came to the Forward Fire party and, pointing to a valve he asked me, "Is there water at that point?" — "Yes, sir, forty-pounds pressure." — "Open it — let me see," he ordered. I gently 'cracked' it and a small jet of rusty sea-water squirted down the front of his pristine-white uniform. He was not perturbed but his entourage were aghast! The Admiral had got wet! But to me he simply said, "Thank you. That's enough," and went on with his tour.

The whole squadron then spent ten days exercising at sea before anchoring off Port Royal for the annual Regatta — the first year that the ship had not been high-and-dry in the Floating Dock during the event. *Exeter* were the overall winners with *Dragon* in second position followed by *Norfolk*, *York* and *Danae*. (What an incongruous assortment for a 'squadron'). May 6th 1935 — The King and Queen celebrated their Silver Jubilee and it was a general holiday throughout the Empire. I took the Senior and his friends across the Great Sound to Hamilton in *Estrellita* for the Grand Review at the Parade Ground and having secured the boat I was invited to join their party to see the show — a March Past of soldiers, sailors, marines and the local militia — the Governor and the Commander-in-Chief jointly taking the Salute. It was a wonderful spectacle with the white and the light-khaki dress uniforms and the bands of the Army and Royal Marines, a delight for the crowds of Bermudans, Americans, Service-men and their families, and me.

The weather was perfect and at the end of the day's work it was really nice to wander around the Yard to the Long Arm breakwater and bathe from the rocks on the outside of the harbour. There was a narrow gap of about ten feet in the Long Arm not far from the shore end and it was straddled by a wooden bridge. Gazing down into the calm, clear water early one evening we watched shoals of tiny fish aimlessly swimming about when suddenly five large horse-mackerel came speeding through the gap from inside the harbour. What a dispersal as those tiny silver minnows flashed out of harm's way, like the burst of star-shell! As the Big Five sped through two peeled off to the left, two to the right while the fifth went straight ahead. A few seconds passed and all five came cruising slowly back through the gap and into the harbour; the tiny ones gradually returned to their original meeting place below us, then — Whoosh! — those same five horse-mackerel repeated the manoeuvre at the same high speed, much too fast for us to see if there was any mayhem or if they were only doing it for 'sport'. The tactics were carried out time after time and it was we who grew tired of watching.

The doll's house, 1935, 1'8" tall.

Dragon continued her winning ways by taking the Water Polo Cup and the Boxing Shield, and our Mess retained the E.R.A.'s Challenge Cup — even though I did not take part.

The Senior — Lt. Comm. (E) C.D.H. Briggs — had recorded many of the events of the commission with his movie-camera and one evening he had a marquee rigged on the jetty with the object of showing his films to "anyone who is interested" — the wording on his Notice — and the place was filled to capacity, the four large reels of 'memories' being enthusiastically received.

I and a number of messmates took up hobbies during these weeks in Bermuda and the machine/work-shop was almost as busy in the evenings as it was during the day. Model yachts — a model of *Dragon* itself — a fire-screen — an electric clock (very intricate, by one of the Chiefs) — while I engaged myself in building a Doll's House for my daughter who would be 3½-years old when we arrived back home. The work helped the evenings along after dark and everyone's thoughts were now of Home.

The C. in C. took the squadron to sea on June 4th and 5th for what he termed "Efficiency Tests" when he boarded each ship in turn. He was carried across to us at 3.30 p.m. on the 4th and immediately ordered us up to 24-knots with all the crew to be at Action Stations between 4 and

5.30 p.m. during which period he ordered all our guns to be fired, every gun we carried, from the 6" main armament down to rifle and revolver! While this was going on he was walking round the ship and I am sure he recognized me when he came to the Engine-room, and recalled the wetting he had received a few weeks earlier. It was the sort of look he gave — or was it just my guilty conscience!

On completion of the exercise we were detached from the squadron to go to Hamilton, I think it was partly for us to say Goodbye to Bermuda and perhaps give the chaps the opportunity to buy souvenirs in that very expensive town, but the real purpose was to embark 250-men of the Manchester Regiment and 60-marines from the rest of the squadron and to carry out a surprise Night Attack on the islands. We steamed out of Hamilton on June 10th and crept back around 3 a.m. with the ship darkened to land them at another spot and then we returned to the Dockyard.

On the 12th. the C. in C. came on board to say "Goodbye" and "Thank you" and at 4 p.m. we sailed from Bermuda with a rousing send-off from the other ships and the Yard personnel. We were on our way home — but not directly. Steaming westward on a sea as smooth as glass we arrived in Norfolk, Virginia, on the 15th. This was another U.S. Navy Yard and Base and the town — which was quite a distance from our berth — was pleasantly small, neat and quiet, but my only interest was to purchase a set of lights and fittings and other tiny accessories such as door-hinges and some red-brick- and red-tile paper for the Doll's House, and then spent the evenings in the workshop with the other model-makers, carving a wooden staircase and making furniture and furnishings. The ship's painter made stained-glass windows for the porch.

We were ten days there and then moved south to Nassau, a small town in the Bahamas, with just a couple of streets, a few yellow-brick houses and many wooden ones, and it was HOT. A Tropical Routine was worked by turning to at 7 a.m. and finishing at 1 p.m. when the non-duty watches could go ashore. There was not a lot to do except sport in the warm, clear water from white sandy beaches and in the evenings to walk along the dusty road and drink in one of the shanty bars, listening to the clicking of cicadas. The Nassau Sports Club challenged the ship to a water-polo and swimming contest at the Colonial Hotel pool and a crowd of us went along to watch our teams win every event. Then there was an Inter-department Aquatics gala held alongside the ship, in water so clear that the sea-bed at a depth of more than 20-feet could be seen as plainly as if it was only a couple of feet deep — our anchor and cable and lots of gaily-coloured fish (and tons of rubbish!) all shimmering on the sandy floor.

After a week at anchor we steamed a thousand-miles to the south-east and the American-owned island of St. Croix in the Virgin group,

95

remaining just four days before moving overnight to anchor on the morning of July 13th in the bay at Plymouth, the capital town of the beautifully green island of Montserrat. The sulphurous smell of the island's volcano deterred most from going ashore and I had no intention of making the trip until the Comm. (E) came into the Machine-shop accompanied by the Manager of the island's Cotton Mill who was carrying a small but very worn part of the Mill's engine. I was asked if I could make a replacement before the ship sailed, and next morning I took the new part ashore to the Mill and with the Manager watched the coloured fitter put it in place and get the engine working again. I lost no time in getting away from that awful smell and back to the ship even though it was just as strong on board, but before leaving the shore I filled the pockets of my white uniform with the grey volcanic sand from the beach, and that became the rough-cast upper storey of the Doll's House.

Our next move was further south — to the French-owned Martinique, another of the islands where I had no desire to land, for two reasons. The first reason was because we could smell the place even though we were lying about two miles off shore, and the second was that it rained steadily and heavily for the whole of the six days we were there — and there is not much fun in sitting or standing in an open boat, in very hot weather and pouring-rain on a very long trip in to the landing-stage. Besides, everyone in the ship was now thinking only of getting home. This was the final leg of our commission.

At 7.30 a.m. on July 25th our anchor came up and we moved off over a glassy sea with not a ripple ahead of us and only our wake astern, and next morning went alongside the oiling jetty at Port of Spain, Trinidad, where fuel and stores were taken on board and at 4.30 p.m. sailed again. This time our bows were pointed towards England and from then on my time was to be taken up in mustering all tools and checking stores and spares ready for turning over to the new crew at Chatham, and with making trays, fruit-bowls, trinket-boxes, napkin-rings and ash-trays — requests from officers, Captain to Middies, — from messmates and stokers, stewards and marines, and anyone who happened to come into the Machine-shop and ask. I was using the stocks of different woods which had been sent aboard as gifts by various islands, woods such as lignum-vitae, rose-wood, mahogany and cinchona. (Quinine).

The Atlantic was as calm as a mill pond. Everybody happy; smiles and cheery 'Good mornings' every day, and there was a magical moment as we approached the Azores on the morning of Sunday, August 4th with the sun glinting on the deep-blue ocean waters and on the islands whose hills had the appearance of a patchwork quilt with contrasting colours of fields of blue hydrangeas, of the different shades of green of the vineyards, the yellows of the various stages of ripening corn and the browns of the fallow

96

farmland, every one clearly defined and separated by the dark lines of dividing hedges — indeed a wondrous pictures, and had an artist painted the scene in its true colours and definition — so exaggeratedly clear-cut — the result would have been received with some cynicism.

Sandy and I landed at Fayal for exercise and a meal in the small, clean and very hilly town. In the restaurant we asked the waiter for the menu. He replied with, "Soooup — feesh — cheeek!" We said, "Well, what goes with the chicken? Potatoes? Peas? Anything?" But again it was, "Soooup — feesh — cheeek!" Neither of us spoke nor understood Portuguese but a German customer noticed our dilemma, came over and ordered for us a most delicious dinner. (We paid, of course!) Quite a treat after ten days at sea. I also bought a singing canary to take home and at 9 a.m. on August 6th we began the final stage of our journey and commission with it becoming colder and rougher, but with the kind words and the smiles remaining and the canary-bird blithely singing in the Machine-shop all the way.

We anchored off Sheerness late on the 11th and proceeded up-river next morning — my sixth Wedding Anniversary — to be met and greeted by a large crowd of wives and families as the ship entered the Dockyard. On the 15th *Dragon* paid off into Dockyard control and those of us who had served the full two years eleven months and one week of the commission were granted 40-days Foreign Service Leave.

The Doll's House was a great success and gave enormous pleasure to both my children and their many friends. The canary moved into a new and bigger cage and carried on singing, and during my leave we bought and moved into a new house in the town.

Time passed all too quickly and I was back in barracks and doing the routines once again and wondering — Where next? and When? It did not take long for me to find the answers!

CHAPTER 11

'You Never Know — — —'

I had three days with a working-party to complete the refit of the 700-ton minesweeper *Sutton* in the 'Yard and three more days stripping and re-assembling the engine of the Naval Stores' motor van before receiving an emergency draft on the afternoon of October 3rd — to join the destroyer *Vivien* at Portland — and was despatched by train to arrive on board at 8 o'clock that evening and take the place of a man who had reported sick. At that time she was a unit of the 20th Flotilla whose duties were to operate with submarines from Portland and Portsmouth and with any ship wanting exercise partners during their "Working-up" period. Portland weather was as bad as it usually was at this time of year and more often than not we had to keep steam on main engines while in harbour, but I thought it might be worth while to have my family come to Weymouth for a couple of weeks.

I met them on arrival on Saturday, October 19th and settled into a comfortable guest house. Next day, Sunday, I was Duty Watch but the Chief agreed to stand in for me from 1 p.m. till 5 p.m. (he would not do more because it was the Duty E.R.A's job to start the dynamo at 5 p.m. and shut it down at 11 p.m.) but an afternoon ashore was better than being on board.

The battleship *Ramillies* arrived at Portland for her Working-up period and we were at sea with her in the Channel, chasing and picking up torpedoes when at 2 p.m. we received a signal ordering *Vivien* to proceed to Chatham "at once"! I asked *Ramillies* to send a telegram to my wife as soon as they returned to harbour telling her to "Pack up and return home", and the ship arrived there next morning. What was it all about? No one knew. *Vivien* paid off on October 28th and re-commissioned immediately with a new crew except for me, and two days later we left Sheerness — in spite of a 'severe gale' warning — and battled our way down Channel to Portland, taking more than 24-hours on a voyage which normally took less than twelve and during which we heard radio messages saying, "All Channel shipping has run for shelter from the storm."

So — we were back at Portland and now it was *Vivien* working-up with her new crew, none of whom knew what we were supposed to be doing. They were asking me where the ship had come from before they were rushed aboard at Chatham but all I could tell them was, "Here. Portland, and the weather was not quite as bad as it is now!" (There had been no communication with the shore for three days!)

Then, late on November 20th we suddenly connected all three boilers, weighed anchor and steamed at full speed and at midnight dropped the anchor again — at Sheerness! (You never know where you might be from one day to the next). At daylight we moved up-river to Chatham 'yard and into dry-dock to refit and prepare for service in the eastern Mediterranean because Italy had attacked Abyssinia.

Each Watch was given 14-days Draft/Christmas Leave and when the 2nd Watch returned on December 27th the ship was ready to leave for Gibraltar but sailing was postponed for 24-hours. Next day it was put back again and "The ship will sail on the 31st." December 31st came — and passed, and our sailing date was again set, this time for January 7th so 1936 began, still full of uncertainty and the 7th came — and went, and we still did not know what was happening, but ready to leave for Gibraltar at almost any minute until on January 11th, *Vivien* was reduced to Reserve and we put her into a state of preservation. On the 17th she Paid Off and everyone returned to barracks — and the Joining Routine once again. (You never know —) I think we must have been just emergency stand-by until a flotilla of more modern boats was available.

On January 20th King George V died and I received a Draft to the *Scout* — my second time with her. She was still in the Emergency Flotilla with *Tempest* and *Scimitar* and during the next week all three boats were employed separately dashing across the Channel and the North Sea, escorting foreign Royalty and Heads of State into the Thames estuary or to Dover, ready for the funeral, which took place on the 28th.

Scout's only trip after the burial was to escort the King of the Belgians over to Ostend and when we arrived back at our berth in the river we collided with and sank an un-lit crane-lighter (fortunately there was no-one aboard it) and then over-ran our buoys in the darkness. It was well into the early hours before we finally secured and were able to shut down. We finished our week as Emergency Boat by working with the cruiser *Curlew* as she carried out post-refit trials in the North Sea.

There were great economies in force in the country at this time so our operations were rather limited to the occasional trips to the Thames estuary with a class of Boy Seamen for training in the lowering of the sea-boats (whalers), pulling away from the ship to pick up a raft or lifebelt which had been dropped to simulate 'Man Overboard', then hoisting the boats back onto the davits. There might also be a little gunnery practice if we could afford the ammunition, and some signal drill.

At 1 a.m. on April 10th we had a tryst with the P. & O. liner *Ranpura* at Tilbury (Port of London). She was carrying Chinese Art Treasures worth more than £10-million being returned to China after being exhibited in London. We escorted her down the Channel.

Our next 'outing' was on April 19th when we had to proceed to Dover to pick up the coffin containing the body of the German ambassador, Baron von Hoeth, and embark his widow and his valet for their return to Germany. It was a very rough crossing to Wilhelmshaven where we arrived at 1.30 p.m. the next day to a mass of "Heil Hitler" salutes by black-arm-banded men and youths lining the banks of the canal. As soon as our cargo and passengers had left us we departed for an even rougher voyage home.

On April 30th we had to go to Dover again. This time it was to escort the cross-Channel ferry carrying the King of Greece across to Calais and that was followed on Monday, May 4th by five days at Harwich, taking classes of Boy Seamen from the Training Establishment *Ganges* to sea each day from 0830 until 1630 — but reverting to that Monday morning — I went to the engine-room for "Lighting-up" with my Leading stoker and two stokers at 0530 to do the usual checking of all machinery before calling through the voice-pipe to the Stoker Petty Officer in the boiler-room to "Carry on. Flash up." I then went to the top of the ladder to the hatch for a breath of morning air and I suppose it was a miracle that I did so at that moment because as I reached the top I caught a glimpse of the top of a man's head disappearing down the inside of the after funnel. I shouted and yelled as loud as I could but he failed to hear so I dropped to the engine-room plates in almost one step, grabbed the handle of the boiler-room telegraph and feverishly swung it round and round until its clanging brought the S.P.O. to his end of the voice-pipe, asking, "What's the panic?" I shouted back, "Stop! Stop everything!" and heard his call to the stokers manning the hand-operated oil-fuel pump to "Stop pumping!" How fortunate that a flaming torch had not been applied to the sprayers, to send volumes of thick and heavy black smoke up the funnel! The man would certainly have been overcome — probably asphyxiated. The S.P.O. explained that he had sent a stoker to the upper deck to "Check that the intakes in the side of the funnel are open" — (the air-inlets to the boiler-room forced-draught fans, situated in the funnel-casing on deck) — and the man, apparently a New Entry from the Depot especially for this trip had interpreted the order as 'inside the funnel'. Had I not caught a glimpse of a disappearing head the man would have been 'missing'! Had he fallen overboard? Had he jumped overboard? Would anyone have thought of climbing the funnel to look inside? I doubt it, but in any case it would have been too late. He now knew where the fan intakes were located.

When the classes from *Ganges* came to sea with us they were usually introduced to the engine-room at some time while the ship was under way and we would endeavour to arouse in them some interest in the machinery and its workings and perhaps influence their future by suggesting they might like to transfer to the Engineering Branch. After lecturing one of the classes following a tour of the works I grouped them on the manoeuvring platform for "Any questions?" session. "Yes, sir. What time's dinner?"

We were given ten days Summer Leave, which was very nice until we received telegrams recalling us to the ship at the end of the week. This was an odd occurrence for peace-time and made us wonder what was afoot — another case of "You never know—'.

When everyone had returned we steamed round to Dover and embarked a section of Royal Scots Guards; took them to sea and then landed them at four o'clock one morning on the Kent coast. We then returned to Chatham only to steam back to Dover later the same day and remain there overnight — Goodness knows why, because nothing happened and there was no activity of any sort. And if 'Goodness' did know why, she did not pass the message on to us! So we went back to our berth in the Medway for a few days before we had to escort and minister-to the County Class cruiser *Cumberland* on her post-refit trials in the North Sea.

On September 30th 1936 I re-engaged for a further ten years service to qualify for a pension, having completed twelve years from the age of 18, and as a result I was making myself immediately available for Foreign Service and fully expected to be called at once. I had had a happy period in *Scout* in spite of the hard work entailed in keeping her in first class running order and the long hours of watchkeeping in two-watches at sea, plus the uncertainty — the possibility of being called back to barracks at any time of any day. (One never knew where one would be tomorrow!)

November 7th — and another very rough passage to Harwich for the *Ganges'* boys' training during which, on the 10th the disturbing news came to us that the King — Edward VIII — was abdicating and we were ordered back to Sheerness forthwith. Thick fog prevented any movement then but we eventually arrived at midnight on the 11th with everyone on edge and wondering what would happen. Nothing happened! We quietly proceeded up-river next morning.

Scout was Emergency boat for the Christmas season and did a Training run to sea on the last day of 1936.

1937 began well with ten days belated Christmas Leave for each of the two watches — except that I suffered a severe bout of bronchial 'flu and recovered just in time to return aboard, back to the routine turns of Emergency duties with *Scimitar* and *Tempest* and of taking Training classes to sea.

At the beginning of May the Admiralty decided *Scout* should be taken in hand for a major refit to prepare her for service on the China Station and while mustering and checking stores and engine spares I found several items wrapped in newspaper dated "December 25th 1916", proving she was more than 20-years old — and still going strong!

The Engineer wanted me to volunteer to remain with the ship and go to

Hong Kong with her, offering the 'bait' — "It will mean 4- to 6-months in Chatham with the ship in Dockyard hands; no duties to keep, and you could be ashore every night and every week-end over that period!"

Tempting — but — "Thank you, sir, for the offer but I will take whatever comes my way. No volunteering!" She was a pleasant little ship and I had spent sixteen happy months with her, but would not relish doing a foreign commission in her, so on May 7th I left *Scout* and returned to barracks for the usual Joining Routine, some Parade Drills, a visit to the Gas School and then some work in the Barracks' Machine-shop which kept me busy until — — —

CHAPTER 12

South America

July 26th 1937. My name appeared with those of four other E.R.A's and one Chief E.R.A. on a Draft list for Advance Party to *Ajax* at Portsmouth, and we started our Draft routine. At the Medical inspection my temperature was 104° with an inflamed throat and I was confined to Sick Quarters for five days as the others went on their way.

On reporting at the Drafting Office for my instructions I was called in by the Drafting Commander (E) — D. H. Tollemache (of *Valiant* and *Dragon*) — who said, "How lucky you are to be going back to the West Indies. I wish I was going, too, but I've just been appointed to the cruiser *Bonaventure*, building at a private Yard up north." We wished each other "Luck for the future" and I was given my Travel Warrant to join *Ajax* at South Railway Jetty, Portsmouth, on August 17th.

Ajax — a light cruiser of 6,850-tons — had just returned home from her first commission (with a Pompey crew) and was to be refitted in Portmouth 'yard and would then re-commission with a Chatham crew for further service with the 8th Cruiser Squadron, America and West Indies (South American Division). The prospect therefore was for her to be at home for at least three months, so I would have my family with me in Southsea for the remainder of the summer! They arrived and two weeks later we — the Advance Party — were sent on 10-days Foreign Draft leave at the end of which my children had returned to school.

There were very few Chatham ratings in the ship and most of the previous company had left, leaving a handful to transfer the reins to us, so life was quite comfortable. There was plenty of work to be done and we also had to become acquainted with everything to do with the ship — the engines, layouts of compartments and pipelines, etc.

One morning the senior officer on board came to ask our Chief E.R.A. if he could raise a team to represent *Ajax* at the Port Rifle Competition and as we had all at some time or other gone through a week's Course on the Range at Chatham, 'Hughie' (Chief E.R.A. Hughes) agreed and we formed a team of six. We presented ourselves at the Whale Island Gunnery School and Range where the Lieutenant-Commander in charge asked if we were "A" Class or Open Class. 'Hughie' supposed the "A" meant "First class" as marksmen and answered "Open, sir!" so we were directed to the butts to be issued with ten rounds of ammunition for our .303 rifles. Targets were set at 200-yards for us and we got down to business — a disastrous business because there was scarcely one hit from the six of us. We were then given ten more rounds and the targets set at 500-yards with results even worse. They were catastrophic enough to bring the Gunnery Officer over to ask. "Did you say you were Open Class?" Hughie said, "Yes, sir. But what exactly is the difference between Open and "A" Classes?" and it was explained to us that competitors for the Open had previously taken part in the Bisley National Competition!

We had a good laugh at our ignorance and were out of the tournament. No glory for us as we were sent back to our ship.

1937 ended with the Advance Party given ten days Christmas leave and on January 11th 1938 the ship paid off and re-commissioned with three-fifths complement of our Chatham crew with Captain C. H. L. Woodhouse in command and Commander D. H. Everett as Executive Officer, and our department had Engineer Commander L. C. S. Noake and Lt. Comm. (E) P. M. Rouse in charge. Stores and ammunition were embarked on the 19th and we proceeded to sea for trials in the Channel until February 14th when our nose was turned towards our home port, into the teeth of a north-easterly gale which held back our arrival until the 16th. when the ship was brought up to full complement. My advancement to Chief came through at the same time, and we now had five chiefs on board instead of the normal four and I expected to be drafted from *Ajax* before she sailed.

March 1st was our sailing date and the C. in C. (Nore Command) — Admiral Sir E. R. G. R. Evans, — "Evans of the *Broke*" — came on board to wish us God-speed and to inspect the ship, and then sailing was delayed until the morrow to enable a Court Martial to take place on board, so it was on the 12th — after a rough passage that we arrived in Bermuda for the start of our 2½-year commission and were immediately sent to anchor in Grassy Bay, in quarantine because of an outbreak of measles on board!

That did not prevent the ship from spending a few days in the Floating Dock while we did a mini refit but instructions were strict and implicit. We must not associate with anyone outside our own ship's company nor visit the Club or Canteen, and "If you see any old friends who happen to be serving in other ships of the Squadron simply hail them from a distance and arrange to meet them later."

The rest of the Squadron came in from their Spring Cruise programme and it now comprised of *York* (Flagship of Vice-Admiral Sir Sidney Meyrick), *Exeter*, *Orion* (our sister ship), and *Apollo*, and the two Town Class sloops — *Scarborough* and *Dundee*.

Quarantine was lifted on the day we undocked; the C. in C. came to welcome us to his Command, and we were free to meet and talk with other people and have a drink at the Club — and of course — purchase transport, the jolly-old £2 bicycle. But we were still in our Working-up period and, with the others, put in quite a lot of sea time at exercises, day and night, while in harbour we had plenty of sporting activities.

Apollo won the Fleet Road Race on April 30th. and *York* took the Boxing Shield in early May, but the E.R.A's Relay Race — that old 'Annual' — was won by us and it was a pleasure to see that old lump of brass, on its rough wooden base, secure on a shelf in *our* Mess.

There were still five chiefs and it was assumed that I was being kept for a period because I had been "Advance Party" and knew the ship, my Daywork job had me in charge in the boiler-rooms — including the latest and most up-to-date Robot Feed-water Regulators — and all fittings and valves on the steam lines to the engine-rooms. At sea I took my turn with the other chiefs (except the senior chief who did not keep a Watch) in charge of the Forward Engine Room.

At 0800 on May 24th the squadron proceeded to sea for exercises which were scheduled to last over a five-day period but as we prepared to anchor in Five Fathom Hole at 4 p.m. on the first day, *Ajax* was ordered to proceed 'with all despatch' to Kingston, Jamaica. Speed was increased to 30-knots and maintained until the early hours of the 26th and was only reduced so that we should arrive at dawn — 6 a.m.

There had been serious rioting in the town but just the presence of a cruiser in the harbour had a quieting effect and we were actually welcomed in the streets and could safely walk out to Up Park Camp to help the sergeants of the Manchester Regiment consume their beer while playing them at snooker on their table.

The ship had berthed at the Banana Wharf on arrival but it became too hot so we moved to anchor in the harbour just as the Governor of the Island — Sir Edward Denham — died, and at 4.30 p.m. next day, June 3rd — we buried his coffined body at sea south of the island at sunset. After the Service we carried on to Montego Bay to advertise our presence and

104

"Show the Flag", remained anchored for a couple of days before returning to Kingston which was still quiet and peaceful.

The Army asked the ship to put up a team of boxers against them and we obliged, and although it was only a one-night affair it cemented a good bond of friendship between the two services and was thoroughly enjoyable. There were three or four of us in the Mess who liked walking, and as a Tropical routine was being worked we could land by 4 o'clock boat and take a walk as far as Stony Hill or Constant Springs, small hamlets, quite a distance out of town — where we sat and drank ice-cold beer and watched young Jamaicans — boys and girls of all ages between two years and fifteen years — playing cricket in the dirt roads all around us. Anything would do for a wicket and anywhere would make a pitch.

On June 20th we headed back north to Bermuda at a more leisurely pace than on the voyage south and taking four days against the 36-hours and H. H. Harwood — Commodore of our South American Division — who wore his Flag in *Exeter* — came on board to congratulate the ship's company on a 'job well done'. Then we had to resume our Working up with high-speed exercises with the other ships, day and night until it was time for us to prepare for an extended cruise, the circumnavigation of the South American continent.

Ajax sailed on July 16th and our first call four days later was to oil at Point-a-Pierre, Trinidad, and then to Port of Spain where I developed a melancholy mood with no desire to go ashore or even leave the ship, a mood which prevailed during our ten-day sojourn in Barbados and a further four days at Grenada. We oiled again in Trinidad and began the journey south on August 12th, crossing the Equator on the 18th.

King Neptune with his Queen and Court boarded us at 9 o'clock, a canvas bath having been rigged on the upper deck complete with dais for the King and his retinue and a Barber's chair. I was below on the Forenoon Watch as news filtered down that the Ceremony had started well but soon degenerated into a rough-house and had been wound up before it got completely out of control.

We stopped for oil at Ceara, Brazil, on August 19th and then started to 'roll' our way down to Sao Sebastio, also in Brazil, and it certainly *was* rolling — even as we lay at anchor off that port for 48-hours we rolled twenty degrees each way, non-stop like a pendulum. It was most uncomfortable trying to walk, work, eat, and even to relax in the Mess. Everyone was really thankful when we got under way on the 27th to move forward into an easier sea.

Off Punta del Este, Uruguay, at 3.30 p.m. on the 30th we met *Exeter* which had just come out of Monte Video and had mail for us — the first since leaving Bermuda. A tremendous cheer heralded its arrival in-board as most waited expectantly and somewhat impatiently for letters and parcels to be sorted and distributed as both ships steamed in company to Puerto Ingineiro White, the port for Bahia Blanca, Argentina, where the ships secured on either side of the mole on September 1st.

With one of my 'walking' chums I went by bus to Bahia and we were somewhat surprised to find such a clean, neat and fair-sized city with big shops and stores. We had our walk and then visited the Palacio Cinema to see the film, "Four Men and a Prayer", the dialogue being in English with Spanish sub-titles but the whole was totally ruined for us by the loud crying and sobbing of the women in the audience. It was as though some dreadful calamity had struck the city and the people had taken refuge in the 'church', so we soon left.

Both ships sailed together on September 8th for two days of exercises before parting company again when *Ajax* entered Monte Video and *Exeter* crossed the estuary to Buenos Aires.

Our berth was a marvellous one alongside a main street and immediately opposite the Novedades Hotel which served splendid meals, and it was possible for us to walk across the road at almost any time — provided we were correctly dressed for going ashore — and treat ourselves to 'big eats'.

This was a big and bustling city of wide streets and avenues and huge white buildings — banks, offices and stores — and a beautiful sea-coast road (promenade?) which seemed to stretch for miles and was very inviting in the warm Spring sunshine.

The English Society of Uruguay invited members of the ship's company to a Musical Evening at the Parque Hotel Ballroom but unfortunately the current Munich Crisis curtailed our visit and we sailed to meet *Exeter* somewhere off the estuary and carried out a series of drills, one of them being the despatch of a Boarding Party to search an 'enemy vessel' which might be trying to break a blockade. Two such parties were required to man the whalers and I was a member of one crew as part of the engine-room squad with a Webley pistol tucked in its holster on my khaki belt and a wheel-spanner grasped in my hand. It all appeared such a waste of time having to clamber into, and out of a boat hanging at its davits and maybe dropped into the water to pull round the ships and be hoisted inboard again. We patrolled in the south Atlantic with both ships darkened at night and crews at Action Stations, until on October 7th when we anchored and oiled off Punta del Este and were due to 'have a rest', but at 8.30 p.m. *Ajax* received the order — Steam for 25-knots — and moved away at 11 p.m. with a host of rumours flying around of "Riots here and riots there", "We're off to Sierra Leone- or Rio" — even to having to pick up a load of bananas in Jamaica and take them to the Falklands! The rumours were finally dispelled when the Captain announced that we were to search for a 'suspicious vessel', and speculation became rife again as to whether we were after gun-runners or slave-traders as the ship careered over the ocean at 25-knots during daylight hours with our Sea-Fox seaplane reconnoitering far and wide, and at dusk we reduced speed and ambled along at 6-knots all night with the ship completely darkened. That went on for four days and nights and on the fourth night at 11.30 the engine-room revolution telegraph started dinging its way up to indicate an increase to 13-knots — our economical speed — so we guessed the search had been called off. Normal sea-routine became the order as we turned back towards the coast and arrived at La Plata on October 14th — three days behind our 'programmed' date, and the proposed visit to Rosario which was to follow was cancelled. The reason for the cancellation was because Rosario lay about 200-miles up the narrow Parana River and we would have had to proceed stern-first up stream and having arrived there the state of the tide would have controlled our exit, and we could have been trapped if another 'crisis' had arisen. So, Rosario time was spent at La Plata, the home of the two biggest meat-canning factories — Swift's and Armour's — both companies issuing invitations for fifteen men from the ship to visit their respective canneries on Saturday morning. I put my name together with that of a chum on the list for Armour's and both names were lucky enough to be drawn from the large number wishing to go.

While at Buenos Aires a list containing the names of a number of ratings who were to be sent home 'on arrival of reliefs' was received from Chatham and apparently my name was included although I was really surplus to complement and did not require a relief — and had no inkling of the list being in the ship.

Towards the end of October, 'Bill' — one of the other chiefs — announced that he would be leaving us without a relief, and with a number of other ratings would be sailing on the 27th aboard the *Highland Brigade*.

The Mess in general thought it strange that he — not I — should be leaving but he duly left on the 27th, and a few days later I was talking with the Master-at-Arms who casually remarked, "That was a dirty trick played on you, wasn't it", and when I asked, "What trick was that?" he said he assumed I had known that my name had been on the Draft Note, "To be sent home without relief" but apparently Bill — who had recently been in a spot of bother in the ship — happened to be in the Engineer's Office when the Note arrived in front of the Senior and suggested he should go in my stead. Ah, well! Too late now, but imagine my feelings when some weeks later Hughie received a letter from Bill to say that he was 'standing by' a sloop being built in a private yard and still on the stocks. It was a job which might have been mine but Fate had intervened on my behalf for, early in 1940 the sloop struck a mine and sank, and Bill lost a leg in the explosion. I suppose I should have felt satisfaction that I had been preferred to remain with the ship but at the time it rankled when I thought of what might have been.

We sailed in company with *Exeter* on Nov. 5th, exercising all the way down to the Falklands where we arrived on the 10th and during the 24-hours prior to anchoring in Port Stanley harbour we were steaming at 5-knots through shoals of seals, and a few sea-lions which barked at us as we passed as though they were warning to keep away from their territory.

It was cold with rain and sleet even though it was summer, but our biggest bugbear was the kelp which continually blocked the inlet valves in the ship's bottom and clogged the condensers so that we were frequently employed changing from one auxiliary plant to the other and opening-up the first condenser to clear the weed from the tube-ends. Tough stuff. We went to sea again on Nov. 18th towing a target for the Local Defence Force to get some gunnery practice. It was a most uncomfortable trip because we had to steam so slowly with the ship rolling 30-degrees each way all the time, we were glad to get back to harbour *and* the weeding. Our next move was to cruise round the islands, calling at remote hamlets and cattle-stations, staying at each for about 24-hours. Leaving Port Stanley — which lies at the most easterly point of East Falkland — it was only five hours steaming into Choiseul Sound to Darwin, and at 7 p.m. next day (Nov. 23rd) another 12-hours to Fox Bay on West Falkland. One officer and two petty officers landed officially at each place to make contact with the locals — that is if the weather allowed. From Fox Bay it was just four hours to Port Stephens during the afternoon of the 25th in almost blizzard conditions with our decks four inches deep in large hailstones which had to be shovelled over the side, so that was one place where we didn't make contact with the shore. We had 'shown ourselves' but whether we had been seen was another matter. We left at 7.30 that evening and after an extremely rough passage round the west coast we anchored at Hill Cove on the Sunday morning (Nov. 27th) and I managed to get ashore for some exercise in the afternoon. What a desolate place! Four houses, no roads, no trees, just mossy scrub on spongy ground whch made for very tough walking conditions, and I did not see any other person except for the three other members of the crew who had landed by the same boat and for the same purpose — to have a walk. We had come ashore at 12.30 and we had all walked on the lower slopes of Mount Adam, the highest point of the Falklands at 2,300-feet — and it was with aching legs that all four of us returned on the 4.30 boat. Next morning the ship moved eastward along the north shore to anchor at San Carlos, the northern entrance to Falkland Sound. San Carlos was 50-miles as the crow flies from Port Stanley but as there were no roads the crofters had quite a ride on horseback to collect their supplies. It was certainly a spartan existence, in a very harsh climate and cut off from the world. We had arrived at 1.30 p.m. on the 28th and we left at noon on the 29th for the two-hour trip across the Sound to Port Howard — yet another tiny settlement of about half-a-dozen people and

Both Seaplanes in Flight. H.M.S. 'Exeter' in background.

'Ajax' at Falklands, December 1st 1938. After the Hailstorm.

only the one officer and two P.O's went ashore to let them know they were not forgotten. We left at noon on the 30th and had some gunnery practice on the short trip back to Port Stanley where we were to spend a quiet few days — except that it was not quiet for our department as we still had to cope with the kelp menace, clearing the weed from the condensers every few hours. The weather was ghastly too, with almost non-stop heavy and cold rain, but one brief bright interval did allow me ashore at 1.30 on Saturday afternoon for a walk in the small town for just 20-minutes before the rain, sleet and wind drove me back to the comparative warmth and comfort of the ship. A mess mate bought a penguin's egg with the instruction that it had to be boiled for 25-minutes and he said it was just like eating a lump of codfish.

On December 8th we left to continue our cruise, passing through the Straits of Magellan to Punta Arenas, the southern-most city in the world, seeing many seals, sea-lions and whales during the two-day voyage.

We stayed for less than 48-hours but I wanted to go ashore to see what it was like and just before I landed there was a terrific downpour, turning the main road (there seemed to be only the one) into a sea of mud — and I think the most comfortable means of transport was by horse-back. There were a few bullock-carts floundering through the mud as motor-cars slithered, slid, bumped and jolted along sending showers of mud and water to either side. But easily the very best of the bunch was a very old "Tin Lizzy" (Could have been the absolute first one made by 'Henry'!) which literally bounced its way along and looked as though it was held together with elastic. It spread itself wide at every bump on the muddy road as if it would split asunder and then, when it got 'airborne' it pulled itself together again. It was like a Keystone Cops film and I wanted to just stand and laugh. And the people! They were so different from any I had ever seen. They were all so short and they seemed to glide along the sidewalks as though they were mounted on flat trolleys. It was because of their squat build and the bulky clothes which reached to within an inch of the muddy ground and hiding their feet. It was really comical. I did not walk far; the dismal day drove me back to the ship and we sailed at 4.30 next morning, December 12th.

I had had the 'Lighting-up' watch from midnight and went to the upper deck as we got under way, surprised to find that it was broad daylight, and stayed on deck instead of going to my hammock. And I am so glad I did. The air was clean and clear as we exited from the Straits, passing amongst the many islands with snow-capped mountains rising directly from glassy-calm water and almost touchable — reminiscent of my *Dragon* days in western Canada.

We anchored that first evening at Otter Ridge but had to keep steam all night because the weather could not be relied upon and the anchorage was confined, moving off again at dawn for another day of flat-calm progress with magnificent scenery all round. Everyone marvelled at the beauty and serenity of our surroundings, urging each other to 'nip up top (to the upper deck) and see it now!'

At 7 p.m. the 'hook' went down in Molyneux Sound but once again steam had to be maintained on main engines, and when we got under way next morning it was only for four hours when we anchored in Alert Harbour — a natural harbour with just a few dwellings dotted at random around its shores — and we waited for *Exeter* to catch up with us. She was 24-hours behind and I don't know where she had been but as soon as she came in sight we joined her out in the rough Pacific, both ships dashing about at 28-knots in the heavy seas and engaging in 'Throw-off shoots' at each other until 4 p.m. on Dec. 17th when we both anchored at Ancud, a small port at the northern tip of Chiloe Island. Two days later we again parted company as *Ajax* made the 8-hour trip across to the mainland port of Puerto Montt — a big sheep-farming district — where we were to spend Christmas 1938.

Christmas Day was also a Sunday with the usual harbour-routine of Divisions and Captain's inspection. Church was rigged on the quarterdeck and the sailors' voices lustily echoed the words of our carols all around the harbour. All messes were decorated with bunting and tree-branches brought off from shore, and the day's menu was:- Breakfast — Rolls, coffee, bacon and egg, marmalade and fruit. Dinner:- Tomato soup, roast turkey with grilled sausages, stuffing and roast potatoes and cabbage, followed by Christmas Pudding with white sauce, fruit and nuts. Tea:- Bread and butter, Christmas cake and biscuits, and for supper there was cold roast pork with Pan-yan pickle, hot mince pies and coffee. The cooks certainly did us well and on the whole it was a good day — quiet — with some silly games in the Mess and some fresh air on deck. In the evening we had a darts match and some card games.

Boxing Day was another 'take it easy' day and I landed at 1.30 p.m. for a long walk in the foothills outside the small town. It was nice to be able to stride out but from the time I stepped ashore until the time I boarded the 6.30 p.m. boat back to the ship I doubt I saw more than a dozen people, including those who were eating in the Hotel Astral where I stopped for tea.

The next two days were work-days although both afternoons were taken over by a 'skylark' Regatta which I think had been specially organized to burn off some of the Christmas spirit. At 5 a.m. on the 29th we left for Coronel, arriving there at 6 p.m. the next day and from our anchorage the small town did not look very inviting, so I gave it a miss — and 1938 came to its end.

We left Coronel on January 3rd 1939, and rendezvoused with *Exeter*

Concepción, Chile. Energetic Chilean —
earthquake San. 24th 1939.

Royal Marines demolition party. Earthquake January 24th 1939.

After the Earthquake of January 24th 1939. One building that
stayed 'up' and some that didn't.

only to anchor off Talcahuano later that day. It was another smallish town but also a Chilean Naval Base. With one of my 'walking' chums I landed on the Sunday at 12.30 and we were not really surprised to find it just as grubby and poverty-stricken as a lot of other places on that stretch of coast, so we decided to go to Concepciòn, a bigger town a few miles away. We boarded a smelly old bus and after what seemed a very short ride we were there. Actually we thought it was just some other small town on the route but as the bus had emptied and reversed direction we alighted — in the Main Street, Concepciòn! Half the width of the street was taken up by tramway tracks, the vehicles being such odd-looking contraptions — as tall as they were long and a dull, dingy red in colour, all drab and battered. The street itself had a good surface and was lined by large and well-stocked shops and stores, but it being Sunday — they were shut. After walking about five minutes in both directions Main Street came to an end and petered-out to become just rough track, so we returned to the town centre for coffee in the very clean Ritz Hotel on the corner of Main Square. A taxi had us back in Talcahuano in time for the 4.30 p.m. boat and next morning we sailed northward in company with *Exeter*, exercising with day and night action and simulating gas-attacks on each other until *Exeter* left us on the 12th to go to Antofagasta and we continued north to Iquique, Chile's northernmost port, where we anchored at 0700 on the 13th. We were now in the Tropical zone and it was very hot. Iquique had been the centre of a prosperous nitrate industry and very ambitious plans had been under way to turn it into a beautiful holiday resort. Parks had been laid out with ornamental lakes and the beaches were clean and ideal for the sport of surfing on the gigantic rollers which came thundering in from the Pacific. But the trade had collapsed and the place was more like a ghost town. It lies on a coastal plain about two miles wide before the ground begins to rise into the great Andes mountains. I went ashore on the Sunday afternoon and found it very clean with good roads (of course the sunshine and warmth are great assets when one compares them with the grim, dank and cold south of the country).

I walked up a road leading inland until the metalling ended and disappeared into a sandy waste, and from there I more or less plodded up a sandy mountain, my right foot advancing 18-inches up the slope but by the time it found a firm foundation would be just about six-inches ahead of my left foot. It was certainly tough going until I reached a railway track running 'north-south' 200-feet above sea-level and firmly built into the hill-side. This was the main line which stretched from its southern terminus at Puerto Montt to La Paz, the capital of Bolivia, to the north, and in parts of its length is reputed to be the highest in the world, but no train disturbed my appreciation of the view over town and harbour. Downward progress was faster although not easier and I walked in the quiet town, noticing that no building other than a couple of very old churches and a modern hospital was more than two storeys high — probably due to the risk of earthquakes — and for the same reason most were of timber construction, one exception being the hospital. That was of white stone and it had never been used. It stood empty. When trade died, the town followed suit — a great pity.

We moved south on leaving Iquique on the 17th and met *Exeter* for 48-hours of intensive exercises before both ships anchored off Coquimbo. First reports from members of the Captain's party who landed for his official arrival visit placed it on a par with Coronel so I decided to give it a miss. (Actually there were many in the ship who rarely went ashore at any place we visited.). We stayed for four days then both ships moved overnight to anchor inside the harbour at Valparaiso at 0900 on January 24th.

Several Chilean Navy ships were in the harbour and all day long bugles were sounding "Attention" and "Carry on" as official boats passed to and fro and back and forth, the Commodore, H. H. Harwood of *Exeter*, calling on the Chilean Admiral afloat and the Intendente on shore and then visiting other senior vessels, and our Captain waltzed about in his boat to call on all and sundry. Every call was reciprocated by Chilean admirals, captains and Port Officials, so that our 'Guard and Band' — and that of the *Exeter* — were in demand and on deck the whole of that sultry day with buglers sounding the "Still" every few minutes, the Guard called to 'Attention', a few bars of a National Anthem and then the "Carry on" — and woe betide anyone moving on the upper deck while a 'personage' was arriving, leaving or passing!

I was on Duty on board that evening and was on the point of sleep at 11.30 when the ship shuddered, shook and rolled. Startled faces peered over the sides of hammocks (from which we had almost been ejected.) What was that? What had caused the sudden movement? Had some other vessel bumped us? Then came another violent rocking and we guessed it must be earth-tremors, probably under the Pacific. They lasted but a few minutes, quite long enough for us to voice our feelings that we would not have wanted to be any closer to the epicentre.

Men returning by the midnight boat said the shocks had been felt severely on shore and that they had had to plant their feet widely apart to keep their balance as civilians ran screaming and crying in the middle of the road, many being thrown to the ground. Copings fell from buildings and men who had been in cinemas reported the whole structure swaying and the audiences stampeding for the exits.

We then slept.

The incident rather upset plans for the ship to grant 48-hours General Leave to each Watch while in port, and some of us had intended to travel up to Santiago some fifty-miles inland, but in the morning news began coming from affected regions — Concepción, Tome and Chillan were in ruins and thousands of people were dead. More towns and villages in remote areas were devastated and thousands injured by falling debris while many more had been rendered homeless.

Both ships immediately went to short notice in case we should be required for relief work but at noon Leave was granted for the afternoon "Subject to recall" so I decided to go ashore while I had the chance, and landed in the 1.30 p.m. boat to find an odd sort of city. There were three streets running parallel to and on the level of the waterfront but beyond that it was hills — steep hills — with funicular railways to transport people up or down. I rode to the top to walk in the upper echelons of the city and found a variety of districts, some fair, some bad, and some very bad, and all piled atop of each other. To my left as I walked there was the basement of a house while on my right were the chimneys of the one next below it. Then there would be the crossing roads, steep hills leading to even higher levels on my left and dropping sharply to the city 'heart' to my right. When I came to the next funicular I returned to sea-level and those three main streets of fine big stores, grandiose Squares and beautiful gardens. A very pleasant late afternoon.

My chum came ashore at 6 p.m. and we could see *Exeter*'s recall signal flying — she sailed at 7 p.m. — but we went for a meal and then to a cinema, the city had seemingly forgotten the earthquake.

Our recall signal was being sent out just as we returned aboard and at 7.30 in the morning we sailed for Talcahuano at 34-knots all the way and arrived at 5 p.m. as *Exeter* with several hundreds of refugees on board was leaving for Valparaiso. Two Consular officials came on board and told us that conditions at Concepciòn were worse than anyone could imagine, saying that the earth must have opened up to swallow about 200 children in the ruins of a Convent and hundreds of people lay buried in the wrecked Roxy cinema; only four buildings had seemed to survive and there was little food and no water for people who wandered lost on the streets. We landed demolition parties of marines and sailors and sent supplies of blankets and tons of drinking-water and in the morning received a message that the city must be evacuated within 24-hours, so the ship was prepared to receive 750 refugees. The demolition parties came back with gruesome tales of digging for any survivors, and pulling out bodies and knocking down the shakiest of tottery buildings.

Refugees began coming on board, pathetic figures who had lost everything, including family and friends. There were mothers carrying small children and there were teenagers, and everyone clutching at the small bundles of whatever they had managed to salvage. About 15,000 bodies had been given burial at Chillan which was thought to be the epicentre of the 'quake, and transport between there and Concepciòn and Talcahuano was no longer possible but we had 540 refugees on board when we left, most of them having been collected from villages along the coast by four small tramp steamers and transferred to us.

Valparaiso could not accept them after 10 p.m. so we reduced speed to arrive at dawn on Sunday, 29th. While off watch during the trip back I was speaking with a doctor who had gone to Chillan from Santiago. He told me there was nothing anybody could do as the town was absolutely devastated, and he had managed to reach Talcahuano. (Supposing disaster had struck a couple of weeks earlier! There would certainly have been casualties among crews of both *Ajax* and *Exeter*.)

As soon as the refugees had landed we took on fuel and loaded more stores ready to leave but *Exeter* returned with a further 600 evacuees and we were not required to go south again. Next day it was announced that 48-hours General Leave would be granted to each watch, starting at one o'clock that afternoon but stipulating that no-one depart the local area and should keep alert for any recall notices. That was disappointing because the doctor I met on the ship had invited me — and a friend — to stay with him and his wife if we could manage a few days in Santiago. I had asked my 'walking' chum — (I might as well give his name) — Frank I. Shaw, known as "Fiz", who was also in the 'Advance Party' (see p. 102) — and he had welcomed the chance to visit the capital, but of course it was not to be. We took advantage of our leave by taking a bus-ride to Vina del Mar, a beautiful suburb a few miles up the coast with wide, clean, and palm-lined avenues and large squares surrounded by splendid hotels and office buildings. We went into the Casino to watch the afternoon gaming session before walking further along to Miramar, another resort and equally as nice and which gave us the exercise we needed. We returned to the city by the high hill-side route which gave us a wonderful view of the city lights.

Next day we met a messmate who had landed with us but had spent the evening in the city and we advised him to go and see Vina del Mar — and then decided that we would go with him as it was worth a second visit. On entering the Casino we got to talking to one of the directors who took us on a tour of the building — the Card Room, Roulette Room, Board-room, Club Room, the Bedroom suites and the Restaurant, all the very essence of luxury. We had arrived at the Club Room by way of a curtained stage on which stood a grand piano with the open music of "William Tell" overture on its stand. I sat and played the first page of music unaware of the presence of a dozen members armchair-bound on the other side of the curtain but suddenly aware, and embarrassed by their applause. It was all a lovely experience and we finally left the Casino at 8 p.m. taking the same scenic route back to the city and again appreciated the myriad lights, sparkling like jewels below us. A Chilean Navy picket-boat gave us a lift out to *Ajax* at midnight.

On February 3rd we sailed for our next scheduled port, Huacho, near Lima, Peru, but on the 6th our destination was changed to Chimbote, which was 200-miles further north. We were still in company wth *Exeter*, doing a lot of high-speed steaming and exercising — General Drills, Evolutions and Action Stations, sub-calibre and full-calibre shoots — with the ship battened down for long periods and making conditions even hotter below. *Exeter* went in to Huacho while we steamed on to Chimbote where she joined us two days later and for some unknown reason we were being rationed in our use of fresh water. There was no fault in our distilling plant so we could only assume it was to conserve fuel. We also had a 'spot' bedding and locker inspection by the Supply Officer trying to find some of the blankets which went missing when the refugees were on board. Each had been issued with one for their comfort during that night and could easily have tucked it into their small bundles of salvaged belongings. Both ships left Chimbote on Feb. 11th and steamed 300-miles north to Paita, another little place with no harbour. Fiz and I went ashore at both Chimbote and Paita; an hour at each place was quite sufficient as it was so hot and there was little of interest to see on shore, and on the 14th we moved a few more miles north to the oil refinery port of Lobitos where I think every worker in the whole complex came on board to patronize our *Naafi* canteen.

Our next scheduled call was to Guayaquil in Ecuador but a message from the consul in Quito stated "Heavy rains have made the place unhealthy and it is inadvisable for *Ajax* to visit the port. Proceed to Salinas with *Exeter*". It was all very mysterious as we left Lobitos that night with both ships darkened — but because of the heat scuttles could be left open provided that no lights were shown! We anchored off Salinas next morning (Feb. 18th) and had to remain at short notice owing to disturbances in parts of Peru. Maybe that was the cause of disruption to our programme and the subsequential dashing hither and thither, to spread ourselves in case we should be needed to protect our nationals. No leave was given at Salinas because of the short notice, and when we sailed at 5.30 a.m. on Feb. 21st we remained at Action Stations for twenty-four hours, changing watches at the regular and proper times but going directly from station to station — Engine-room to Fire & Repair Party to Magazine Flooding position and back to the Engine-room — having our meals at our stations. We crossed the Equator and arrived at Balboa in the U.S.-controlled Canal Zone on the 23rd. where the local "Y" — (Y.M.C.A. — which is much bigger out of England) — arranged a sight-seeing tour at 60-cents per person for the afternoon of the 25th Fiz and I and about 50 others from the ship were picked up by bus and with an American soldier as our guide were taken over the hills to the ruins of Old Panama City which had been sacked and burned by the British pirate, Captain Morgan, in 1671. He was after the cathedral's solid gold altar but, when the people heard of his approach they dismantled it and covered it with mud. Morgan was mad and had the city razed. Years later another church was built for the altar in a new city and some distance from the old and we went there to see it — 25-feet tall and magnificently carved, but a lot of the original gold had had to be sold to finance the building of the new city so that the altar is mostly gilded wood, but still very beautiful.

When Bill left us there was a switch in daywork jobs and I was moved to be responsible for machining and the main workshop as I was in *Dragon*, thus keeping me off the watchbill during some periods at sea and this was the case as the ship passed through the Panama Canal on Monday, February 27th when I spent a lot of the day relieving the watchkeepers in both engine-rooms that they might go on deck to see something of the scenery and our progress through the locks and lakes because it was possible, if not highly probable, they would not come this way again and I had already passed through the canal twice before. We oiled at Colon and then ran into rough seas as both ships went into War Routine for 72-hours with Dusk- and Dawn-Action Stations and being called to Instant Readiness at any time of day or night, all culminating in a mock attack on the coast of Jamaica before entering Kingston harbour at dawn on March 4th.

Leave was severely restricted owing to the amount of maintenance work to be done before we could sail for Bermuda on the 7th and arrive on the 11th — back to the Base we had left eight months ago. The North American division ships were returning from their Spring Cruise to the islands and as soon as all were present and correct the whole squadron went to sea for five days of exercises — stops and starts, firing guns and torpedoes, General Drills and Action Stations.

The C. in C. — Vice-Admiral Sir Sidney Meyrick — transferred his flag to *Berwick* and *York* was given a rousing send-off as she left for home at the end of March and the end of her commission. *Ajax* moved into the Floating Dock for a week.

The Squadron was now made up of *Berwick*, *Exeter*, *Orion*, and *Ajax*, and there were all the usual sporting activities except for Water Polo — the water being deemed too cold for swimming, and the cold wind and the rain continued through April and into May.

Our position at the head of the Football League was usurped by *Exeter* which also won the Governor's Cup, whacking *Orion* 7 − 0, and *Berwick* won the Road Race. Friendly rivalry in all sports continued between all ships through all commissions just as they did on all Stations; the Royal Marine Bands gave their excellent concerts at Club and Canteen and the massed bands performed the ceremony of Beating the Retreat on Moresby Plain with an appreciative audience of ships' companies, Dockyard staff and their families, and guests from Hamilton. All these events were great morale boosters to help commissions along. There were few occasions at this time when it was possible to walk much further than Club or Canteen because of the atrocious weather, and the threat of war must have been getting stronger as the first two weeks of May can only be described as 'frantic'! All ships left the harbour and as soon as they were well clear went their separate ways. We — *Ajax* — steamed round the islands to anchor in one of the many bays at 7.30 p.m., then at after midnight all hands were called to Action Stations and the ship got under way. We remained closed-up until long after dawn with apparently nothing happened and no explanations, then anchored for a few hours during that day before moving off once again. Things livened up then and we must have met some — if not all — of the others because guns started firing and we fought a Night Action. We were not told whether we were supposed to have been damaged but two days later *Ajax* alone went into the port of St. George's at the north-west corner of the Bermudas — the point where the original settlers had landed — for 48-hours. I managed to get ashore for a walk in the quaint old town but there wasn't time to do or see a lot except visit the Old Fort and Somers Gardens (Sir George Somers led the first colonizers.).

As soon as we left port we reverted to the same pattern of high-speed steaming and anchoring, now in company with the Squadron and the Commodore spending a day and a night on board each ship in its turn to watch the men at work and at Day- and Night-Action. (Sir Sidney Meyrick was ill on shore).

Our mysterious excursions and frantic fortnight ended when all ships entered the harbour to act as hosts to the crew of the cruiser — the USS *Sacramento* — with *Ajax*'s Concert Party playing a prominent role.

On May 31st we (*Ajax*) sailed from Bermuda for our second circumnavigation of South America and in normal times we would have gone the reverse way round, but times were not normal and we kept to the eastern shores. Our first call was at Turks Island where we arrived early on June 3rd and found the water was too deep for us to anchor while the Captain went ashore to consult with the Governor. No-one else was allowed ashore; we steamed slowly to and fro all day with the ship becoming hotter and hotter, and it did not help matters much when he did return and we proceeded at full speed to Kingston, Jamaica, arriving there at midnight. I had just gone below to take over the Middle watch when the ship anchored outside the harbour and as it was not worth shutting-down main engines we split the watch and I left my senior E.R.A. in charge until 2 a.m. when I would relieve him and I went to the upper deck, to the cool refreshing air and brilliant moonlight, and witnessed the phenomenon of a wonderfully clear 'night rainbow'. At dawn we moved to anchor inside the harbour and it was still very hot.

We left Kingston on the 14th and had a fairly rough passage to Aruba where we arrived on the 16th Aruba? I'd never heard of the place until the name appeared on our itinerary but now realised it to be one of the most important islands in the world. We secured at a jetty with oil refineries all round us and many enormous tankers discharging crude oil from Venezuela while equally as large boats were loading with the refined products and leaving for all parts of the world. It was indeed very busy.

Several members of our Mess joined a party of a hundred invited by Esso and Lago, the two biggest oil companies, to attend a Baseball game and the American Legion's barbeque afterwards. Company lorries collected us for ten-minute ride to the ground and we had hardly settled to watch the game when a typical tropical shower struck — with no shelter to hand. Some Americans sitting in their cars called for us to "Come on over and jump in", so I, with a Stoker P.O. and a Seaman got into a car with a man, his wife and her woman friend. Our host was a jolly sort while the women-folk were snooty and nasty individuals who obviously resented our presence. The rain lasted only a few minutes — enough to have soaked us but for the chap's kindness — but when we made a move to thank him and leave he said, "No! Stay here and see the game in comfort," much to the disgust of his wife and her friend who both began making snide and sarcastic remarks, which we ignored as we listened to our friend trying to explain the rudiments of the game. Then he trotted to the Pavilion and returned with several bottles of beer and four glasses and we were even more comfortable as his wife continued nagging for him to "Leave this lot and let's drive over to the Marine Club. The English officers are playing tennis there." He eventually lost patience and shouted at the two women, "Shut up, damn you. And damn the officers. I've no time for them and I am quite happy in these boys' company!" They almost cried with rage as the game went on for another 16-innings (whatever that meant! for none of us knew the final scores) but they drove with us to the Barbeque Field where a whole cow and two pigs were being spit-roasted and were ready when we arrived at 6.30 p.m.

Luscious beef and pork was sliced; tables were laden with bread rolls and pickles and there was no limit on what we could eat — or drink, from the six medium-sized barrels of beer supplied for liquid refreshment. When the eating finished the serious drinking began, and when two more barrels were brought out at 7.30 I could see a rowdy evening developing and did not relish the thought. I noticed one of our shipwrights standing apart from the crowd, obviously sharing my forebodings, so I suggested we leave and walk back to the Esso Club which I thought I could find in the dark.

Of course we lost our bearings among the houses in the Concession and asked directions from a man sitting on the lighted verandah of his bungalow who immediately got his car and took us to the Club and then suggested that instead of waiting there we should return to have coffee with him and his wife. It was an idea which was very acceptable as we would rather be sitting with two strangers in private than with a crowd of them in their own Club. So — fresh coffee was made and the four of us sat and talked until 11 p.m. when they ran us back to the ship. They were Belgians; had been married three years but she had only arrived in Aruba in February while he had been serving there for eight years. Neither were enraptured with life as they felt penned up in the Concession with little to occupy their spare time. On the credit side they appreciated the two or three clubs, cinema, their well-furnished, rent-free bungalow and the beautiful bathing-beach close by. They said the pay was good at $400 per month (about £20 per week in our money) and that food and other necessities could be purchased at the Company Store, but their sole aim was to save for their retirement. A charming couple nevertheless.

Next morning, June 19th, we steamed 15-miles along the coast to Orangestad to take in fuel, and where we were to remain for 24-hours. I would see what Orangestad was like. I would take a walk that evening! What a walk! First I had more than half-a-mile of pier to traverse before reaching a vast stretch of sandy wilderness and a long road threading its way between hundreds of oil storage tanks eventually coming to the gates of the English Concession. Then followed another trek of nearly two miles along an ill-lit sandy trail to arrive at the lighted street called Orangestad! The place was dead. There were only three people beside myself moving and I asked the only white one of those three, "Why?" His reply was, "Ja! Effrybody iss a-sleepin!" so I wended my long, dark and weary way back to the ship and in the morning we steamed for 6-hours to another Dutch island — Curacao — and went alongside at Willemstad. A clean town of narrow streets, brightly-coloured houses and stores but once off the main streets the buildings seemed to degenerate into a series of tiny huts each housing a whole family.

Ajax left Curacao — we were on our own — on June 27th and during the ensuing 48-hours on passage to Martinique the ship's company were kept at Action Stations. We lay at anchor until July 3rd and during that period Fiz and I picked a dry moment (and it was only a moment!) to get ashore for a walk. We landed by the 4.30 p.m. boat and had walked but a few yards when the skies opened to allow a deluge to descend on us. We dived for the only shelter — the Scent Shop — and bought a bottle of perfume each to send home and then sat drinking coffee with the French owner until the 8.30 boat came in.

From Martinique it was an overnight trip to Grenada for just 24-hours at anchor before another 8-hours steaming to Port of Spain, Trinidad, and a berth at the jetty — with the convenience of being able to walk ashore. The main drawback was the rain, which could come so suddenly and fall so heavily. Fortunately the local Police Sergeants' Mess gave an 'Open Invitation' to us to make use of their facilities and thus provided a convenient umbrella for which we thanked them by beating them at billiards on their own tables. They retaliated by issuing a Chess challenge which they easily won. Quits!

On July 16th we anchored off Georgetown, Br. Guiana, not crossing the Bar as in my *Dragon* days but anchored about 11-miles off-shore and if anyone was keen enough to want to go ashore they had the prospect of a two-hour trip each way, and for the whole time of the five days we were anchored the ship was rolling 15 to 20 degrees each way, making life most uncomfortable. In addition it was hot and it rained, so it was a great relief to all when the anchor came up and we were on the move once more and had some air circulating, but as soon as the ship was aired she had to be battened down again for more long periods of Action — until we anchored overnight (July 24/25th) off the Amazon Delta. Practically the whole of the 25th was spent progressing up the Para River to the port of Belem, 80-miles from the sea. Quite a big town with good shops, a fine residential area and beautiful parks all of which Fiz and I walked through on the Saturday afternoon before visiting the main objective on our itinerary — the Botanical Gardens and Zoo. There was a vast assortment of tropical flora and fauna, our attention focused on the numbers of snakes — giant anacondas and Bushmasters — and the huge tank of electric eels. Copper rods were available for visitors to use to touch the water and feel the 'shock'. Several rods lay in the bottom of the tank and we could understand why, for when we 'tested for current' Fiz's rod touched the surface and an eel about five feet long with a girth of twelve inches or more poked its snout above water and barked loudly, just like a dog, at us and another rod went to the bottom.

We left Belem and the Para on August 1st and crossed the Equator on the 2nd, and the ceremony was very low-key this year — just a little 'something' to placate King Neptune for our intrusion into his territory — and then we assumed full War Routine with Dawn and Dusk Action whereby we were at full state of readiness half-an-hour before dawn and sunset, and remaining closed-up until half-an-hour after sunrise, and until really dark at night, dropping to 2nd or 3rd degrees between those times depending on the prevailing circumstances.

We passed the Fernando Noronho Islands at dawn on the 5th and arrived at Salvador, Brazil, on the 7th.

During our stay the British Club invited us to a Concert, laying on special trams to convey us to their Hall. There were some excellent turns interspersed with items by our own Concert Party and refreshments were served before we left.

We sailed on August 14th and after the usual exercises in our War Routine arrived at Rio de Janeiro on the 17th. This was a very big city of tall buildings, wide streets and avenues, parks and squares and marvellous shopping facilities which I intended to take advantage of when I walked ashore at 1.30 on Saturday, 19th. Instead — I went by tram-car and then two successive cable-cars to the top of Sugar-Loaf Mountain, a thrilling experience which afforded a wonderful view over the city and the vast harbour — an experience later surpassed when I went to the even higher vantage point, the Corcavado, on the 24th. On that afternoon I went by tram-car to Cosme Velha and by 'cog-wheel' train to a point near the summit of Corcavado which is 2,300-feet high, and walked the final hundred-yards to the base of the 100-feet tall figure of Christ — the Monumento y Christo Redemptor. The day was beautifully clear and sunny to give a vast panoramic and uninterrupted view over the sprawling city and its suburbs, the harbour and the miles of beaches and the surrounding mountains. Unforgettable! On the return ride I left the train at Silvestre and boarded the tram-car for the Scenic Route back to the city. I was wearing white uniform and after our long sojourn in the tropics I was feeling rather cold in the hills and so was glad to get back to the relative warmth of city streets as I made my way to the waterfront where the ship lay — but did not go directly aboard. I entered the a'Noite building — the tallest in Rio — which had everything; restaurant and shops at ground-floor level; offices of one of the main daily and evening newspapers, its printing-presses and editorial suites of offices, and a Radio Station. I introduced myself at the Manager's office and asked if it were possible for me to go to the roof to see the "City by Night" and was duly escorted to the top. It was a most fantastic sight looking down on glittering, sparkling lights of every colour of the spectrum, all appearing to be strung together like jewelled necklaces lying on dark blue velvet cushions in Asprey's.

CHAPTER 13

War

The crisis in Europe was becoming worse and it seemed war was not only inevitable but imminent when on August 26th the ship came under "Sailing Orders", so I walked ashore at 5 p.m. to buy the curios I had intended to get before the day we were due to leave (August 31st) and when I returned at 7 p.m. I learned that the 'last mail will close at 9 o'clock and all letters will be censored from now on', and that I had the First Watch in the Forward Engine-room. At 9.45 p.m. we slid out of the harbour with the ship darkened and steamed at 18-knots away from the coast for about six hours to get well clear of the shipping routes and during daylight hours we drifted along at slow speed with look-outs keeping an eye on all directions; if a ship was sighted on the horizon we sped away so that our position — or even our existence — could not be reported. Watch also had to be kept for any aircraft either flying the Atlantic or just out from coast. In the middle of the night of the 28th speed was increased and at noon we entered Rio de Janeiro to oil and take in provisions, and when it was dark we were off again at 20-knots with everyone to remain at 1st Degree of Readiness. At 6 a.m. on August 31st we 'spoke' to a British merchant ship bound for B.A. and we were beginning to assume this crisis would evaporate as that of last year had done, and we would be able to relax — but . . .

Sunday, September 3rd. The Morning Watch was finishing and I was handing over the reins of the Forward Engine-room to my relief, C.E.R.A. Frank Pearce, at 8 o'clock when a voice came on the Tannoy, "D'y'hear there!" and the Captain announced: "We are now at war with Germany. I am confident that you will all do your duty." So. It had come! The War. What would it mean? The Admiralty message had ended with, "Commence Hostilities" but there was no-one for us to start on, so we went looking and two hours later we fired our first shot of the war — a blank — to warn an oil-tanker to stop. She was the *San Nerandha* — British, and therefore allowed to proceed on her 'lawful occasions'.

Meanwhile *our* first casualty of the war was the ship's piano. It had been located in the port shelter-deck and I had enjoyed many hours playing it but after our meeting with the tanker our next challenge might be an enemy raider whose shells could send piano-wires flying and cutting anybody in the way, so it was moved quite ceremoniously along to the waist then quite un-ceremoniously dumped over the side for Davy Jones to strum. It was just an hour later — at 11 a.m. — that another vessel was sighted and failed to stop when signalled and when a blank was fired, but soon hove-to when a live round went over her bows. She was a trim and very new-looking craft of some 4,000-tons, wearing no national flag and the only sign of a name were the two letters — ND — on her port bow.

Our Boarding Parties were piped and ready to be lowered when the Captain decided only seamen and marines were needed and my party of E.R.A's and stokers were stood down. He would not take a 'Prize' because he could not spare any of our complement to steam her to the nearest British port — Port Stanley — more than a thousand miles away.

It was established that she was the motor-ship *Olinda* of Hamburg with a cargo of copper and nitrates bound for the port and her captain "did not know that war had been declared" — although his crew had been busy painting-out her name when we arrived on the scene — hence the 'ND'. Her crew and passengers were ordered to abandon their ship — which they certainly took a long time in doing (It was an hour before her boats were lowered and escorted over to *Ajax*) but as soon as they — and every bit of their belongings — and our own boat were safely inboard, their life-boats were set adrift, we stood-off and put a few 4″ shells into *Olinda*'s hull at the water-line and down she went. A sad sight! Any ship sinking is a sad sight — even that old hulk *Ravenswood* — but this was almost new! Such a waste.

We then steamed at 30-knots to overtake the *San Nerandha*, bound for Monte Video, and transferred our prisoners to her so that the German nationals could be interned in Uruguay. Next morning we heard of the sinking of the *Athenia* by a U-boat in the North Atlantic without warning and costing the lives of many children evacuees. What a difference in procedure! and that affected our procedure because — that afternoon we chased another German, the *Carl Fritzen* of Emden, 6,000-tons, an older vessel and in ballast. A blank was fired and she was given five minutes for her crew to leave their ship. They, too, wanted to take their time but a live round fired over her bows soon had their boats pulling hard towards us, then a few 4″ shells sent *Carl* to join *Olinda* on the bottom. Quite a heavy sea was running and created some difficulty in getting the prisoners from their boats and one old chap fell between his boat and the ship's side and everyone thought he was a 'goner' — that he would be crushed — but our seamen with skilful and judicious use of boathooks staved off the boat and fished him out to recover in our Sick Bay. Although they had been given little time to salvage their belongings (because *we* could not afford to wait around like a sitting duck) they did manage to bring their two cats and a collie-cross dog with them, but as the animals could not be accommodated they were injected and 'put down' by our doctor, and the prisoners were put under armed guard in the Recreation Space on the fo'c'sle as we chased yet another ship. It was becoming a habit; two 'bags' on successive days, the first two days of the conflict promptly earned the Captain (C. H. L. Woodhouse) the nickname "One-a-day Wimpy". (I know no reason for the 'Wimpy'). The object of our present dash proved to be a Finnish collier and further chases in the next few days turned out to be false alarms — although we did learn later that one vessel was a valuable prize but had been sailing under false colours, using the Greek flag.

On September 9th we met *Exeter* again on her arrival back on the Station. She had returned home in August after nearly three years away and was to pay off but had only been in Devonport five days when her crew were re-called. She took over our patrol area while we steamed southwards — transferring the nine Dutch members of the German ship's crew to a British ship going north — and landing the Germans at Port Stanley for internment, on the 12th. After oiling we anchored in the harbour but war and weather made it necessary to keep steam on main engines, guns manned and look-outs posted. We had arrived during a snowstorm, the whole countryside white, and the tremendous drop in temperature affected us all. Those whose work kept them on the upper deck endeavoured to keep warm by wearing jerseys, overcoats, stockings, sea-boots, woollen helmets, ear-muffs, duffel-coats with hoods, gloves and scarves.

Recreational leave was given on the 13th — two hours ashore in the forenoon for one watch, two hours in the afternoon for the second and two hours in the Dogs for the third watch, and the deck-hands returned aboard laden with all kinds of knitted-wear, sheep-skin-lined boots and coats for their outer warmth, and tins of cocoa for the inner man — for we had run out of pussers 'ki' on the ship.

We left harbour again the next day at 5.30 p.m. to encounter the worst weather yet experienced during the commission. Mountainous waves crashed hundreds of tons of water onto us with the noise of a giant power-hammer and buckled the supporting stanchions below the upper deck — 4″ diameter steel bending like a dog's hind legs and dropping the level by inches. It was bitterly cold with the gale coming directly from the South Pole and we were being battered and jolted so much that we wondered if she would stand the strain. And goodness knows where we were going — but three days later we began calling at some of those 'outposts of Empire' visited last year — Fox Bay and Hill Cove, Port Stephen and Darwin — at each place landing stores which we thought could have been wireless transmitters and receivers.

On Sept. 18th we learned that the aircraft-carrier *Courageous* had been sunk. The ship we used to admire when she was a battle-cruiser lying opposite *Fisgard*. It was unbelievable! Was the war being taken seriously at home?

We steamed northward towards the River Plate area, where, on the 25th we rendezvoused with the *R.F.A. Olwen* for oil and stores and while we were secured on one side of the supply ship the destroyer *Havock* tied up on the other side, so there was contact between crews. She — like *Exeter* — had also just arrived home from a commission (Mediterranean) when war broke out and she had now just come from a 48-hour 'break' in Rio. *Ajax* was then ordered to patrol the Rio area and proceeded at 20-knots through more heavy weather, questioning a few 'friendly' ships and escorting some of them until they were well clear of the coast. October 1st — we heard that the British ship *Clements* had been sunk off Pernambuco by the pocket-battleship *Admiral Scheer*, so we were ordered south to rejoin *Exeter* who was now in company with *Havock* and *Hotspur*, and the four of us spent the next week escorting British and neutral vessels sailing out of B.A. and Rio on the first part of their voyages. At dawn on the 9th *Ajax* was dispatched after a ship spotted on the horizon — another 'friend' — and on the 10th we slipped into Rio harbour for oil and stores — and received our first mail for 8-weeks. Leave was given in two watches, the first from 1 p.m. till 7.30 p.m. and the second from 8 p.m. until 6 o'clock in the morning. My 'turn' was the latter, but my day had been extraordinary. I had come up fom the Middle Watch after 4 a.m. At 9 a.m. the Chief of the Forenoon Watch was injured in an accident and carried to the Sick Bay and I had to take over. Then the ship entered the harbour at 10.30 and by the time we had shut down one engine-room and left the other 'ticking over' in case of emergency it was 12.30 when I got to the Mess for my dinner. So we had one Chief in the Sick Bay and the other one went ashore at 1 p.m. and then the Harbour Master wanted *Ajax* to move closer inshore and the Watch had to go below once more. By the time we anchored again it was 3.30 and a well-earned cup of tea was ready in the Mess together with a message from the Senior: "Would I go below to supervise a change-over of boilers and engine-rooms to maintain a balance in the number of steaming-hours on each set". That was completed by 7 p.m. and I had been below almost without a break since after midnight, so now for a quiet five minutes! Optimistic thought, for at 7.30 all the drunks came back and the other watch went off for their 'fill up' and there was no 'quiet'. Only one man failed to return at 6 a.m. as we steamed out to continue our patrol. There were two German ships in the harbour and if either had decided to leave while we were there, we, under International Law, would have to remain for another 24-hours.

We moved 200-miles south to pick up the liners *Almanzora* and *Highland Brigade* off Santos and escort them to Rio — where we learned that one of the Germans had virtually followed us out of the harbour — cheeky b . . .! We searched in all directions for four days but it was pretty hopeless because she had had time to travel up to 400-miles any which-way and even our Sea-Fox, airborne for most daylight hours of search failed — Well, the South Atlantic is *vast*!

We continued escorting or guarding ships leaving or travelling between South American ports; met *Olwen* on October 27th for more oil fuel, then *Exeter* appeared and the Commodore (H. H. Harwood) transferred his flag to *Ajax* while his ship proceeded north to join *Cumberland* in a search for a raider off Pernambuco. Later that night we met *Achilles* — sister ship to *Ajax* — of the New Zealand Division and here to help guard Trade Routes of the South Atlantic, and we carried on patrolling in our separate areas, every time a ship was sighted by day or picked up on the screen at night the alarm rattlers sounded and everybody was at "Full alert" as a full-speed chase ensued and continued until the identity of the quarry was established.

A short respite came on November 6th when we slipped into Buenos Aires for a 48-hours break. Frank Pearce, whose watch I had kept while he was sick in Rio, came down to the engine-room to relieve me just after we arrived at 1.30 because Ian Gordon had sent a message asking if I could meet him and his wife at 3 p.m. "and bring half-a-dozen Messmates for an outing!" Leave was granted at 4 p.m. but I got permission for our party to land at 2.30 when our hosts had a small coach waiting to take us to Retiro where we entrained with a group of English people for a trip to the Country Club at Saens Pena a few miles out of the city for a barbeque. After a plenitude of appetising food and some amusing entertainment the coach was ready to take us on a tour of the City by Night and then deposit us at St. George's Hall where the British Argentina Society had arranged a Dance for the ship's company, a large number being already present and enjoying themselves. Then we were at sea again with the continuous round of watches, of Dawn and Dusk Action, and frustrating chases; of meeting and oiling from the tanker *Olynthus* on the 10th and 23rd; of rough weather, and on the night of the 25th increasing to 28-knots driving through rain and fog to anchor at Port Stanley on the 27th of November.

Within an hour Action Stations sounded and there was a mad rush to get the ship to sea again as all the guns were fully manned, but just as the anchor was being weighed the "All clear" came. A report had come from coastal look-outs on the north of the island — "A cruiser has been sighted steaming throught the mist towards Stanley!" It was *us*!

The weather was now near perfect and recreational leave was given, but our department were much too busy with maintenance to be able to take advantage, and we always had the kelp to contend with — clearing it from valves and condenser-tubes.

Exeter came in on the 29th and it was like old (peace) times for us both to be in harbour together again. Three days of this summer sun tempted Fiz and me ashore for a walk on the 30th but we had only done a couple of miles when we became engulfed in a thick mist which turned to heavy rain when *we* turned back and plodded our way to the town to be told "No boat for another two hours!" We went and stood in the pavilion at the Sports Ground — wet through and watching a Rugby match being played in a sea of mud — Local Volunteers versus *Ajax*. We did not know who was worse off but we certainly said, "No more shore!"

The Local Defence boat — the drifter *Port Richard* — came alongside to have a 3-pounder gun fitted on her bows by an Ordnance Artificer but it was necessary for the winch to be re-sited — a task given to me and one E.R.A. working out in the typical Falklands wind and snow and completed by 7 p.m. so that she (and we) could go to sea to test the alertness of her crew in a night-encounter exercise. With satisfaction achieved she returned to harbour and we proceeded north at 22-knots to our patrol area, increasing to 28-knots on December 5th to overtake a 9,600-tons German liner — the *Ussukuma* — at 8.30 p.m. Her crew forestalled us and were already abandoning their badly listing ship which they had scuttled and was too far gone for any attempt at salvage, so we picked up the 107-people (men and women) from the four boats which we cast adrift and then departed the scene with the sinking liner still above water. There was no trace of her when we returned to the area the next morning and later in the day we met *Cumberland* on her way to the Falklands and transferred our prisoners to her and then carried on our patrol.

When we met our oil-tanker on Dec. 7th she had some mail for us and one of the newspapers dated Oct. 21st 1939, carried a story by a Mr Barnard of Southampton claiming he was the only Britisher in the *Olinda's* crew — (our first-day-of-the-war victim). He told of how the Nazis locked him in his cabin when they left the ship; of how he had hammered on the door and shouted and when he realised she was going down he tore a brass fitting from the bulkhead and used it to smash the door panelling to get out and "Even then I did not know how long she would remain afloat so I dived into the water as the ship sank beneath me, and about two hours later the British cruiser returned and picked me up." What a load of rubbish! The ship had been boarded and searched. Her manifest and other documents were collected by our Boarding Party so that passengers and crew were accounted for and almost before they had even arrived on our deck *Olinda* was gone, and we were going — to continue our business. Propaganda? or Daily Mirror sensationalism!

On Sunday, Dec. 10th we met *Achilles* somewhere off Uruguay and next day *Exeter* joined us, the three ships then stayed together on patrol with the Commodore still wearing his flag aboard us.

(On the 2nd of the month and just after we had parted from the *Port Richard* there was news that the British ship *Doric Star* had been sunk off the South African coast by 'a pocket-battleship' and the Commodore told

River plate action 'Ajax' Starboard side. Capt's Cabin. December, 1939.

H.M.S. 'Ajax' December 14th 1939.
Heat Blackened Guns of 'A' Turret, but 'Still Ready!'.

our ship's company that he now expected the enemy ship to make her way towards the Rio or River Plate area for richer pickings, and if the latter area we could expect to meet her about Wednesday, the 13th. How prophetic!)

At Dawn Action on the 13th as on many other mornings there was no sign of any other ship so at 0600 we reverted to our 2nd degree of readiness status and those of us not actually on watch returned to our hammocks for another hour's rest, but twenty minutes later the Klaxons sounded for "Urgent Action!" We jumped from our hammocks to hastily pull trousers over pyjamas, grab overalls, gas-mask, torch, anti-flash gear and inflatable lifebelt and dash to our stations again. As we ran along the deck my neighbour, Spud Slater, said, "It's the *Scheer*! She's ten yards astern of us" I thought perhaps the morning was foggy and that the enemy had suddenly loomed out and was in danger of ramming us! But Spud had apparently returned to sleep very quickly and was dreaming when the Klaxons blared, the morning actually being clear and sunny. Our three ships had been fanned out to cover as much ocean as possible with *Ajax* at the centre, *Exeter* far out to starboard and *Achilles* to port, and it was *Exeter* who had sighted the masthead of the German apparently at exactly the same time as the enemy spotted her for she opened up with her 11″ guns at a range of 12½-miles — her third salvo hitting *Exeter* and causing a lot of damage. *Exeter* continued to close the range so that her own 8″ guns could be more effective. We had all worked up to full speed and *Ajax* began firing at half-past six, my Station — until (normally) eight o'clock — was "B" Magazine Flooding and the guns had only been firing for ten minutes when the hoist from that Shell-room was put out of action and the ammunition for "B" turret had to be carried up by hand — more than a hundredweight each shell — and trundled throught the mess-deck. "A" turret was working O.K. and the rate of fire was so fast that it sounded more like a Machine-gun. A Wireless rating passing through my station at 7.15 told me, "*Exeter* is out of the action and our main-mast has been shot away, carrying the aerial with it. One seaman has been killed and several have been wounded." In order to keep myself occupied I helped in the man-handling of the shells along the deck. Then a seaman told me that an 11″ shell has hit "X" turret killing all six Royal Marines gun's crew and all the time we were doing 30-knots, the ship throbbing and vibrating as we ran in towards the enemy, closing the range to 3,000-yards, plastering her with 6″ shells in an attempt to wean her fire from *Exeter*.

We must have been successful because the German turned and ran and during this part of the action our speed was 36½-knots, our fastest ever! In order not to get too close at this point we veered away and fired four torpedoes but unfortunately the firing order was misheard and all went simultaneously instead of singly or even two-and-two, and the fleeing battleship was able to avoid them.

Achilles was firing from another angle and could not use her 'fish' for fear of hitting us. She, too, had had many killed and injured, a lot by shrapnel from the enemy shell-bursts.

Firing ceased at 0900 with the enemy running at 22½-knots and we two tailing her at the same speed until about 0930 when she made to turn as though to meet us but it was so that she could loose six torpedoes in our direction. One of our Sea-Foxes had been catapulted at the start of the action for the pilot to report 'fall of shot' and was able to warn us and *Achilles* of the impending danger. 'Avoiding action' was taken and advantage also of her broadside presentation to us as both ships hit her with salvo after salvo of 6" shells.The hits could be clearly seen but could not penetrate her thick armour-plating as she resumed course for Uruguayan territorial waters.

During a slight lull in the action during late forenoon we were able to facilitate a change-over of watches — a switch which should have taken place at 0800 — and my watch took over in the engine-room where we then remained until 8 p.m. The German eventually reached shelter at 7.30 p.m. and with a final bit of impertinence, from her refuge fired a couple of 11" salvos at us. A signalman told us that one salvo had fallen "about 20-yards short", the other fell some 200-yards astern, both causing terrific water-spouts. Our cooks kept us amply supplied with corned-beef sandwiches, hard-tack biscuits, hot soup, tea and cocoa throughout the long day, but it was not over yet. For the next three days we and *Achilles* kept up our patrolling just — only just — outside the territorial zone. (On the afternoon of Friday, 15th of December, we both steamed into the estuary of the River Plate and within five miles of Monte Video to see where the enemy ship was lying, and to let *her* see that we were waiting.)

Meanwhile we received news that *Exeter* had managed to reach Port Stanley under her own power, and during this waiting period — in the daylight hours when we were at 2nd degree of readiness — opportunity was taken to carry out some repairs.

The 11" shell which wrecked "X" turret had jammed both "X" and "Y" when it hit, smashing the training gear so that neither turret could be moved. Another shell had exploded in the Captain's Day Cabin just for'ard of the turrets; the mainmast had been carried away and the second Sea-Fox, parked ahead of the catapult, was shot to pieces. Pipe-lines (fire-mains, fresh water, high-pressure air, steam and hydraulic) were fractured and torn apart as was the electrical wiring for lighting, power, gunnery circuits and telephones. Then there was the debris and the mess of all the oil and water — all had to be cleaned up. It seemed a colossal task. Our dead were committed to the deep individually with brief "Burial at Sea" services presided over by the Chaplain and attended by as many officers and crew as could be spared as the clearing-up went on. E.R.A's were using blow-torches to cut the jagged metal and to weld patches on bulkheads and decks; they were re-siting pipe-lines and re-making joints. Ordnance artificers dismantled the shattered turning mechanisms of the two turrets so that they could be man-handled into their fore-and-aft positions, the broken equipment was passed to the enginesmith who forged replacement parts and the whole lot then brought down to the machine shop where I and my assistant (Ernie Carr) machined and fashioned the actuating contours of the apparatus — which prevent the guns being fired beyond a certain angle — ready for the O.A's to replace. The Electrical artificers saw to the renewal of the wiring. The whole crew worked hard and long hours to get the ship back to as near normality as possible because we did not know when the *Admiral Graf Spee* — we now knew the name of our adversary — was likely to venture out. The Captain told us re-inforcements in the form of the battlecruiser *Renown* and the aircraft-carrier *Ark Royal* had been detached from the Home Fleet to assist us but they had a long way to come. (We said, "Hurry up!")

The Admiralty congratulated the Commodore and asked for a list of names of men who had distinguished themselves in the action. His reply had been, "Every man in all ships carried out his task with courage and efficiency." Their Lordships were not satisfied and requested that a comprehensive list of names be forwarded, so there were hurried conferences and consultations in ships' offices and a list was sent. While this was going on Commodore Harwood was promoted to be a Rear-Admiral from December 16th and awarded the K.C.B., and the Captains of the three ships were made Companions of the Bath (C.B.). At a later date there were a number of D.S.C's (for officers), and D.S.M's (for ratings).

When I came up from the Morning Watch on Sunday 17th there was a welcoming sight. *Cumberland* was with us! The help we needed. Radio broadcasts from shore, put out specially to be digested by the Germans, spoke of "massive re-inforcements" arriving in the estuary almost every night and we hoped they were being believed. Now — we had *Cumberland*. Anyway, we were at 2nd degree all day as usual and at dusk the Sea-Fox was catapulted for reconnaissance and almost at the same instant (8 p.m.) the shore radio spoke of "activity aboard the German battleship", then came our pilot's confirmation, "*Graf Spee* is under weigh!" and our alarms sounded for 'instant readiness'. It was still daylight so — we wondered as we waited. Would we steam away and make it a Night Action? or would we fight it out there-and-then? (I learned later that we had formed up in Battle Formation steaming directly at the enemy.) Below decks we waited — every one tense — expecting a salvo of 11″ shells to come at any second

133

and to hear our own guns start blazing away as we felt the vibration building with our speed. Then — it was about 8.45 p.m. — the word passed round, "She's blown herself up!" A spontaneous cheer ran through the ship — Hooray! What a marvellous relief after five stressful days. Those of us who were not actually on watch were allowed to leave our stations and go to the upper deck where, eight miles ahead a dense cloud of smoke rose high in the sky. As we stood there *Achilles* overtook and passed us and we cheered each other. Then *Cumberland* came by and cheered both of us, and it was a grand feeling as crowds of men just stood around, reluctant to go below again, simply gazing at the fading column of smoke now silhouetted by the setting sun. As it got darker the leaping flames became more apparent and we steamed in to within two miles — and then it was time for me to go below for the Middle Watch.

When I came up at 4 a.m. I climbed into my hammock for the first time since the previous Tuesday midnight, and it would be for less than two hours because Dawn Action would sound before 6 a.m.

I spent the whole of that Monday forenoon with many others on the upper deck as we kept in sight of the still-burning battleship and was amazed at her size. The thought came to me then, supposing history had been repeating itself! For, in September, 1914, at the beginning of the First World War my father had been 33-years old and here, at the start of this war I was of the same age. In 1914 my father was a Petty Officer Naval Policeman in the cruiser *Cressy* which, with her two consorts *Hogue* and *Aboukir* had been torpedoed by a German U-boat on September 22nd and was one of many hundreds who lost their lives. Now — I was alive but the *Graf Spee* was a smouldering giant aground in 24-feet of water off the port of Buenos Aires. It did really seem miraculous that we had survived confrontation with such a monster.

Tentative arrangements were made for *Ajax* and *Achilles* to have a 48-hour rest period in Monte Video but there were doubts as to the sort of reception we might get. Friendly or hostile? The issue was resolved by both ships proceeding at 18-knots to Port Stanley where we arrived at 5 p.m. on the 21st.

A battered *Exeter* was anchored in the harbour with a heavy list and her bows low in the water, more than sixty of her crew had been killed and many more wounded. Now, too, we could see the extent of *Achilles'* damage and learn something of her casualty list. Her director-tower had been hit, killing twelve men and bursting-shell fragments had wounded several more and peppered her bridge and funnel.

We sent some E.R.A's and shipwrights to help *Exeter* with her repairs while the rest of us got on with getting ship-shape before we and *Achilles* went on patrol again, a patrol from which we were relieved by *Cumberland* and *Dorsetshire* on Dec. 24th and were back in harbour on Christmas Day

— our second on the Station. The weather was bright and cold and all Messes were decorated with bunting, and some tinsel and baubles saved from last year — all of which had to be taken down before 'lights out' — but there were no fun and games or singing as in previous years and ships. (Harking back to December 18th — On that 'day after Battle' the Cable and Wireless Company arranged for a "free, reply-paid telegram" to be sent to the next-of-kin of all surviving members of the three ships' companies, the 'homeward' message being, "All's well. Best love. Happy Christmas." When we met *Cumberland* on the 24th she had brought many replies and I heard someone ask if all were the same!)

Rumours began floating around that we were to escort *Exeter* to Simonstown dockyard — to England — to Monte Video, and were enhanced on the 28th when a consignment of stores designated for us were diverted to *Achilles*. Next came an Admiralty Directive — "Admiral Harwood will transfer his flag from *Ajax* to *Achilles* on January 3rd 1940." and that convinced everyone that we would soon be on our way home.

At 10.30 p.m. on the 29th we were leaving harbour for the River Plate area patrol because it was thought the German liner *Tacoma* would try to leave with the *Graf Spee* survivors and get them back to Germany when both condenser inlets became choked with masses of kelp and the only remedy was to shut the main valves in the ship's bottom, remove the end doors of both condensers and clear each of the hundreds of tubes individually, then 'sight' every single one before the doors were replaced — a very hot task which we finished at 4 a.m. and then sped north. We saw nothing of *Tacoma* so on Jan. 3rd we entered Monte Video, and what a rousing reception we were accorded as thousands of Uruguayans lining the harbour walls clapped and cheered as the ship went alongside. Red carpet was laid as the Admiral and our Captain walked ashore to be welcomed by local and National dignitaries and our Ambassador, Mr. E. Millington-Drake. Ian Gordon was over from B.A. and sent a message inviting me to dinner at the Hotel Noraro that evening "to hear all about the battle", and I think everyone had a great time ashore that and the following night. We sailed at 0900 on the 5th and when we were outside territorial limits the Admiral transferred his flag and his Staff by launch to *Achilles* — which had spent the two days at Buenos Aires — and at 4 p.m. it was "Goodbye and Good Luck" as we parted company, we steaming northwards and meeting up with my old ship, *Shropshire*, patrolling with *Dorsetshire*, and after a few hours with them we suddenly went off at 25-knots on a two-day fruitless search for the German ship *Rio Grande* thought to be somewhere in the area; the two ships we did intercept after 30-knot chases turned out to be neutral. On Jan. 11th there was another brief contact with the other two cruisers before we went in to Rio de Janeiro for oil and provisions, sailing again on the 12th with course set due east at 19-knots and still at War Routine.

On the 15th we met *Renown* and the a/c carrier *Ark Royal* with destroyers *Hasty* and *Hero* with whom we engaged in a series of exercises warding-off simulated air-attacks and had a passing contact with *Neptune* (another of our sister-ships) before calling at Freetown, Sierra Leone, 19th to 22nd for oil. Vice-Admiral G. H. d'Oyly Lyon, C. in C. South Atlantic, came on board to inspect the ship and crew and the two destroyers escorted us as far as the Bay of Biscay where their task was taken over by three boats from Western Approaches — *Whitshed*, *Acasta* and *Active*. At noon on Jan. 30th their Asdic gear picked up a U-boat and while *we* increased to 30-knots they hunted and sank U55 — accredited to *Whitshed* in co-operation with the sloop *Fowey*.

On January 31st we were safely ensconced in Devonport dockyard to be fitted with de-gaussing gear for our eventual passage up-channel, and on February 5th one Watch proceeded on 14-days leave.

Exeter arrived home on the 15th to a tumultuous welcome in her Home port and from Winston Churchill, First Lord of Admiralty, the Lord Chancellor, Sir John Simon, and the First Sea Lord, Admiral Sir Dudley Pound who came aboard both ships and told us we were to be honoured by the City of London at a lunch in Guildhall on Friday, February 23rd. Two special trains carried the ships' companies to Waterloo station on the 22nd, and overnight accommodation was provided for those who needed it; others could go home on condition they were back and on the station forecourt before 9.30 a.m.

I and seven other chiefs were sent in advance to Horse Guards Parade to be 'markers' for the main bodies of troops who were marching via Westminister Bridge and when they arrived the King (George VI) inspected and then presented the medals and Orders to those nominated. On completion we marched off via Trafalgar Square, Northumberland Avenue, Embankment, Queen Victoria Street, Queen Street and King Street to Guildhall, with thousands of flag-waving and cheering people lining the route. The Lord Mayor, Sir William Cowen, received and welcomed us and in the Banqueting Hall we were joined by some of the Merchant Navy Captains who had been prisoners on the German battleship. It was a splendid lunch with the captains of both ships — C. H. L. Woodhouse, C.B., of *Ajax*, and F. S. Bell, C.B., of *Exeter* — responding to the Toasts and Winston Churchill winding up the proceedings with his customary eloquence. It was a great occasion and every officer and man received a leather cigarette-case embossed with the City coat of arms and containing twenty cigarettes. A fleet of buses took us to Waterloo and the special trains back to Plymouth, back to work and war, and on the following evening *Ajax* set off at speed up the Channel and to Chatham

136

Dockyard where she was taken in hand for refit and many men left the ship. Those of us who remained were given 28-days leave and returned to a very busy work-load, refitting all machinery and every valve throughout the ship, with a reduced complement.

During this period Norway and the Low Countries were invaded and France had surrendered; our armies had been rescued from the beaches at Dunkirk — every member of the ship's company having been told he could be called upon to leave at a moment's notice to go to another ship. Some did — and were lost.

We were made up to full complement early in July and on the 17th oiled and ammunitioned to proceed to sea on a familiarization exercise for new crew-members, and came under enemy air-attack several times, thus giving our guns and gunners good experience. On the 28th we left Sheerness and headed north to Scapa Flow with three very heavy attacks and bombs coming quite close to us on that day, but a Full Power Trial — an hour's run at 34-knots — helped us to reach the Flow at 2 p.m. next day ready for another strenuous working-up period. Every time we went to sea for practice the 'practice' was for real because the Germans — via 'Lord Haw-haw' on wireless — vowed to 'get' *Ajax* in revenge for *Graf Spee* and their planes certainly tried their hardest to fulfil that pledge. The weather was variable with some halcyon summer days, some stormy ones and even days of thick fog, but on the night of August 14th, a most severe gale struck the Flow. We had steam on main engines as is usual in such conditions, as did (presumably) the new cruiser *Naiad* lying ahead of us but it availed neither ship when she dragged her anchors and came crashing broadside-on across our bows with an almighty bang. Our stem-post buckled and side-plates in the bows were sprung and we began taking in water for'ard, our nose started to drop. Only continuous pumping could maintain the status quo so it meant we had to dock, and next morning poor old *Ajax* — nose well down — steamed out and down the west coast to arrive in Cammel Laird's Yard at Birkenhead on the 16th. The whole stem, a couple of ribs and several plates had to be renewed and this was Friday afternoon! It was quite a big job but the ship-yard workers toiled non-stop to complete the work by Monday afternoon and the ship undocked that night but unfortunately massive air-raids on the Mersey with mines being dropped on that and the following night made it impossible for us to leave until mine-sweepers had cleared the path. It was August 22nd before we could get out — to find ourselves a unit of the escorting force to a huge convoy of troopships and cargo vessels. "Hallo! Where are we off to?" everyone wondered. Certainly not back to Scapa for as soon as the armada was clear of the Irish Sea the course was due west for 24-hours and then all turned southwards. Our Sea-Fox was catapulted morning and evening at Dawn and Dusk Action Stations; one morning we received an S.O.S. when it plopped into the sea several miles off and made a 30-knot dash to rescue it. Back with the convoy we had a couple of U-boat alerts which the escort handled so that they failed to develop.

I came off watch at 4 a.m. on August 30th with pain in my groin and both feet swollen so reported at the Sick Bay after breakfast. On examination the Doctor just said, "All right," — no mention of treatment and I assumed it was a case of "Go away and forget it", so at noon I went below to take over the Afternoon Watch and an hour later the Medical staff were searching the ship for me! I 'should have turned-in in the Sick Bay'. "Why had I ignored the Doctor's orders?" A relief came down and I was duly put to bed with my feet still puffed, the Doc's verdict was that nothing could be done for me in the ship and that I would be sent back to U.K. from Freetown, Sierra Leone, where we were due on September 2nd. I was stretchered over to the Hospital ship *Oxfordshire* and cot-bound for two days with my ship and the convoy gone. A week later I was discharged to the Depot-ship *Edinburgh Castle* — to await passage to rejoin *Ajax*.

During my two-weeks wait I met several 'old ships' — people I had served with before — who were either waiting passage home or to other ships throughout the world. The crew were native Sierra Leoneans and it was quite amusing to see them going ashore and returning aboard, every one carrying his huge, badly-rolled umbrella and all in tropical uniform of white shirt and shorts with black stockings and shoes. Then there was the 'Side Party' — a squad of ragged natives who kept the side of the ship clean — with a 'Fellah' in charge of them. The 'Fellah' wore a black silk topper, a white sleeveless vest with a separate white, winged-collar round his neck, white calf-length trousers and nothing on his feet, and was being 'paddled' around the ship in his own canoe by his two 'henchmen'. He certainly kept his 'boys' on the move.

One afternoon a large snake about ten feet long came swimming down the river and slithered onto the catamaran floating alongside the ship and from which the 'boys' operated. What panic! Those 'boys' literally ran up the ship's side, scrambling up ropes, their eyes wide and bolting from their sockets, voices shrieking in alarm. Amid the commotion an R.N. Petty Officer was issued with a revolver to dispatch the poor old reptile and push it into the water with a boat-hook. 'Fellah' soon had his 'boys' busy again.

On Sunday, Sept. 22nd the new C. in C. South Atlantic, Vice-Admiral R. H. T. Raikes, came on board to introduce himself to, and inspect the men in transit, and the next day was "Coal ship day" with much the same hustle and bustle as the old E. of I. days and coal-dust getting everywhere, and midst all the turmoil I, and Chief Painter Trelease were told to have our kit on the gangway by noon as we were going to the Armed Merchant Cruiser *Carnarvon Castle* for passage south. (Trelease was to join

Shropshire — eventually). We sailed as part of the escort in charge of a massive convoy of troop- and supply-ships on the 25th — southwards. The A.M.C. was a beautiful and modern Union Castle liner taken over by the Admiralty and fitted with four 6" guns, and we two were the only passengers and were not required for any duties. We each had a large and comfortable cabin and ate with the ship's officers; spent most of our time pacing the deck or reading, and watching the progress of the famous liners in the convoy. Our guns were fired on a few occasions to keep the gunners in trim and re-assure the troops that their escort was alert. All arrived safely in Cape Town at 5 p.m. on October 4th with rain pelting down and no news forthcoming as to the whereabouts of either of our ships, so after dinner Trelease and I walked ashore. The city was well-lit and the rain had stopped but all public houses and places of entertainment were shut! The local authorities were under the impression that the incoming troops were Australian and would be flooding ashore and did not want a repeat performance of the antics of a previous crowd whose exuberance had prompted them to bodily lift a small car off the main street, carry it into the Main Post Office and ask for it to be wrapped and sent 'home'. They were taking no chances.

The following morning was sunny and warm and we two were despatched by train to the Naval Base at Simonstown on the other side of Table Mountain — "To await arrival of your ships".

As we walked through the gates into *Afrikander* 1 at 1.20 p.m. I was told to return to Cape Town by the next train and report to the R.T.O. (Railway Transport Officer). I asked about some lunch and was given an Expenses Chit for use at the local hotel and had just started eating when Trelease came in. He too had to return forthwith, so after lunch and a brief walk in the pleasant little town we boarded the 5.53 train back. The R.T.O. gave us our orders and we parted company. He went to the *Durban Castle* and I to the *Dominion Monarch* — the largest motor-vessel in the world — and was just in time for dinner!

Now this ship was sheer luxury. The Admiralty had taken her over for 'trooping' but had not 'converted' her. All her frills and fittings were intact — as were her full peace-time crew, and I was conducted to a suite comprising of a lounge, bedroom, bathroom, dressing-room and a shower-room on the Boat Deck, and had a personal steward to look after me. (Perhaps they thought that C.E.R.A. meant Chief Engineer Rear Admiral!)

We sailed at 1 p.m. on Sunday, October 6th — a massive convoy of big liners fully laden with troops, and a number of large cargo ships all guarded by the one A.M.C. Among the liners were *Durban Castle, Andes, Orion,* the French *Pasteur, Britannic* and *Athlone Castle,* and on *Dominion Monarch* we had a few thousand soldiers and their officers, several

Midshipmen and one senior naval officer, Captain F. Howard, but I was the sole naval rating.

My steward brought a cup of tea to my bed at 0700 and prepared my bath. A 4-course breakfast was served at 0800 after which I reclined on the Lounge Deck with colonels, majors and captains (when they were not drilling or lecturing the men) and at 1100 the stewards brought glasses of sherry to us. The bell for lunch rang at noon for another 4-course meal and the afternoon was for 'rest' before dainty sandwiches, cakes and tea were served at 4 p.m. Between tea and dinner we swam in the Pool, played Shovel-board or Deck-hockey on the Games Deck. It was obligatory to dress for dinner and everyone congregated in the Smoking Room for aperitifs before sitting down to a 5-course meal served with wines and brandy. How the other half . . . !

But the Army were great fun with their impromtu concerts and a Boxing tournament — to which we were all invited — and the crew still had their peace-time concert party intact, one of its shows being a version of the Radio programme "In Town Tonight" which was broadcast round the ship and news had that day come through of *Ajax* having been in action in the Mediterranean, sinking two Italian destroyers and setting fire to a third (subsequently despatched by *York*), and Captain Howard — knowing I was rejoining *Ajax* — roped me in as one of the 'interesting people who are "In Town Tonight", October 12th 1940' to answer questions about my ship, the River Plate and the Navy in general.

Another of their shows was a "Henry Hall's Guest Night", in which a Sergeant Thornton of the Royal Artillery gave a splendid piano recital and the Regimental Band orchestra played dance music with some good 'vocals'.

On the 16th my old ship *Shropshire* — a perfect picture on a calm Indian Ocean — met us and took over from the A.M.C. which then went south again, and two days later as we approached the Bab el Mandeb Strait the anti-aircraft cruiser *Carlisle*, the destroyers *Kingston* and *Kandahar*, and the sloop *Flamingo* joined the party — just in time! The 'fun' started next morning and lasted for three days as our escorts protected the convoy from several attacks by high-level Italian bombers. The concentrated and intense fire from the ships stopped the enemy from pressing home his attacks although some of his bombs fell a bit close to some of the troop-ships but all anchored safely off Suez at 0930 on October 22nd.

Everyone was ready to leave even before the ship stopped but there was no movement of personnel until late in the afternoon when a small number of soldiers landed. Next morning the main bodies of troops began disembarking and by evening all that were left were two sergeants and fifty men, Captain Howard and the Middies and me, and of course the crew. How empty and quiet it was after sixteen days of movement and life. At

8 p.m. Captain Howard called me — "Arrange for a call at 0600 and be ready to go ashore at seven. Our train leaves at eight."

At 9 p.m. one of the Middies said, "You know we have to be up at three-thirty in the morning, don't you?" but before I could say anything the Purser arrived. "Ah, Mr. Gurr, Captain Howard would like to see you," and he confirmed, adding that we would leave the ship at 4.30 a.m. and the train would depart at six. What a time to have to rise after six weeks of luxury living!

We were all at Assembly in the Dining Room at 4 a.m. for tea, coffee, toast and marmalade, and there were packets of sandwiches made ready for us together with an apple and an orange, and the stewards had filled gin bottles with iced water — strict instructions being given to be sure to take them with us because the water ashore was not fit for drinking and "you will certainly need a drink during the long journey across the desert." In darkness our baggage was moved to the Well-deck and we landed with it at Port Tewfik as dawn was breaking at 6 a.m.

An Egyptian State Railway train backed into the station; Arab porters put our baggage into the vans as we took our seats in the First Class compartments and expected the train to pull out. It didn't. An Army Embarkation Officer told us to "Relax. We have to wait for a big Naval Draft to come ashore from *Athlone Castle*." We vacated, leaving the train to the millions of flies which had invaded it but did not move far because it seemed there were just as many Arabs hovering about as there were flies. At 9 o'clock a tatterdemalion collection of some 400 to 500 seamen, stokers, marines, etc., arrived, their baggage was loaded, they boarded and the train moved off at ten o'clock. It had been a long, boring wait but now we were moving — slowly — along the streets of Suez, the men leaning from the windows, singing and shouting.

There were no glass windows to the carriages but wooden, slatted shutters for when it rained and sun-blinds which could be lowered when necessary. We had our compartment wide-open in order to see as much of the country as possible — and hoping that any breeze would blow the flies away (but it didn't, and they still pestered us.)

We crossed a deal of rough country and then ran alongside the Suez Canal almost as far as Ismailia before the line turned westward and into the desert proper. Sand — and more sand; a dirty grey sand as far as the eye could see, and we passed a few camel-trains wending their way southward. At one point a Tarmac highway crossed our tracks (no signals or crossing-gates!) and standing on the road, proudly displaying the 'Invicta' rampant horse badge of Kent on the front of its boiler, was a steam-roller built by Aveling & Porter (Engineers) of Strood, Kent. A "homely" sight. The train stopped at many wayside 'halts' — for no apparent reason, there being only a few mud huts ranged beside the line — but within seconds

141

crowds of men, women and children appeared, all calling for 'baksheesh' and 'ceeg-rets' though most of the women (dressed overall in long black robes, their faces hidden by scarves and hoods) remained well back. The desert seemed never-ending as we passed many nomadic bands of Arabs on camels, mules and asses with pack-animals piled high with bales and bundles and slung panniers and the women and children trudging along beside them.

Moving on through cotton plantations and fields of rice and maize, the country was criss-crossed with irrigation canals and ditches from which the farmers drew water for their land, using water-wheels — some worked by hand but many by blind-folded oxen, mules or asses plodding round and round for ever.

It was dark when the train got to Alexandria at 6.30 p.m. and a Working-Party from the cruiser *Liverpool* unloaded the baggage — placing mine with that of the officers but I hastily retrieved it before it vanished. My *Dominion Monarch* companions had disappeared; the main Draft mustered in the subway below the station, none knowing the name of the ship they were to join until an officer and a Master-at-Arms came with lists of ratings' names and began calling — "Petty Officer 'So-and so', Able Seamen Alfred 'Whatname', William 'Thingummy', Leading Steward Jack Dusty — to *Eagle*. Get your kit up to the yard and report to the Transport Officer", then another batch of names and another ship — on and on.

Nothing was known about me for I had no Travel documents or Draft Note, my only identification being my Service Certificate which I had been carrying since Freetown and I had to wait until the last. It was after 8.30 before I was dealt with when I was directed to a bus for the twenty-minutes ride to the Docks and they would signal for a boat from *Ajax* to pick me up.

142

CHAPTER 14

Mediterranean Theatre

The boat came at 10.30 and I was soon back among my messmates who had thought I was back in England. They jumped from their hammocks and there was much hand-shaking and many questions as to where I had been. It felt good to be back, and the next day I caught up with news of what had been happening since I left and was able to see the damage incurred in, and learn details of, the skirmish — or action — with Italian destroyers on October 12th.

Ajax had not called at Cape Town but had spent a few hours in Durban and three days in Aden before passing through the Red Sea and Suez Canal to join the 7th Cruiser Squadron, Eastern Mediterranean Fleet at Alexandria on September 30th.

On October 8th the Fleet sailed to cover an important convoy of four ship along to Malta, arriving on the 11th. *Ajax* and *Orion* then left to carry out a patrol and were operating 20-miles apart when, at 2.30 a.m. on the 12th. *Ajax* was attacked by Italian torpedo-boats and destroyers. Two of the t-b's were sunk and one destroyer badly damaged before the enemy broke off the action, but *Ajax* had been hit and 13 men were killed — including the Flag Officer, the chief Yeoman of Signals and the R.M. Bugler when a shell hit part of the bridge — and more than twenty were wounded. A serious fire burned out the Central Store and a Fresh Water tank was shattered. (The damaged Italian being towed by another was sighted next morning by the *York* at whose approach the tow was slipped and *Artigliere* — for such was the Italian's name — was left to her fate. *York* gave her crew five minutes to leave their ship and then sank it with one torpedo and radioed Italian Naval Command to "Come and pick up your comrades", then beat a hasty retreat because in a similar situation on July 12th when the Australian cruiser *Sydney* stopped to pick up survivors of the *Bartolomeo Colleoni* which she had sunk, the enemy sent out planes to bomb her!)

I was back now, having missed all that, but the ship was still a bit of a shambles with my Forward Fire Party position badly smoke-damaged and blackened.

Italy invaded Greece on Oct. 28th and after dark on the 30th the ship went alongside at Alex. to embark 854-men of the Yorks and Lancs Regiment, their motor transport and Whippet tanks. We sailed at 4.30 next morning doing 25-knots to arrive in Suda Bay, Crete, at 0830 on November 1st and went alongside a new jetty — the only change I could

143

notice since my last visit in 1931 when there was no jetty.

As the troops were disembarking the air-raid warning sounded. I was shutting the scuttles and dead-lights in my Mess and saw five bombers flying directly at us. I ran to my Station as a terrific barrage of shells was put up from us and by *Carlisle* lying out in the harbour as a hail of bombs descended. The 'All Clear' sounded half-an-hour later and I went on deck to see clouds of dust still hanging over the hillside, a gunner telling me that 15-planes had attacked, their bombs falling close and that two soldiers had been wounded by blasts from *our* guns! We quickly moved from the jetty out into the bay so that we could cover the troops as they moved their equipment to safer surroundings. More spasmodic raids followed and even came after us as we sped back to Alex. where we arrived on Sunday afternoon, Nov. 3rd to oil and take on ammunition. We had been at Action Stations during daylight hours and at 2nd degree of readiness at night, fully clothed for instant action every minute since leaving Alex. and now, on completion of ammunitioning we proceeded at 30-knots to Port Said to embark more than 600-troops — men of the Royal Artillery who had been on the *Dominion Monarch* and I invited the R.S.M. (W/O Milner) and Staff Sergeant Sutton to come to the engine-room when we got under way for Suda at 4 p.m. on the 5th. Both were very impressed as we went to 27-knots but said they still preferred Army life and commented — "Not as comfortable here as the *Monarch* — but 'Boy!' — what speed!"

Troops landed without incident at Suda on the 6th and we anchored in the bay until the next evening with not one raid to mar the equanimity of the day. In fact — that 7th day of November was a perfect day with clear blue skies, clean air, and not a ripple on the surface of the water. There was Peace in the World — it seemed. But not for long, as we left Suda at 9 p.m. and met the Fleet next morning. And what a glorious sight that was with destroyers, cruisers, battleships and aircraft-carriers strung out as far as the eye could see, as we joined them for a sortie to the west — Dusk and Dawn Action and 2nd degree of readiness when not at full alert, and fully-dressed at all times.

Enemy planes attacked the Fleet on Sunday afternoon (10th) but fighters from our two carriers drove them off before they could do any damage, and on Monday our Squadron, under Vice-Admiral H. Pridham-Whippell in *Orion*, with *York* and *Sydney* and a flotilla of destroyers was detached to enter the Straits of Otranto as a distraction while planes from *Illustrious* bombed the Italian base at Taranto. At 0130 on Nov. 12th we made contact with five enemy transports on their way from Brindisi to Albania escorted by destroyers. Our ships opened fire damaging one of the escorts — which abandoned their charges — and then sank three large transports before being recalled to the Fleet.

Enemy planes were out early in the morning looking for us and had four of their number shot down by our fighter planes and the rest driven off. It seems that the whole — or main — purpose of the 'sortee' was to pass a convoy through from Port Said to Malta and Gibraltar at the same time as another was coming eastwards from Gib. and anything else was just a diversion. The raid on Taranto resulted in the sinking of three Italian battleships in the harbour for the loss of one "Stringbag" (Swordfish torpedo-bomber) from *Illustrious* with its two-man crew, the Observer being my cousin Harry — Lt. H. J. Slaughter, R.N., "Missing presumed killed".

The raids on the Fleet continued all the way back to Alex where the enemy kept up their harassing tactics with high-level bombing through the night (14th/15th) and 'Repel Aircraft' stations maintained all night. The Squadron then left harbour to escort a troop convoy from Port Said to Piraeus, the port for Athens, taking the ships right into the harbour where we remained overnight, no leave being given. No sooner were we back in Alex and topped up with oil than we were off again with the Fleet covering another convoy along to Malta. *Ajax* was detached to escort two supply-ships to Suda Bay on Sunday, 24th and even as the ships entered the harbour a flight of enemy bombers swooped from over the hills to release sticks of bombs. Our a/a fire affected their aim and their targets were missed. We topped-up with oil and sped off at 26-knots to catch up with the Fleet on Monday afternoon just in time to help with the terrific barrage being put up against another force of enemy planes approaching from the north. None got through that curtain of fire. After dark *Ajax* with another cruiser and some destroyers were detailed to accompany the carrier *Eagle* on a diversionary dawn bomb attack of the Italian-occupied Libyan port of Tripoli. This was rated 'successful', as was the delivery of the convoy and our sweep round the island and all were back in Alex by Friday evening (29th). *Ajax* went alongside the jetty for extra anti-aircraft guns (Oerlikons) to be fitted and while there an opportunity was taken for a film-show on board. The screen was rigged on the quarterdeck but unfortunately a strong wind was blowing the tail-end of a sand-storm directly into the faces of the audience. We could not keep our eyes open. I gave up after 20-minutes and next morning there were lots of sore and bloodshot eyes amongst those people who had stayed until the end.

Our new guns were tried out when we went to sea on December 5th. R.A.F. planes towed sleeve-targets for us until we met the transports we were to escort to Piraeus where we arrived at lunch-time on Sunday, 8th. Leave was given from 1.30 p.m. and I think almost everybody except the actual Duty Watch took advantage for there were only five of us left on board in my Mess. We sat at table waiting for our supper to be served and the Air-raid alarms sounded off. We dashed to our stations and within 15-minutes the "All Clear" came. We returned to the Mess only for the

145

"Alarm" to sound again, but this time I had only just reached the engine-room when the "All Clear" came for the second time. What was going on? The answer to that came to me by messenger from the Duty Engineer Officer, — "5,000 Italian prisoners have been brought in — hence the general din ashore which we poor English took to be an 'air-raid warning'. Regrets — J. Linnell."

When the chaps returned that night they said it had been absolute bedlam ashore. Bands were playing — people were cheering and singing and some Britishers had been carried shoulder-high through the streets. There had obviously been a considerable victory somewhere.

For the next couple of weeks we were passing transports and supply-ships between Suda and Piraeus in particularly squally weather and saw some terrific waterspouts one of which reared up suddenly and directly ahead of us on December 16th and was of such gigantic proportions that emergency orders were piped for everybody to get below decks, all screen-doors and hatches to be shut and everyone to make certain that *all* water-tight doors are shut and secured. There was no way of avoiding it. Later in the day we met the Fleet and steamed westward, guessing that some stunt was in the offing, and we were right. The battleships were to bombard the Albanian port of Valona during the night and the Squadron with some destroyers searched for any Italian shipping crossing between Bari and Durazzo. We found nothing and rejoined the Fleet at dawn with a convoy which had come through from Malta. We were at full alert the whole time as enemy reconnaissance planes watched from a distance as the Fleet and convoy wended its way towards Alexandria, but there were no develop-ments and we arrived on December 23rd to have Christmas in harbour.

The actual day was not as 'bright' as it had been last year in the Falklands. I suppose the constant pressure of high-speed steaming in three-watches coupled with the air-attacks, the bombs and gun-fire were taking their toll and wearing down the men's humour, but there were one or two simple, but amusing incidents to lighten the 'gloom' of the day. The custom of the most junior member of a Mess donning the uniform and assuming the duties of the President or Head of a Mess meant that a young 4th Class. E.R.A. was in charge of us. A Sunday routine with Divisions and Church on the quarterdeck was worked and when the 'Chief' called the E.R.A's Division to "Number" — in order to report to the Officer of the Day — we did so in our South American Spanish — much to the amusement of other Divisions.

Then there was the dog — a small black-and-white cross Spaniel/Terrier which had been found straying in the docks at Alex when we had our extra guns fitted and had been brought on board by stokers (Who else?) and had been allowed to stay as a mascot. It was trotting about during Divisions, dodging between legs and wondering why no-one was taking notice of him

146

when somebody inflated a sausage-shaped festive balloon and dropped it in front of him. The atmosphere changed in the ranks. What fun that dog had! And what amusement it gave to all sections as we waited for the Captain — E. D. B. McCarthy now — to begin his inspection. The dog sniffed at the strange object which had fallen in front of him and backed-off suspiciously only to advance again as a slight breeze wafted the object along the deck. He chased it and tried to sink his teeth into it but only succeeded in pushing it further away. He crouched and wiggled his backside and crept up to the balloon as a playful kitten might and then skidded along the deck. Eventually the teeth won the battle and there was a 'pop!' and his toy had disappeared. The amazement on the dog's face was plain to see as it walked slowly through the ranks of all the Engine-room section as though it was searching to find the individual who was hiding his toy, and there were smiles on all faces when the Captain walked by. He must have thought he had a happy crew! But the day had been made a bit brighter by that dog's presence on board.

There was a short Carol Service and then Messes were decorated with last year's paper chains. Christmas dinner was just as good as usual, and there was a bottle of beer supplied for every man.

At 3 p.m. on New Year's Eve *Ajax* unexpectedly left harbour for Suda Bay and the following morning I was on deck as we steamed westward along the south coast of Crete. The sun was bright, the sea flat calm, the air was clean so that the true beauty of the magnificent scenery of rugged, snow-covered mountains could be thoroughly appreciated, and war was a million miles away — until that is — we anchored in Suda Bay. Almost as soon as main engines stopped a squadron of Italian bombers swooped down from over those same snow-capped mountains to deliver their cargo harmlessly into the calm water. We oiled and left to meet the rest of our squadron to patrol between Crete and Piraeus until January 9th when we took up our positions, 'screening' ahead of the Fleet and a small convoy bound for Malta. The attacks began next morning when hordes of high-level and torpedo-bombers appeared on the scene and resulted in the *Illustrious* being hit by six 1,000 lb. bombs and near-missed by several more. It was quite a scrap but she survived and we escorted her as she limped into Grand Harbour at Malta. The destroyer *Gallant* had her bows blown off by a mine just outside the harbour and *Mohawk* took her in tow so that she could beach inside the harbour.

Meanwhile, another convoy which had been brought through from Gibraltar was arriving at the island — having cost the loss of the cruiser *Southampton* and severe damage to the *Gloucester*, both by dive-bombers — and we were to take part of that convoy for through-passage to Alex while the Western Med. section returned to Gib with the ships we had brought through. It was all part of a massive operation and we did not linger at

Malta but steamed back towards Alex with our new charges. When it became quite dark our squadron was detached to increase speed to 30-knots, take in oil at Suda and then, at the same speed get into position to cover the battleships when they bombarded Tobruk before dawn on Sunday, Jan. 12th. It was another successful foray (they said!) and when we neared Alex the convoy and Fleet went in and the cruisers went to Suda Bay for a quick 'top-up' with oil before the night's operation, an attack on the island of Stampoli. Fleet Air Arm planes were going to drop flares to illuminate the scene and then they and we were due to blast and strafe the Italian aerodrome on the island. Unfortunately low cloud made it impossible for the airmen to define the target so the operation was called off at the last minute — 8.30 p.m. — and we withdrew at speed to join up with the Fleet next morning for another foray to the west. During the afternoon our reconnaissance planes spotted an Italian convoy many miles ahead; a force of torpedo-bombers from our carriers was sent to destroy it as the Fleet turned to the south-east and that night the battleships plastered Benghazi with 15″ shells, the destroyers shielding them on the 'land-side' — and adding a few salvos of their own — and the cruisers guarded them from any seaward intrusion.

When that job was finished our squadron ploughed through bad weather for more fuel (we burn it very quickly at high-speed) and rejoined the Fleet the next afternoon with the weather still bad. It was during my Last Dog Watch that evening as we were doing a steady 18-knots at 7.30 there came — "Emergency — Full Astern both engines". Our reaction was immediate and collision with the carrier *Eagle* averted, for in the pitch darkness with all ships darkened we were headed straight for her — and disaster. All arrived off Alex 24-hours later but enemy air activity over the city made it too risky for any ship to enter the harbour until after daybreak. Everyone turned-to on maintenance work and in storing and ammunitioning the ship, and all had the thought that at least they could look forward to sleeping in a hammock that night for the first time in more than two-weeks.

At 2 a.m. — being the Duty Chief — I got a call to get "Full Watch below — at once!". A full gale had sprung up and we had to raise steam and keep the main engines running slowly so that we would not drag anchor. We remained below until 6.30 and then carried on with our maintenance jobs while riding out the storm all day Sunday and at midnight sailed with the squadron and a flotilla of destroyers. At 3 a.m. on Tuesday all ships oiled at Suda and then swept to the west of the island — evidently a preliminary to another operation for we returned to Suda on Wednesday evening, oiled through the night and sailed at 0530 on Thursday 23rd. We were to meet and escort *Illustrious* from Malta where she had been docked since her battering in November and had been the

Saturday March 1st 1941. Ajax — Eastern Mediterranean. Taken by 'Perth'.

target of intensive bombing by German aircraft based in Sicily, and get her back to Alex. She was leaving Grand Harbour under cover of darkness that night so *Orion* — flag of Vice-Admiral Pridham-Whippell — led us with *York* and the Australian cruiser *Perth* towards the island. We met and passed the carrier which was managing 22-knots and the destroyers turned to accompany her and guard her from any U-boat attacks while the cruisers carried on westward before turning to take up station 100-miles behind. Then followed one of the worst days ever as from dawn onwards high-level bombers — too high for our guns to reach — rained bombs all around us. They were falling everywhere, sending great columns of water high into the air (according to my signalman contact) and it was a miracle no-one received a direct hit. But there was worse to come at 5 p.m. when the German Stukas took over and for one-and-a-half hours dive-bombed the squadron non-stop, more than fifty planes at a time. Bombs crashed down all around as we steamed at full speed, twisting, turning, heeling — and jolting — (from explosions below the water). It was really hectic. I had relieved Frank Pearce for the First Dog Watch at 4 p.m. and his watch, which had endured four hours of the 'hecticity', were happy to be leaving the heat and the noise of the turbines, pumps and fans, but the Stukas made things even worse. We were saying, "Surely it must be nearly dark

149

by now," and "For Christ's sake hurry up and get dark up there and maybe they'll go home!". There was no hope of trying to change over watches while the planes kept coming with their lethal loads and our guns blazed back at them with the ships writhing like demented snakes, but about seven o'clock ("It *must* be dark by now, surely!") the revolution telegraph began to ring down the revs and our speed gradually reduced. Pumps and fans could be eased down and a sort of peace came to the engine-room. Anti-climax. The "All-clear" sounded at 7.40 and the watches could be relieved, and I think *everybody* was relieved and thankful we were still alive, and afloat.

At dawn no enemy planes were about so we increased speed to catch up with the destroyers and our 'charge' — which was shepherded into Alex harbour at 6 o'clock that Saturday evening.

During Sunday we took in provisions, ammunition and oil, and on Monday embarked a crowd of R.A.F. and Fleet Air Arm personnel with their equipment, stores, a large number of bombs and several drums of aviation spirit and left harbour at 2 p.m. — and at 25-knots. The seas were very heavy and we reduced speed for a time but as they didn't moderate we increased to 27-knots in order to arrive at Suda on time. What a battering the "Old Girl" took! And how those poor airmen suffered! They were so happy to set foot on terra firma when the ship went alongside the jetty. The squadron patrolled in the Aegean for three days, at Action Stations the whole time because of the constant air activity, and as soon as we entered Suda on Friday morning we were ordered to sea to find and escort a stricken oil-tanker back to harbour. She was the *Desmoules*. Her engine-room had been hit by a U-boat's torpedo and the destroyer *Dainty* had her in tow. She was well down by the stern but stayed afloat long enough to be beached in Suda Bay on Saturday morn. Italian high-level bombers came over and spent the day trying to hit at least something in the harbour. They didn't and we left at 10 p.m. to meet the Fleet on Sunday morning and steam westward for 24-hours when suddenly we — *Ajax* only — turned away and proceeded to Piraeus, stayed for 24-hours and then left for Alex at 23-knots. Why? Everyone was asking. Why? We were not told, but Dame Rumour had the answer. 'The Suez Canal, which had been blocked by three sunken ships was now clear and the *Illustrious* is to be passed through on her way to U.S.A. for repair. *We* are to escort her through the Red Sea.' Who makes them up? We were to arrive in Alex at 6 p.m. on Thursday but during the afternoon a sand-storm reduced visibility to 50-yards and our speed to 10-knots so it was Friday morning when we entered — and then lay at anchor for four days getting rid of the sand which had found its way to every part of the ship *and* engines. There were a few 'alarms' when Italian reconnaissance planes approached, but no raids. They were probably keeping an eye on *Illustrious*.

150

On Wed. 12th we left harbour and that night rejoined the squadron to cover the battleships while they bombarded Benghazi at the request of our armies on shore, and at dawn the squadron was ordered to patrol north of Crete, thus giving rise to more speculation. What were we doing? and Why were we doing it? Generally we were 'in the dark' but perhaps an independent operation involving our ship alone, or with one or two destroyers, would prompt the skipper to give us an inkling of what we were hoping to accomplish and what opposition we would be likely to meet. Maybe it is just as well not to know too much beforehand. Sunday afternoon (16th) and not far from Piraeus when two Italian torpedo-bombers swooped out of the sun and straight into our line of fire which definitely put them off their aim, and two days later south of Crete we came across a submarine surfaced. It was one of ours which had suffered some mishap and could not submerge but was making good progress towards Alex and refused our offers of assistance, so *Ajax* carried on to Alexandria, entering harbour at 6.30 on Wednesday morning and immediately embarking 400 men of the Hampshire Regiment with their equipment and a number of Maltese stewards and at 5.30 p.m. left harbour at 29-knots for an uneventful voyage along to Malta. When the passengers had disembarked the ship moved to anchor in the middle of the harbour whence we could see some of the damage done by the enemy bombs, mostly it seemed, to properties outside the Dockyard which made me wonder about my friends of 1930/31 — but I had no means of finding out.

Two more raids occurred while we were at anchor with all the bombs falling into the water as a terrific barrage of fire was put up by shore batteries and ships, and as soon as it was dark we left, again at 29-knots and arrived in Alex at midnight on Sunday where, even before we could 'shut down' we were ordered to sea again. What now? We passed through the Boom Defence only to turn and re-enter less than an hour later. (We subsequently learned that our mission was to have gone to the assistance of the monitor — *Terror* which had been bombed off Benghazi and was being escorted back to Alex but was reported "Has now sunk" just as we cleared the harbour.) *Ajax* moved into the Floating Dock for an examination of her hull and a time limit of 24-hours during which the whole company worked, with seamen scrubbing the sides and bottom of the ship and cleaning the propellers, and the engine-room department refitting all underwater valves and clearing the inlets. As soon as we were floated out we embarked a 4" anti-aircraft gun with its mounting and a ton of ammunition all destined for Suda and at 6 o'clock on Friday morning, Feb. 28th we left harbour with an arrival time of 8 o'clock next morning but — what weather! A storm developed into the worst — the fiercest — gale known for many years in the Eastern Med and we could not make headway. Two stokers simply vanished. They apparently were standing by the screen of the Shelter-deck and there was not the slightest hope of finding them again. In the six hours between noon and 6 p.m. the ship advanced just 15-miles, and we were 30-hours late arrriving in Suda Bay.

There was the usual air-raid soon after going alongside. Queer things — those raids. Our radar picked the enemy planes up late because of the mountains and the bugler would be sounding "Repel Aircraft" as our guns started firing at the planes which were on the point of dropping their loads while we were dashing to our stations. The bombs inevitably fell into the water as the planes disappeared over the hills on the other side of the harbour. Then — ten minutes grace before the bugler sounded the "All Clear" and we returned to our jobs and waited for the next lot to come over. (Analogous to those little minnows and the five big horse-mackerel in Bermuda years ago).

We had a short patrol in the Aegean before returning to Alex on March 6th to top-up with oil and immediately began embarking 650 New Zealand troops, some of whom had difficulty getting from their camp through a severe sand-storm and delayed our sailing until 12.30 next day, then it was 27-knots to Piraeus where they disembarked 24-hours later. Sailing after dark for another patrol we passed eight fully-laden troopships entering the harbour and spent Sunday, March 9th covering another huge convoy of supplies to Greece and Crete, then oiled ship on Monday in Suda Bay, but now the Germans had their Luftwaffe in the zone and as we left at 4 p.m. we came under very heavy attack by dive-bombers, an attack which lasted an hour as we twisted and turned at 30-knots dodging the hail of bombs. Another wave of Stukas came at 5.30 but by then it was nearly dark (thank goodness!) and we were able to get away. At 8 o'clock on Wednesday morning (12th) we arrived at Port Said just as *Illustrious* was entering the canal en route to U.S.A. and were able to wish her "God-speed and Good Luck". The Hospital-ship *Atlantis* with many sick and wounded soldiers, sailors and airmen on board followed her through and were given a big cheer by our company. Our reason for calling at Port Said was for the giant Floating crane to lift out our redundant sea-plane catapult to allow room for more anti-aircraft guns to be fitted for additional protection against dive-bombers. The job finished, we sailed again at 5.30 p.m. and were back in Alex next morning to be welcomed by a wonderful surprise. At anchor lay the aircraft-carrier *Formidable* — replacement for *Illustrious*.

We remained in harbour for four days, working 18-hours a day and hampered by another of those sand-storms which left a layer of fine sand in and over everything, all gritty underfoot and bringing back memories of 'Coaling ship', but certainly not as dirty.

At 6 a.m. on Monday, March 17th we embarked 800 New Zealand troops and sailed before noon at 27-knots to land them at Piraeus 24-hours later and remain alongside overnight, another chance for some to get a decent meal ashore. On our way to Suda for more oil we endured an hour-long dive-bombing raid until the merciful weather came down to protect us. Unfortunately it protected the enemy on the Dodccanese Islands too because by the next evening we had met the Fleet with the intention of giving the islands a plastering but the exercise had to be cancelled at the last minute (9.30 p.m.) owing to low cloud, torrential rain and gale-force winds. Instead we whiled away the time waiting for the second part of the exercise which was to escort a large convoy coming through from Port Said for Malta. We certainly felt safer with *Formidable* in company, seeing her planes flying far ahead as the eyes of the Fleet. Our squadron with a flotilla of destroyers was sent ahead of the Fleet during the afternoon of Saturday (22nd) to help with another big convoy coming through from Gibraltar, to be met south of Sicily — the worst point in their voyage because of the proximity of enemy air bases.

The attacks began in earnest as we rejoined the Fleet on the 24th when, due to the proximity of German air bases in Sicily we came under continuous attack from scores of Junkers 88's raining bombs for more than two hours. Miraculously (again) no ships were hit but there were many near-misses and at dusk another swarm tried to catch us off guard but their coming was anticipated by *Formidable* and her fighters were airborne and waiting for them, thus frustrating their plan. We were once again thankful for the cover of darkness which then enabled our squadron (only three ships during this operation) to be detached to link up with a flotilla of destroyers out from Suda for a sweep south of Greece for any enemy shipping. Dawn found enemy reconnaissance planes keeping tabs on us as we rejoined the Fleet and convoy but a few shells from all of us gave them warning that we knew they were there and there were no developments, the only scare coming during the First Dog Watch while doing 20-knots — "Emergency! Full Astern both engines" — and learned when I came off watch that the destroyer *Ilex* had crossed our bows and narrowly missed being sliced in two (in broad daylight).

The Fleet and convoy continued on to Alex as our squadron went into the Aegean to patrol our vital supply routes, going into Salamis Bay on Thursday, 27th to oil from a tanker and to learn that *York* — the fourth ship of the squadron which had remained in Suda for boiler-cleaning when we left on the 21st — had been severely damaged by Italian 'human-torpedoes' and was beached.

As we left Salamis later that night the Captain spoke over the Tannoy — "Be ready. We can expect to be in action against Italian surface craft within the next 48-hours!" Again we wondered. Was their Fleet at sea? Were we about to attack one of their bases?

At 10.30 p.m. we assumed 1st degree of readiness; at 4 a.m. I took over the Morning Watch in the forward engine-room and Dawn Action lasted from 5 o'clock until a quarter past six when it was well daylight. Our radar located enemy planes on the screen at a quarter to seven and "Repel Aircraft" was sounded, that alarm lasting another half-hour to make the 'watch' somewhat hectic, but just as the Forenoon Watchmen were coming down "Action Stations" sounded at the same time as a voice over the Tannoy announced, "Enemy surface craft in sight!" — so, this was it! The Watch was transferred and I hurried to my station in charge of the Forward Repair Party on the Stokers Mess Deck where I learned that the enemy force consisted of three cruisers with four destroyers, and that they had turned away when they sighted our ships comprised of *Orion* (Vice-Admiral Pridham-Whippell), *Ajax*, *Gloucester*, and the Australian-manned *Perth*, plus three destroyers.

Our speed increased to 30-knots and *Gloucester* opened fire with her longer-range guns as we took up the chase but we could not tell whether hits were scored. At 10 a.m. another enemy force appeared on the horizon beyond our quarry — a force consisting of two battleships, with more cruisers and destroyers which was a signal for us to have second thoughts, so we turned to run just as the battleships opened fire with their 15″ guns, the salvos falling fairly close to our ships. (A signalman told me that at times the other ships of our little band had been completely hidden behind the spray of the bursting projectiles.) None were hit but below decks we could feel the below-water explosions getting closer and the order was given to "Make Smoke", enabling us to escape in the black fog which was created.

At noon the enemy ships turned to the north and we followed suit at extreme range to shadow them until our main Fleet (which had only sailed from Alex the previous day) could catch up with us.

Conflicting reports filtered through, such as "The battleships (ours) are only 75-miles astern of us", and half-an-hour later, "The Fleet's only 90-miles behind us now" — frustrating because it seemed they were going backwards but probably explained by the fact that we were shadowing at 25 to 30-knots while the Fleet could only make 22 to 24-knots and we began to ponder the outcome.

Twice during the afternoon the enemy turned towards us, forcing us to turn and increase speed to keep out of range of their big guns and it was then that we felt glad that *York* was not with us, considering that she would have been more liability than asset as her maximum speed was about 26-knots and "The speed of a Fleet is the speed of its slowest member!" We could not have remained out of range of the superior fire-power and would probably have suffered hits and casualties and perhaps even worse. So — "It's an ill wind. . . !"

Watches had been regularly changed during the day and I was back at my Repair Party when heartening news came at 7 p.m. "A squadron of bombers from *Formidable* has passed overhead on the way to attack and slow-down the enemy" — which were now silhouetted by the setting sun ahead of us and it seemed they were taken by complete surprise according to accounts which filtered down to us which told of guns firing in all directions and of "Flaming Onions" being sent up (Flares which illuminated them even more!) Our planes must have slowed them because as it grew darker we were able to shorten the range to less than three miles, steaming on a parallel course and at roughly the same speed (10-knots) the C. in C. (Admiral Sir Andrew B. Cunningham) in *Warspite* having signalled the squadron to — "Keep the enemy in range. Shadow them but on no account open fire. Let the big ships finish the job!"

So we steamed along with them — we shrouded in darkness — they bathed in the light of their own flares. Suspense! Everyone tense and the ship was almost silent as everyone spoke in whispers. It was eerie as a very subdued voice came over the Tannoy from the bridge giving a running commentary of what could be discerned in the darkness — "We are passing a battleship. It is stopped and it looks as if a cruiser is lying alongside". A few minutes later — "We are now passing another battleship which appears to be doing about 8-knots". "There's a ship on fire some miles ahead — possibly the result of the bombing". "Our battleships are only nine miles astern now". — "We are now passing three cruisers which seem to be disabled. There is a destroyer standing-by them". So the hushed bulletin — and the suspense went on as we steamed 'silently' at 10-knots just about three miles distant.

Then a signal from C. in C. ordered the cruisers and destroyers to move away from the area so as not to complicate matters when the Fleet arrived. Watches changed again at midnight and I was back in the Forward Engine-room. A few minutes later came a message — "The battleships have opened fire!" the hushed voice intoning as we purred along at 12-knots. We thought of the terror and chaos in the enemy ships at the surprise of receiving salvos of 15" shells from guns of *Warspite*, *Barham* and *Valiant* at almost point-blank range.

Leaving the scene as ordered we actually passed through and amongst an enemy flotilla. Our guns were loaded and trained but fire was held for fear of confusing our battleships and shortly after that the quiet voice from our bridge announced, "The boats we just passed are now firing at their own burning ships", and "There are ships blowing up, and there's smoke and flames all around in the blackness."

As we came off watch in the engine-room at 4 a.m. an unofficial 'brief' gave a tally of "One battleship, four cruisers and one destroyer definitely sunk, and a battleship, cruiser and destroyer damaged." That seemed a good night's work as our ships were given a rendezvous position to

"Rejoin at 0800 Saturday March 29th 50-miles south-west of Cape Matapan". Disappointment came at 0800 when the Captain said, "It is not known — but is 'practically certain' that one destroyer has been sunk, and one battleship and three cruisers 'hit'". It was like being hit in the face with a wet deck-cloth!

During the forenoon our ships steamed through tons of wreckage and hundreds of bodies as our destroyers picked up survivors from boats, rafts, and from the water as all other ships formed a protective ring to guard against attack by submarine or aircraft or possibly any surface craft. At 11.30 a.m. squadrons of German bombers appeared and began bombing so any further rescue attempt was abandoned with enemy planes still diving. *Formidable*'s fighters shot three into the sea and damaged a number of others (according to our informant on the bridge) as the raid lasted an hour, and during the lull we were able to change watches again and I was back in the engine-room for the Afternoon Watch. At 3.30 p.m. more waves of dive-bombers came out to face the terrific barrage and our man on the bridge telling us of seeing many planes crashing in flames. That onslaught continued until five o'clock when advantage was taken to change watches once again — just as the Captain announced, "Expect another raid before dark!" Sure enough, at 5.20 p.m. out they came again but, likewise, *Formidable* had also 'expected' and her planes were up and meeting them well clear of the Fleet. Darkness came and the carrier's brood landed back on. Our squadron was detached to patrol north of Crete and top up with oil in Salamis Bay. *Ajax* was still oiling on Sunday (30th) afternoon when the squadron was ordered to "Raise steam for full speed". Now what? But half-an-hour later the order was rescinded, and we learned the reasons. "When the Germans had bombed our rescue efforts Admiral Cunningham sent a signal to Italian Naval Chief to send a hospital ship to pick up any survivors we might have missed. Our reconnaissance had (mistakenly) reported the Italians as sending a cruiser and destroyer to do the job.") We relaxed and at 6 p.m. listened to a B.B.C. News report that, "Three 10,000-ton Italian cruisers — *Fiume, Pola* and *Zara*, and one large destroyer — *Vincenzo Colbierti* and a smaller one, the *Mistrale* — were sunk in yesterday's battle." A later bulletin reported the Italian battleship *Vittorio Veneto* "badly damaged in the action", so there had been some success!

Next morning we picked up a huge convoy arriving from Port Said and shepherded it safely into Piraeus, then went to meet the next one on April 3rd. but were not as successful for at dusk that evening the Germans mounted a formidable assault on the supply vessels with their dive-bombers with the result that one received a direct hit, caught fire and sank. I suppose we had been really lucky in losing just one ship from such a big convoy — although one was one too many, but the rest were delivered safely into the harbour at Piraeus and we followed the last one in on that Saturday morning, April 5th and berthed alongside the jetty — which meant we were going to stay overnight. Shore-leave was given from 1.30 until 11 p.m. but I spent the afternoon on the fo'c'sle watching thousands of troops and hundreds of lorries, guns and Bren-carriers being off-loaded from the many ships we had escorted in over the past days, and saw men and vehicles moving away from the port. Next morning — Sunday — came news that Germany had declared war on Yugoslavia and Greece and at 11 a.m. and 3 p.m. air-raid warnings sounded and we closed-up to Repel Aircraft stations, each 'alert' lasting about an hour with no raid developing and I think we were lulled into a false sense of security — for shore-leave was again piped "from 4 p.m. until 11 p.m."

The beautifully sunny evening tempted me ashore at 5.30 to walk along to Phaleron Bay where I had a couple of beers at the quarters of some New Zealand troops who had just landed. We sat in the garden of the big house (their barracks) on the sea-front and they said they were "itching to have a go at the Huns." I then went by train to Athens for a meal at the British Services Club. As I left the Club at 9.20 the sirens were sounding their warning "Another False alarm?", but as I arrived at Omonoia Station guns began firing all around the city; traffic stopped and the station was already filled with people, most waiting for the trains to start running again and a goodly number of our ship's company were among them.

"All clear" sirens wailed at half-past-midnight and there was a mad rush to the platforms by the thousands anxious to get to their homes in the suburbs. The Piraeus train was packed tighter than the proverbial sardine tin as it crawled along the track to eventually disgorge us at 2 a.m. after a journey which normally took 20-minutes. As we hurried towards the ship the sky was bright from the flames of a ship burning furiously in the harbour. She was the *Clan Fraser* — one which we had brought in yesterday morning — berthed across the basin from us and now glowing white-hot! The Germans had been dropping mines into the harbour and its approaches and one had landed on her deck and — she was laden with ammunition! Even as we raced along the dockside the flames leapt higher and there were a number of minor explosions as of small-arms ammo going off, and there was no apparent effort being made to fight the blaze — no fire-float with jets of water — and the Captain of the Port had refused to allow her to be towed out of the harbour lest she hit one of the mines and blocked the harbour altogether.

Arriving on board I and my watch donned our overalls on top of our shore-going uniforms and went below to relieve those who had been on watch since the raid started (9.20) the previous night. The ship was ready to get under way and we stood awaiting orders. At 3 o'clock the 'Old Man' (Commander "E") came down to the engine-room and told me to "Revert to one hour's notice" — which virtually meant "Shut down" and we were doing just that when, at ten past three a terrific explosion rocked the ship. It was as though a 1,000 lb. bomb had passed through and exploded beneath us as she lifted, rolled, rocked and shook herself. Half the lights went out and clouds of asbestos dust from steam-pipe lagging filled the place with thick white fog. My starboard throttle watchkeeper was suddenly at the top of the ladder on his side at the same time as the 'Old Man' dropped down the port ladder, dressed only in pyjamas, and "Get ready to get under way as soon as possible!" (We moved out of the harbour at 3.40 a.m.).

The *Clan Fraser* had been burning for some time and when she blew up white hot metal was scattered over a vast area to start many more fires. Several fires on our decks were quickly dealt with by our Fire Parties but those occurring on other and smaller ships in the harbour — and there were scores of them, cargo and fishing vessels — took firm hold as did the fires in the dockside warehouses and dwellings in the vicinity and the whole area was ablaze.

We had a number of casualties — a corporal of marines died instantly when struck by a white-hot lump of steel, and a lot of men who had been ashore remained on the upper deck "sight-seeing" when they returned even after an order, "Only guns' crews to be on the upper deck. Every-one else remain under cover" was piped and were 'peeking' from behind the screens. One man had his left arm torn off from the shoulder and several others suffered lacerations and burns, and I would think casualties among the civil populations must have been high.

Our teak deck-planks (quarterdeck and fo'c'sle) were literally torn to pieces by the great lumps of metal which rained down and gouged and set fire to them. One huge chunk of metal which must have weighed at least half-a-ton had struck our tripod foremast, bending the supporting and strengthening bars and lodged itself behind the bridge and during the forenoon I watched as eight hefty seamen struggled with the aid of ropes and pulleys and massive crowbars to free that now-cold, buckled, inch-thick ship's plating and finally dump it over the side.

But, to revert to the early hours of the morning. "Slow Ahead" came at 0340 and the order was given "Everybody not actually required below for steaming the ship or for other duties should be in the Shelter-decks because of the danger from magnetic- or acoustic-mines, and all watertight doors and hatches are to be kept shut and secured."

The ship's de-gaussing gear was adequate protection against magnetic mines but for the acoustic type a heavy machine-gun was rigged on the bows with a gunner posted to fire short bursts ahead into the water every few seconds, then, as we cleared the entrance another explosion shook us as the warehouse which held *Clan Fraser's* off-loaded ammunition blew up. (Our report from the bridge said, "It's like Dante's Inferno up here!") The ship anchored in Salamis Bay after 5 a.m. and our Watch could be relieved after our gruelling night but we still kept at one-hour's-notice all day — a day which saw seamen clearing the debris from the upper deck, and the stokers getting rid of all the rubbish which had fallen from the pipes in machinery spaces — and at 5 p.m. we steamed slowly and gingerly through potentially mined waters and when well-clear of land the body of the R.M. corporal was given proper burial at sea before we rejoined the squadron in Suda Bay.

We then began to spend most of the daylight hours in the harbour and the nights patrolling between Crete and Greece and every day there was some sort of raid or attack from the air — either by a lone high-level bomber dropping his bombs at random into the bay, or by several dive-bombers coming at us from all angles. One morning we returned to harbour at 6 and as I came off watch I went on deck for a breather and stood looking at poor old *York* lying all forlorn and awkwardly beached about two-miles distant when a solitary German plane dropped out of the clouds directly above us. I don't know who was more surprised — he or we — but he managed to release his load before a shot was fired and his closest bomb which fell about ten yards from the ship's side entered the water with a tremendous splash but failed to explode — Luckily for us!

On Saturday, April 17th we swept the Aegean coast of Greece as our destroyers entered every little bay and cove in a search for "E" boats and U-boats; on Sunday morning we joined with the Fleet for a westward sweep and had *Formidable* in our midst with her planes soon in action shooting down a reconnaissance plane which had been watching from the northern horizon. Later in the forenoon four German troop-carrying planes were spotted on that same horizon being escorted by three fighters and apparently on passage from Italy to Greece. They were no threat to us so men off watch were allowed to remain on deck to see Fulmar fighters take off from *Formidable* and about five minutes later shoot all seven into the sea. One must have had a cargo of aviation spirit for it simply exploded in mid-air and floated down as a ball of fire into the sea about five miles from the Fleet. We saw it all on that bright, sunny Sunday and probably the enemy knew nothing until they were hit because our men were flying in from the sun.

That night the squadron were the covering force while the battleships bombarded Tripoli with the carrier's planes dropping flares to illuminate the target area. On the 23rd (St. George's Day) we entered Alexandria harbour, our squadron's first time back since we left on March 17th during which period we had ferried troops to Crete and Greece, covered convoys to Malta, taken part in the Battle of Matapan (as it had become known), been under air-attack many times and very nearly been blasted out of Piraeus. Now — we learned from people who had been in harbour all that time that *Ajax* had four times been reported 'sunk'.

In Greece our troops were being steadily driven back by the Germans and as it was St. George's Day we were somewhat anticipating a call for a Patriotic Epic — a Feat of Arms to help stem the retreat — but we remained at anchor for three days to see units of the Greek Navy steam into harbour having evacuated their home base. The 3-funnelled cruiser *Giorgis Averof* with destroyers and submarines moored astern of *Ajax* and we wondered what was happening. We were working all hours on maintenance and repairs until the morning of Saturday, 26th when we left harbour, oiled at Suda on Sunday and learned that all troops were to be evacuated from Greece. Many ships were engaged, cruisers and destroyers ranging up the coast to rescue the rearguard which was fighting a delaying action to allow the bridge over the Corinth Canal to be destroyed but German paratroopers had forestalled them so they had to go north again. *Ajax*, with the destroyers *Kingston, Kimbereley* and *Havock* went to Raphtis, a tiny place 25-miles N.E. of Athens, after midnight and in pitch darkness with enemy troops barely three miles away, *Ajax* picked up 2,560 soldiers — Australian, New Zealanders, British and Greeks, and three women in battledress; the destroyers embarked about 600-men each and we all left at 4 a.m. to steam at full speed and disembark the troops at Suda at 10 a.m. and all four ships sailed again for Greece that same evening. Having brought out the 'rearguard' we had assumed the operation had been completed in one night so were rather surprised — and a little shocked to learn we were on a more difficult mission as, under cover of darkness we again dashed northwards to another tiny place, Monemvasia, collecting a variety of troops (after they had set fire to the equipment and stores they had to abandon), and then cruised slowly around several small islands picking up odd groups here and there — the destroyers continually coming alongside silently in the blackness to transfer their human cargo and then just drift away to find more.

Eventually *Ajax* had on board 1,203 evacuees, men and women of many nationalities, as well as General Freyberg of the N.Z. Forces, and Rear-Admiral Baillie-Grohman of the H.Q. Staff. One destroyer entered a small bay in her search for stragglers and was fired on by a German battery. She withdrew at full speed — astern! It would have been extremely foolish for her to have returned fire and perhaps let the enemy know exactly what was afoot — a handful of small ships packed with thousands of troops! What havoc could have been wrought by the dive-bombers when daylight came!

Our small force arrived safely back in Suda Bay at 8 a.m. and found it to be full of ships — cruisers, destroyers, sloops, troop-transports and supply-ships — and *Ajax* went alongside a transport to transfer 800 passengers, keeping the remainder on board and at 1 p.m. all ships steamed out on a course which took us along the northern shores of Crete towards the enemy-held islands of Scarpanto and Rhodes, the cruisers and destroyers guarding and 'shepherding' the flock (Yes, it was very similar to a "Sheepdog Trial") — the convoy only making about 8-knots with the escorts continually circling it at 25 – 28-knots, wanting no stragglers and wanting all to pass through the Kaso Strait during darkness and be well clear of the whole area by dawn.

About 11.30 p.m. there was gunfire on the far side of the convoy! Were "E" boats out from Scarpanto? We dashed round behind to investigate and a torpedo missed us by a few yards! It all happened when a destroyer on the port flank mistook a small island for a ship and had opened fire when it failed to respond to a recognition signal, then, spotting our luminous wake had loosed a torpedo at us — luckily only one!

The Fleet was there to protect us at dawn and *Ajax* was told to proceed independently (at 29-knots) to Alexandria to land our distinguished passengers and the remaining troops that same night. The other ships arrived safely the following day and all stayed in harbour until May 6th — mainly because enemy planes dropped mines inside and outside the harbour every night. A path was swept on the 6th for the whole Fleet to exit and when clear *Ajax* with the destroyers *Havock*, *Hotspur* and *Imperial* went ahead at 30-knots as a scouting force. There was a hot desert wind, damp and full of sand which was carried into every nook and cranny in the ship and found its way into our food and drink — and eyes. Everything was gritty.

Our sprint ahead — whatever its reason — ended the following morning when we turned back to meet the main body and found it had gathered a number of merchant ships and all were steaming westwards. We took up station and remained until late afternoon when we were dispatched to investigate shipping spotted by *Formidable*'s reconnaissance planes apparently 'hedge-hopping' along the Libyan coast towards Benghazi. At 1 a.m. on May 8th two vessels of about 8,000-tons were picked up as they were about to enter harbour and both blazed furiously when hit by our first few shells. Our destroyers ignored them, passing them in the glare to put a few salvoes into the port installations at close range. One of the enemy ships suddenly blew up and by the light of the flames from the other a motor-lorry was seen to sail about 80-feet over the top of our mast. When both ships had sunk the only lights were the blazing buildings on the dockside and we withdrew. Dawn broke with rain and thick mist so we were safe from any retaliation from the air and we overtook the others in the late afternoon as they were nearing Malta, in the vicinity of which a 'change-over' of convoys would be effected, so after dark we were dispersed to patrol to the north and the shore-line of Sicily. All was quiet in the Middle Watch as the ship ambled along at about 8-knots when just after 2 a.m. we heard two distinct 'whirrs' in rapid succession beneath our feet, followed some seconds later by two explosive thuds simultaneous with our telegraphs ringing "Full Ahead" and in a very short time we were doing 34-knots — away from whatever may have threatened — and rejoined the Fleet and new convoy now steaming eastwards. (It was generally assumed that our noises-in-the-night emanated from torpedoes aimed at us but set to run too deep and had exploded when they hit the rocky shore).

Before we closed up at Dusk Action in the Dog Watches I went on deck for a breather and it was very re-assuring to see *Formidable*'s fighters circling the skies above like Guardian Angels. The night passed peacefully and the next afternoon our squadron, with destroyers, was sent forward probably because of the proximity of enemy bases now set up in Greece and we had barely lost sight of the others over the horizon behind us at dusk when we were attacked by a squadron of dive-bombers for the last half-hour of daylight. Their bombs fell close but I think finding us had been a surprise and a bonus as their prime target had been the convoy which the carrier's planes had defended so ably (we later learned that several Stukas were destroyed without loss on our side) and the Fleet's guns had also wrought havoc that the enemy decided to 'call it a day' and go home. Fleet and convoy arrived safely at Alexandria on Monday and I decided to go ashore for a meal and a walk — landing by the 4.30 p.m. boat and returning at 10.30 comfortably tired and ready for sleeping in my hammock only to find the ship under "Sailing Orders" and I had to pick up the Middle Watch.

We left harbour at 1.15 a.m. wondering "Where now?" — in company with the Australian cruiser *Perth* and three destroyers, the first part of the day being uneventful and the real fun coming when we went down on the Afternoon Watch. "Repel Aircraft" sounded at 1 o'clock and from then on we had no idea of what was happening up top for more than an hour of frantic movements of telegraphs and revolution indicators, the ship weaving and slewing, stopping and starting. Word came down to us that squadrons of Italian high-level bombers were raining their cargoes everywhere. Miraculously none of the ships were hit but we knew we could expect further attacks before the day ended and sure enough at dusk we became the target of 13 German dive-bombers. They seemed to have changed tactics now by concentrating on one ship at a time and as they came at us every gun in the ship was brought to bear on the diving planes. The first blast from our 6″ guns fragmented one plane and its load to crash into the sea as we sped past. The others released bombs and then climbed to turn and swoop onto *Perth* and as she was engaging them on her starboard side our starboard gunners spotted a Stuka diving towards her port side and concentrated their Bofors and multiple pom-poms' fire at it, causing it to crash within a few yards of her side. The action lasted about

162

30-minutes with no hits or casualties on our side (but several near-misses) and definitely two enemy shot down, others seemingly hit and faltering as they departed. *Perth* signalled "Thanks, *Ajax*!"

We could relax a little now it was dark and were given a brief outline of our night's task. R.A.F. planes were to bomb installations at Derna and would then indicate and pin-point a special target for the two cruisers to plaster. But —

As we approached the port at 28-knots we could see the flares and the exploding bombs, the flashes of A.A. fire and the 'flaming onions' but we waited in vain for the R.A.F. spotter-plane to signal our exact target. We lay off while the destroyers took advantage of the lighting effects to enter the harbour and sink a large oil-tanker, then put a few 4″ shells into the burning warehouses and workshops before we all withdrew at 2.30 a.m. to distance ourselves from the scene at top speed. Torpedo-bombers found us at 10 a.m. and another frenetic Forenoon Watch followed but our luck held and after they had discharged their 'fish' there were no further attacks and we arrived in Alex at 2 a.m. May 15th.

Saturday, 17th and another trip ashore, landing by the 1.30 p.m. boat to visit the new and recently opened Chief and Petty Officers Club, finding a very comfortable and relaxing establishment where one could get a cooling drink and a good meal and be away from ship-noises for a while. Then comes the worst part of a run ashore — the return trip to the ship! All boats embarked their liberty-men at the one landing-stage at the same time so there were hundreds of men in varying conditions of 'wear and tear' waiting in the black-out for their ship's boat to come alongside. As each boat comes in there is a surge forward to find out whose it is (Usually not yours!) and someone in the crowd yells, "*Ajax*?" — (Is it *Ajax's* boat?). All Ajaxes then scramble and push their way through under the impression it was the Patrol Chief who had called the name, meaning it was "*Ajax* boat alongside". The men clamber over the gunnels of the launch until the Cox'n, by the light of a dim torch realises they are all strangers to him and says, "No, — this is *Orion*" — or *Dido*" — or any one of the cruisers, mine-layers, battleships or 'carriers lying in the harbour. So there is an about-turn by those Ajaxes who have boarded the launch and a struggle against the incoming tide of others whose boat it could be. Eventually things get sorted out and hopefully everyone manages to get 'home'.

Sunday, May 18th. We were boiler-cleaning when the orders came — "Proceed to sea at once!" The job was abandoned and the boilers hurriedly closed and the next night found us patrolling in the Aegean north of Crete as it was thought the Germans might attempt a sea-borne landing on the island. We remained at Action Stations all that night and the next with no signs of enemy activity so we withdrew, and it was then that the excitement began. Waves of dive-bombers came out to attack — in groups of six, one group after another — and we were near-missed several times while the destroyer *Juno* in close proximity received a direct hit and sank. We dare not stop to pick up survivors; we had to keep moving — fast — to dodge the Stukas and their deadly cargoes. (A destroyer did return to the area after dark to look for any boats, rafts or individuals but I do not know if any were found.)

The last attack of the day came at dusk with just four Stukas and *Ajax'* gunners were given the credit — and satisfaction — for shooting down three of them.

For the whole of that day it had been impossible for any sort of routine to be kept. Watches were changed as and when there might be a short lull in attacks. It had been chaotic and very wearing, and then in pitch blackness at 11.30 we ran into the middle of an enemy troop convoy north of Crete. It was being escorted by a destroyer and several torpedo-boats and consisted of troop- and stores-transports, and a large number of caiques (large Greek fishing boats) tightly packed with fully-accoutred German troops. Our force consisted of *Ajax, Orion, Dido,* and four destroyers. Fire opened at 11.38 p.m. and our watch had been below since 8 p.m. but no chance of being relieved until the end of yet another hectic period of "Full Ahead's — Stops and Full Astern's" on port and starboard engines, singly, together or against one another as the ship avoided torpedoes. There was a crash and a jolt as we rammed something and the telegraphs went to "Full Astern Both", together with a telephoned message from the bridge — "Give it all you've got!" as every gun in the ship was firing — 6″ — 4″ A.A. — mutliple pom-poms, Maxim and Lewis-guns — (and from what I heard later — rifles and revolvers were included.) The enemy destroyer was sunk by the first shots and two of the larger transports set afire, their flames illuminating the scene for our ships to carve a way through the mass of caiques, ramming and raking them with small-arms fire and even using the bigger guns at their maximum declination to blast the enemy out of the water, some carrying stocks of ammunitions being blown sky-high. None escaped and it was estimated that more than 4,000 were accounted for by the time the action ended at 1 a.m. Then the watches could be relieved and I went to my Forward Repair Party where the shipwrights were shoring-up a 'sprung' bulkhead. Dawn Action sounded at 5 a.m. and the air-attacks began as soon as there was sufficient daylight for the planes to see us — heading through the Kaso Strait with a 30-feet length of heavy timber from the caique we had rammed during the action still stuck firmly across our bows and sending up a magnificent 'wall' of water. It could not be dislodged. A lull enabled watches to change again at 8.30 and I was in the engine-room before the attacks resumed with even greater ferocity and continued until after ten o'clock, during which time the destroyer *Greyhound* and two cruisers —

Fiji and *Gloucester* — had been sunk by the dive-bombers. They had spent the night in another search area and were withdrawing with us.

The attacks eased off until just one Stuka would come out, either to try to become a hero or else to see if we had any ammunition left to shoot with. The baulk of timber had vanished but our bows were twisted almost as badly as when *Naiad* bumped us in Scapa Flow and we were running low on fuel and ammunition. At dusk we (*Ajax*) and the destroyers *Kandahar* and *Kingston* were told to return to the area where the other ships had sunk to look for survivors. We picked up several hundreds and when it was felt there were no more we left at 30-knots to arrive in Alex at 8 o'clock next morning. Survivors were landed, we oiled, and then ammunition-lighters came to both sides of the ship for the seamen to work like slaves to fill the magazines and lockers before dark.

"Repel Aircraft" sounded at 5.15 next morning (May 24th) with a very heavy raid on the harbour. My station was Forward Engine-room and as the Watch was complete I was told, "Be ready to leave harbour at eight o'clock", and that night found us again passing through the Kaso Strait in another effort to stop sea-borne re-inforcements from Greece getting to Crete or Rhodes. (German parachutists had already landed in considerable numbers in both places).

We saw nothing during the night and withdrew through the Strait at 5.30 a.m. just as the Chief of the Watch in the engine-room collapsed. I was called to replace him until 8 o'clock and then had to carry-on and stay down for my own Forenoon Watch as wave upon wave of Stukas came out to attack, diving and zooming while we and the other ships weaved and writhed, dodging the rain of bombs with all guns firing the whole time.

Things quietened towards the end of the Watch and just before our reliefs came down at noon the Captain (E.D.B. McCarthy) addressed the ship's company over the Tannoy saying that *Ajax* with two destroyers had a very dangerous mission that night. He said we were to pass through Kaso Strait after dark and proceed to bombard the airfields at Heraklion and Maleme. "We will not be able to get clear of the island before dawn and can therefore expect much heavier attacks than any so far experienced. I want to thank all of you for the way you have fought the ship and played your part in serving me so well. Good luck and God bless!" Perhaps it would have been better if he had not spoken — to have let matters take their course, for we had already taken practically everything (and anything else) the Germans could throw at us by day or night. On the other hand we did appreciate having some idea of where we were going and what to expect when we got there but, in the event we passed through the Strait and went to full Action Stations at 11 p.m. only for the weather to deteriorate so quickly that visibility became virtually nil and the mounting seas made it impossible for the destroyers to keep with us — and

German parachutists over Crete, May 1941.

German parachutists — ready to leave Greece for Crete invasion. (negative and camera taken from German at Crete). 1941.

apparently we needed them for the mission to be a success. The operation was aborted and it was with mixed feelings that we heard the news. Thankfulness that we could relax and disappointment that we had not carried out our assigned task — especially as we were emotionally keyed up. Now we had to see what the dawn held. Would visibility remain poor enough for us to clear Kaso before the Stukas found us?

Dawn Action — Skies fairly clear and no sign of enemy planes as the three ships sped on. Then, later in the forenoon came the welcome sight of *Formidable* and the battleships *Queen Elizabeth* and *Barham* with other ships, and it was then that the enemy decided to strike. Wave after wave of dive-bombers swooped down at all angles, concentrating mainly on the carrier with the occasional side-swipe at the battle-wagons and the rest of us, continuing all afternoon. *Formidable* was hit on her bows and *Barham* on her stern both by 1,000 lb. bombs and there were near-misses on the rest of us but considering the ferocity of the attack damage and casualties were relatively light. All arrived back in Alex at 11 a.m. on May 27th and topped up with fuel and ammunition.

The Commander-in-Chief, Admiral Sir Andrew B. Cunningham, came on board to speak to us, his message being "Don't worry about air-attacks as only one of a thousand bombs hits its target," (and that was just two days after *Gloucester*, *Fiji*, *Kashmir* and *Kelly* had been sunk by bombs!) and "Don't play the Germans' game because we must hold Crete at all costs!" WE MUST HOLD CRETE — — So, at six o'clock next morning we left harbour thinking we were to cover a landing by our troops on the island. Instead we were to take them OFF! Our force of cruisers and destroyers was doing 25-knots when at 5 p.m. there came an attack by what seemed to be hundreds of bombers. They came from all angles in an onslaught lasting an hour and it was almost dark when it became quiet and we thought "That's the last for tonight" and were able to change watches. I and my crowd went to the Forward Engine-room for the Last Dog Watch just as another wave of Stukas arrived on scene. A 1,000 lb bomb dropped close on our port side causing considerable damage and almost lifting us out of the water. Torpedo-bombers joined the attack at the same time as did Italian high-level bombers and we had more near-misses. (I learned later that we had been narrowly missed by two aerial torpedoes and that one had actually passed beneath us.)

It was after nine o'clock when it became a bit quieter and we received a very surprising telephone message from the bridge — "We are returning to Alexandria. Maximum available speed, please!" and at 10.30 p.m. we could change watches again. Our 2-hour Last Dog had lasted 4½-hours. I went forward to relieve Frank Pearce at our Repair station before he could proceed to Magazine Flooding position, and we were exchanging our notes on 'current state' when he said, "Poor old Ben's gone!" I did not grasp the significance of his remark and said, "Gone where?" His reply was, "He's dead!" The full story was that the Germans were dropping anti-personnel bombs containing shrapnel some of which had exploded close alongside and perforated the ship's side-plating. By the break of th fo'c'sle we were carrying two "Invasion Craft" (re-named "Evacuation Boats" by the 'lads') both fully fueled, so while we were at Action an E.R.A. and two stokers had to be at hand with fire-fighting equipment. The job had fallen to Ben Foord, E.R.A. 4th Class, a quiet and pleasant young chap who had married a few days before joining the ship in June, 1940. Ben together with 3 stokers and a seaman had been killed instantly and a fire started in the Shelter deck.

Another of the bombs had peppered the ship's side by the Stokers Mess Deck and all the men in the Repair Party on that side of the deck had suffered leg injuries in varying degrees. A stoker who had both legs shot away was being tended on a mess-table by Medical Staff but they could not save him and he died soon after I had taken over from Frank. Mostly the Repair Party sat on that side of the deck and during the afternoon I had been sitting there talking to the Leading Stoker — discussing music — and when C.E.R.A. Ken Wingrove relieved me at 4 p.m. (to go to my Magazine Flooding position) we arranged to continue our conversation when I returned at 8 p.m. after my Last Dog Watch in the engine-room. Sadly though, I did not return until 10.30 and by then he was being operated on to remove a ton of shrapnel from both legs and regrettably he died in hospital in Alexandria shortly after we arrived back. Ken sat in the seat I vacated at 4 o'clock and he later told me that about five minutes before the 'fatal' bomb fell he — for no reason — had walked to the other side of the deck. Fate? Guardian Angel?

Six bodies were buried at sea next morning and 26 seriously wounded men were whisked away to hospital on our arrival in Alex where our feelings were very mixed — thankful to be safely in harbour but — had we let the side down? Of the 'force', comprising *Ajax*, *Orion* and *Perth* and three destroyers, the Germans had concentrated their fiercest assault upon *Ajax* with the result that, apart from damage, we had expended virtually every bit of ammunition and would have been a 'sitting duck' target had we remained to take part in the evacuation of troops from Crete, a suicidal act.

Phoebe and *Dido* — the latter cruiser had arrived on the station just a week earlier — and three other destroyers had gone to another part of the island to pick up troops. We waited anxiously for all to return safely and our entire ship's company were on deck when they came in that evening — and what a fearful and tragic sight it was.

They had rescued thousands of soldiers and had then been under attack from first light by hundreds of high-level- and dive-bombers. *Orion* had received two direct hits, one 1,000 lb. bomb going down her funnel and exploding in the boiler-room killing hundreds of her crew and passengers. *Perth* had a 1,000 lb. bomb go through her decks which were packed with troops and casualties were horrific. *Dido* had one of her five turrets lifted bodily out of the ship by another direct hit — ("Only one of a thousand bombs hits its target" he said!). Two of the destroyers — *Imperial* and *Hereward* — which had been in our group had been sunk — by direct hits, and every ship had casualties and damage from near-misses. It had been a terrible two-weeks in which hundreds of men had been killed or injured and many good ships sunk or damaged.

On Saturday, May 31st all ships in harbour 'cheered' *Dido* out as she departed to be repaired in the U.S.A. and that evening I hied myself ashore for a walk and a meal. The first was easy, the second impossible because absolutely everyone who was not Duty Watch on board a ship had come ashore. The town was teeming with hungry sailors and every eating-place had a long queue; the Club had the longest queue of them all so my only option was to catch an early boat back to the ship — and arrive on board just as an air-raid started and then be tied to my station until the "All Clear" at 1 a.m. (which was probably better than being ashore because while the raid was in progress there was no movement of ships' boats allowed in the harbour and all those who were ashore had to wait in the vicinity of the pier in the darkness.)

We remained in harbour all the week — ostensibly to 'rest' but it was an opportunity to carry out maintenance work and a long-overdue boiler-clean. (We had been six-weeks overdue in mid-May but when permission was sought for "up to 48-hours to clean boilers" the C. in C's response was — "This is no time for any ship to be broken down!")

During this rest period more than a hundred men reported 'sick' and were referred to hospital suffering from 'mental stress' as the result of constant gunfire, bomb-blasts and lack of sleep. Those who left did not return, replacements being drawn from the Base 'pool' or from ships undergoing repair and the Captain addressed the ship's company on the quarterdeck thanking again everybody for the way they had stood by him and played their part in the actions of the past "gruelling fortnight" — (his words) — and saying that it had been a "harrowing time" for everyone.

Air-raids were a regular nightly occurrence to remind us that the war was still with us, one raid during the week costing the lives of more than a hundred people in the dock area and landing stage.

CHAPTER 15

Syria and Palestine

On Saturday, June 7th we were dispatched in company with *Phoebe* and *Coventry*, (anti-aircraft cruiser) and a number of destroyers to forestall any attempt by the enemy, with the help of Vichy French forces, to reach the Suez Canal through Syrian territory. We were to support a small number of troops which were operating on shore and a day later our ships were spaced out along that coast. Enemy planes did not take long to find us and two boats — *Isis* and *Janus* — were near-missed and suffered minor damage but we were able to call on R.A.F. planes from an Egyptian land base to scare the predators off. On Monday the same two destroyers came into contact with Vichy French destroyers out from Beirut and in the skirmish that ensued *Janus* was hit and badly damaged but by the time we reached the scene the Vichy boats had vanished. I do not know what their shells were filled with but *Janus'* side and upper works were splashed with all colours of a rainbow. She was taken in tow by one of the other boats and we escorted both to Haifa and then anchored for the night — and entertained some surprise guests. A number of soldiers — survivors of a larger group which had been put ashore at night near Tyre but on the wrong side of the Litani River — had lost all their equipment and supplies, so we gave them supper and accommodation for the night. They went off to a transit camp at dawn when the ship moved north again after a long night of enemy air activity against the Oil Storage Depot at Haifa.

Later in the day our destroyers went close in-shore to shell Vichy positions while we stood-off to fire at the same targets and protect the boats from any seaward attack.

Before I went below for the First Watch I went to the lower bridge and borrowed binoculars to see what was going on, and what I witnessed was almost funny. An armoured car was speeding northward on the coast-road dodging the destroyers' 4" shells which fell just behind it and then passed a long, barn-like building. The destroyers' guns crews waited for the car to emerge; it didn't, so the guns demolished the 'barn' with one salvo and the car went scuttling on like a scared rabbit with more 4" shells falling behind and ahead — but never 'on' it. Then a stone wall maybe about a hundred yards long obscured the 'target' and our 6" guns were brought to bear to systematically destroy the wall and the car (most probably) for it was not seen again.

Two more days were spent bombarding bits of the coastline — doing some good for somebody I suppose — and on June 12th we were back in

Haifa. Surprisingly shore leave was given from 4.30 p.m until 8 p.m. but very few men were interested, and the next day our little group was relieved by another force of cruisers and destroyers and we returned to Alex on the 14th.

The enemy had maintained their nightly attacks on the harbour during our short absence by dropping mines and a day or two before our re-entry one of *Illustrious'* motor boats had over-run one, killing all the crew. And two days later it was discovered that *we* were almost sitting on top of one and had to be gently towed clear for it to be detonated. (*Illustrious* had completed her repairs in U.S.A. and returned to take *Formidable's* place.)

The weather was hot now and we began a routine of working from 7 a.m. until 12.30 p.m. when the men could go ashore — (provided they were not Duty Watch or the ship was Duty Cruiser and ready for sea at short notice) — all leave expiring at 10.30 p.m. so it was nice to have the occasional afternoon ashore for a walk and to see something different — such as Nouzha Park and Zoological Gardens with their beautiful flowers and trees and a wide variety of birds, reptiles and animals, including an elephant which was very adept at collecting money by using its trunk to take coins — ever so gently — from the outstretched palms of visitors while its keeper was even more adept at transferring the coins to his pocket.

The new club in Alexandria was a boon and a blessing for chiefs and petty officers, comfortable and relaxing, where a four-course dinner cost 11-piastres (two shillings and ninepence). Then back to the ship and the prospect of being at one's 'Repel Aircraft' station for most of the night. The usual pattern was for the alarms to be sounded at 3 a.m. and the raiding would continue until about 5 o'clock but the terrific barrage put up by all ships in the harbour kept the raiders too high for any precision bombing although bombs did fall close to ships and the Floating Dock. But those that fell on shore in the poorer-class districts round the docks devastated vast numbers of the lath, plaster and mud houses.

One of the main conversations during this period was: "Do you think we shall be going home soon?" Rumours had begun to circulate soon after our bows were damaged when we rammed the caique and had increased after every near-miss we sustained and each time a new cruiser arrived on the Station it was "Our relief!" — but usually as soon as it joined the squadron either it or another unit would be sunk or badly damaged and have to go away for repair. So — we were still 'operational and going strong' with our bows still buckled and twisted and forward compartments flooding every time we went to sea, yet still capable of knocking up 35-knots in emergency. When *Orion* left for repair we took over as flagship while waiting for *Arethusa* to come through from Gib, but she was damaged by German aircraft before reaching Malta, so docked there and we waited for the next rumour.

171

July 3rd — At 1 a.m. we left harbour and steamed at 27-knots to Haifa to relieve the force which had taken our place two weeks earlier and for the next four days we bombarded Vichy positions south of Beirut, returning to Haifa on Monday night and to a very heavy enemy air attack during which magnetic mines were dropped into the harbour. Two mines fell too close to the anti-aircraft cruiser *Carlisle* and her whole company had to vacate their ship and spend the night on the breakwater.

In the morning a tow-line was attached and she was slipped from her buoy to be inched gently clear. The mines were then blown up and her crew could return. We remained at sea the following night (to dodge any raid?) and when we came back at 7.30 a.m. our Chaplain organized an afternoon motor-trip to Nazareth for some sixty men.

Landing at 2 p.m. we boarded small buses and were soon clear of the town and rolling hills and passing through Arab and Jewish villages — really communal farms where a number of families or individuals banded together to work the land, build their houses, every member producing for the benefit of all. One could easily tell the difference between the two nationalities, the Arab districts and dwellings being straggling and shabby, the Jewish orderly, neat and clean.

Corn-threshing was in progress and being done in exactly the same manner as it had over the past two-thousand years — the stalks being strewn over a large circular patch of ground with a horse or mule tethered to a stake in the centre and being driven round and round all day long, trailing a wide, flat piece of wood (the 'thresher') on which the driver stood while other members of the commune stood round the circumference of the 'ring' and used long-handled scoops to push more corn under the thresher.

The Chaplain halted the buses on a hill about 20-miles from Haifa to point to the Plain of Jezreel, a vast green and fertile valley stretching for miles between the hills where Christ had fed the multitude, and also to the distant Mount Tabor — the scene of the Transfiguration. We reached Nazareth at 4 p.m. expecting it to be a small 'modernised' town instead of the small dusty village of straggling narrow streets perched on a hill-side with a few camels and donkeys roaming about, and we realised we were looking at a Nazareth almost unchanged over 1941-years (except for the small cinema which now adorned "The Street".)

Alighting from the buses we visited the Church of St. Mary and the Annunciation built over Mary's Well where she was visited by the Angel Gabriel, and drank water from the Well. The church was small, very quaint and dark with many altars of various denominations — so many in fact that there was little room for any worshippers.

We meandered through narrow cobbled streets of shops — shops which were really just the open fronts of houses and in one such street the upper storeys almost met overhead to turn it into a tunnel. The shops themselves were only about six-feet square with their souvenir wares displayed on domestic tables, chairs and hung on walls.

At the end of the 'tunnel' was the Synagogue where Christ had preached — small — but more roomy than the Church of St. Mary — and its original walls were still standing.

Boarding our buses at 5.30 we thought our outing was more or less over but while we were waiting the Chaplain had telephoned the ship and obtained an extention of leave until 7.30 p.m.

The buses sped along the road through the evening scene of workers homing from the fields and olive-groves with their horses, mules and cattle. War was a million miles away.

Then the buses suddenly turned onto a secondary track for a couple of miles and we came to a Jewish Community Training Centre, a model farm being run entirely by girls of many nationalities and mostly refugees from the Nazis. The girls receive a 2-year Course in Botany, Agriculture, and Domestic Science to fit them for their part in the national life and can then form themselves into small groups on farms or marry and be given their own little plot, the training ensuring their becoming good citizens. There had been little prior knowledge of our arrival but we were warmly welcomed by the Matron who showed us round the remarkably clean place. Each of the girls had her own room with a single bed, easy chair, writing desk and book-shelf, and the privilege of choosing her own decorations, books and pictures. There were Studies and a Main Dining-room, a Reading-room and a special room for Sewing, but the girls themselves were presently engaged in their evening duties with the animals and while we were in the Dairy they actually brought in huge churns of fresh milk to tip into the Separators, a cooling-plant keeping it fresh until the morning when it would be sent in to Haifa.

We were in the cheese-making room and I was speaking with the Matron when the Chaplain said we ought to be going so I asked Matron if I might purchase one of the mature cheeses from the shelf. She told me to choose any one I would like and I picked a small white and creamy 'round' weighing about a pound which she wrapped in a white cloth and presented to me as a gift, refusing any payment. (I shared it with the Mess — most of them vowing they would definitely buy a cheese should another opportunity to visit Nazareth arise.)

Now comes the sorry part. We arrived back at the jetty to find *Ajax* ready for sea — urgently — and all had to sprint the last 100-yards 'in ten-seconds flat' but men on one of the buses had acquired bottles of wine in Nazareth and consumed the liquor on the way back with the result that they had to be assisted along the jetty under the steely gaze of the Captain on the bridge and the Commander and O.O.D. on the quarterdeck. Result

— "Should there be any further visits to Nazareth they will be 'straight there' and 'straight back'."

Next day, Saturday, July 12th an Armistice was signed in Syria and we expected to leave the area and rejoin the Fleet. Instead we did some more patrolling and were back alongside in Haifa again on Monday.

After another night-patrol along the coast we left Haifa on July 22nd to join the Fleet on a westward sweep and were soon at Action Stations when enemy aircraft found us. Fortunately we had the umbrella of *Illustrious'* fighters for protection, forcing them to keep their distance and a few days later we were back in harbour when it was felt that our bows should be repaired. On the 29th *Ajax* went into the Floating Dock for our stem-piece to be straightened, some side-plates and internal bulkheads renewed and were in the dock for ten broiling days. The normal temperatures in Alex were above 100 degrees and in the dock there was no air circulation. It was stifling and we had a heavy work-load in the engineering department, everybody working late each night to get the daily jobs closed up lest the dock had to be flooded or should be damaged during the nightly raids. In one such raid bombs fell close and magnetic- and acoustic-mines were dropped, and a day or so later a motor launch was blown up and all aboard were killed. The victims were French seamen from units of their navy (4-cruisers, a battleship, 3-destroyers and a large submarine) which had been in the harbour when France fell and had opted to join the Vichy Government side, so had been immobilized by our forces.

We became operational on August 20th when we left harbour with another ship of the squadron on what was to become known as the "Tobruk Run" — a sustained operation of support and relief for our besieged troops in Tobruk. Our task was to guard three destroyers and a fast mine-layer carrying men, stores and equipment to the garrison and bring out any casualties and relieved men and the importance of our mission merited an R.A.F. fighter escort during daylight hours from our time of leaving Alex at 0830 — to protect us from air attack and warn of any U-boats in the offing. We zig-zagged westward at speed to arrive off Tobruk at 11 p.m. and the relieving ships entered the harbour to effect the change-over — all in total darkness — while the cruisers stood guard outside until completion at 2 a.m. when we all withdrew far from the coast before turning eastward for Alex.

On this (our) first "Run" the R.A.F. were either late in arriving or the Stukas were early, for the dive-bombers got to us first and scored a 'near-miss' on the destroyer *Nizam* and reduced her speed — an injury which could have had calamitous results had not our tardy escort appeared to save the day and shoot down five of the enemy without loss to themselves. The only consequence being that we were six-hours late getting back with our lame duck.

174

A regular shuttle-service was being run between Alex and Tobruk with the other two ships of the squadron operating with a similar relief force and it could have been almost a 'published' time-table. We wondered how long it would take Jerry to work it out. Not long! For as we came back from our third run on August 27th we received an emergency call to proceed 'with dispatch' to stand by the cruiser *Phoebe* which had been torpedoed off Tobruk while on *her* run. Lucky for her she had been hit in the bows and was not in imminent danger of sinking and could move under her own steam and did not require our assistance. Our 'shuttle' party therefore kept to the 'time-table' and left for Tobruk at 8.30 in the morning and then for most of the day were subjected to very heavy attacks. Our signalmen and gunners told later of the many dog-fights which took place during the day — and even after dark the enemy planes came looking and dropping flares but we held our fire and kept quiet until our 'charges' came out from Tobruk and then belted back to Alex at 29-knots on August 29th.

When we returned from an uneventful Tobruk Run on Sept. 15th an R.A.F. plane towing a target-sleeve came out to meet us so that we could have some shooting practice! and the next afternoon *Ajax* left harbour in company with the Australian-manned cruiser *Hobart* to arrive in Beirut on the afternoon of the 18th. Why? Both ships berthed alongside and next morning *Ajax* embarked 800 troops (I suppose *Hobart* embarked a like number) who had just come down from a place called Homs. They said they had been given only a few minutes notice to "Pack up and go" that very morning and had abandoned stores, equipment and vehicles to the value of more than £3 million in the desert. We asked the soldiers where they thought they were going now — because we wanted to know where WE were going — but they had no idea and hoped "Not Tobruk! We've had some of that." We sailed at noon and disembarked then at Alexandria at 6.30 next morning — then we did another incident-free Tobruk Run followed by a jaunt with the Fleet to cover a large convoy through to Malta and another back to Alex and Port Said. I've called it a 'jaunt' because things seemed to be quiet all round — very few raids and little opposition — and back in harbour all ships' companies received their monthly pay at the end of September so that the town was packed every evening, with bars, restaurants and cinemas all showing "House Full" signs. It was not very pleasant amongst the milling crowds — just a case of an hour's 'exercise walk' and an early boat back, but there was compensation when we were visited by an ENSA Concert Party. Just seven members — two male and five female — and a really enjoyable treat. There were also two different films shown on board during that week. Then — October 10th the quiet spell ended when the Fleet went to sea for a westward sweep and we were met by scores of dive-bombers in a prolonged attack. Our carrier's planes were airborne and circling us while all ships put up an 'umbrella barrage' and rumours spread that the Italian Fleet was at sea. With darkness the attacks ceased and we assumed 2nd degree of readiness until 9.15 p.m. when the alarms sounded. "Ah! This is it." but it wasn't. A flashing light had been seen in the distant night and destroyers were sent to investigate and picked up the three-man crew of an R.A.F. bomber from their inflatable dinghy. They were based in Malta but their next landing would be in Alexandria and we were on our way back with no signs of attacks — just steady steaming until in the middle of the Afternoon Watch we got — "Emergency! Full Ahead." Throttles were flung wide open and the helm went hard over with the ship heeling heavily to starboard as we hung on to valves and pipes to prevent us being catapulted over the top of the distilling plant. Scare tactics! Torpedo-bombers had swooped out of the sky and released their missiles before anyone in the Fleet was even aware of their presence. No ships were hit but it had been a narrow escape and was generally assumed that the look-outs must have been asleep — a verdict, apparently, of the C. in C. too, for "Because of this laxity all ships will remain at sea overnight instead of entering harbour," — a signal which enhanced our opinions that the Italians *were* at sea, and further enhanced when, during Dawn Action "Repel Aircraft" was sounded and the guns of the Fleet started firing. More excitement! But only a few rounds were fired before news filtered down to us that it was meant to scare off a reconnaissance plane watching from a distance, but just before noon there was near catastrophe as three of our own planes came flying in low towards the Fleet. The battleship *Queen Elizabeth* and the cruiser *Galatea* opened fire with our ship being sandwiched between them and their target and there was great danger of our bridge and funnel and general upperworks beng shot away before identity of the aircraft was established. It was another narrow escape, perhaps understandable in the circumstances with the guns' crews being slightly trigger-happy after the previous day's lapse.

In harbour that evening *Ajax* was allocated a film (The Santa Fe Trail) for two-nights showing on board, which was all very nice except that up until a week or so ago we had been in the fortunate position of having two projectors enabling us to enjoy 'continuous film', but during our previous sojourn in harbour we had to pass one of them to the fast mine-layer *Latona*. It happened because our Chief Electrical Artificer had been one of the men sent to hospital suffering with stress after Crete and when judged fit for duty had been drafted to *Latona* — which happened to be awaiting the arrival of a projector from England. He remembered our having two — (one had been a gift from Gaumont-British Film Company when they filmed on board after the River Plate action) — and made representation to the 'powers-that-be' resulting in our being ordered to hand one over to her. I suppose it would have been very churlish of us to have kept both but parting with one (we retained the G-B gift) made a difference to our 'viewing pattern' by leaving a gap between each reel. Men would wander away to their messes for a cup of tea and forget to come back!

We did another Tobruk Run on October 20th and while the destroyers went into the harbour with relief troops and supplies the Army asked us to oblige by putting a few 6″ shells into some enemy positions which had been annoying them. We did — and three days later we were sent along to bombard the German Depot and Tank Repair Workshops at Bardia in daylight. A nearby shore battery replied but their shells fell short, so about 2 o'clock in the morning we moved quite close in-shore and when *we* opened fire their retaliatory shells passed well above us but *our* gunners were able to pin-point the enemy gun emplacements and a few 6″ salvoes effectively silenced them.

At the same time just along the coast *Latona* was engaged in a routine Tobruk Run when she was hit by a bomb and had to be abandoned — and was then sunk by our own forces as she could not be saved. Our projector went down with her.

When we arrived back in harbour a two-feet diameter steam-pipe manifold was leaking steam into the boiler-room and I was put in charge of the repair work. The whole casting had cracked (probably caused by near-misses) and was too big a job to be undertaken in *Ajax*'s workshop, so with the help of a couple of stokers I took it across to the the Repair-ship *Resource* to have the necessary welding done, and then all their lathes were in use and the only other lathe big enough to accommodate the manifold for machining was in the battleship *Barham*. I obtained permission for it to go on board but they stipulated that I did all the work — that *Barham* took no responsibility.

While I was doing this, other E.R.A's were working eight-hours shifts round-the-clock surfacing the pipe-joints to the manifold on the pipe-lines in situ, and when I finished the machining and got it back to the ship everyone 'mucked in' to get us ready for sea again. The job had taken 48-hours from start to finish with virtually no sleep.

Air-raids were still regular nightly events to maintain the 'no sleep' pattern, the ploy being to come over for an hour or so at 9 p.m., then go away but come back in greater force about 2 a.m. to aggravate for a further three hours.

On November 17th *Ajax* with *Hobart* and three destroyers were assigned to bombard the Halfaya Pass area that night but when darkness came — well — it didn't come! There was a fierce storm illuminating everything for miles around, making it too risky for ships to get close to shore so there was nothing for it but return to Alex and were only a few miles from harbour when we met the Fleet and joined up for a westward sweep. It was dark enough that night for bombarding of Halfaya to be carried out by the cruisers *Naiad*, *Euryalus* and *Galatea*, and the following night all ships engaged in shelling the coastal roads between Bardia and Tobruk. It seemed that our Army had started an advance out of Egypt and intelligence had reported an enemy column moving along the coast to meet it so an R.A.F. spotter-plane located the column and obliged by dropping flares to assist the ships.

The enemy replied at dawn with a concentrated air-attack, successfully fought off by the carrier's fighters as we steamed well clear of the coast and we were back in harbour on the night of Saturday, Nov. 2nd. *Ajax* was Duty Cruiser which meant we had to keep steam to go anywhere at short notice and at 4.30 on Monday morning we had orders to intercept an Italian convoy reported by R.A.F. reconnaissance to be bound for Benghazi. We dashed off and searched for two whole days and nights without success and assumed that their reconnaissance had seen us first. We got back to harbour on Wednesday night to receive the shock news that the *Barham* had been torpedoed 'last night' while operating off Tobruk. A U-boat had penetrated the destroyer screen and its torpedo struck the battleship's magazine, causing her to blow up and sink within twenty minutes with enormous loss of life, including I suppose, many I had met in their machine-shop just recently.

CHAPTER 16

Sojourn in Malta

At 10 o'clock that same (Nov. 26th) night *Ajax* oiled and took on many tons of ammunition and a large number of torpedoes as cargo and at 4 a.m. we — just *Ajax* alone — left harbour steaming at 28-knots along to Malta. Enemy reconnaissance soon found us and sent torpedo-bombers to attack but our speed and manoeuvrability enabled us to survive all their efforts and we entered Grand Harbour early on Saturday, 29th to discharge our cargo at the Armament Store before the air-raid warning stopped all movement, and that afternoon Captain E. D. B. McCarthy said "Goodbye" to us.

"I thank every one of you for your co-operation through all the trials and tribulations, and I know you will give the same devotion to my successor. Goodbye, and God be with you all." (His successor was Captain S. L.

Bateson, whose ship *Latona* had been sunk on October 25th.) At 4 o'clock next morning we left harbour in company with the cruisers *Neptune*, *Aurora* and *Penelope* and three destroyers "to try to stop four oil-tankers from reaching the enemy in Benghazi. They're being escorted by a battleship, 3-cruisers and 9-destroyers so it shows how important they are. We expect to make contact at 7 p.m." (The general concensus was 'Old Mac' had picked the right time to leave the ship!)

During the afternoon we had a report that the R.A.F. had attacked the convoy and a little later we were attacked ourselves by two torpedo-bombers, making it obvious that the enemy knew we were looking for them. "Action Imminent" came at 5.30 p.m. and everybody was ready and waiting. We were still 'Ready and waiting' at 9 p.m. when it was reported that the enemy had split into two sections so we did likewise — *Ajax*, *Neptune* and one destroyer in one section, the other two cruisers and two destroyers in the other, each section going in an opposite direction in ever-increasing circles. *Aurora* and *Penelope* found one large tanker and a destroyer and sank both but there was no other contact made and at 4 a.m. the R.A.F. reported having damaged some ships of the convoy which had now 'gone to earth' among the Greek islands. We extended our range but eventually had to return empty-handed to Malta.

Ajax was 'booked' to go into dry dock then and I had to scout around the dockyard to locate a donkey-boiler which would connect with the ship's galley and heating system, assess the amount of flexible piping required and make the necessary adapters ready for connecting up, but each day we lit up and went to 1-hour's notice for sea with no idea why — until December 5th at 7.30 p.m. when we four cruisers and the three destroyers sailed from Grand Harbour to escort the Fleet Auxiliary — *Breconshire* on her way to Alexandria with vital supplies. Air attacks began at 1.15 next afternoon and continued non-stop until it was too dark for them to see us at 8.45 p.m. during which time it was impossible for the watches to change. At midnight we were met by units of the Fleet from Alex who took responsibility for our charge and we turned back towards Malta with the enemy resuming the attack on us at first light. I went below at 4 a.m. to take over the Morning Watch and was greeted with the news of the Japanese attack on Pearl Harbour, then had the whole of the day until after dark being bombed. There was no respite; it seemed even worse than the ordeals of the evacuations from Greece and Crete with the hectic movements of telegraphs regulating the ship's speed and direction; the violent motions as she veered and dodged and the everlasting noise of blazing guns and of bombs bursting below water — the best place for them! We had had breakfast, dinner, tea and supper (when they could be got to us) at our stations — ours the engine-room — and we were thankful for darkness. But even as we neared the island at 1.15 a.m. on Monday the air-raid sirens were wailing to signify yet another attack on Valetta, the "All Clear" sounding as we entered harbour at 3.30 a.m.

Ajax moved into dry dock but as the Yard had not known when we were returning they had not brought the donkey-boiler nor any of the equipment I had prepared for its connection, so as a matter of urgency I journeyed forth with my stokers to re-locate it and arrange towage to the dock and for a supply of coal to come alongside as the heavy rain fell all day.

Rumour spread round the ship (Who starts it?) that we would be leaving Malta as soon as we undocked because "we are officially unfit for operational duties owing to mechanical defects," and when the Paymaster called for all Egyptian currency to be handed in and exchanged for Sterling — Well (they said) it must be official! Anyway, it was nice to be using 'tanners and bobs' again instead of milliemes and piastres (ackers).

Malta was being continuously plastered with bombs by both German and Italian dive-bombers, high-level bombers, and by mine-dropping planes, making it necessary for ships' companies not actually required for duty aboard their ship at night should sleep in the shelters in the Yard — and excellent shelters they were! They were built into the solid sandstone rock giving some 50' of protection and cutting off all noise of bombs and gun-fire so that men could sleep well and safely — except for on that first night when the Maltese dockyardmen made more noise in the shelter with their incessant jabbering than there was outside. The workmen were brought into the yard every night for urgent work on the ships but whenever the sirens sounded tools were immediately 'downed' and there was the rush to the shelter — and most nights the warning came at 9.30 and remained "Red" all night, and practically the whole of that first night was taken up by the navy shouting at the workers — "Shut up!" — "Turn it down!" — "Put a sock in it!" Mutual complaints were made and the workmen were moved to another part of the shelter for the period of our docking, the 'dry' part was only for 30-hours and then we stayed there after flooding (and started another spate of rumours.) But these could be said to be warranted because — to revert to the near-misses the ship had suffered in our many brushes with the Luftwaffe, our main engines had been badly shaken and on our way back from a Tobruk Run in September a harsh roar and grating noise came from the reduction gear of one set. Opening the gear-case on arrival in Alex we found much of a tooth had broken from one pinion, had damaged other teeth on it as well as on the main wheel and the other pinion. We lifted out the worst-damaged one and had it trimmed and machined aboard *Resource* and when it was back in place the Fleet Engineer decreed that our speed should not exceed 25-knots "except in an emergency" — and we had certainly had many of those since then! A new set of gearing was ordered from home. Now that we were afloat in the graving-dock the opportunity was taken to open all four sets of gearing. All were found to be in a parlous state with cracks and our whole department worked 'round the clock' four days and nights, filing and honing (with carborundum stones) to get as near perfect a mesh as was possible, finishing on December 14th to raise steam and run a 'Trial' in the presence of top Engineers from the Yard. The verdict was — *"Ajax* is unfit for operational duties and her speed should be limited to 22-knots!"

Then came the news of the loss of *Prince Of Wales* and *Repulse*. Worse and worse!

I had my first trip ashore in Malta since 1931 and saw many bomb-craters as I passed through the Yard but most of the destruction seemed to be outside the walls where all was ruination. The district of Senglea where I used to visit the Simms ('Soapy' Hudson's relatives) was a waste-land of rubble. All civilians had been evacuated and everywhere any bit of wall left standing was daubed with the words, in huge letters, "Bomb Rome" and "Bomb Roma".

I crossed the harbour by ferry to Valetta and made my way up to Strada Reale — which had been re-named Kingsway — the narrow streets seeming more narrow than the last time I had walked them — but my greatest shock came when I reached Kingsway. The German and Italian airmen must have flown up and down the street hundreds of times dropping bombs on everything. Scarcely a building was left standing or recognizable as such. The Cathedral (St. Paul's) which stood back from the main street was gutted, but the statue of Queen Victoria was still there in the Square — definitely *not* amused!

Massive sandstone blocks and blackened timber lay everywhere with the rubble, a scene of desolation. It was getting dark so I made tracks towards our E.R.A's Club at Floriana for a meal. The Club had been built when I was serving in *Shropshire* and was a select, comfortable place to rest, write, read, play billiards, eat, sleep, meet old class-mates, messmates and shipmates. Now — damaged by bombing — it was an island amidst the derelict properties all around with no character or cosiness — more or less abandoned but able to supply me with a snack.

It was quite dark when I left to pick my way over and through the rubble in the black-out and arrive at the jetty to find that our 8.30 p.m. boat had returned to the ship — and no ferries operated after dark. Fortunately our Captain was waiting for his boat and invited me to travel back in the comfortable cabin. The night's air-raids started as we walked aboard.

On Monday, Dec. 15th we heard that *Galatea* had been torpedoed and sunk off Alexandria which meant we were another cruiser short in the Eastern Mediterranean, and following hard on the heels of that news came a report that the Italian Fleet had put to sea.

Aurora, Penelope, Neptune and the destroyers dashed off out of harbour and later in the day we heard that a battle was 'imminent'. On Wednesday 'the battle has started' was the message but during the afternoon all our ships came into harbour for more fuel and ammunition, leaving again as soon as they had topped up. Nothing further was heard of a 'battle' so we think it must have been air-attacks which had induced the 'battle had started' report.

There was one rather sad result which affected us when they came in to re-fuel. *Neptune*'s Chief Shipwright had been injured, taken ill or perhaps 'lost in action' but whatever the reason they needed a replacement urgently and the most convenient candidate was our Bill Batt, a popular Chief and very nice chap who filled the gap at very short notice.

The raids on the island were far more frequent by day and by night as we worked to get the ship ready for sea again with everyone disregarding the "Take shelter" warnings and carrying on with the job. Then on Friday morning we were warned to prepare to receive about 200 survivors from *Neptune* and *Kandahar*. Rumours abounded — One of them had been sunk! — Both had been sunk! They have been hit — and are being brought in at 5-knots — or 8-knots — or 11-knots! Every one knew — and they all knew something different but the tragic truth became known when *Jaguar* came in with 168 survivors from *Kandahar* and told us that they (the force) had been searching for the Italians when *Neptune* tried to cross a mine-field off Tripoli at 30-knots, had struck a mine — blown up and sunk. Despite bad weather *Kandahar* sought to rescue any survivors but she in her turn hit a mine and although she did not sink the damage prevented her moving under her own power, so *Jaguar* ventured alongside and took off her complete company of 168 men before sinking her by gun-fire and withdrawing in the darkness.

As the incident had taken place just a few miles from the coast it was hoped that at least some of *Neptune*'s 600-plus crew managed to reach the shore. Regrettably Bill was not heard of again and we missed his cheery presence about the ship.

I had been doing a job on the capstan on the fo'c'sle at about nine that morning as two R.A.F. fighters flew eastward over the harbour and a couple of minutes later the sirens sounded with the A.A. guns on shore immediately opening fire. I could see their shell-bursts to the west and then the enemy bomber they were shooting at coming in towards the harbour entrance. The guns ceased firing as suddenly as they began and I wondered why — until I realised that the R.A.F. had circled to get on the Hun's — or Wop's — tail and it was fascinating to watch. The bomber obviously had no idea of impending danger until both fighters swooped with blazing cannons — rat-tat-tat-tat-tat-tat — and he plummeted into the middle of the harbour with a terrific splash and explosion. After tea that evening Frank Pearce and I took a fresh-air stroll on the fo'c'sle and were walking towards the capstan as I was relating my morning's 'thrill' when the sirens sounded their tenth warning of the day and an almost identical situation developed — except that now we could actually see the tracers leaving the Hurricane's guns *and* entering the fuselage of the enemy bomber which erupted in a ball of fire and hurtled to destruction in the harbour — leaving just a trail of smoke as its epitaph.

Four more were shot into the harbour next morning — four out of a squadron of fourteen (counted by our gunners as they flew in) — and another four went down in the afternoon raids. Three more succumbed in the nine o'clock raid on Sunday morning, and in the 11 a.m. raid an enemy bomber got in the way of a 6″ shell from our guns at exactly the same time as another was hit by shore batteries, both victims hitting the water simultaneously about a hundred-yards apart. (The harbour must be getting full of bombs and planes — all the planes were 'certainties'!)

The enemy was making more determined efforts to neutralize Malta as a British base and all ships' companies were urged to be on the alert all times and watch out for one-man submarines or 'human-torpedoes' which could creep into the harbour through the Boom Defences. ("Rumour" had already caught one!) Small boats began patrolling the entrance all night and dropping explosive charges at regular 15-minute intervals.

December 19th was a 'Red Letter' day — a cheer for everyone — because good old *Breconshire* had braved all the hazards yet again, escorted by units of the Fleet, to bring much-needed stores and provisions through from Port Said. She also had mail for the ships — the first we had received since leaving Alex.

Her arrival signalled an intensification — if that were possible — of raids and the further littering of Grand Harbour floor with carcases of enemy planes.

In one of the raids on Christmas Eve a bomb fell just 20-yards from the ship on the dockside and showered the decks with bricks and rubble, three planes being shot down, one of them accredited to *Ajax*.

Dido came into harbour that Christmas Eve evening, passing through to rejoin the Fleet after being repaired in U.S.A., and I went aboard to see my old chum, Frank 'Fiz' Shaw to hear about his four-months sojourn in New York.

Earlier while working on board I had asked a Dockyard Charge-man if he had known Mr. (Joe) Simms whose home I used to visit in 1930/1 and learned that he and Mrs. Simms had returned to U.K. in 1936. I remembered names of other people I had met and asked about them. One — who lodged with the Simms' for a period during my visits was still in the Yard and would actually be on duty that night, and another family who had been neighbours and friends were still on the island, so after an hour with Fiz I walked to the office of Mac (Mr. MacCarthy) who was the duty

Inspector and found he had just gone to arrange for his Christmas dinner to be sent in for him on the morrow, but his assistant recognized and remembered meeting me at the Simms' so we had a talk about those times and he mentioned that Mr. Cornish was at that moment 'Duty' in charge of the Ship-fitting shop. I made that my next call and had another happy welcome with tea being brought in for us and we reminisced over those picnics at St. Paul's Bay and Mellieh and the care-free days. He was the duty Warden that night and while I was there he logged "Raid No. 1087".

He said it had been a terrible time when Italy entered the war and arrangements were made for the English workmen and their families to move to a 'Fort' about two miles from the Yard. The Cornishes moved most of their belongings to their allocated rooms and when the first raids came he said to his wife, "Let's go to our 'fortress'!" "As we got to the entrance the bombs began to fall. Several friends who were already there were killed. We were badly shaken, bruised and covered by debris. Practically all our possessions were lost but we were alive and managed to get back to our house for the night and were evacuated to a Camp-site on the other side of the island and are still there — living in one room in a wooden hut and take all our meals in the Camp restaurant. Ian (their son, a babe-in-arms in 1931) is at school in England. Come out to see the wife on Sunday (28th) — she'll be pleased to meet you again — there's a bus — etc."

So it was arranged. I was to catch the 8 a.m. bus. We would take a walk before lunch and then go to a beach. After tea there was a bus at six o'clock to bring me back to Valetta. Yes, it sounded fine as I took advantage of a lull in the firing at 1.15 a.m. and walked back to my ship.

It was Christmas Day, 1941, with no Santa Claus, but the Italian radio had broadcast a threat of a 24-hour blitz as a 'present'; In fact it was a very quiet day with shore-leave given from one o'clock and it seemed that everyone not actually Duty Watch (I was Duty Chief) went ashore. Next morning the enemy certainly made up for the laxity — the attack started at 8.30 and waves of planes came over at half-hourly intervals — high-level, low-level, and dive-bombers, — the latter strafing everything with machine-guns and cannon-fire while launching their bombs. Several were shot down, at least one falling to our guns, then at 2.30 p.m. my Watch was ordered to raise steam ready for sea. At dusk *Ajax* steamed out of Grand Harbour with four merchant ships to escort to Alexandria. There was no opportunity to contact Cornish but I am sure he soon knew we had sailed.

Among the four ships of the convoy was the Blue Star liner *Sydney Star* which had been with the pack we had brought out from Liverpool in August, 1940, and while on watch that night the Commander (E) Glynn Hearson remarked, "Well, Chief, *we* brought her out, so I think it is only

184

fair that *we* should go through to Port Said with her and see her safely home again!" I said I could not agree more!

Saturday, 27th was uneventful as with our four charges we wallowed in rough seas eastwards towards Alex. Then — Sunday — the day of my lunch appointment with the Cornishes and a nice afternoon on the beach. How different it was now!

The day began with Dawn Action at 6.15 when we were picked up by enemy reconnaissance which signalled continuous attacks throughout the day, not only from the air but from the presence of U-boats off the Libyan coast. Our guns were firing non-stop — all calibres — and there was the blast from bombs and the periodic rumble of depth-charges.

Men could only change watches in ones and twos; there were no meal-times but at opportune moments an individual from a party, a turret or A.A. gun's crew, or from an engine- or boiler-room, etc., would be sent to the galley to collect a 'fanny' of tea or soup and some bread, corned beef or cheese.

There was a wonderful feeling of relief when early in the afternoon we were met by units of the Fleet out from Alexandria which included fighter cover by *Formidable* although the ferocity of the attacks did not lessen and at 4.30 p.m. four torpedo-bombers swooped towards the convoy with fighters on their tails all of them flying directly into the face of a terrific barrage. One of the enemy received the blast of a salvo as he released his torpedo and was blown into little pieces but unfortunately the fighter also crashed and although a destroyer picked the pilot from the water he was dead. Then a two-seater Fulmar fighter pancaked almost alongside us with once again a destroyer nipping in to pluck both men — this time to safety as their craft sank.

Darkness came as a great relief but we kept closed up at our stations against possible U-boat attack — which we thought was imminent when our alarms sounded at 10.15 p.m. as the radar picked up a tiny 'bleep'. — A U-boat lying on the surface? No — it turned out to be upon investigation (by destroyers of course!) a schooner, one which had been captured from the Italians in Benghazi and was now manned and being run by the Navy to carry personnel and stores to Tobruk. (My old *Dragon* messmate, George Hammond, turned out to be the engineer of the schooner). It had been another long, hard day, but all arrived battered but safe at Alex next day — and — What a sorry sight met our eyes!

We had wondered why there were no battleships with our protective force and now we had the answer. *Valiant* was in the Floating Dock and *Queen Elizabeth* was resting on the bottom of the harbour still at her buoy. Nearby lay a Fleet Auxiliary vessel low down in the stern while a short distance off was a huge Dutch tanker with her bows under water. What could have happened?

It appeared that about a week before Christmas an Italian submarine had penetrated the defensive mine-field at the entrance to the harbour and released several one-man submersibles which had then followed a ship — or ships — through the Boom Defence and attached limpet-mines with delayed-action fuses to whatever targets they could find. Luckily the water was not deep and the unfortunate victims settled on the bottom in an upright position and did not founder — and the enemy did not realise how much damage had been caused. It did mean, however, that there was even less chance of *Ajax* leaving the station, and it accounted for those orders we had received in Malta — "Keep alert for one-man subs trying to enter the harbour!" — a case of "locking the stabledoor—" — surprising too since I believe we (the Navy) had been doing precisely the same sort of thing to their ships in their harbours and the Italians had certainly been successful against *York* at Suda. But we never learn.

The next evening *Ajax* again left harbour — alone — and at dawn on December 31st we were shelling German positions at Bardia for an hour before returning, without incident, to secure at our buoy at 9.30 that night — the end of 1941.

1942 came in with a full-force gale which lasted for four days, bringing rain and cold weather — and a crop of buzzes. "We're leaving the station in a few days." "We'll be homeward-bound next week!" "We're going to the east— (or west—) coast of America to be repaired." All would fade and die in their turn and the cycle begin again, perhaps in different order, but while *Valiant* remained in dock we secured at her berth in order to fox enemy reconnaissance into thinking *we* were the battleship — straining at the leash!

We were still wearing the flag of Rear-Admiral H. B. Rawlings but on Jan. 14th he left us to return to U.K. He thanked us for taking great care of him and his staff, and for serving him well, then added, "I wish *Ajax* was taking me home and I know lots of rumours are flying round but take no notice of them. Nobody knows what is going to happen to the ship but the new pinions are on their way and I think they are at Aden and should arrive here in about a fortnight." So now we knew!

CHAPTER 17

McCarthy of the "Ajax"

(An Appreciation of Captain E. D. B. McCarthy, R. N., by W. F. Harris, Special Correspondent, "Daily Mail". Published on the day he relinquished command of *Ajax* — November 29th 1941).

Whether the *Ajax* has been lucky in her captains or her captains have been lucky in their ships is a question we can consider officially resolved by the news that Captain McCarthy has been awarded a bar to his D.S.O. We never had any doubt, though it must have been about as easy to take over command of a ship already immortalized by her action against the *Graf Spee* as for an unknown singer to make a success of his marriage with a prima donna. Perhaps it never occurred to Captain McCarthy as a problem at all, for so completely did he impress his personality on the ship from the first that on this station his name and that of his famous cruiser have long been interchangeable words.

What happens on the bridge communicates itself like the nervous reactions of the human body to every part of the ship, and McCarthy is a man I have never met off his bridge at sea. Indeed, the *Ajax* must be unique in having a structure, which he had built, rather like a large rabbit-hutch on the back of the bridge. It is just a wind-break and inside it you will find sometimes a mattress but more often a deckchair. That is where the captain sleeps. He does not go even to his sea-cabin which, as in all warships, is on the deck just below. Nor have I ever seen him eat at sea, though I have heard him say to his Maltese steward when the menu is brought up to him on the bridge, "Anything you have got, but kill me quickly".

Yet this tall loosely built man with fair straight hair and the typical pale blue eyes of a seaman, always appears the least pre-occupied person on the bridge. He will squat down on the edge of the compass platform and yarn away as if oblivious of everything else, but a word from his signal yeoman will bring him to his feet instantly. In that moment he is already immersed in the orders that have come to him by signals. He seems to know instinctively about the course, the speed, or some intricate point of the moment, and his orders are rapped out with a joke at the end of them that set signalmen or messengers grinning.

From a battleship I have watched the *Ajax* during these days of ceaseless bomber versus warship fighting off Crete. "Hullo, where's that fellow? — *Ajax* is firing," was a remark I heard a dozen times in different ships, and, sure enough, *Ajax*'s puffs of bursting shells would soon point out the position of a microscopic enemy high in the sky.

Grim humour — in fair weather or foul, when bombs are falling or enemy coastal batteries come whining back in answer to those of *Ajax*, you will always find her captain ready for quips, jokes, or grim humour to fit the occasion. But don't deceive yourself that he cannot hand out what sailors have always called "a bottle" and the cockney "a raspberry". I once heard one being addressed to an officer which made me wilt and slink away. Yet back in harbour that night McCarthy was, as usual, the centre of a group of his officers in the wardroom. The recipient of the bottle, now holding the contents of another sort of bottle, was listening to one of those stories of McCarthy that an after-dinner speaker would give a fortune to tell like he does. In the group I was probably the only person who remembered the incident of a few hours ago, but then I was only learning about McCarthy. He has that quality essential to leadership — the ability to talk to you straight and be done with it.

How his ship's company appreciate their captain is best illustrated by a signal sent this morning on their behalf. It read, "Congratulations. Ruth chapter one verse sixteen". For the benefit of those unfamiliar with their bible an industrious signalman found the quotation and appended it to the message. It reads, "Entreat me not to leave thee, and return from following after thee, for where thou goest I will go."

Good luck to Captain McCarthy and his brave ship's company. They are worthy of him.

CHAPTER 18

Self Repairs

A critical situation arose at 9.30 p.m. on January 16th when — with no prior warning a most severe gale struck the Alexandria area. Lots of men were ashore and it was quiet on the ship as I sat writing in our Mess beneath the fo'c'sle and suddenly heard the pipe, "Close all watertight doors. Stand by for collision." I went on deck where several men were standing and in the darkness could see the towering stern of a large merchant ship bearing down on us as she was dragging her anchor. I recalled the damage caused by *Naiad* when she dragged at Scapa and realised this could be infinitely worse for us because of the size. I was not Duty Watch but I knew that no orders for "Watch below" had come to the Mess so I made my way to the Engineers' Office which I found deserted and with no signs of "Steaming Orders". In the present circumstances I wondered "Why?" It was like the "Marie Celeste", and to my mind serious so I went to the Forward Engine-room and with the help of the auxiliary watchkeepers proceeded to open up steam to warm the main engines.

I knew a number of messmates had gone ashore but had no idea how many officers were out of the ship and it appeared that those remaining on board had repaired to their cabins unaware of the intensity of the wind. The Officer-of-the-Watch's first reaction was for the safety of the ship by having all watertight doors and hatches closed but eventually the Duty Engineer became aware of the situation and issued Steaming Orders only for the Office messenger to have considerable difficulty finding the Duty C.E.R.A. and Chief Stoker who were among the crowd watching proceedings on the upper deck as seamen dispensed fenders along our starboard side. The Duty Chief relieved me at 10.30 just as the telegraphs went to "Slow Ahead' on both engines. (The engines were kept running throughout the night).

The merchant ship 'dragged' past with a minimum clearance of about three-feet — sufficient for my initiative to be acknowledged by Comm. (E) and the Executive Commander next morning.

All men should have been back on board by 11.30 p.m. but it was impossible for any boat to go alongside the jetty so the Shore Patrol directed liberty-men to another lying beyond a mountain of coal and this description was garnered from messmates the following day. It was pitch-dark with the wind whipping coal-dust all about them, and it was not a jetty but a dock-side wall from which they had to drop or jump about four feet down on to lighters alongside which some libertyboats had arrived — their cox'ns directing with hooded torches. By now the storm was even worse and it would have been rash, or possibly suicidal for any small boat to venture into the harbour so the only alternative was for them to travel the short distance to *Valiant* lying in the Floating Dock. Even that was not without hazard because on the lee-side where they had to board lay a sullage lighter which the men had to cross by 'walking a plank' to reach the Dock. One man had missed his footing and fallen into the water at the coal wharf, and another fell into the muck — both being instantly pulled out — and their final ordeal was the long climb — about fifty-feet of stairs or steps inside the Dock to reach the brow across to the battleship's deck and then find shelter for the rest of the night.

When they eventually returned during the forenoon all were as black as chimney-sweeps — a vivid reminder of 'Coal ship' days in the *E. of I.* By mid-afternoon the harbour was as calm as the village pond, which was a blessing because in the darkness that evening *Valiant*'s launch over-ran our 2nd motorboat and sank it. Fortunately they were able to pick up its crew and nobody was hurt.

The Senior Engineer walked past me as I was working in the engine-room on Wednesday morning and whispered, "Leave here 5 p.m. tomorrow — Through the Canal on Friday", the first rumour to come 'straight from the horse's mouth' so to speak, on the strength of which I went ashore to Alexandria in the afternoon to buy things to take home, and as I was having tea in the Club a messmate who came ashore later joined me at table with, "I think we must be moving tomorrow because they have brought all our Sick-cases back on board from hospital!" I kept my counsel and all was normal on board next morning with the usual daily working and it being voiced around the ship that "All hospital cases have come back to the ship because beds are required for a lot of new patients."

How strange! Normally a similar situation would have had everybody going about the ship building their own interpretation on the happenings and the ship would have been half-way round the world and even when a seaman knocked that story on the head by saying that he had just visited his brother (from another ship) in the hospital and the Ward had been almost empty for quite a time no-one latched on and said, "We *must* be leaving then!" (Unless everyone knew and thought they were the only one who did know!)

At 2 p.m. the messenger brought the Steaming Orders — "Full Watch below at 1430" — we sailed at 5 p.m., so the Senior had been right and when the ship was clear of the harbour the Captain told us we were going to Port Said to have four of our Oerlikons taken out next morning. (We had had ten of the guns fitted when our redundant catapult was removed — see page 145).

The guns were out by noon and the ship moved off to pass through the canal and — the sign of a long voyage ahead — the Department was put into 4-watches for steaming!

My afternoon was free so I spent it on the upper deck, comparing the scenery with that of our (and my) passages through the Panama Canal. We had miles and miles of sand both sides but with relief to starboard as there was a road and a railway both carrying a fair amount of traffic. There were also a number of Barrage Balloon and Anti-aircraft-gun sites from which the soldiers cheered us and shouted, "Good old *Ajax!*" while those manned by Australian troops echoed with, "Look after Aussie for us!" — probably under the impression we were on our way to Singapore! The canal for the most part is not very wide and for ships to pass one another they have to slow down and pull over to one side, but the dhows (mainly laden with bricks and gravel and very low in the water) held merrily to their course and it was amusing to watch the antics of their Arab crews, dancing, gesticulating and shouting as though they wished us to go slower. They probably did, but we maintained a steady speed and course, making exception only for the deepest-laden at the narrower points or on a slight bend, and when passing the Canal Stations situated at regular intervals along its length.

The Stations are control posts for signalling the approach of ships and give orders as to precedence.

The movement through the canal caused the water-level on both sides to drop some four or five feet, the drop keeping pace with the ship and following on behind us was a curling wave which towered about six-feet above the normal level and the usual result would be the sound of a dull thud as a well-laden dhow hit the canal-bottom only to be lifted almost level with the top of the bank a minute later. I suppose they get used to it — especially when warships are passing through. The Stations were guarded by Egyptian soldiers and twice during the afternoon we surprised one of them as he was doing his dhobeying in the waters of the canal, the reaction being the same in both incidents. The soldier would be standing in about six-inches of water on the bank and only become aware of our presence when the water-level suddenly fell away from his feet. His bowl of laundry rested on the sandy bank at waist level beside him so he immediately grabbed it and threw it further up while trying to scramble up after it but I suppose we were moving faster than most ships do through the canal because neither man made it without a soaking at least to his midriff by the following surge. I wonder if either said, "Good old *Ajax*"?

We anchored for the night in Bitter Lakes and close to the half-submerged wrecks of two merchant ships which had been mined during transit and subsequently dragged clear of the fairway and then we received a bit of a set-back. The Captain, speaking over the Tannoy told us, "We

191

are going to Suez as anti-aircraft Guardship for three weeks and will then return to Alexandria". 'Bit of a set-back'? It was great disappointment. All had been convinced this was the start of our homeward journey. Well, we *had* gone into four steaming watches, hadn't we?

Some one soon thought of a reason for the change of plans — "The ship bringing our pinions has been sunk!"

We moved south in the morning and anchored in Suez Bay. Three days later I walked into the Sick Bay to ask for a tonic — was put into a cot where I remained, full of aches and pains and very weak for four days. From my bed which was level with a scuttle I saw — on successive days — great liners arriving with thousands of troops — *Ile de France* — *Mauretania* — *Orcades* — and more, and as soon as their troops for the Desert War had landed the liners began embarking others, Australians and New Zealanders for passage to Malaya. And — our new pinions arrived! My final night (Sunday) in the Sick Bay was filled with incident. First a man was carried in unconcious and on examination by the doctor was diagnosed 'drunk' and was put on the floor to recover in his own good time. Later the doctor was called for again when a seaman was brought in suffering from knife wounds sustained in a fight on shore. Fortunately they were not too serious and after cleansing and dressing he was able to go to his Mess.

Round about midnight there came a call for the Emergency First Aid Party to go away in the motor-boat as a Wellington bomber had crashed into the sea. At the same time I heard the pipe for the Duty Searchlight crew to 'Man their light', but their reaction — for some reason was so slow that the motor-boat was searching in the dark for quite a while before the scene was illuminated, and then it was a boat from Port Tewfik which was closer to the crash and picked up four of the six-man crew, the other two being lost. Our First Aid Party were very distressed and saddened by the incident when they returned to the 'Bay'.

During my sojourn in Sick-quarters shore-leave was being given to organized parties to travel to Cairo, leaving the ship at 6 a.m. they would reach the capital by 10 and have the whole day and a night and the following day until 6 p.m. and were to be back on board by 11.30 p.m. but as I returned to duty the big and heavy task of fitting the new pinions began and I was in charge of one of the three teams working 'round the clock' to lift out the defective units, lower in the new and then — turning the main engines by hand — painstakingly examine the whole length of every tooth on the main wheel and both pinions with the help of magnifying-glasses, and using fine carborundum-stones to rub off the 'hard' marks and so obtain perfect mesh. The working team had to carry on with the job through any raid or alarm.

Life on board seemed slightly boring now after the excitements of the

192

past months; our excellent Concert Party had been broken up when the ship returned home in January 1940 and now, when opportunity arose for some light entertainment we relied on the occasional film-show or 'Sods Opera'. During this spell away from the battle-zone there was a ship-wide craze for the game of Uckers so it was decided to have a knock-out tournament to find an Uckers Championship Pair and it all turned out to be as exciting as the Football Cup Final.

By the end of February we had the new pinions well bedded in and gave them a good trial by running the main engines slowly as we cruised in a giant circle round Suez Bay for 48-hours, stopping many times to open the gearing cases — checking for any 'hard' marks and rubbing them down. The movement of the ship also started the rumours moving with everyone feeling more certain that we were on our way home, but there were others floating about like — "One chief and four E.R.A's will be leaving at the end of this week", which caused speculation as to who would be the unlucky ones. I felt reasonably 'safe'. Then I heard similar tales of people leaving from other parts of the ship. Goodness knows who starts the ball rolling but it's "Did you hear that . . . ?", or "I've just heard that . . ." or "Some-one's just told me that . . .".

My Leading Stoker of the Watch who had been with me in the engine-room most of the time and actually lived in the same street as me when I was at school and had been helping on the pinion job was always saying to me, "I bet *I* will be one of those leaving the ship," and I would say, "Don't be daft. It's only rumours about people leaving the ship. Take no notice!" A little later, again — "I bet *I* won't be going home with her!" It became an obsession — or was it a premonition? — for even if we met about the ship and spoke together the same subject came up — "I feel sure I shan't go home with the ship", and again I would try to convince him otherwise. "They won't take *you* away, Charlie. You've been here almost as long as I have — so don't think about it!"

On Wednesday, February 25th a number of people were detailed to pack their bags and be ready to leave the following afternoon and Charlie was one of them!* The poor chap (he was a bit older than me) was sorely upset and vowed that 'wherever he was going he would make a nuisance of himself, lose his Leading Rate and be *sent* home.'

That evening I talked long with him, trying to tell him that it might not be all that bad and maybe not for long, and anyway not to ruin his whole career — jeopardize his pension — but to think of his wife and children waiting at home. He seemed brighter in outlook, more resigned, when we

---

*I met Charlie a year later when we occupied adjacent beds in the Royal Naval Hospital, Chatham, where we had both undergone surgery. Regrettably he died a few days later — from emphysema p. 203.)

parted and asked me to deliver a small parcel to his wife in Chatham. He would leave it in my Mess before the Draft was called. I was working on the slow-moving engines the following afternoon when I heard the Draft was about to leave the ship. I could not leave my post so sent a messenger up to ask Charlie to come down to say 'Cheerio'. The messenger returned to say, "Leading Stoker Ward is very ill and is being sent to hospital right away!" so I sent him to my Mess to ask one of the other chiefs to relieve me urgently for a short period. I dashed along to the Sick Bay to find Charlie certainly very weak, lying in his cot, and he told me that he had been feeling ill for a long time but feared reporting sick lest he be sent to hospital and not go home with the ship. I collected his parcel, wished him "Speedy recovery and a safe and early return to England" and he was stretchered over the side. (The steward told me that he was on the danger list and his wife had been informed.)

Amongst the draft which left us that Thursday were six E.R.A's — to ships at Alexandria, and one chief E.R.A. to take up a shore job in Port Tewfik, and on Friday morning *Ajax* steamed northward through the canal to Port Said where our catapult was returned to the ship.

More changes in the ship's company took place during the day as men arrived from other ships — men who were being sent home for various reasons and who took the places of those who had just left us.

Then — at 5 o'clock on Sunday morning, March 1st — another chief E.R.A. and six more E.R.A's got a 'pier-head jump' — having been replaced by new arrivals the night before.

An hour later *Ajax* edged away from the jetty to pass through the Suez Canal once again, and this time the Captain told us, "We are now on our way home!"

CHAPTER 19

Homeward Bound

It became hotter and hotter as we moved south through the Red Sea and even hotter in the ship when we stopped for four hours at Aden for oil and fresh water, and when we crossed the Equator on March 8th it was extremely hot but after keeping the Middle Watch that night and then Dawn Action from 6 till 7 a.m. I went to the upper deck to savour the beautiful air which was filled with the scent of forests although we were many miles from land. The surface of the sea was as a sheet of glass except for the faint ripple made by our steady progress at 13-knots, and the sky a mass of wonderful colours. During the forenoon we stopped at Mombassa — just long enough to take in more fuel — and although it was still very hot it was the scenery — the greenery — which made the difference as it was so restful to our eyes.

In the course of the next night we were called to action three times, each being a false alarm through a merchant vessel failing to answer our 'recognition' signal and after investigation proving to be 'friendly' (We hope!)

It was generally assumed that we would not stay long at any port and on arrival at Durban on Friday, March 13th every one was agreeably surprised, and happy at the news that we would be staying until Monday. A very welcome rest after the rigours of watchkeeping and the heat. Shore leave was given from 4.15 p.m. and a Ship's Notice advised that each man could purchase up to 25 lbs. weight of foodstuffs to take home, so there was quite a rush to get ashore.

I was Duty Watch on board so as we arrived in harbour I went below to relieve the chief of the Afternoon Watch that he might go ashore — and then spent the whole evening with the remainder of the Duty Watch opening the main gearing case ready for a detailed inspection of pinions and main wheel when they cooled.

Those who went ashore that evening had quite a rush as it was more than a mile to the city from our berth and the shops closed at six o'clock. Leave was from 11 a.m. on Saturday to enable men to beat the 1 p.m. closing dead-line of the shops and Sam Locke and I struck it lucky as we stepped ashore to be given a lift in a South African Government car (which had brought an Official Visitor to the ship) to the centre of the shopping area. Sam was an old C.E.R.A. taking passage home with us from the shore job in Port Tewfik. There was no time to pick and choose but we managed to purchase the amounts of tinned foods we were allowed and returned with our 'booty' before going off again to find an absolutely deserted city; all stores and shops had shut and practically the whole populace departed to their surburban homes for the week-end.

We walked along the Beach Promenade — where defences were being erected against a possible Japanese invasion. There *were* one or two people taking advantage of the last of the summer to bathe from the beach but Sam and I were attracted to the Snake Pit which was quite fascinating with its many varieties of reptiles — vipers, pythons, black mambas and green mambas, puff-adders, tree snakes and King cobras — big snakes and small snakes — thick ones and thin ones, and all only separated from us by a three-foot-high wall and a narrow water-filled moat. The 'native' keeper was quite at-home walking amongst them and lifting them to give us a closer view. He was safeguarded by thick leather gloves and gaiters — long ones — and used a hooked stick to lift each exhibit before transferring it to his hand, and to entice the cobras to stand on their tails and spit at us.

We tramped both main thoroughfares seeking to find an eating-house open but failed and on enquiring from about the only Durbanite left in the city we were directed to a road-house about a mile outside the City limits for a nice, hot meal, at a reasonable price.

Back to the city and we found it was hopeless trying to get beds for the night as there was also an "R" Class battleship (*Ramillies* — I think) in port, but in the foyer of one hotel we saw an advertised "Motor Coach Tour to the Valley of a Thousand Hills" — leaving at 10.30 a.m. on Sunday and returning at 5.30 p.m. and booked two seats — despite the fact that leave would not be granted until much later — and as soon as we returned to the ship I approached the Commander for permission to go ashore at 10 a.m.

The driver of the 20-seater coach was also our guide — a very good one — who, as the bus climbed the higher road out of the city pointed to the New Dockland which was a vast area recently re-claimed from swampland. A few miles along the way and we came to Pinetown, a district entirely devoted to fruit-growing with the roads lined with stalls displaying oranges, apples, peaches, pears, grapes — a wonderful show and we got the driver's promise that he would stop there on the way back so that Sam and I might purchase a stock of goodies to take aboard. The route took us through the Bamboo Forest with its tall, straight and slender trees; the road winding continuously around the hills and valleys, allowing magnificent vistas of the beautifully-green scenery. When we entered the Valley of a Thousand Hills we were more than 2,000-feet above sea-level and the view stretched for miles along the wide valley dotted with small hills (mounds) and scattered Zulu kraals — *and* lots of massive boulders, some of which must have weighed more than 200-tons and probably from meteorites deposited in antiquity.

Our fare included a marvellous lunch at the big hotel on the Peak, after which we travelled a good many miles further to the Umgeni Waterworks Project, a gigantic scheme to build a reservoir by erecting a dam to divert the courses of two rivers — a task which was expected to take another couple of years to complete.

When we were about a mile short of our next 'port of call' which was to visit a Zulu kraal in the Nature Reserve the driver stopped the bus because he could smell burning rubber. He had everyone leave the vehicle "as quickly as possible please, because 'nine people were burned to death yesterday' when a bus caught fire in the city!"

Smoke poured forth as he lifted the bonnet and I could see flames behind

196

the dashboard inside so grabbed the extinguisher to douse them. The wiring was totally destroyed and we were stranded, more than 50-miles from Durban!

The driver's solution was for us to walk towards the Reserve and hope to meet another vehicle of some description along the road. We did and flagged it down for our driver to request the other to telephone the City depot when he reached the next phone box down the road and acquaint them of our plight.

The kraal comprised of a dozen-or-so wattle huts and a compound for goats, and the next hour was most interesting, especially for Sam and me as we were joined by a fellow-passenger who could speak and understand the Kafir language. He was elderly — although *I* would have said 50-to-55-years — saying that he came out to Africa in 1880 and had spent most of his life in the Transvaal.

The people were clad in loin-cloths, beads and bracelets and our first stop was at the Head-man's hut which was clean but dark and smokey — the only furniture to be seen was a couple of blocks of wood which apparently served as pillows. The inside walls were adorned with an assortment of symbols each having some superstitious connotation for the 'house' and its inmates. Egg-shells above the entrance were to make the home fruitful and a wooden spoon in another position ensured a plentitude of food while an arrow, some bits of straw, a large feather and various other items all had their own significance for the family.

I suggested to the driver/guide that this was a 'show house' but he assured me otherwise and 'Transvaal' must have voiced my doubts to the Head-man who beckoned me and Sam to leave the main party and with our Kafir-speaking friend we visited other huts. They were smaller but the furniture — or the lack of it! — and the adornments were much the same. Above the entrance to one hut a stick with a few beads dangling from it protruded in the direction of another hut and our translator elicited from the 'lady of the house' the fact that her daughter had set her heart on a boy who lived in the other hut, and it was her way of telling the other girls in the kraal to "Lay off! He's mine!" We also had some of the rules of 'courtship' explained, such as — a girl would make a little 'flag' of beads, stringing them together in a pattern and presenting it to the boy of her choice as a sort of love letter. Of course, she was the only person who could read it so they had to wait until the night of the full moon when they would meet at some trysting-place and he would be told the meaning of every bead and pattern of beads. The 'flag' was roughly two-inches square and on accepting it the boy had to wear it on a string about his neck at all times to show that he was 'spoken for'. (The Head-man said it could take many hours to explain the meaning of every bead!)

The old man was very friendly — and he *was* old! (Many moons, he

197

said!) Then he introduced us to *his* mother, and she was "many, many moons" — he did not know how many, but she certainly looked twelve to fifteen hundred' moons. She sat outside her hut at the centre of a circle of her other sons and daughters — two of each — and one daughter-in-law, plus several grandchildren either squatting in the circle or running and playing with each other, all visiting from their various kraals in the surrounding hills as a sort of Sunday get-together. (The daughters had been sold to their husbands for "Six cows and two goats apiece") We three — Sam, 'Transvaal' and I — were quite enjoying ourselves among these quaint, innocent folk when the relief bus arrived and we had to leave, much later than scheduled. The "Full tea" laid on at Hillcrest Hotel had to be foregone with just a brief stop for a cup of tea — all the other passengers buying huge bunches of flowers. It was dark and the driver apologized to Sam and me for being unable to stop at Pinetown.

Back in the city Sam suddenly remembered a letter he was carrying from the Chief Writer at Port Tewfik who had asked him to deliver it to his wife in Durban "should the ship happen to call there, if not, maybe you could post it in Cape Town." He decided we would take it before going for supper and found the house at the end of a 20-minute trolley-bus ride. It was in a seemingly pleasant suburb — as far as we could sense in the black-out — and Mrs. "Chief Writer" welcomed us with a thousand-and-one questions (the questions fired at Sam of course). 'How was he (her husband) healthwise? What was the environment like? Is the accommodation comfortable? What are his workmates like? Is the food good? etc., etc." She was so taken up with her questions — quite understandably — that she failed to ask if we would like a cup of tea, but we were eventually able to excuse ourselves at 9.30 p.m.

Ajax sailed at mid-day on Monday and we called in at Cape Town two-days later (March 18th) but only for oil and then left on the next stage of the journey home — course, north-westerly.

During the Morning Watch on Friday, 20th I noticed the rudder-indicator in the engine-room showing that we were making a 180-degree turn and on ringing the Steering compartment it was confirmed that our course was now — south-east! By the time our watch was relieved at eight o'clock the rumours had begun to circulate — "An enemy raider is making towards Cape Town!" — "We've been ordered to the Far East," and when "Action Stations" sounded in the afternoon and the ship increased to its maximum-permitted speed of 22-knots we all thought "this is the reason for the 'about-turn', but it was a false alarm for an innocent Greek tramp-steamer. Or was it? There were so many cases of enemy raiders fooling our ships by pretending to be innocent neutrals, using any subterfuge or camouflage.

Saturday afternoon found us back in Cape Town and four hours shore-leave given. Sam and I took a walk and when we returned we found that leave had been extended till 11.30 p.m.

We were still in the harbour on Sunday, (22nd) and learned that we had been recalled to 'cover a convoy to Colombo' but when the 'director' awoke to the condition of our ship another cruiser was assigned to the job.

We went to sea on Monday evening and spent the next three days wallowing in heavy seas about 300-miles south of Good Hope searching for that evasive (probably mythical) enemy raider, and when we arrived back in harbour again on Thursday evening I was fortunate enough to get ashore and perhaps see more of the city. I chose a top-of-the-bus ride out to the suburb of Wynberg on the other side of Table Mountain but unfortunately there was no time to leave the bus when I arrived there; it certainly was a pleasant-looking, superior sort of district of neat detached houses and bungalows with tidy and well-kept gardens.

Ajax sailed at 8.30 next morning — March 27th — and one hour later we were back in harbour to land an emergency appendicitis case. An ambulance was ready to rush the man to hospital and we sailed again at 10.30 a.m. — with new rumours already in existence that we were going to Simonstown to have our propellors examined, these rumours emanating from the fact that odd noises had been heard along the propellor-shafts when we were in those mountainous seas south of the Cape, but now I was below on the Forenoon Watch and the Senior showed me the signal which was sent ahead to Freetown, Sierra Leone, requesting "fuel, fresh water and eggs" to be available for *Ajax* on arrival.

The heat and tropical rain-storms were the only banes during this part of the voyage until we entered a danger zone where U-boats were presently active — a liner 300-miles ahead of us had been torpedoed the previous day.

We anchored off Freetown at noon on Easter Saturday, April 4th and shore-leave was piped only to be immediately cancelled and prompting the next rumour — "We're going to be based here to patrol outside the port."

As shore-leave was cancelled the quarterdeck was rigged for a cinema show for the ship's company but as soon as the film started there came a signal from the C. in C. ashore ordering it to be shut down, and we sailed at dawn (5th) to call in at Bathurst, Gambia, to top-up with oil the following day. From then on for the remainder of the voyage we worked War Routine — fully alert at all times against U-boat attack and from long-range aircraft. The Captain said, "We will be arriving at Chatham on April, 16th" — a destination which was changed on the 9th to Greenock, near Glasgow. The weather gradually worsened each day as the temperature fell and then we had the comforting presence of aircraft of Coastal Command escorting us from Western Approaches all the way up to the Clyde which we entered on April 14th — passing the battle-cruiser

199

Renown and a light Fleet Carrier on the way. We immediately started boiler-cleaning and a mass of running repairs as one Watch was sent on a week's leave.

Greenock held no attractions. It was cold and dismal but I ventured ashore by the 4.30 p.m. boat one day with two suit-cases filled with goodies brought from South Africa to despatch them 'Advance Luggage' to my home and returned by the 6 p.m. boat. Besides being cold there was a gale-force wind and, to make matters worse the pinnance's engine broke down completely as we neared the ship and the fast-flowing ebb carried us a mile down stream before we were noticed, and even further by the time a tug-boat was able to reach us and haul us back.

The first Watch returned from leave and our 'Chief', the Commander (E) — G. Hearson — said "Goodbye" to the Department with the usual word of thanks for our support and left the ship on April 26th. I landed with the 2nd leave party in a force-nine gale, thankful that I was travelling 'light' and did not have to manipulate heavy suit-cases from boat to jetty to train. Our Watch were to have three-weeks leave and then return to steam the ship to Chatham.

Leave passed all too quickly. I delivered Charlie's parcel and learned of his favourable progress, still in hospital at Suez, and on May 19th I was back aboard *Ajax* at Greenock to sail next morning via the Pentland Firth to be met by a destroyer Escort Group for passage down the east coast. Our only encounter with the enemy was during the afternoon of the 22nd when a large number of bombers attacked our small force, failed to score any hits with their bombs but did some damage with cannon-fire. Our bridge personnel told me afterwards that the enemy had suffered considerable punishment themselves from the massive barrage put up against them and from the small-arms fire. We anchored safely that night at Sheerness and de-ammunitioned. Captain Bateson left next morning after thanking the ship's company for all they had done for him and the ship, then on the 26th we proceeded up-river to be taken into Dockyard control and most of the crew left us. The Engine-room department remained to muster and check spares and stores until June 16th 1942, when *Ajax* finally paid off and we returned to Depot. I had been with her for four years and ten months; she was a fine ship and had had good crews; there had been happy times and some hard times. There had also been lots of action. Now what?

CHAPTER 20

Motor Torpedo Boats

On joining Depot a Medical examination found my weight had fallen considerably since my previous visit and as a result of a further check-up in the hospital I was diagnosed Category "C" — (Not to be drafted for One Month) — a month in which I was employed in the Depot workshop machining items for the maintenance of Services such as galleys, bakery, laundry, general heating and the transport vehicles, and on re-assessment was given a follow-up period of "Six-months Home Shore Service" and on October 1st was detailed in charge of a Working Party of about fifty E.R.A.'s, Mechanicians and Stokers to carry out the refitting of all auxiliary machinery in the paddle-steamer *Jeannie Deans* lying in the Yard.

The appointment was short-lived for, after getting everything organized and running smoothly for nine days I was suddenly called back to Depot and that same afternoon I arrived in Gosport to report at the main Motor Torpedo Boat Base — *H.M.S. Hornet* — for a course on Packard Engines.

There was no accommodation at the Base so I was placed on L & PA — Lodging and Provision Allowance — and told to find lodging in the town and report at the Base at 0830 on Monday.

For six weeks with nine other chiefs I attended lectures every morning and "Practical experience" in the Gun-boat Yard and in the confines of the boats in the afternoons while most evenings were spent writing-up lecture notes and making sketches.

The boats were powered by three 18-cylinder Packard engines and a Ford V-8 motor for auxiliary cruising all compacted into the smallest space and part of the Course was to be able to dismantle both types of engine and to reassemble them. A written examination was set at the end followed by each of us having to give a practical demonstration of partially dismantling either a Packard or a Ford in a boat. We were then ready to be drafted to different bases.

My move came on December 7th when I was sent to Lowestoft with a mandate to "Take over responsibility for the Service and Maintenance of the 22nd M.T.B. flotilla" at the Base — *H.M.S. Mantis*.

As at Gosport no accommodation was available and I experienced some difficulty finding lodgings in a strange town.

Reporting at Base I found I was to relieve C.E.R.A. Christmas who had been in *Dragon* with me. No one had told him about a move; he was quite happy to remain and keep mum until he was told to go, and there was plenty of work to be done. Between us we supervised the removal and overhaul of all three engines of M.T.B. No. 234 while also doing running-repairs on Nos. 83 and 93 and on Anti-Submarine Boat No. 33.

No. 234 was an 'Urgent' job and our whole party worked flat-out to get her ready for service, not even stopping for meals — and when she was ready with her engines running sweetly we were not allowed to take her for a trial run because her guns had not been put back on board! The days and nights were really hectic — the evenings especially so as the boats were being prepared for their nightly marauding patrols, and checking on the reported damage and defects of those which were out during the day.

When the weather was too bad for any to put to sea — and it frequently was — their crews 'rested' in the huts and the Maintenance staff visited all boats at regular intervals, checking the engines and giving them short runs to ensure they were kept warm and ready should conditions improve.

'Albert' was still with me at the end of December and when the Base Commanding Officer realised the fact he told him he might as well stay, and to me said, "The 6th Motor Launch flotilla is coming from Grimsby in the New year — you can look after that".

The six boats of the 6th M.L. flotilla came into the harbour and their own C.E.R.A. arrived with them — which was just as well because they were entirely different sorts of boat with entirely different sorts of engine (Hall-Scott) and meant for a totally different sort of work.

On January 19th 1943 we had fitted one of the new engines into M.T.B. No. 238 and I went to sea with her for trials, a very bumpy ride at 40-knots with the roar of the engines louder than the noises of the Messerschmit and its cannon-fire when it came out of the sun spraying shells at random.

A young 'makey-learn' R.N.V.R. lieutenant supernumary on the bridge had apparently been feeling a bit under the weather and squatting on the floor of the cockpit, more or less comatose before the attack and not even the frantic movements of the boat — zigzagging, stopping and starting — in the skipper's effort to shake off the predator, and the rattle of our replying guns had any effect on him. The enemy eventually flew off and it was then that the skipper (also an R.N.V.R. lieutenant) discovered his second-in-command had been severly wounded by a cannon-shell, possibly one of the first to hit the boat during action. He was whisked away to hospital as soon as we entered harbour and when the boat was examined more than a dozen holes were found in the bridge casing and the torpedo-tube canopies, but luckily none through the engine-room although all the engines had to be taken out again.

I think the wounded man survived to tell the tale — if he could remember anything about it — but everybody was kept so busy, and there was no close contact between the Maintenance staff and the crews of individual boats. It was all so impersonal.

A few days later while running a trial on M.T.B. 100 we were called by radio to meet and escort home another boat which had been shot-up while operating off the Dutch coast during the night.

We met her through the mist and stood by her as she was making about 5-knots with her Ford V8, her main engines being out-of-action. The sea was flat-calm and we were not spotted from the air.

In mid-February I had to visit Sick Quarters for re-survey of my medical condition and was sent to hospital at Chatham for a 'probe' and on the 16th was about to go on the 'table' when the operation was hurriedly cancelled with no explanation. Two days later the 'op' went ahead and when I came-to I found myself in a bed next to one occupied by Charlie Ward — whose 'op' had taken place on the 16th. (See p. 193).

Air-raids occurred almost every night and patients were moved to the basement each and every time and remained there until the "All Clear" sounded.

On March 5th I was moved to convalesce at Joyce Green hospital at Dartford from which I was discharged to Category "C" (for two-weeks' observation) on April 24th and arrived in Depot to find my name on a Draft List for the repair ship *Maidstone*, which was also acting as Base ship for spare crews for submarines and destroyers in the Mediterranean. My "C" status blocked that draft and I was given charge of a Working Party to prepare the destroyer *Holderness* for sea. That job took us a week and I was then told to "take your party across the Basin to the *Cottesmore* (a Hunt Class destroyer) and start refitting", but before we could collect our tools I received another directive, to take the party to another part of the Dockyard and carry out the refit of the destroyer *Vivacious*. Ten days to complete that job was followed by a week refitting the Hunt Class destroyer *Cattistock* and was then given control of a much bigger working-party to refit the cruiser *Dauntless*, in dry-dock and being converted to an Anti-Aircraft ship. This was a longer-term effort with considerably more responsibilities for in addition to arranging work schedules and supervising the jobs I had to organise a Duty roster of those who had to stay in the ship overnight as Fire Party and also make out Pay Lists and keep a record of names and rates of a constantly changing and fluctuating gang.

On reporting at Sick Quarters for re-assessment on August 27th I was up-graded to Category "B" and returned to the ship only to be recalled to barracks for draft, this time it was to the Repair-ship *Greenwich*. No one could tell me where she was but I was given seven-days Draft Leave so it was somewhere 'foreign'.

CHAPTER 21

Back to Work

Over the next few months I was kept busy on non-operational duties, which mostly consisted of escorting prisoners, though (luckily for me) the journeys were interesting which satisfied my love of travelling. I set out on the giant Cunarder *Queen Mary* on Friday 3rd September with many service personnel travelling to Canada for training. My first escort duty was from New York to Quebec, after which I travelled to London, Ontario via Toronto which enabled me to visit my brother; then to Halifax, Nova Scotia, and eventually I reported to Manhattan Island in New York for passage to Iceland. The whole range of Atlantic winter weather accompanied us and after 18 interminable days I arrived at Reykjavik where I reported to the Naval Depot, *Baldur* to arrange transport to *Greenwich*.

Greenwich was a very old 'coal-burner' of some 8,000-tons which had begun life as a Greek merchant ship building in England at the start of the First World War in 1914 when she was taken over by the Admiralty while on the stocks and converted to a Destroyer-repair-ship. She had been destined for the scrap-yard in 1939 but this war gave her another lease of life when she was sent to Iceland to service and repair the drifters and trawlers of the Minesweeping flotillas operating from there, and during my service with her we gave help to any type of craft which needed or asked for our assistance.

My task was to supervise the Outside Working Parties but it was easier to work with them to get the jobs finished, and we often worked all through the nights on the decks of the boats, refitting capstans, steam-winches, safety-valves, and frequently working away from 'mother' on a ship having to go into the Floating dock where we would remove a damaged propeller and fit the spare — very heavy work — while icy winds laden with rain, hail, sleet and snow whistled through the open-ended dock, our only shelter being a roped-up tarpaulin whose principal raison d'être was to shield our dim lamp from the prying eyes of enemy reconnaissance planes.

Frequent gales made it extremely hazardous getting to the boats, even those tied up alongside, and impossible during the more severe storms.

The Engineer or the Skipper of a boat coming for refit or docking would submit the Defect List beforehand and I would then go aboard to check the items listed and estimate the requirements in the way of materials, machining and time. Some of the lists were made out comprehensively and were straightforward; others needed a lot of deciphering — especially those written with an unsharpened pencil on loose sheets of signal-pad resting against oily pillars of main-engine cylinders. One such which is particularly called to mind was for the trawler we subsequently nick-named "Needen Fixin"! Every single defect on the list was "needen fixin" — "towing winch is needen fixin, bilge pump is needen fixin, boilers needen fixin, dynamo needen fixin, galley steam is needen fixin", — a score of items all "needen fixin" and on some boats all machinery, both main and auxiliary, was in most parlous condition as though no repair or even adjustment had been made for a number of years — if ever! — and in some cases it was almost a miracle they managed to steam at all!

Anyway, *Greenwich* was well-equipped with workshops and material to cope with most jobs. We had 'heavy' and 'light' machine-shops, pattern-making and moulding-shops, a foundry, power-hammers in both the boilermakers' and enginesmiths' shops, and of course the fitters' benches and the Instrument-makers' room.

Daylight — such as it was — lasted between 10.30 a.m. till 2.30 p.m. and then it was "Darken ship", when dead-lights, doors and hatches had to be closed with no light visible to the outside world.

1944 began in the middle of one of Iceland's most severe of winters with blizzard conditions which lasted for many days without let-up but work had to carry on regardless of weather and our 'outside' gang spent more nights working in that bleak'n cold climate, handicapped in our movements by the many layers of thick outer- and under-clothing we wore in our efforts to keep warm and on a couple of occasions whilst working on non-urgent craft and looking forward to a warm evening with 'mother' the weather deteriorated so much and so rapidly that it was impossible for us to get back and we had to take pot-luck in the boat, scrounge some food and a mug of tea and kip-down on lockers or in the wheel-house for the night and hope to get home next day.

Leave Parties departed — and returned — as and when they could and generated much excitement, especially on the immediate close days as men packed their cases ready for the morrow with 'hail fellow well met' attitude to all others and hoping nothing would prevent their departure. On the day normal work had to continue as they listened somewhat impatiently for the pipe "Leave Party to muster in the Well-deck", and when they had gone a silence descended on the ship as the thoughts of those left on board travelled home with them or waited for the returning Party, all agog for first-hand news from Blighty. "What was it like at home?" "How are people coping?" "Did you have a good trip?" "Much damage where you live?" and many other questions. Then the next day when all life should be back to normal but for those who had just returned from four-weeks at home it was the bleakest of days as reaction set in. A bad time for everyone. Now it was March and my 6-months of Category "C" was ending so I was sent ashore to the Hvitanes Sick Quarters one Sunday morning to trudge through snow twelve inches deep and heavy rain to the Nissen-hut for the doctor to tell me to "See a Specialist at a later date", arriving back on board to find my name on the "7th Leave Party List — which will apply when circumstances allow". The rider was necessary because of late the enemy had stepped up his reconnaissance activity and Red and Yellow alerts were becoming more frequent, always entailing everyone going to Action Stations in case of a follow-up by the real thing.

One such alert came at 11 o'clock on the morning of Friday, March 31st and we closed-up and waited quietly for any development when, out of the blue came the pipe "7th Leave Party to clean and fall-in on the Well-deck." There was a mad rush to change out of our working rig, the raid suddenly far from our minds as *B. O. Davies*, our ship's Drifter, waited alongside, and we left the ship at noon but only to secure at Hvitanes jetty until the "All Clear" sounded two hours later. By that time it was dark and we steamed out of the fiord passing the returning 6th Party and giving them a 'cheer', and at 9 p.m. transferred to the C.P.R. liner *Empress of Russia* for the three-days uneventful voyage from Reykjavik to Greenock and a 24-hours delay before the ship could proceed up-river and we could land for our trains (south in the majority of cases).

During my leave my 12-year-old daughter suddenly contracted German measles and our doctor duly notified the authorities of the fact which resulted in my being told to report to the Sick Quarters at Naval Barracks for 'Clearance' on the day before I was due to travel back.

Fate struck again in the form of a 'Recall' telegram received the following day: "Report Greenock at 1000 27th" and on reporting at the Sick Quarters my temperature was checked, I was put into a cot — "Unfit to travel — has Mastitis" and was prescribed 'hot fomentations'. Another doctor doing the rounds next morning advised "cold compresses morning and night" and on the morning after that a third doctor came to the ward and, "This man must go to hospital right away" and I was promptly on a stretcher and into an ambulance and wondering What's going on? What *is* wrong?

In the hospital next morning the Ward doctor tapped my chest and listened with his stethoscope for a while, then departed to return later with two colleagues and all three then took turns to tap, listen, prod and poke. They then went into a huddle against the screen around my bed — 'Mutter — mutter' — until one came over to me and asked, "How do you feel?" I said, "Fine! I'm here because my daughter has German measles". There was another consultation, then — "O.K. You can be discharged to Depot at 1 p.m."

I reported at the Drafting Office to enquire about returning to Iceland and was told to await clearance from the hospital — a clearance which eventually arrived on May 10th and when I returned to the Drafting Office for instructions was told "The post has been filled. You're probably required somewhere else." I asked for my kit, hammock and tools to be sent for.

May 18th — "Report for urgent draft."

At the Drafting Office I was told to proceed to John Brown's shipyard on the Clyde where the cruiser *Euryalus* was refitting, "as Senior Chief E.R.A". The move was so urgent that an official car rushed me to the railway station for the 5.15 p.m. train to London and the night-train to Scotland and I walked aboard my new ship at noon next day, sans kit, sans hammock, sans tool-box, and found myself totally unexpected. There was a reduced complement and the ship was still in the hands of the repairers. The Commander told me the ship would not be ready for service for another month and when she was she would be going "anywhere in the world, so you had better take 7-days' Foreign Draft Leave while you can." I collected my Travel Warrant and was on the next train south.

Just after I arrived back on board on May 28th I received a list of names of all Engine-room personnel who were to re-commission the ship so that I could prepare their Commissioning Cards and organize balanced Duty Watches, fitting the new-comers in with those already on board and apportioning Daywork jobs provisionally — putting myself in charge of the Machine-shop with an assistant/deputy.

CHAPTER 22

To The Pacific

Captain R. Oliver-Bellasis assumed command of *Euryalus* on June 17th 1944 and the new crew re-commissioned the ship on the 28th and in his welcoming speech to them the Captain also gave praise to the men who had done so much work during the past few weeks of the re-fit preparing the ship to take her place in the Fleet and promising them four-days leave before the ship put to sea.

He kept his word and on July 6th I travelled south yet again and while at home had experience of Hitler's latest civilian 'terror' weapon, the Flying Bomb or "Doodlebug", numbers of them passing over the Medway-towns by day and night. We watched the sparks emanating from their spluttering engines and when those engines suddenly stopped we wondered where they would fall as they were not targetted and simply fell at random, some on residential properties but most falling harmlessly in open country — although a close neighbour was killed when one of the missiles struck the home of her daughter less than a mile away while she was visiting for the afternoon.

On the 10th we began an even busier period in the ship with engine trials and speed trials taking place in the Clyde combined with all the necessary Exercises and Drills for the ship's company to work towards full fighting efficiency and know their ship.

This working-up continued even more earnestly on joining the Fleet at Scapa Flow on August 4th, with some opportunities to prove we were succeeding, for on the 14th while exercising in the North Sea an air-craft from one of the carriers hit our fo'c'sle, killed its two occupants and caused damage on deck. On the 18th a freak storm in the Flow swamped *Vivien*'s motor-boat and sank it; our life-boat's crew were first on the scene to rescue the four men from turbulent waters, and there was more drama next day when the Warrant Officers' galley caught fire. It was under control within a few minutes of the alarm being sounded and gave confidence and satisfaction generally.

As I had no kit, tools or bedding I had been allocated a spare cabin and this seemed to engender some resentment, or maybe jealousy? — among the members of the Mess. It meant that I did not sleep with them and by virtue of my job there was plenty of paper-work to keep me busy each evening and therefore did not spend a lot of time with them. Perhaps they considered me 'stand-offish'.

Early in September we were carrying out Night Action gunnery exercises with other units of the Fleet when suddenly — on the 9th — *Euryalus* was ordered south to Swan Hunter's Yard at Wallsend for the long-awaited repairs to our fo'c'sle and arrived there on the 11th.

We were told the job would take 36-hours but on each succeeding day the time was extended until on the 16th of September the Captain granted 24-hours leave to each of the two watches — leave that was of little use to anyone living outside the environs of Newcastle — but I was immediately inundated with requests written by my members for me to pass to Commander (E) asking for "48-hours leave because they were working in 'four' watches, not two!" It was a daft request and of course all were returned — "Not granted" — and the Mess were under the impression that *I* had refused them! (Many were H.O's — Hostilities Only ratings —

and not conversant with the ways of the Service, especially not with its traditions and certainly not with its sense of comradeship. No-one seemed willing to help another in any way and right from the start of the 'commission' there was general discontent throughout the ship. One complaint was about the food — or the lack of it — as instanced by a stoker who had been slack turning-out one morning and gave as his excuse, "I could not stand, sir!" "Why not?" asked the 1st Lieutenant. "I did not have the strength to, sir. I was feeling starved!" and it may have been pure coincidence that on the following day something comparatively edible — Spam, mashed potato, peas and sliced beetroot — was served but things soon reverted to the norm when we went to sea. And she was not a good sea-boat because her narrow beam caused her to roll inordinately in even a moderate sea and the water managed to get everywhere below decks, sloshing about in passages and across messes. We rejoined the Fleet at Scapa on September 20th and made frequent forays, accompanying and covering the aircraft-carriers *Furious*, *Formidable* and *Indefatigable* to bomb and bombard enemy positions and shipping in Norway, usually in atrocious weather — and one evening in October as we ploughed through a force-nine gale the ship's company was issued with — Tropical kit. That started everyone talking — "We're off to Murmansk or Spitzbergen!"

In the morning we rescued the pilot of a crashed plane from the escort-carrier *Trumpeter* and in the afternoon picked up the three-man crew of an Avenger which had ditched, landing all four at Scapa that night. A few days later with the same three carriers and the cruisers *Kent* and *Bellona* and a flotilla of destroyers we were again off the Norwegian coast and while we bombarded the enemy gun-batteries and our planes attacked the harbours the destroyers were severely mauling a German supply convoy which had been creeping along the coast. It was another very rough passage back and we were about to enter the Flow when *Euryalus* was ordered to Rosyth dockyard and as soon as the ship secured alongside on November 16th one watch was sent on ten-days leave, a complete surprise to all but with the issue of our tropical kit we knew we would soon be off to warmer climes.

The second watch returned on December 12th ready to sail the next day, "Immediate destination unknown. Ultimate — Trincomalee — to join the East Indies Fleet".

Speculation was rife as to our immediate destination with the strongest buzz being "Liverpool — staying for four days!", and some men even arranged for their wives to meet them there.

Euryalus sailed from Rosyth at 5 p.m. on Wednesday, Dec. 13th — the anniversary (day and date) of the River Plate battle five years before — and two days later anchored in mid-stream at Liverpool. Dame Rumour had been right but only up to a point, for no leave was given and the crew were busy embarking stores and provisions through the night and the following day and when we sailed at 8 p.m. on the 16th it was without a couple of seamen who secreted themselves aboard the last tender to leave the ship before we weighed. They were 'posted' as deserters. After the usual testing of all communications, fire-fighting equipment and so forth, the Captain broadcast details of what we were doing — '*Euryalus* was to be the senior ship of a small force escorting Their Royal Highnesses the Duke and Duchess of Gloucester who were travelling aboard the N.Z.S.N.C's ship *Rimutaka* to Australia where the Duke was to be Governor-General and we will arrive at Gibraltar next Thursday.' Our force consisted of seven destroyers and frigates; the 8,000-ton *Rimutaka* was old and slow so the boats were able to circle her quite easily. On the sunny Sunday evening a destroyer way out to starboard began dropping depth-charges as the rest of us veered to port, shepherding the Royal party away from danger. There was no official report at the time so we surmised it was a demonstration for the benefit of our wards but later we learned that "U-400 was sunk by the frigate *Nyasaland* south of Cape Clear, Sunday December 17th" so it had been for real.

We zig-zagged slowly on southwards and on Tuesday five ships of the escort force wished us 'Goodbye and Bon Voyage' as they turned for home having helped us through the most hazardous area — the Bay of Biscay — and we were left with two destroyers, *Ulster* and *Urchin* who, like us were to join the East Indies Fleet. We anchored in Gibraltar Bay on Thursday afternoon and three hours leave was given from 4 p.m. — strict instructions being given to libertymen "no mention to be made of the presence of the Gloucesters while on shore!" (Members of my Mess walking in Main Street saw the Duke and Duchess alighting from an open car in Town Square to inspect a Guard of Honour!)

Leaving at midnight we steamed through the Mediterranean with no fears from air attack or threat from U-boats and although our ships were 'darkened' all navigation lights were in use because of the huge amount of traffic, the long lines of U.S. Landing-craft on passage between North Africa and Sicily, and Malta was reached on Christmas Day with rain bucketing down non-stop for the first three hours; then it stopped and the sun shone to reveal the ruins of Valetta. The destruction was bad enough at Christmas 1942 but now it was infinitely worse with almost every building reduced to a heap of rubble by the German and Italian planes.

We were anchored in the middle of Grand Harbour and one hour's leave was given — scarcely a dozen men from the whole company deigning to take advantage — and there were no celebrations on board and only a weak attempt at decorating one or two messes, everyone being much too busy with work about the ship.

Leaving Malta at 5 p.m. we ran into bad weather on the voyage along to

Port Said where we were due to arrive at noon on the 28th but by the time we entered the port at 8.30 p.m. the 'Welcoming Party of Officials and Dignitaries' had tired of waiting and had gone home, so we all steamed on through the Suez Canal during the night to anchor off Port Tewfik at 8.30 a.m. to embark provisions and stores before sailing at noon for a very hot passage through the Red Sea.

Every day and most nights throughout the voyage we had exercised our various drills, evolutions and Action Stations with plenty of gunnery practice and certainly felt the Red Sea heat.

At 3 p.m. on January 2nd 1945 we oiled at Aden. No leave was given but the Royals could be seen being received ashore by plumed-hatted officers in the dusty heat and when we sailed at midnight all ships were 'darkened' for the first time since leaving Port Said, with a rapid rise in temperature for it to continue swelteringly hot all the way to a hotter Colombo where we arrived at 5 p.m. on the 9th.

The Duke and Duchess signalled their thanks for safe conduct thus far and wished us good luck for the future as *Rimutaka* continued on her way to Australia escorted by the cruiser *Suffolk*; we followed a few hours later to round the island to Trincomalee, our Naval Base in Ceylon to join the newly-formed British East Indies Fleet.

There was much speculation as to what our future role would be as it was thought our steaming-range would limit us to convoy duties with no Fleet Operations in the Indian Ocean but on the 12th we were told that on leaving Trincomalee we, with other ships would form the nucleus of a new British Pacific Fleet and would proceed via Australia.

My kit had caught up with me before we left U.K. so I felt more comfortable especially during this present busy maintenance period as the ship embarked stores and ammunition and topped-up with oil.

Vice-Admiral Sir Philip Vian (Captain Vian, of *Cossack* fame and now in command of Aircraft-carriers) came aboard to welcome us to the Station and the fact that it would be a different sort of warfare than that versus the Huns in the North Sea and the Atlantic, and there would be long periods at sea during which both ships and men must be kept 100% efficient and "With other ships ordered to the Pacific we shall leave within a week and carry out two one-day air-strikes against Japanese-held oil-fields in the Palembang area of Sumatra and proceed via South Australia to the Pacific."

We steamed out of Trincomalee on January 16th in company with the battleship *King George V* and four carriers — *Victorious, Illustrious, Formidable* and *Indomitable* — the cruisers *Black Prince, Argonaut* and *Gambia*, and six destroyers and when we crossed the Equator on the 18th our 'apologies' were duly signalled to King Neptune with a promise that homage would be paid later "when the business of His Britannic Majesty

King George VI was completed". (All ships were preparing for the Strikes and also had to be alert for action against Japanese surface craft operating from Sumatra.)

Then it rained non-stop for five days, a constant deluge — and the very air we breathed was like warm water. The deck-heads dripped and the bulkheads streamed. Visibility was virtually nil and flying impossible so that the Strike proposed for Monday, 22nd had to be postponed until the rain eased a bit on the 24th. In the interim we met up with three large oilers with their guardian frigates and escort-carriers and the whole Fleet oiled at sea, then — on the day — all the planes taking part in the operation were air-borne at 0530 and all ships and men at Action Stations. The attack lasted for six-hours and nine planes were lost — some by shore 'flak' and some in accidents while flying back on — but Japanese radio, broadcasting in English, claimed "104-British aircraft shot down". (I doubt we put a hundred into the air in the whole day!)

Late that night our radar picked up a bleep on the screen and all ships went to Action Stations on the assumption that a 'snooper' had located the position of the Fleet and we waited for the illuminating flares to be released above us, but when nothing happened the 'bogey' was logged as yet another of the heavy rain-storms which tended to plague the radar screens.

All ships oiled again and returned to the 'Strike' area on the 29th when our planes met with very tough opposition both from shore batteries and Japanese fighter-planes and while they were pressing home their attack on the enemy oil installations the Japanese sent six torpedo-bombers out to attack the Fleet. All six were shot down before getting within striking distance.

For our part we lost seven planes by enemy action and eight through accidents as they returned, mainly due to the sudden freak rain-storms, the 'solid' walls of water which reduced visibility to zero. They were responsible for many calls to Action at night as they appeared on radar screens; when the object vanished we could re-assume our 2nd or 3rd Degree of Readiness with the explanation — "It was a rain-storm" — "a cloud-burst" or — "some floating debris" and "It is better to be safe than sorry!"

The Fleet moved south after the second 'Strike' and we anchored off Fremantle on the 4th. Tankers brought fuel out to the ships but we — *Euryalus* — waited in vain for one to come to us so we moved to berth at the Oiling Jetty — and night-leave was given to one Watch. A lot of men landed and made tracks to Perth, which was about five-miles by train or bus, but Australia on a Sunday night is really 'dead'.

All ships sailed for Sydney in the morning.

Our days and nights were crammed with evolutions and exercises as we crossed a rough and chilly Great Australian Bight to enter Sydney Harbour at 9 a.m. on February 11th and berth at Woolloomooloo. It was Australia and it was a Sunday! Nothing to do on shore and about ten-thousand sailors to do just that — Nothing but amble around the streets. All bars and cinemas were firmly shut but as we were to remain in port for 17-days we had ample time to adjudge the merits — or otherwise — of the city, and were to find a huge metropolis where the majority of ships' companies enjoyed their runs ashore.

On the 13th *Euryalus* passed under the famous bridge to enter the dry-dock at Cockatoo Island for necessary maintenance, and a very busy period for the whole crew.

While we were in dry dock each Watch was given 24-hours General Leave — from 12.30 on one day until the same time on the next, and the Australian Government issued 15 Clothing Coupons to any man who wanted them so I took advantage of the offer and the leave and landed at 12.30, then had to window-shop until 2 p.m. while the stores had their lunch-hour- or more! (Probably a 'heat-wave routine').

The assistants kindly helped-out with coupons when it was found my fifteen were insufficient to cover my purchases and then made up a neat parcel for me to leave at the British Centre — a Club for Servicemen — while I took a ride out of the city to Pennant Hills, a name which had taken my fancy to visit.

As I deposited my parcel "For safe-keeping until tomorrow while I have a trip to Pennant Hills", the lady in charge asked, "Have you a place to stay when you get there?" I said I only had 24-hours and would be returning to the city that night. "Oh! You mustn't do that. Here's my address — I live about a mile from there and my husband will be at home. You can have dinner with him and I shall be home at seven, and there is a nice bed on the verandah". I said she was very kind — but — well— How could I walk up to somebody's house and say, "I've come to have dinner with you"? Perhaps it was 'natural' for Australians?

It was an hour's ride on the train through pleasant rolling country but the brilliant sunshine played havoc with my eyes and caused me a most severe migraine so that when I left the train I could not face the further bus-ride to Pennant Hills Park, my objective. I walked very gingerly along the road the bus had taken, fearful that my head might fall off if I strode out and when I came to a low wall separating the lawns of a mansion-sized bungalow some 30-yards distant from the side-walk, I sat to rest with my eyes closed for a few minutes and when I opened them there were three Scottish terriers examining me. They had been lying close by the house when I sat down but their inquisitiveness had proved too strong and they decided to inspect in a very friendly manner. Then the lady of the house came down to see what was happening and I asked if I might have a glass

213

of water — and perhaps an aspirin. She invited me to cross the lawn and produced water and aspirin and as I sat on the steps leading up to the verandah a gentleman came up the path, recognized my uniform with a welcoming handshake and the lady explained the reason for my presence. He was concerned and asked if I would like a bed — to rest and recover. I thanked him and said that actually a kind-hearted lady at the British Centre had given me her address so perhaps I should go there, and showed him the card I had been given. His reaction was immediate — "That is my wife's. I am Mr. Vine-Hall!" It was a remarkable coincidence; I had had no notion of where I was, having not even looked at street-names after deciding to follow the bus instead of riding it and had walked almost blindly along the route. Mrs. Vine-Hall arrived home and was very solicitous; she had the housekeeper — for such was the position of the other lady — make up the bed on the verandah for me and I was asleep by 8 p.m!

It was an effective cure and next morning after a shower and breakfast and some sport with the dogs I thanked and took leave of my generous hosts, and returning to my ship without seeing Pennant Hills Park.

Amongst the mail awaiting me was a letter from home bearing a request, "Mrs. 'A' " — a close neighbour — says "If you ever get to Australia and to Sydney, will you try to see her sister, Mrs. 'C' who lives in Campbell Street with her husband."

Well, I was in Sydney and Campbell Street was easy to find — except that it was in a depressed Down-town commercial area of warehouses with no residential properties at all!

At the office of the City Registrar I learned there were nineteen streets of that name within the City Limits but on mentioning the family name I found they were located in the north-west suburb of Eastwood. They were not listed in the telephone directory so I took a chance (and a train) and made the 25-minute journey to that pretty Garden suburb of wide avenues, smart houses and bungalows, well-kept lawns and gardens massed with flowers — mostly roses.

When I reached the gate of the house I was seeking the matronly figure tending the blooms paused at my inquiry and self-introduction and beamed at the mention of her sister's name. As we were speaking her husband arrived home and I was invited in for tea and to be asked many questions about the 'Old Country', from which they had emigrated early in 1914 and never returned.

To hear more they invited me to spend the coming week-end with them — providing the ship was still in port! — and on Saturday afternoon I sat with them in the rear garden of their bungalow, amongst the shrubs and vines and beside the tiny stream which trickled through it, and under a hot, summer sun, as we talked about the country they both yearned to see again. It was an idyllic setting, away from the noises of the city — and away from the Navy for a short while. But on Sunday morning, February 25th I took Mr. 'C' down to the ship for a complete tour and a taste of old England, while Mrs. 'C' cooked the Sunday lunch ready for our return.

CHAPTER 23

British Pacific Fleet

The Fleet comprising the battleship *King George V* — flagship of Admiral Sir Bruce Fraser — the aircraft-carriers *Indefatigable*, *Indomitable*, and *Victorious*, the cruisers *Argonaut*, *Black Prince*, *Swiftsure*, and the *Gambia* (New Zealand Navy); we — *Euryalus* — were wearing the flag of Rear-Admiral Sir Philip Vian, commanding the ten destroyers which made up the number — left Sydney on February 28th and assumed War Routine on clearing the harbour. The ships were battened-down more or less permanently as we were called to Action Station exercises at any time of day or night and carried out Night Encounters as the temperature rose higher every day to help make conditions even more uncomfortable. Then, on March 7th all ships anchored in the lagoon at Manus, an island in the Admiralty Group north of New Guinea. We were now to be known as the British Pacific Fleet and were placed at the disposal of the United States Commander-in-Chief. We lay there for ten days in the tropical heat and with non-stop rain during which time we had plenty of maintenance work and I had to visit the *Oxfordshire* (last seen at Freetown) for a medical check-up.

To help relieve the monotony a Water Sports afternoon was organized but just as the event began there came the fiercest of rain-storms and after more than thirty-minutes of the heaviest, continuous rain any of us had ever experienced the idea was abandoned — because there was "too much water!" And it did not ease up; it was a blinding rain which prevented any ship from moving. *Euryalus* was getting low on fuel and it took the tanker 24-hours to find us and when she did so and came alongside her hose-connections would not match ours and oiling was delayed a further four-hours while I made the necessary adapters. At last, on Sunday, March 18th the cruisers and destroyers were able to depart from Manus, leaving the big ships at anchor, and two days later we arrived at Ulithi close to the

Japanese-held island of Yap in the Caroline Islands. The big ships arrived later in the day and we were happy to see that the fourth carrier — *Illustrious*, which we had left in Sydney — had rejoined and that another of our latest battleships, the *Howe*, was with the *K.G.V.* and it was a most impressive sight as they came to the anchorage with yet another destroyer to boost our numbers.

The American C. in C. Admiral Chester Nimitz had decided our ships should be used to neutralize the Japanese islands of the Sakishima Group south of Japan's main islands while U.S. marines landed on Okinawa. Our Fleet weighed before dawn on March 23rd and rendezvoused with the replenishment tankers before steaming to our target area. The whole of the 26th and 27th was spent at Action Stations as the 16″ guns of the two battleships and planes from all four carriers plastered the enemy's air-fields and gun-positions while the rest of us fussed about on the alert for any attack by submarine or surface craft and fighting off the non-stop onslaught by high-level- and dive-bombers and thankful for the darkness when it came each night. Our attack was to continue through the 28th but the signalled approach of a typhoon made it imperative the Fleet should oil before conditions became too bad so we adjourned to the rendezvous point. While there R.A. "D" (Vian) transferred his flag from us to *K.G.V.* — the destroyer *Cambrian* coming alongside to effect the move — then we oiled throughout the night and during the next 48-hours the cruisers and destroyers steamed north, east, south and west in a protecting screen while the big ships filled their tanks, following which the rest of us had to top-up again before we could carry on 'neutralizing' on March 31st. The American landings continued and our return was a signal for the Japs to try even harder to 'neutralize' — eliminate or exterminate — us as their bombings became phrenetic with wave upon wave of Kamikazi (suicide) planes diving directly at our ships from every angle. One crashed onto *Indefatigable*'s flight-deck in an explosive mass of flame. The Fire Parties quickly had the fires under control and the steel deck had withstood the force of the explosion so well that her planes were taking-off and landing normally within a very short time. *Ulster* — one of our companion-ships all the way from Liverpool — suffered damage and casualties when a Kamikazi hit the sea a few feet from her side, and another destroyer had casualties caused by the shrapnel of our own shells. Yet another enemy pilot misjudged his aim and plunged into the sea ahead of *Indomitable* with a brilliant flash and a terrific waterspout. In the general melee four Corsairs from our carriers were lost.

Our bombardment went on over the Easter week-end but on Monday afternoon the weather became too bad for our planes to operate.

Euryalus was rolling onto her beam-ends and all ships were having a hard time, expecially the destroyers which were being hammered by huge seas towering above their bridges, as we searched for our tankers. We found them two-days later and during that respite we were able to borrow some sugar from the *Swiftsure*. (Please, Mrs. Swiftsure, may we borrow a cup of sugar? We'll return it on pay-day!) Actually we had been without for quite some time. We also had a pleasant surprise when a corvette of the tankers' Escort Group passed bags of mail to us which she had brought up from Sydney.

On Friday we were back to our allotted task at Sakishima with the Kamikazis out in force to attack the Fleet but I think our fighters had the measure of them and those which were not shot down on their approach usually ended in a harmless (to us) dive to the ocean-bed.

Information was received late on Saturday that a Japanese Fleet had left port and was steaming south at high speed and we closed to our Action Stations as we increased to 30-knots. The Captain broadcast over the Tannoy System that we were speeding to re-fuel and should be ready for battle on Sunday!

Everyone was tense as we steamed northwards on Sunday morning, still at 'battle-stations', until we learned that the Japs had been met and almost annihilated by the American Task Group 58, losing their 60,000-ton battleship *Yamata*, two cruisers and four destroyers.

We were not required! Our feelings were mixed — relief, and a reaction to the tenseness of impending battle — as we turned back for more fuel before resuming the Sakishima job.

Now that the risk of imminent action had passed it was decided to take advantage of the lull and effect repairs to one of our three forward 5.25" turrets which had been damaged by a glancing blow from a crashing Kamikazi on Saturday so I with my workshop-assistant E.R.A. and an Ordnance Artificer began stripping the blasted section of the turret at 7 o'clock that Sunday evening and then worked through the night machining and shaping pieces of steel ready for our enginesmith to weld into a composite lump which we could then machine to its proper configuration.

The welding was completed by 7 p.m. on Tuesday just as our ships were assigned a new target by Admiral Nimitz.

Our softening of Sakishima had apparently been successful enough to force the Japs to switch their planes to the airfield of northern Formosa whence they were now taking off in their efforts to prevent the Americans consolidating their hold on Okinawa. Our target now was to be the Formosan airfields and the Captain wanted the turret to be ready by dawn! Fortunately (for our little working-party) the weather at dawn and throughout the day was too bad to allow any flying at all, for even though we worked non-stop through the night we did not have the turret working until 4 p.m.

All was well for the next two days — April 12th and 13th — as our shells and bombs rained down on those airfields, and many of the planes which they put up against us were shot down by our carriers' protective fighter screen and the only four Japs to penetrate that fell victims to the ships' gunfire.

Gloom was cast over the Fleet on the 12th with news of the death of President Roosevelt but no relaxation of effort until the 14th when we withdrew to meet the oil-tankers — and — a Fleet Train!

This was something new — a mobile Base to bring all manner of stores and provisions to the Fleet, instituted for use in the event of our distant 'fixed' Shore Bases being bombed. Now it would not be necessary for us to leave the war zone and steam about 3,000-miles to Sydney. Oiling and the transferring of stores, etc., was carried out while the ships were under way and on completion we were returned to our Sakishima target where for the first two days of our bombardment there were no retaliatory attacks by Kamikazis. Then there was a day or two with the occasional plane coming over to perform its ritual suicide and we were warned that the lull was because the enemy had a new weapon — a rocket-bomb which could be launched from a plane and then guided to its target by remote-control, It was a worrying thought and we wondered when the first one would hit us.

On April 21st we left the area and on the 23rd anchored in the Gulf of Leyte (Philippines) and our main engines were stopped for the first time in 31-days.

We lay at anchor for seven days cleaning all boilers and working most evenings on essential maintenance which is only possible at such times. No shore leave was given as the seamen were busy hoisting ammunition and other supplies inboard, but on the 26th there was a special welcome and well-deserved treat of a bottle of beer for every man. Yes, very welcome in the hot weather.

Having replenished — and practically refitted the ships — we all steamed north on a new assignment to carry out a bombardment of air-bases at Miyako north of Tokyo on Honshu, Japan's main island. It was a somewhat complicated operation with the *K.G.V.* and *Howe* standing about eight miles off-shore, blasting away with their 16″ guns as we, the cruisers (including *Black Prince, Swiftsure, Uganda*, of the Royal Canadian Navy, and *Gambia* — New Zealand Navy) went further in to assist with our smaller-calibre armament and some of the destroyers went even closer to shore. The other destroyers remained to seaward protecting us all from submarines, and planes from all four carriers helped by dropping a few bombs, spotting 'fall of shot' for the battleships and keeping Japanese planes away from the Fleet.

The Kamikazis came out in waves of up to about thirty in each group but our fighters had the measure of them and shot most down although slight damage was caused to our ships. However, weight of numbers did allow three Kamikazis to penetrate the screen; one crashed itself onto *Formidable*'s flight-deck to destroy several parked planes and starting fierce fires. A second suicide pilot hit the deck of *Indomitable* at too shallow an angle and bounced straight over into the ocean while the third missed his aim — and the *Indefatigable* by a few yards — to enter the water and disappear in a spectacular explosive splash and once again we were thankful for the kindly darkness.

On Sunday, May 6th we found our oil-tankers again and spent a couple of days licking our wounds — patching bullet-holes in our superstructure and in the ship's boats hung in the davits, and repairing their motors.

When we returned to the attack on Miyako, *Euryalus* and *Black Prince* were detailed to remain with the carriers for their extra protection from Kamikazis but heavy rain brought visibility to zero, cancelling all operations. The day also brought the heartening news of Germany's capitulation of the previous day. It was no relief for us though as we were moved south again to ensure the Sakishima airfields remained unusable, and on May 9th Action Stations sounded at 5 a.m. and our bombardment/bombings went on all day with virtually no opposition from the enemy and therefore very little for we two cruisers — protecting the carriers — to do until about 4.30 p.m. when a large number of Kamikazis descended on us from the Japanese mainland to the north. The carriers' fighters were air-borne to meet them and shot down some twenty or more before they got near the ships but a few managed to get through. Thank goodness our fighters did not follow them into the 'ring of fire' which was put up! I think all guns of all ships were firing at once and all five of our 5.25" twin turrets were rattling away as fast as machine-guns, downing the enemy (who were intent on death anyway) — except for two which miraculously penetrated to crash onto the flight-decks of *Formidable* (yet again!) and *Victorious*, resulting in the loss of many parked aircraft in the ensuing fires. The Fleet then adjourned to the oiling and replenishment area after dark and we were regaled with the news of the great jubilation and celebrations of Victory taking place all over Europe, which we participated in the following evening when "Splice the Main Brace" was the order of the day — an extra tot of rum or a bottle of beer for everyone that night.

May 12th and 13th found us mounting further strikes against army barracks and the airfields on Formosa, with scant opposition, and on the 16th and 17th it was "Give Sakishima another wallop" before withdrawing on the 18th — when *Euryalus* spent two days ferrying bombs from *Formidable* (which was going to Sydney for repair) to *Indefatigable*.

On the 20th — Whit-Sunday — we returned to the attack on Sakishima until thick fog blanketed the area and the destroyer *Quillan* collided with *Indomitable*, the destroyer getting the worst of the argument and was escorted away by *Black Prince* and the destroyer *Norman* for repair. Better weather on Monday enabled our attacks to go on from 5 a.m. until 9 p.m. with only an occasional 'hero' Kamikazi attempting to break in but with quite a few high-level bombers hoping to score hits. Returning to meet the Fleet Train for a two-day replenishment period we said "Good-bye and God-speed" to *Formidable* as she steamed away, and Vice-Admiral (Cruisers) Sir. B. Rawlings transferred his flag from *Gambia* to us but apparently he was not comfortable for as our considerably reduced force was moving north a couple of days later he and his staff suddenly decided to move to *Indomitable* and May 24th and 25th found us bombarding the airfields and shore installations at Miyako with no opposition whatever. Evidently we were being successful in our task of denying the enemy the power to strike back.

We retired to re-fuel and surprisingly continued steaming southwards to anchor in the lagoon at Manus — where it was *still* raining hot rain (it seems it never stops!) — on May 30th, and after 24-hours in that cauldron we all moved off through heavy seas and the endless rain, and on June 3rd *Euryalus* parted company with the rest of the Fleet — which was bound for Sydney — and we arrived at Brisbane on the 4th with rain still teeming!

CHAPTER 24

Respite in Brisbane

Having been long at sea and away from civilization men were anxious to get ashore on that first night in port but whether it was rain or the apparent 'reserve' of the local people which induced most to return on board quite early I do not know, but their reports were disappointing.

On Friday — 8th — I took the day off when a party of 30 from the ship was invited to a Fruit Farm and, landing at 10 a.m. we were picked up by an open truck with wooden planks laid across (empty) crates for seating — most uncomfortable! — took us about 18-miles out of town to Cleveland where we were welcomed by the Shire Council chairman who led the way in his car to a Pineapple and Banana plantation at Redlands a few miles further out. We were regaled with ice-cold beer and after an hour of walking amongst the plants and trees we were conducted to the local hotel where a salad lunch was set for us. Everybody there was most kind and the lunch very tasty as the Deputy Chairman concluded the meal with another "Welcome to the Navy" speech. Fred Barratt, Chief E.R.A. — my 2nd in charge — whispered to me that he had overheard one of our hosts saying "We are now going on to have a big dinner at Miss McCarthy's" and after a few more miles of those hard seats we came to the beautiful Colonial house, the home of Miss McCarthy, which had been built by the first Lord Linlithgow more than a hundred years earlier and was being maintained as closely as possible to its original character.

A very old retainer — I would have said he was as old as the house! — took us over the vast estate, showing us where the old convict labourers lived, worked, ate, died and were buried. There was a banyan-tree growing in the Compound, its branches spreading over a vast area of a hundred-feet diameter and could have concealed a whole army. Our guide took us through acres of sugar-cane to show us giant anthills and some giant ants, and demonstrated the insects' industry by placing pieces of cane across the entrances to their nests and we observed how they organized themselves to remove the obstructions and place them beside their 'road'. And at another — older — 'hill' we saw ants on the march — thousands of them, marching on proper roads they had made for themselves and keeping to the left as they went to collect food and carried it back along the same road, still keeping to the left. It was fascinating to simply stand and watch. Fred and I returned to the house and Miss McCarthy took us over it to see the priceless collection of period furniture and many relics of the past including a number of aboriginal weapons — spears, axes and boomerangs — and all the time telling stories of her life on the Estate over the past sixty-years; tales of her father and grandfather and of native 'boys'. She had certainly lived an exciting life. At the end of our tour she went to help the old man as he carried trays of buttered scones, sandwiches, cakes and tea to serve the whole party. It was just as acceptable to us as Fred's "big dinner" would have been, I'm sure!

We returned to the city by a different route and stopped at the farm of another Councillor who gave us the run of the place and told us to pick as many pineapples and custard-apples as we liked to take back to the ship. (At our other stops we had permission to eat as much as we liked.)

Rain fell steadily over the week-end but on Monday (11th) I took advantage of the 72-hours General Leave granted to the two Watches.

I booked a room at the Naval House and on Tuesday morning the rain was as persistent as ever so I spent a most interesting and absorbing day in the Queensland Museum and Art Gallery.

On Wednesday the sun shone and I boarded the first tram to come along when I left the House. It took me to Lutwytche — a scattering of houses — no shops — at the end of the line a few miles outside the city limits where a single-decker bus waited to take people onwards to Sandgate. There was no driver in evidence as I boarded with other would-be passengers to sit and wait.Ten minutes later another tram arrived and disgorged its load most of whom came aboard the bus. Another ten minutes and another tram and more people for the bus. Many were now standing. I gave up my seat and asked, "Does anyone know what time this bus leaves for Sandgate?" No one knew but a man volunteered, "No — we just have to wait until he feels like it!" — so I left and began walking but had not gone far when a lorry overtook me, the driver asking "where was I going?" and gave me a lift in that direction. He had a mate in the cab and his load was three 25-feet-long electric-lighting poles which were to be dropped off at different locations in the Bush. I said I was only sight-seeing so they suggested I go along with them and could drop off at any time.

We travelled for miles along the rough road through wild country of scrub and small trees, stopping to off-load each pole at its proper position and not seeing a single dwelling nor any other human. It was certainly off the beaten track but they were good company and when the last pole had been dropped at the appointed place we came to a junction where a rough signpost indicated Sandgate lay to our left and we parted company as they took the road back to Brisbane.

I had been walking for about twenty minutes when a Royal Australian Air Force car overtook me and its Wing Commander driver gave me a lift to Sandgate just a few miles further along the road. It was unexpectedly quaint with tiny cottages — clean and smart — and oh so quiet. It was on the coast and I suppose it would be classed a 'watering-place' rather than a seaside resort but there were no other people to be seen anywhere until I found "The Tea Shop" and was able to satisfy hunger and thirst before boarding a bus back to Brisbane by the direct route.

A lot of work had piled up in the workshop during my short absence and almost all the crew had taken advantage of the break, visiting a number of different resorts within the specified radius and all returning with their own, varied feelings. Six members of my Mess had gone together to one place — and had become bored with each other's company. Two others had joined the organized party to Gympie and their reaction was, "Too much 'Navy'! Might just as well have stayed on board!"

Now it was a return to Action . . .

CHAPTER 25

The Atom Bombs

After three weeks of relaxation plus a lot of work, we sailed from Brisbane at 0630 on June 28th and were soon into War Routine when we met some of the ships which had been to Sydney and began exercising as all steamed northward, splitting into two groups at times to come together later in a 'Night Encounter' action with plenty of high-speed running and gunfire. Unfortunately one of our boilers developed leaks so the ship was diverted to Manus — the "Oven" — arriving there on July 3rd and then working almost non-stop in the humid climatic heat and the sweltering heat of the boiler, cutting out the faulty tubes and fitting and expanding new ones into place, then a full pressure test on the repairs before we could 'flash up' and sail to rejoin the Fleet. We left Manus at speed early on the 6th, the Captain telling us we were on our way to Tokyo — catching up our ships on July 13th and on the 16th we met and combined with the United States 3rd Fleet about 300-miles from the Japanese capital. There were a hundred ships in the American Fleet, and twenty-five in ours and we all closed up to Action Stations at half-past three next morning as planes from all carriers took off to attack airfields around Tokyo. All day long there was a shuttle-service of bombers flying from the carriers with full loads and returning to re-arm for another attack, also fighters being kept airborne to protect them and the ships from opposing aircraft.

At 5 p.m. the carriers withdrew and the rest of us — battleships, cruisers and destroyers — were ordered in-shore to bombard the industrial suburbs and shipyards which we did throughout the night. Shells of all calibres pounded the area until we withdrew just before dawn when the air-men took over again, thus giving the Japs a dose of their own medicine and at the end of that second day both Fleets retired to replenish and ran into the tail-end of yet another typhoon.

Oiling was hazardous and difficult in the rough seas and as there were many more ships the process took much longer and it was four days — and nights — of continuous activity before all ships were ready to resume. On the 23rd the massive armada attacked the naval bases of Kobe and Kuri and their airfields with much the same pattern as at Tokyo except that on the second day of our attack the enemy planes which came out seemed more intent on their own destruction than in destroying us for they flew directly into the terrific barrage of fire put up by the ships and all fell like flies in front of D.D.T. spray-guns. The consensus of opinion was that the pilots must have been trainees who had never flown solo before but we

223

were still very relieved when "Secure" sounded at 9 p.m. and we had the shield of darkness after another long day.

The target for the morrow was Tokyo but as we started to move north there came warning of another typhoon causing the cruisers and destroyers to return to the attack on the Kobe shipyards through the night of July 29th while the battleships bombarded the town of Osaka and when daylight came on the 30th with no opposition our ships moved closer inshore actually into their Inland Sea to deliver close-range shelling to all three industrial centres — Osaka, Kuri and Kobe. A few enemy planes appeared but seemed to be more 'reconnaissance-minded' or perhaps 'sight-seeing' and had no stomach to attack. At dusk we moved out to sea to find the Fleet Train and re-fill magazines and fuel-tanks.

Typhoon conditions again affected operations when a planned attack against Hitachi could not go ahead on August 4th so all ships retired to top-up with fuel and returned to the fray on the 8th.

We closed to our Action Stations at twenty-to-four that morning ready for the air-strikes and bombardment of Hitachi just north of Tokyo but were frustrated again when thick fog blanketed the target area and we moved away from the coast, remaining at our Stations until 5.30 p.m. because of frequent radar alerts of approaching enemy planes and it was then that we heard a brief report on a wireless set — "An Atomic Bomb has been dropped on the city of Hiroshima". That was all — no details whatsoever.

The fog cleared during the night and Action Stations again sounded at 0340 as planes took off for the postponed attack on Hitachi, and on this day enemy planes were much more active than of late. It was seemingly a last desperate effort to inflict maximum damage on the ships for they were sending out every type of aircraft they possessed from ancient Trainers up to their most modern fighter-bomber — one of which managed to penetrate the screen and score a direct hit on an American destroyer, causing serious damage and casualties.

When we secured at 8 p.m. we heard that a second Atomic Bomb had been dropped, this one on Nagasaki but it did not interfere with our planned third day of assault on Hitachi as once again we closed to Action at 0340 on the 10th for what turned out to be an uneventful day, and when "Secure" sounded at 8 p.m. the Captain also spoke over the Tannoy — "The Japanese have asked for Peace but that does not mean the war is over. We must not relax, not even for one minute."

Our further strikes were cancelled pending developments as both Fleets withdrew to the replenishment area and on Sunday, August 12th our Force divided; *King George V, Indefatigable, Gambia, Newfoundland* and some of the destroyers were to remain with the American Fleet ready to enter Tokyo harbour when the official Surrender came; *Implacable,*

Euryalus, Swiftsure and the rest of the destroyers were ordered to Manus. So we headed south through mountainous seas and temperatures soaring to make life almost unbearable in all ships and absolute hell in the destroyers. *Euryalus* was running short of fuel and attempted to take some from *Implacable* and she had only transferred enough to ensure a margin of safety when the hose broke in the rough seas.

On the evening of the 14th the ship's radio picked up a broadcast from San Francisco, "Japan had accepted the Allies' terms of Surrender" but the Captain immediately came on the Tannoy to say that we must wait for official confirmation which came next morning with yet another message from the Captain. "We must all remain alert against any 'Death or Glory' attacks!" But everyone was feeling happy! It was Peace at last and we were thankful at having survived nearly six-years of War. But — what now?

We had been plodding along at 10-knots, wallowing in the heavy seas, but on receipt of official signal from C. in C. speed increased to 25-knots with the ships battened down against a combination of tropical rain and mountainous waves so that not many men could enjoy the bottle of beer or extra tot of rum when the Main Brace was spliced that night, August 15th.

It was very hot and very wet below decks, and too dangerous above them so that even Manus was a relief on Saturday, August 18th when the ship secured alongside the giant oil-tanker *Assa Maersk* to fill our nearly-empty tanks, but before oiling could start I had to make the necessary adapters to connect her hoses to our inlets. Then *Assa Maersk*'s chief engineer brought a broken valve from his engine-room for me to repair — as an urgent favour.

Euryalus at this time was in a very sorry state with scarcely a scrap of paint on her hull, funnels or superstructure and almost red with rust. She must have appeared like some old hulk which might be found rotting in a breaker's yard, and her internal condition was much the same, and that was reflected in the attitude of a lot of the ship's company.

We were to have remained with the oiler overnight but at midnight received orders to move to anchor and I was called to get the Steaming Watch below as soon as possible. Unfortunately, while I had been engaged in the machine-shop those men who had not consumed their beer or extra tot when it was issued on the 15th had done so this afternoon and evening, with disastrous results, for, whether because they had been 'dry' for a longer time than normal or that it was 'fighting beer', it had certainly affected many of them. Fist-fights occurred in some messes with smashed crockery and broken bottles lying about the decks in the vomit and 'bodies' sleeping just where they had passed out. It took time to locate and rouse those needed for the lighting-up Watch and had just made sure that all were below when I was called to the Office (at that hour of the night) and presented with the latest signal to be received — "Hostilities-Only ratings in Age Groups 18 to 20 are to be discharged to the Supply-ship to await passage to the U.K." — and two of the men I had sent below were in the Group. I had to find and rouse reliefs for them at once in order to give them time to pack and as with all the others I had had to detail — none felt like turning-out. "Why me? Can't you find somebody else?"

The ship moved to anchor at 2 a.m. and at 9 a.m. all the men in the specified age-group left us and we weighed anchor with orders to proceed to Leyte, Philippines, and thence to Hong Kong.

It had been a relief to arrive at Manus but it was much more of a relief to leave the place, to get moving and have some air circulating through the decks.

Coming off watch at midnight I went to the upper deck where it was so cool and peaceful. A million stars filled the sky, many shooting about all over the place while brilliant flashes of lightning lit the horizons and a swelling moon gradually sank behind some low-hanging clouds — shedding a few more rays before slipping into the ocean and leave the myriad twinkling diamonds and incessantly-flashing lightning as the sole illumination of the night sky for, being virtually still at war there were no visible lights on the ship. In peacetime bulkhead lights on the upper deck were sufficient for men to read or write by and to pace the deck without tripping over ropes, wires, cleats or bollards. But we could not relax.

At Leyte on the 22nd we oiled and then steamed through the Mindanao Strait passing many places which had featured in bulletins connected with General McArthur's re-taking of the Philippines from the Japs — Mindoro — Bataan — Corregidor — Subic Bay — and anchored off Manila on Friday, August 24th to embark stores during the week-end, and to enjoy our "Victory Dinner". What a farce!

The refrigerated chickens were brought while we were at Leyte but it was decided the celebration meal would not be served until we were anchored at a place where it was considered most of the crew would be able to sit down at the same time. The birds were taken from the cold-store on the morning of the *day before* they were to be cooked and — in that terrific heat they began to sing!

The Special Menu included "Sakishima Soup" and "Chicken à la Tojo" — which should really have been "Chicken à la Kamikazi" because it was a 'killer' — not that anyone died from eating it, but so many were very ill, too many to be accommodated in the Sick Bay and had to remain in their hammocks where the over-burdened doctor and his staff attended them. The actual colour and the smell of the meat had offended my palate and olfactory senses so I refrained from eating the stuff but I was reminded of a similar incident which occurred in *Shropshire* in 1930 when we were in the dry dock in Malta and calves' hearts had been served for supper one night. My stomach turned at the very off-putting smell and the thought of eating

226

but others' stomachs were less sensitive and they ate — with dire results, for in the middle of the night the majority were stricken with diarrhoea. Unfortunately the heads (toilets) were located on shore and quite a distance from the ship, a long way to run in those circumstances and many runners did not stay the course. No one died but lots reported sick and "An Inquiry will be held to look into this matter".

Now — *Euryalus* was afloat and at anchor in Manila Bay and those who were taken short during the night had not far to run, but it was as much a nuisance. Of course, there was to be an Inquiry, which probably ended with the same kind of result as the 1930 one (whatever that was!)

Sunday Divisions were held on the 26th for the first time in many, many months but the Engine-room department was very conspicuous by its absence; we were far too busy on general maintenance, boiler-cleaning, and machinery examination.

Another odd incident. At Leyte an Official Photographer had joined the ship (with the chickens!) and one day the Executive Commander called me to be introduced to this chap with the words "You *must* have pictures of our chief E.R.A. in his 'Palace of Engineering'," and to me "When would it be convenient, chief?" Next morning they came and a number of flash-light photographs of me and my assistants and the various machines were taken. Then we toured engine-rooms, boiler-rooms, gun turrets, plotting-room and bridge, with his camera flashing at every object in sight but afterwards I wondered whether he had film in it, for no one in the ship ever saw any results of his work. Perhaps he forgot our address, for he left us a few days later when we arrived in Hong Kong.

We had sailed from Manila at 4 p.m. on August 27th in company with *Indomitable* (Rear-Admiral C.R.J. Harcourt, who had been Commander of *Shropshire* — 1929/32), the light fleet carrier *Venerable, Swiftsure,* and three destroyers. All ships went to Action Stations and remained closed up against any treachery as we approached Hong Kong and on the 29th met the battleship *Anson* with two more destroyers.

Admiral Harcourt transferred his flag to *Swiftsure* in order to lead the force into harbour without jeopardizing the big ships should the Japs have mined the entrance, and at 0630 on Thursday, August 30th he led the way in closely followed by us and three destroyers in our wake. *Indomitable* entered in the evening and on Friday morning came three more destroyers and a Hospital-ship; *Anson* — which according to the B.B.C. had "led the British Fleet into Hong Kong" — entered on Friday evening to the ironic cheers of the crews of ships which arrived 36-hours earlier.

From our anchorage could be seen a barracks on shore with Japanese flags flying over them and it was known there were about 20,000 troops stationed in the colony so the guns of all ships were trained on them. (Prior to our entering harbour we had heard — via the lower-deck grape-vine —

227

that a plane had taken off from the carrier to land at the local airfield to collect a released P.O.W. Naval Commander and a Japanese envoy from the barracks and fly them out to the carrier to confer with the Admiral and the story was that the Jap had said he had no orders from his Government to surrender, to which Harcourt had responded, "My ships are going in and it is up to you to control your men. The Official ceremony takes place on Sunday, September 2nd.")

Well, we were in and all ships had fire-hoses rigged on their decks ready to keep Chinese sampans at a distance from their sides; those coming too close got a drenching. It seemed cruel but there were so many, each containing between 20 and 30 people of all ages, from tiny babies to wizened old men and women, all actually living in their craft, and had they managed to secure alongside in any number could have overrun us.

To revert back for a moment to our recent brief stop at Manus — when it became known that *Euryalus* was to visit Hong Kong a Petty Officer serving in one of the carriers was transferred to us because his wife had been captured and interned by the Japs when the Colony fell to them in January 1942, and he had neither seen nor heard from her since then. Now it was Saturday, September 1st and I was 'Standing' Rounds as the Captain inspected all Messes when the Commander asked if I would like to visit Stanley (Internment) Camp that afternoon? I would — and at 1.30 p.m. landed with the small party which consisted of the Commander, the Commander (E), the Gunnery Officer, Paymaster Commander and the Navigator, the Master-at-Arms, Chief Bo'sun's Mate, Chief Electrical Artificer, myself and the carrier's Petty Officer.

All of us carried revolvers and ammunition as we boarded a Japanese-made lorry driven by a Leading Seaman from our ship and had two additional guards — a seaman and stoker each with automatic rifles — to ride 'shot-gun'!

The Dockyard was a shambles. Much had been destroyed by our own people before retreating in 1942 and aerial bombardment during recent months together with possible sabotage by the Japs when they knew the end was nigh had certainly taken toll, and remarks were passed to the effect that "It'll be a long, long time before *this* will be usable!"

The Chinese quarter outside the Yard was even worse as most buildings had been destroyed or gutted by fire and it was almost impossible to get our lorry through the rubble in the narrow streets. There were thousands of destitute natives squatting or standing about in the heaps of masonry, and the stench was awful. Then we passed what had been the Naval Hospital and it was in the process of being looted. Hundreds of Chinese were streaming out like crowds from a football match or those giant ants of Queensland — men, women, and children — down to the tiniest tot — all laden with chairs, tables, beds, doors, cupboards, window-frames, in fact anything that *could* be moved and carried was being taken.

The Camp was about ten miles distant but a short way outside the town we came to what had once been the Headquarter Office of one of the big firms of the Colony. The Navy had already taken control and the carrier's Petty Officer made it known that the belongings of himself and his wife had been stored there at the end of 1941 and he wondered whether they had survived. He and the Commander went inside to check and, remarkably, some of it had and that was heartening for him. While they were inside the rest of us alighted to stretch our legs just as a small patrol with rifles, and with a Japanese prisoner in their midst, marched past.

We resumed our journey in the hills and about ten minutes later the sound of rifle-fire echoed round — and we glanced at one another! It might not have been what we thought it was! Perhaps it only sounded like it?

The shaky old lorry caused some alarm when, at the top of one of the hills on what was becoming a lovely drive, smoke began pouring from its engine and we thought disaster had struck. Fortunately it was only that the radiator was running dry, but even more fortunate was the fact there was a small stream tumbling down the road. Fresh, clean, sparkling water topped up the radiator and we journeyed on to our next mishap! Our driver took a wrong turn on the narrow mountain-road and we all had to alight while he gingerly manoeuvred and inched the vehicle to turn it round — there being a drop of 200-feet on one side and a rise of about 500-feet on the other side and at some points much of the road had been blasted away. He was brave, and he was calm, but we voiced the hope that we would not be returning when it was dark! We reached the Camp after three o'clock; some of the inmates ran to welcome us and were as thin and skeletal as the Chinese, having existed for years on a meagre diet of rice, water-spinach and hard-tack biscuits.

We distributed the sweets, biscuits, chocolate, soap, newspapers and cigarettes we had brought, and the Petty Officer was re-united with his Eurasian wife. She was one among the 2,500-plus internees in the Camp. We gradually split into small groups as their stories unfolded — as they told of what swine the Japs had been throughout the three years, eight months and six days of captivity, each and every day having been religiously ticked-off on the walls of their huts — and that the last fourteen days had been the most dreadful because they knew the Japanese were finished and were giving-in and wondered if they, the internees — might be bayoneted or shot before help arrived.

They had managed to secrete a tiny radio-receiving set on which they got a modicum of news when their guards were well clear but first realised something out of the ordinary was about to happen when a week ago there was no morning Roll Call and the guards got drunk. That was really ominous, but from then on it seemed the Japs were deserting the Camp to hide in the hills.

We left at 5 p.m. and returned to Victoria via Repulse Bay and were on board by 6.30, thankful that we had not had to endure the privations of those we had seen that afternoon.

A Peace Document was signed in Tokyo next day (2nd) and we immediately landed platoons of marines, seamen and stokers (I suppose the other ships did too) to take control of the Dockyard, to patrol the town, and to pick up any Japanese found wandering.

I had to arrange for one Chief and three E.R.A's to go to the Yard each day to try to get the machine-shops back to some semblance of order and every day they were sending broken and sabotaged parts to the ship for us to repair for them; sometimes they would send just a rough sketch of an item they wished us to manufacture, so there was no let-up and all worked long hours.

The Chief O.A. received a message from an old chum and *Fisgard* classmate of his (a Chief E.R.A.) who was recovering aboard the hospital-ship *Oxfordshire* after being a prisoner of the Japanese for nearly four years, and on returning from a visit to him reported that his chum was "just skin and bone — had lost an arm — and thought he would not have lasted many more days had release not come when it did, and he was the sole survivor of a number of engine-room staff captured when Hong Kong fell." It made me wonder how the *Scout* had fared. Had she been there when the Japs landed?

No shore leave was being given because of the conditions on shore but recreational parties were allowed to land on some afternoons if they were accompanied by an officer and kept to specified roads and areas, but even that concession was quickly withdrawn after one party broke the rules (as usual!) and everyone was confined to the ship.

Actually we were still awaiting the surrender of the Japs in Hong Kong for apparently their senior men on shore were not authorized to sign. A General or an Admiral would be flown in — when they felt like it! Meanwhile the Chinese were taking their revenge by killing any Japanese deserters found roaming the islands and many bodies were seen floating past the ship. The sampan-dwellers took scant notice of the corpses except to prod and poke them with boat-hooks and push them beneath the surface as they passed by.

Lots of sampans congregated round the carriers and two 'adopted' us, keeping station a few feet from our starboard side about midships. The larger of the two craft was about 12-feet long and 5-feet beam with a canvas shelter in the middle under which the family/crew lived, cooked and slept, the family comprising parents, two boys of about nine- and ten-years and a girl of maybe 7-years of age. All sat round in the boat fishing most of the day but always alert for any food or salvable item coming down the gash-chute or dropped over the ship's side, their nets ready to hand for lifting the articles into the boat.

The smaller sampan had a crew of three little girls, the eldest of whom I judged to be about 12-years, and the youngest no more than 8-years but they could handle their craft like veterans and would nip in under the noses of the other family and with their long-handled nets scoop up many tasty morsels. Watching them one day after our dinner I saw one of the girls net a lump of pie-crust before it hit the water. She immediately handed her catch to the senior member who halved it and handed one piece to the middle one who, in her turn divided that piece into two equal portions and gave one of them to the junior member, then all three sat contentedly to eat — and seemingly enjoy — the tit-bit. Half-under the canvas shelter of the big sampan stood an iron cauldron into which all the collected food was thrown. It contained water that had been scooped from the harbour (Filthy stuff!) and beneath it was a wood- or coal-fired brazier to keep it warm. At meal-times 'Ma' would throw a handful of rice into the pot and the family then dipped their tins in for the liquor and used chop-sticks to rescue and eat the solids.

After two weeks of lying at anchor in the heat and frequent torrential rains, and with no shore-leave following the rigours of months at sea, there was considerable discontent on board, especially amongst the H.O's (Hostilities Only ratings) — impatient for their Age and Service Group number to come up for their release. There were many in the ship with no basic loyalties to the Service and its Traditions, to their shipmates, or even to their messmates, and instances occurred of men dropping over the side into sampans in the darkness to be taken ashore and (hopefully) return before dawn. Some did not and paid the penalty. One incident concerned a member of our Mess who disappeared one evening and was not missed at supper-time as most of us were working irregular hours, but one of the Duty E.R.A's doing the 9 p.m. 'Rounds' had found the De-Laval turbo-generator 'open' with most of its components scattered about the deck — despite strict and specific orders that "All machinery must be closed up at night in case of emergency."

The Duty chap came to me and I instituted a search in case the man had fallen in another compartment but there was no trace and another man had to be detailed to close the job — a task more difficult by his not knowing why it had been stripped down to almost bare bones. (He and a mate took three hours).

Reporting this to the Senior Engineer I said the last sighting had been at 4 p.m. when a messmate saw him in the bathroom. The Senior said, "He probably got fed-up and left!"

Our man appeared at the breakfast table as though nothing was amiss but I produced him before the Senior at 9 a.m. to explain his actions and when he had finished the Senior said, "Well, as you were not seen going or returning — er — we don't want any more trouble in the ship than there already is, do we, chief? — So — don't let it happen again!" What discipline! and in spite of the sentries who were supposed to be patrolling round the clock to prevent sampans coming too close to the ship!

On September 14th the battleship *Duke of York* with the C. in C. British Pacific Fleet, Admiral Sir Bruce Fraser, on board entered harbour to a chorus of ironic cheers and booing from a considerable crowd of men on our upper deck and as soon as his flagship anchored he summoned our Captain to go on board. This was on the very day a new captain had arrived to relieve Captain Oliver-Bellasis but it was O-B who went — to 'carry the can' and receive the dressing-down and on his return he had the Lower Deck cleared — to pass the 'rocket' to the whole ship's company saying: "The Admiral told me he had had the greatest repect and admiration for this ship until that moment but now he thought us to be the lowest of the low! I feel utterly disgusted". One could tell he was a very sad man, for in addition to that he had attended two Courts-Martial on board earlier in the day both involving marines who had committed offences while on Guard Duty on shore. One had received nine-months imprisonment, the other four-months (Court-martial sentences were always read out to ships' companies).

That night one of the marines together with a stoker who was awaiting Court-martial on the morrow disappeared over the side. What a place to want to desert in! especially as we were due to leave Hong Kong ourselves on Sunday 16th.

On Sunday morning we were told the C. in C. would be coming on board to attend our Church Service and inspect Divisions, and as it was customary for a C. in C. to visit a ship before she leaves the Station and his command (for home!) hopes rose, but before the Admiral arrived, Captain O-B addressed the crew. "He is coming because he wants to see the type of men who can jeer at others against the good order and the discipline of the Navy". And that is just what it was, for after Church the Admiral said he now knew the reason for the booing when his ship came in. "It was the lack of publicity given to this ship despite all the good work she has done, but that is not my fault". He added, "You have been in every operation out here and when the war was finished *you* were sent to Hong Kong — on a very vital duty — while other ships, which have been on only one or two operations went back to Sydney. You are accompanied by ships which have just arrived out here, yet it is *their* names which are blazoned over the wireless and in the newspapers. Mr. Attlee tells me to sign the Treaty of Surrender in Tokyo and I come up here in my flagship which, for one reason or another has not been in one single operation out here — and *her* name is immediately given out over the radio. I appreciate all that but I still think it very ill-mannered of you to jeer and if it was not for the good name this ship bears you would now be towing a damaged oiler down to Sydney. Good-bye and Good Luck to you all!" He left us and we sailed for Sydney at 2.30 p.m. — with the missing marine (who had been picked up ashore) — but no sign of the stoker.

On the following Sunday — the day before we would be calling at Manus — Captain Oliver-Bellasis said his "Goodbyes" and told us: "I'm sorry I am not taking the ship home, but I've heard that the China Station is a happy one to serve on and I wish you all the best of luck!"

On his departure his successor, Captain R. S. Warne, introduced himself with the usual "I hope you will serve me as faithfully — — etc., and I do not know the ship's future movements on leaving Sydney, but even if she does go home you must realise that the lower Age and Service Groups, men who have been out here longest, and those near the end of their Service engagements will be the most probable to sail on her." Well, that sounded hopeful for me as I had just one more year to serve for my pension.

Every day we were steaming past tropical islands, seemingly uninhabited, with beautiful white sandy-beaches lined with palm-trees and on one evening we had what can only be called 'a very pretty picture'. Away on our port beam steaming northwards was a Hospital Ship with all her lights on and her hull outlined in blue-tinted electric bulbs and the Red Cross on her funnel was edged with red lighting. To complete the picture her stern was flood-lit — to give a "Carnival" sort of scene against the background of deep purple night sky and twinkling stars and crowds of us stood fascinated on the upper deck watching until she disappeared over the horizon.

I and other day-workers were still keeping the First Watch — 8 p.m. till midnight every night in order to give the 'standing' watch-keepers a break, and I was also engaged in preparing a Defect List of all jobs to be done while the ship was in dock at Sydney.

CHAPTER 26

Sydney

Euryalus arrived in Sydney on September 30th and another Chief E.R.A. joined the ship. My relief? No! (Shades of *Emperor of India* — 1928) "Owing to the amount of work to be done we cannot let you go." Anyway, the Captain decided to grant 10-days General Leave to each of the two Watches while in port — a very welcome concession in view of our prospective work-load in the Engineering department — so I formulated a new Duty Roster to reflect the depleted numbers available during the Leave period, cutting the size of the Duty Watch for each night to allow maximum opportunity for shore-leave.

I purposely omitted my name as I considered myself fully occupied in regulating the Mess, organizing the work routine and allocating jobs in addition to my machine-shop duties, but our new arrival thought that — as my relief he too should have no Duty Watch to keep. Airing his views to the other two chiefs all three decided to petition the Senior — who promptly sent them packing, especially as the ship was 'dry-docking' on October 2nd and all underwater valves would have to be removed, machined, refitted and replaced, and it was essential that all should be 'boxed up' each night lest the dock had to be flooded in emergency.

Discontent had been growing since the cessation of hostilities but now hackles rose and recriminations began flying.

It was a 'no win' situation with a general malaise in all departments, and the situation on shore was just as bad. There were labour disputes and a strike had cut electical power supplies from the city. There was an acute shortage of foods such as meat, fruit, vegetables and cereals, while practically every wireless report was of trouble somewhere in the world — China — India — Argentina — Greece — so that we began to wonder if we would ever get home.

In the popular British Centre I met a messmate from my *Shropshire* (1929 – 1931) days who had been released from a P.O.W. camp in Japan. His face was scarred from his treatment while in captivity so that I would not have recognized him had he not approached me. He had been serving in *Scout* at Hong Kong (I did not tell him that I had been asked to volunteer to remain with *Scout* in 1938) — had been captured there and shipped to Japan. That ship was torpedoed en route but now he was "going home tomorrow aboard *Dominion Monarch*" — another of the ships I had known. I landed for a walk on Sunday afternoon and followed the crowds pouring into the Domain, a large park on the South Shore, wondering what the attraction was and found a "Speakers' Corner" similar to that of London's Hyde Park and as entertaining. Speakers on all subjects — politics — religion — scholarship— theatre; cranks and maniacs, pros and cons and a lot of heckling. It was hilarious and I stayed until dusk but there was little joy in being in the city after dark. Cinemas and theatres could only open for business if they had their own generators and restaurants had to rely on solid- or oil-fuel to supply hot meals in their candle-lit dining-rooms. The newspapers spoke of more than 200,000-men being idle and losing more than a million pounds a week in wages and forecast that police-pickets would be on the streets to prevent rioting and looting. No, it was not pleasant being ashore in the city. The British Centre had long queues waiting for meals every evening so on my odd trips ashore I made a point of seeing something of the outlying areas such as Parramatta, a quiet, 'dead-as-the-dodo' place; Lilyfields, which I imagined would be as its name implied — a pretty Garden-suburb — but which turned out to be a shanty-town of derelict and dilapidated industrial buildings!

I had been undecided about taking my 10-days Leave but my friends at Eastwood, knowing I was keen to see as much as possible while my ship was in Sydney, invited me to use their home as a base. I accepted and then, as I could have a free Travel Warrant I obtained one to visit Orange, a small town on the other side of the Blue Mountains and some 200-miles distant, without the hassle and disappointments I had experienced at Brisbane.

I landed at 3 p.m. on Tuesday, October 23rd for the 8.30 p.m. train which deposited me at Orange at five o'clock next morning — with two shipmates (Mechanician Prowse and Petty Officer Dyer) who had chosen the same venue. I would not be entirely on my own, which was just as well because the town *was* small, and reminiscent of towns in American Cowboy films — wood-frame houses, dusty, dirt roads, and hotels and shops with hitching posts for the tethering of horses.

We booked into the same (Howell's Tourist) hotel which was clean with large, airy rooms with bath and comfortable bed, and good food. What more could one ask!

When I returned to my ship I was immediately called into conference because *Euryalus* had been un-docked the day after I went on leave to allow for the emergency docking of another ship and had re-docked this very morning — water still being pumped from the dock. I had assumed that all the machining of under-water valves and fitting would have been completed during my absence but returned to find things exactly the same

235

except for the reason of this conference. One messmate was being invalided home and three others — (H.O's in the latest Age & Service Group) — were also being discharged to the U.K. so the work schedules of those remaining, together with the composition of their duty watches had to be re-arranged — much to the chagrin of all, of course!

Work was completed and the ship undocked on November 10th, steam was raised and we were able to leave Sydney at 0600 on the 16th.

I was able to get ashore on the 15th to say my 'Goodbyes' and 'Thanks' to Mr. and Mrs. "C" at Eastwood because I did not know when or *if* we would meet again. Leave expired at midnight and the last boat would depart Circular Quay at 11.30 p.m., and when I arrived at the jetty I think practically the whole ship's company were there with their Aussie friends waiting to see them 'safely off the premises' — so to speak. And what a night that was! A night to remember! A night with everybody singing, the words of "Aloha", "Goodbye", and "We'll meet again" echoing round the harbour, and our ferry-boat delayed as its cox'n waited for the last-minute stragglers, reluctant to let go of, or be released by, their friends, to scramble on board with some clinging to the outer rail as we eventually got clear.

To add to the general scene the liner *Stirling Castle* — brightly illuminated and floodlit — was slowly pulling away from an adjacent pier with more than 2,000-Naval and R.A.F. personnel bound for home. Hundreds more men were boarding the troopship *Nestor* further along the Quay again with lots of people singing 'Goodbyes'.

It was hectic! It was noisy! It was merry! It was GREAT!

CHAPTER 27

South Sea Islands

We sailed next morning and arrived at Brisbane the following day in heavy, tropical rain which continued non-stop for our four-day visit and very few men were sorry to leave on November 21st on what was now an independent cruise to some of our Dependencies in the Pacific Ocean, our first being Fiji where we secured to the jetty at Suva on the 26th.

I walked ashore at five o'clock that evening, and returned aboard at half-past-six after a walk along dirt roads and avenues of coconut trees and neat, clean bungalows. It was strange seeing practically all the male population wearing skirts, part of the national dress, and when one asked me questions about my ship I, in turn, asked about the skirt and established that it is called a 'sula', the equivalent of the 'sarong' in Java, and had other names in other islands.

Ordinary shorts are worn beneath the skirt. The policemen wore navy-blue tunics and white sulas with deep 'vees' cut all round the bottom edge and at sunset they had to change to navy-blue sulas — vee'd the same as the white. During my short time on shore I think I saw more Chinese and Indians than native Fijians.

The ship gave a Searchlight Display the following evening with thousands gathered in the town's open spaces and along the quay-side.

The Torpedo Officer was directing and passing his orders in a low voice over the Armament Broadcast System. The finale was to be the firing of three rockets and as the time approached he quietly said, "Remember, when the lights are doused I want the three rockets to go up at once — and together! Right? . . . O.K. *Douse the lights!*" The starboard searchlight was shut off. In a slightly louder voice he repeated, "*Douse the lights!*" and the port light was extinguished and — Swish! One rocket soared into the night sky, followed at split-second intervals by — Swish! — Swish! — as the others rose in succession.

The appreciative crowd had been silent except for 'oohs' and 'aahs' at the patterns being woven on the night sky but there was an explosion of laughter from the whole mass as the Torpedo Officer obviously annoyed by the contretemps, and in a low voice which was heard all over the town said, "Bloody hopeless!" I bet his face was red!

We left Suva on Friday, Nov. 30th and anchored off (a very long way off) Nukualofa, the capital town of Tonga, the next day, to take part in the Centenary celebrations of the island becoming a Kingdom.

The ship was dressed overall and a Royal Marine Guard of Honour landed to attend on Queen Salote; Native Feasts were arranged ashore for the ship's company and the Sergeants' Mess of the New Zealand Forces invited twelve C.P.O's to a Social on Sunday, Dec. 2nd. "Transport from pier at 2 p.m."

To see something of the town before going to the Mess I landed by the 1 p.m. boat and found it wasn't so much a town as a collection of native huts in lines to form streets, and as it was mid-day — *and* a Sunday — only a few people were about. The men wore mid-calf length skirts (longer than the sula) and the women wore hulas, grass skirts worn over their ordinary cotton-print dresses, with wide, gaily-decorated waist-bands and looking very picturesque.

I met the other chiefs at 2 p.m. for the ride on an Army lorry to the Camp pleasantly set amongst coconut palms about four miles outside town where the New Zealanders were delighted to welcome white faces. There was plenty of talking, some card-playing and table-tennis and billiards, and an ample supply of ice-cold beer, all followed by a set meal of corned-mutton, tomatoes, spring-onions, and fresh, new bread with tasty New Zealand butter — a real luxury!

Darkness fell suddenly at 6 p.m. and we were conducted to their open-air cinema among the palms to see "Captain Kidd" (Charles Laughton). After the show a giant water-melon was cut and served with liberal helpings of ginger and brown sugar and the evening wound up with a group of Maoris singing Native and National songs, in perfect harmony. A most enjoyable day ended with the lorry whisking us through the cool, night air back to the jetty for the 10.30 p.m. boat.

Few men could be spared from the Engine-room department to attend the Native Feast next day because although the ship had spent seven weeks in Sydney her boilers had not been cleaned (probably due to the granting of General Leave) so as soon as we anchored on Saturday two boilers were opened and other work was taken in hand.

The main Celebration ceremony in the presence of the Queen of Tonga was on Tuesday, December 4th and a list of names of men wishing to attend was required by the Commander by 8.30 on that morning.

The notice I posted on the Mess board on Monday was still blank on Tuesday morning. At breakfast I asked, "Does anyone want to go ashore to this Opening Ceremony today?" No reply was forthcoming so I put my name down and immediately two others said, "You can put our names on the list," Three names! As the rest reported in the Machine-shop at 8 o'clock to be allocated their work I again asked if any were interested in the pageantry taking place on shore and another six said they would like to go. (Could it be that they didn't like their job?) I submitted the list of nine names to the Senior and, after some hesitation he agreed saying that it was the maximum number to be spared in view of the work to be done. My list was in the Commander's Office at 8.30. At 9 a.m. a junior Engineer Officer came to say that two E.R.A's working in his department had asked his permission to go ashore and "I have given that permission". I told him he could withdraw it because the Senior cannot spare more than nine and in any case his two had had ample time to make up their minds. By the time I had sorted them out it was too late to be ready to land with the party, so that only eight went from our Mess — which was rather providential as things turned out, for on landing the whole crowd from the ship were kept waiting in the broiling sunshine until 10.45 when they were marched to the Parade Ground to stand and wait again until 12.30 when Queen Salote arrived to take the Salute. All suffered sun-burned faces and arms, and all my crowd blamed me for forcing them to go ashore and then staying on board myself!

In the evening we returned the New Zealanders' hospitality by having them aboard to supper and a tour of the ship before having the pinnace take us ashore to see the merry-making.

Euryalus was fully illuminated and made quite a picture in the distance and even as we gazed back at her all her lights were suddenly doused; star-shell and rockets were fired, and then followed a spectacular searchlight display. Meanwhile our Royal Marine Band played Concert-music in the Town Square, to the further delight and appreciation of the local population, the Army and a large number of the ship's company. The performance and show ended at 10 p.m. with the most orderly and sober dispersal as the gaily-dressed populace walked away, the Army boarded their lorries back to Camp and we our boats back to the ships at 10.30 p.m. I think *Euryalus* and her crew acquitted themselves with great credit and added some spectacle to the glittering occasion.

Rain teemed solidly down all the next day with everyone saying what a mercy it was that the Big Day had been dry.

We sailed from Nukualofa that night north-eastwards through the rain and heavy seas, crossed the International Date Line next morning so that it was Wednesday again, and on Thursday morning anchored off Apia, Western Samoa.

I expected something similar to Suva so took the afternoon off work in order to see it in daylight and return by the 4.30 p.m. boat. However — I had walked less than a mile before I was greeted with welcoming voices by a white woman who gave me directions to her house. "You'll find my husband there," she said "Just call 'Wilson' and he'll wake." Sure enough, he not only awoke and greeted me but produced two bottles of ice-cold beer . . . I had a marvellous evening with all the family entertaining me and making me welcome. The '4.30 boat' turned into 'the midnight boat' . . .

It was just a year ago that we sailed from Liverpool; the war was over and everyone's thoughts were of — going home, and although the Captain had told the ship's company to discount any rumours about leaving the Station — that we would probably be here for several months yet, the 'buzzes' monotonously circulated, each lasting a day or two before dying a natural death only to be replaced by something new, destined to die in its turn. "We're going down to . . ." so many different places and "It's straight home from there via Suez" — or maybe it was Panama. Yes, the rumours came thick and fast like snowflakes and were just as short-lived.

It was now mid-December and an attempt to produce a pantomine failed through lack of interest mainly on account of the large number of men in Age & Service Groups in other ships who had already gone home to be de-mobbed, which made them disgruntled, with no enthusiasm for any activity to do with the ship — including work! December 13th — Battle of the River Plate day, of six long years ago, and now I was steaming on a glassy sea between the large islands in the New Hebrides group, very mountainous and protected by coral reefs — the same as those we had to pass through to reach Nukualofa and Apia. It was at Apia that we saw the wreck of the German ship *Adler* which had lain on the reef since 1889 when a typhoon hit the area and seven of the eight ships at anchor sank with heavy loss of life, the only ship to escape being *H.M.S. Calliope* which managed to sail through the gap to ride the storm outside.

We passed Guadalcanal — the scene of much heavy fighting just a few months ago — and now, in spite of the heat and humidity the 'powers that be' in order to keep the mens' thoughts from dwelling on their grievances had drills and exercises carried out at any time of day or night.

It rained heavily most of the time and perspiration dripped from our bodies especially when below decks. The best part of the day was at sunset when, if it wasn't raining most of those off watch would be on the upper deck to feel the cooler air and watch the glorious colours as the sun went down. Darkness then came within minutes and the sky then filled with millions of bright, twinkling stars.

At 0600 on Dec. 17th we arrived at Manus — where it was still raining and we wondered whether it did ever stop. We didn't! We took in oil and stores and were on our way again at 11 a.m., the temperature rising steadily in a following wind until it was almost unbearable on board. One of the four pet cats which had been with us since commissioning must have been affected by the conditions for it went mad and had to be shot. And amongst the stores embarked at Manus was a ton of potatoes in sacks left piled on the upper deck. They quickly became a stinking, sodden mess and had to be dumped over the side; we continued with the powdered stuff. The food generally during recent weeks had been of very poor quality and most of us seemed to exist on cups of hot tea and slices of bread, especially while it was terrifically hot.

Of course, the rumour-mongers soon had the reason for this state of affairs. "The ship's food allowance was overspent by £1885 (Australian) in Sydney" they said, but no-one understood how that could have happened with so many men ashore each night or else away on General Leave. But it upset morale.

On Dec. 20th we caught the tail-end of yet another typhoon and we were battened down, the ship rolling through 60-degrees non-stop for more than twenty-four hours and everywhere below decks feeling almost as hot as the inside of our boilers while the seemingly everlasting rain lashed down outside.

By Christmas Eve the rain had eased a bit but the sea remained violent and as we approached Hong Kong the temperature fell — as did a monster rat which lost its footing when the ship rolled that extra degree and plomped onto the desk in front of me as I sat writing-up the Daily Register and Work Book in the Engineers' Office that evening. All weighty objects such as the inkstand, ebony ruler, ledgers, etc., usually lying on the desk had been cupboarded so there was nothing to hand for use as a weapon and by the time I recovered from my surprise and shut the Work book the rat had scampered up to the deckhead and was gone. Commander (E) came in to talk about jobs to be undertaken when we reached the port and said, "By the way, the Skipper is very pleased with the tools you made for him. You seem to have 'hit the nail on the head' again". He was referring to the new Captain's hobby of Wood Inlaying for the execution of which the Captain had asked me to make extra knives, tamping and matting tools so I thought this might be an appropriate moment — all 'chummy like' — to broach the subject of him applying for my relief to be sent out to the ship.

He was very conciliatory but said the Admiralty was having difficulty finding replacements for all the men due for release in the Age and Service Groups and then he showed me a Confidential List of names of Engine-room Department ratings who were to leave the ship when we arrived at Hong Kong. The list included eight E.R.A's from my mess!

CHAPTER 28

Shanghai and The Chinese New Year

We arrived at a cold and wet Hong Kong to find a sizable Fleet at anchor including the battleships *Anson* and *Duke of York*, the cruisers *Argonaut*, *Belfast* and *Bermuda*, a small aircraft carrier, four destroyers and some frigates, three or four Repair-ships — and hundreds of junks and sampans.

It was Christmas Day 1945 and my last one in the Navy. Sunday routine and a welcome day of rest after the Carol Service on the quarter deck. There was a bottle of beer for every man who wished to buy one, the senior member of each mess to collect the money and take it to the Paymaster's Office before Mess-men and "Cooks of Messes" could be issued with the bottles. Some of the men who went ashore as soon as we dropped anchor the previous night had smuggled some of the potent local brew back on board and had already begun clandestine celebrations almost before breakfast and some from my mess became incensed when I refused to release the legal bottles until after the Service. I ordered them to clean themselves and vacate the Mess so that it could be tidied by the mess-men.

The Carol Service was well-sung and as we dispersed the Commander invited me to the Ward-room for a drink, and while there the Senior Engineer came over to me and asked if he could put my name forward to be advanced to Warrant Rank, saying "I don't think we can afford to lose you from the Navy!" I said I hoped this would be my last Christmas away from home, and when I got back to my Mess I wondered if I had done the right thing. The Mess was a 'mess'. It was a shambles — a charnel-house. There were bodies lying about, some covered with blood from fist-fights, and there was blood and vomit on seats and deck — a disgusting, filthy state.

With the help of the other two chiefs and some of the few sober members we dragged the bodies of the offensive ones out onto the upper deck to sleep off their excesses.

When the Mess had been swabbed down there were only six of us who were in a fit state to sit at table for our turkey at noon. There was an excellent bill of fare — turkey, roast potatoes and peas, Christmas pudding and custard — well prepared by the cooks and dished-up by our mess-men, the six of us quietly eating and talking when a semi-comatose member lying along a mess-stool pushed his foot into the side of a chap who was eating, and *he* promptly pushed the offender's feet from the stool. An argument developed between the two and culminated in the 'flopper' sitting up and thrusting the other's plate of pudding and custard into his face despite remonstrations. The local brew was definitely 'fighting beer' and the only thing to do was bundle him out of the Mess. When all was quiet again I adjourned to the boat-deck for a peaceful read and some fresher air and discovered that our Mess was not the only feuding crowd. Fist-fights were taking place on the fo'c'sle while two rival gangs battled each other with fire-hoses — (The hoses were permanently rigged to repel the sampans).

Two messmates went ashore to get away from the turmoil on board but returned by the next boat saying it was even worse on shore, with thousands of men milling around, bottles flying and blood flowing. They said it was anarchy and they did not feel safe. Then one came to me to report his locker-door had been forced and his personal belongings stolen.

I went with him to report the robbery to the Regulating Office just as a signal came in — "The Fleet Club has been closed following the death of a rating from the *Duke of York* and to prevent further damage to the premises", and the Regulator told us that a rating from one of the destroyers was being held on shore for the murder of a Chinese girl. It was a sorry state of affairs and there were a sorry lot of faces about the ship the next morning, black eyes and missing teeth, and a messmate who had fallen through a deck-hatch and down a steel ladder suffered facial injuries which required several stitches.

Anson steamed out of harbour in the afternoon on her way home and was followed by one of the Repair ships — the *Tyne* — which was going to Sydney.

On the next afternoon the Senior wanted all engine-room staff to be on the quarterdeck in blue suits with the rest of the ship's company — despite all the work we had in hand — because the Rear-Admiral of the squadron was coming on board to speak to us. I tried talking the Senior away from the idea by saying we had too much to do and that I doubted the Admiral had anything interesting to tell us and was told "Have as many as you can up there then".

And what did the Admiral say? He said, "I have come to tell you how lucky you are to have been out here to fight the Japs, and I am sorry that I only arrived out here two days after it was all over. I have just been up to Shanghai for four months and now I am going down to Australia but will come and see you again when I return. British civilians abroad always look forward to seeing a British warship enter port and see British sailors in the streets, so — maintain your good standards wherever you go!" What standards? I suppose it was intended to be a 'morale-booster'. The Admiral departed and the assembled company were marched off.

I was talking with the Senior as a marine slightly under the influence of a drink or two was brought before the Officer of the Watch on the quarterdeck and when the formalities had been gone through the Regulator gave the order, "Right turn, quick march" instead of "Left turn", and the order was obeyed although the guard-rail was only two paces away. The marine took the two steps, dived over the wire and swam back to the port gangway to come aboard stone-cold sober and brought before the O.o.W. again to be charged with "Breaking out of the ship!" but the humour of the situation was appreciated and he was taken away to be dried off.

Everyone was getting more bored and fed-up as there was very little to do on shore. It was either take a football and kick it about on some of the bare ground between finishing work and darkness, or walk the smelly streets of the town — where parties of seamen and marines were landed each day to render what assistance they could in tidying the place and repairing the Fleet Club.

A Chief E.R.A. with three E.R.A's and a squad of stokers went to help re-habilitate the Dockyard and sent plenty of jobs back to the ship for machining and refitting by me and my workshop staff.

And it was quite expensive ashore (compared with Sydney, of course) — as we were still using Australian currency on board and had to change it into Hong Kong dollars on shore, and losing in the exchange. A snack which would have cost about a shilling in Sydney was priced at six H.K. dollars, the equivalent of seven shilling and sixpence, in the Fleet Club.

Our ship's failure or failed effort to produce a pantomine for Christmas had apparently been duplicated in the other ships but now, in the New Year, practically all combined their talent to produce a good — and very appropriate "Aladdin" — at the Fleet Club and which enjoyed a four-night 'run' with full house every night.

Just after midday on January 7th the motor-boat was called away — "Urgently" — to take the jolly-boat in tow and "Fire Party to stand by". A shipwright and I grabbed a fire-extinguisher each from the bulkhead brackets and stood by. The jolly-boat had burst into flames on her way back to the ship and as the motor-boat brought her close in the Fire Party played their hoses down onto the flames but only succeeded in drenching the two-man crew — and there were 19-gallons of petrol in the tank. Chippy and I both dropped into the boat and set-off our extinguishers directly at the seat of the fire and quickly subdued it. We too were soaked by the hoses, but were also covered with white fluid because the extinguishers had been hanging in exposed positions for so long their casings had rusted and when we fired the cartridge in each one to release the fluid the casings perforated like a collander, but we surely saved the tank although the boat became a charred shell. It was coincidental that the fire should have occurred for on that very Monday morning a signal had been received from Commodore, Hong Kong, — "a Fire Exercise will be carried out on Thursday afternoon. One ship in the harbour will be told, "You are on fire" and all ships will do all in their power to assist the stricken vessel".

During the next two days we overhauled every appliance in the ship. Courts-Martial were becoming commonplace on board and as is usual under the Naval Discipline Act, when the Court reaches its verdict the Lower Deck is cleared for the ship's company to muster on the quarterdeck for the charge(s) to be read out, the findings of the Court made known together with the punishment meted (unless the papers have had to go to the C. in C. for his direction).

The Royal Mail liner *Highland Chieftain* (Peacetime memories of seeing her in South American ports) entered the harbour to collect more Age and Service Groups and brought us a very junior E.R.A. as a replacement for a senior one who was going home.

The new lad said he had arrived in Sydney on the day after we sailed and had been 'kicking his heels' there ever since!

The *Chieftain* sailed again that evening and, just as they had stood on deck and watched numerous other liners and ships of the Fleet leaving for home so the whole company were there to cheer her out — and even as she was leaving the harbour the Senior sent for me. "Sorry, chief. Another one to go. Tell — — — — — to pack his kit and join the mine-sweeper *Moon* tomorrow morning. She is leaving for Malta on Friday," and when I told the chap he wondered why he couldn't have travelled home on the liner. (When he arrived on the 'sweeper' he found that he was a replacement for an E.R.A. who *had* left on her! Crazy?)

On Sunday, Jan 20th *Euryalus* was ordered to Shanghai to relieve *Black Prince* as Guardship and we left harbour at 3 p.m. to take over our duties. On the evening of the 22nd I was told to arrange for special Damage Control parties to be on duty from midnight onwards as we passed through possibly mined waters and there were the usual moans from all those affected, but no sooner had I completed my list than there was another emergency; an S.O.S. from an ex-Japanese liner in difficulties 120-miles away! Full speed was ordered so all boilers had to be connected — and additional watchkeepers detailed. We all dashed about to raise steam in the extra boilers and were doing 30-knots at 11 p.m. when we received the message, "Damaged merchant-ship no longer needs help" and we were now in the danger-zone. Speed was reduced to 5-knots and the D.C. parties took up their positions as the ship slowly crawled through the night and in the late afternoon of the 23rd we oiled from a tanker off Wusung before anchoring for the night in the middle of the fast-flowing, dirty brown-yellowish waters of the river where we were soon surrounded by sampans full of American-speaking Chinese calling for anything we could spare. Sentries had to be posted to prevent boarders in the darkness.

From the tanker's crew we learned that our rescue dash had been to a ship which had struck a mine but managed to beach herself on the jagged shore.

On both sides of the river were scores — maybe hundreds — of American ships, mainly Landing-craft, tied up in long strings bow-to-stern and we passed many more, including cruisers and destroyers, as we went up-river next afternoon, so we guessed there were plenty of Yanks ashore in Shanghai where we tied-up alongside *Black Prince* in mid-stream. Everyone was reminded to be of best behaviour on shore and warned not to drink the local beers or mineral waters, and on no account *whatever* eat the ice-cream! (Fog lay thick over the river — and it was very cold!). *Black Prince*'s chief told me she had left U.K. in July 1944 and that they expected to be home by this coming July "but I'll be glad to get away from this place tomorrow and back to civilization in Sydney!"

I took a reconnaissance trip on Saturday afternoon to look at the shops, landing with 2000-Chinese dollars in my pocket and returning aboard with 2,650. The Exchange Rate on board was 4,300-dollars for an English pound but we were using Australian money so I paid eleven-shillings and eight-pence for my 2,000-dollars. I landed at the Bund to be met by the most awful stench and the sight of the populace using the gutters as a 'public convenience', so with my handkerchief covering my nostrils I hurried along to one of the main thoroughfares — the Nanking Lu — and went into every store and silk-shop I came across, comparing the prices of garments and materials as presents to take home when my time came. It was all very beautiful merchandise but far too expensive for my meagre purse so I ventured into some of the side-streets hoping to perhaps find a bargain! The streets were all narrow, cobbled and crowded, where oranges and pomegranates, dried lizards and live chicken were on sale, the hawkers and other people sitting about on large stones and sucking tea from the spouts of small tea-pots while keeping up loud arguments with anybody and everybody within ear-shot. Dogs and chickens got under my feet and there was garbage all about.

I inched my way through the crowds — all of whom knew me because they addressed me by name "Hello, John " — and one Chinaman bought a packet of 20-cigarettes from me for 1,000-dollars saying he would buy any amount at the same price if I brought them ashore, but I was not interested.

It started raining and the streets became seas of mud so I decided to find the Union Jack club and despite the fact that millions of Chinese had been killed in their long war with Japan there were still many millions left in Shanghai and I think they were all in this street!

Suddenly I was on a busy city road with an electric tram-car service, the cars coupled in tandem of First and Third Class — the latter packed 'as full as an egg' with passengers and the First Class more than twice as full. It was really amazing how many people could be carried, lots of them hanging on around the sides, and perhaps even more amazing that they managed to remain on board the swaying, rattling contraptions. Motor traffic was very heavy, with rickety old cars and lorries and American jeeps, and everywhere was noise! Tram-conductors had whistles which they were continually blowing, and their drivers rang their warning bells the whole time. Policemen controlled the traffic with even louder whistles while the ricksha-boys kept up shouting-matches with each other as they dodged through the mass of vehicles with the bells of bicycle-drawn rickshas adding to the general din of whistles, bells, bulb-horns and klaxons.

What a relief when I entered the U.J.C. at 5.30 p.m. and could relax over a $350 meal in one of the two dining-rooms. Probably the long absence of the China Squadron was responsible for the condition of the Club which was so sparsely furnished and had bare-boarded floors and was poorly lit. But soon the place filled with shouting crews from *Euryalus* and three of our destroyers also in the port; shouts over the Bar to the Chinese barmen for drinks, and shouts across the room as old shipmates and friends were recognized and got together. It was bedlam and as no other activity was advertised for the evening I left and walked back along the road to the American Forces Red Cross Club I had passed earlier and remembered the Notice I'd seen outside — "Band Concert here Tonite" I walked in and — What a different atmosphere! Hundreds of Americans moved about in orderly fashion and many were eating in the bright cafeteria. A row of shops along one side of the foyer had on sale almost anything and everything anyone could wish to purchase in relative comfort.

I ascended the marble staircase to the Ball Room where the concert was to be held, passing through an elegant lounge fully carpeted and furnished with easy-chairs and potted plants. The huge Ball Room was set with canvas-seated chairs ready for the evening's audience.

At the Enquiry Bureau were leaflets and posters detailing activities and entertainments available to the Americans — Concerts, Lectures, Sports, Local Tours, etc., — and I was handed a pamphlet giving details of the imminent Chinese New Year Celebrations which would continue for eighteen days. I copied the 'good wishes' at the end of the leaflet —

WISHING
YOU
PEACE AND
GOOD WILL
HAPPY NEW YEAR

ALL THE THINGS
BACK TO
SPRING AGAIN

(Acknowledgement to the American
Red Cross Society).

****

There was still much work to be done in the ship and when the *Highland Chieftan* came up river on January 30th she sent over some jobs with a request that we machine them for her. Then there was a call for us to make all brass rails, brackets, bollards and other 'showy' bits to brighten our motor-boats, brought about by our Commander noticing the gleaming polished brass of *Black Prince*'s smart craft and comparing with our rusty and grey-painted iron fittings.

Next came a rush job to make various items for the heating system of the Union Jack Club and being asked to go ashore on the afternoon of

February 1st to see them fitted and to instruct the Chinese manager on how to run the plant.

The weather was bad. It was very cold and it was raining most of the time and it was New Year's Eve, and although I had read the pamphlet's version of what to expect I was astonished at all the hustle and bustle. It was so like Christmas Eve in England with thousands doing last-minute shopping and hurrying home, either on foot or by ricksha and carrying their trees, balloons and bundles of red paper.

Fireworks were exploding everywhere with lots of noise and smoke and leaving the air thick with the acrid smell of gunpowder.

There were scores of hawkers selling the red paper and some had tiny books on offer. It was quite fascinating.

Next day Fred Barratt obtained two tickets for a concert to be given by the Shanghai Municipal Symphony Orchestra at the Lyceum Theatre that evening and on landing at 4.30 p.m. we grabbed a ricksha — after several attempts to find a 'boy' who could understand where we wanted to go.

This part of the city had been, until recently, the International Settlement but now things were changing. Anyway, the orchestra was quite big and comprised mainly of European artistes. The guest Conductor for this performance was a United States Navy lieutenant and an excellent programme was greatly appreciated by the full house.

During the following days many things happened, such as a large junk bursting into flames within a few yards of the ship. Fortunately a fire-float from the near-by docks reached her before our Fire Party and boat could be called away. I say fortunately because she was well ablaze and in the fast-ebbing tide both she and the fire-boat were soon far round the distant bend in the river and out of sight. Then the sloop *Black Swan* arrived from Hong Kong to relieve her sister-ship *Hind* and brought yet another replacement for a member of my Mess who was due for 'Civvy-street' and I had the pleasant (for him) duty of saying, "Get your kit packed as soon as you can and get over to the *Hind*. She's leaving for Hong Kong in the morning."

The composition of the Mess and of the whole ship's company was constantly changing and no sooner had *Hind* sailed off down the river than the destroyer *Camperdown* arrived with two more junior E.R.A's as further reliefs, and I had to find and tell another couple of the 'older-stagers' of the Mess to "Pack your bags and be ready to leave on the (destroyer) *Terpsichore* — You're going home!"

It meant more new faces to fit into the scheme of watches and duties — to pick up on the work hurriedly abandoned by those they had relieved, and requiring constant supervision by the very few senior ratings remaining. In addition an epidemic of influenza knocked a large number off their feet, far too many to be accommodated in the Sick Bay so they had to stay in their hammocks in messes and on messdecks thus putting much more work onto the shoulders of we lucky ones who escaped the virus.

On the strength of the amount of typing I had undertaken since joining *Euryalus*, viz:- Defect Lists, Watch Bills and Steaming Orders, — the Commander (E) thought I might do some of the more urgent work of the Engineers' Writer who had succumbed to the virus. This was additional to my Mess duties and machine-shop work and was mainly done in the evenings. Then — when the Captain learned that the Engine-room Department letters and other correspondence was being done I was asked to do confidential work for him as *his* Writer was also in the Sick Bay, and for this purpose I was allocated the cabin I had occupied after joining the ship — sans kit and hammock — with desk and typewriter supplied.

It was quite interesting and involved letters to the Commander-in-Chief, (Admiral Lord Fraser), the Fleet Engineer, the Resident Naval Officer i/c Shanghai, the Commodore, Hong Kong, and to Masters of liners and oil-tankers, keeping me in the know about what was happening, but unable to rebut the rumours about the ship's imminent movements which were always circulating. For instance — "We're leaving for Sydney on the 10th — It's official!", whereas I knew we would still be in Shanghai on the 12th, having just typed a letter to "American Naval Command" accepting an invitation to set up a team of boxers to meet their challenge later in the week at the Auditorium.

On February 13th the ship 'manned' (all the crew dressed in their best uniforms and lining the guard-rails all round the ship) to cheer and salute General, and Madam Chang Kai Chek, the leaders of the new Chinese Government as they passed down the river with the U.S. Admiral in his launch on their way to the *Estes*, flagship of the 7th Fleet. (The American later sent a signal congratulating Captain Warne on the smartness of *Euryalus*' ship's company as they passed.)

A day or two later it was arranged that we should assist *Camperdown* by doing some machine-work for her and two stokers brought a number of valves and castings to our workshop accompanied by Camperdown's Chief Stoker. I began setting the first item up in the lathe and when I looked at the Chief Stoker the recognition was mutual. We were cousins and had not met since before he joined the Navy in 1930, he being some six or seven years younger than I.

We arranged to meet for supper at the U.J.C. that evening and attend the finals of the boxing.

I walked to the Club, again through the Native quarter but chose a more salubrious route — a more genteel area — where every man wore a long gown of blue or grey serge with a high collar, and a small, round, silk hat; and the women either garbed in the same-style long gown or in trousers below short, padded (quilted) silk jackets — but all, always with hands folded into their sleeves.

Our supper was good; the boxing poor — although the "Shanghai Herald" said it was "the finest seen in the city for a long time". The "North China News" however was more honest with its report of "cat-calls and boos after each bout" and "the whole thing was more like a dance or a wrestling match than a boxing tournament".

Back on board I found a signal from C. in C. (Lord Fraser) saying "Hong Kong will now be the Headquarters of the British Pacific Fleet with Singapore the Refitting Base. The Sydney Base will be shut down in April and all staff moved to Colombo where all people for discharge in Age and Service Groups should be sent. We hope it will be possible for H.M. ships to pay periodic visits to Australia." That meant we, *Euryalus*, were a permanent unit of B.P.F. and scotched the latest buzzes of "New Zealand next week and home via Panama" and "We're going to the Med to finish our commission."

More work came from *Camperdown* on the 18th (Feb.) with instructions — "to be done at once as she is leaving on the 20th and we will have left Shanghai before she returns." Was one of the rumours about to become fact?

I knew we had to await the arrival of the cruiser *Ariadne* due on the 24th as she was bringing three more juniors up from Sydney for our Mess, and I had not yet 'shopped' for the silks I wanted to take home so, on the 20th having completed the jobs for the destroyer I took time off — and yet another route through the Native quarter, possibly the oldest part of the Old Chinese City with really ancient architecture and quaint Chinese temples, where even the people seemed to be of a different — higher — class.

I eventually emerged on the Avenue Joffre, recently re-named Ling Sen Road, in the heart of the old French Concession, where I met a Frenchman, an ex-Sergeant-major of the Free French Marines. He wanted information about Australia, hoping to be able to settle there with his wife and two children.

His story was that he had come to Shanghai in 1938 with the French Police but when the war broke out he had to rejoin his regiment and his wife and children had been interned by the Japanese in Shanghai and consequently lost everything. All other relatives in France had been killed and now the Chinese wanted all foreigners out of the country and all concessions to be given up (hence the change of names of all streets and squares) and all jobs were being taken over by Nationals. We drank coffee in his club, the Cercle Francais as I gave a rough idea of conditions in Brisbane and Sydney — the unrest and strikes — and wished him good fortune for his future quest but he could not help me in my quest for silks.

The Club issued an invitation for me to visit at any time. (I doubt I could have found it again!) Prices were high and always quoted in U.S. dollars then multiplied several times to convert to Australian £'s, so my quest for silk-goods at the many shops and stores always evoked my same response — "I'll call back later".

I started off back towards the Bund and a Russian-marked jeep pulled up beside me, its driver asking me in perfect English if I would like a lift to the jetty. On the fairly short journey he told me he worked in the Russian Embassy and did NOT intend going back to Russia but would snatch the first opportunity to get to Australia. He too asked about conditions there and I wished him all success. I hope he did eventually get away.

The price of a bottle of beer at the Union Jack Club was $250 C.N.C. — less than half the cost at any other establishment in the city, and notices were displayed in the Club specifically asking patrons NOT to take bottles away from the premises. Of course there were some men to ignore the request by buying several bottles and stowing them in their greatcoat pockets to take along to the higher-priced "Night-spots" to drink there — and then leave their empties strewn about the floors. This brought complaints from those places to the Club Manager with the result that anybody wanting a drink in the club had to pay for his beer plus a $250 deposit on the bottle, and $500 deposit on a glass from which to drink. It was irksome having to cling to the empty bottle and glass in order to reclaim one's $750 but there is always some-one to spoil an amenity or privilege.

Ariadne duly arrived on the 24th with my three Juniors and a more senior member of the Mess who had been left in hospital in Hong Kong but he was sent back to *Ariadne* because he was in Age and Service Group 35 and should have been back in England by now — and *Ariadne* was leaving on the 26th.

Camperdown had returned prematurely on the 23rd towing a Chinese steamer whose engine had broken down. Repairs took 24-hours then both ships sailed again, the destroyer escorting because of pirates operating all along the China coast. All merchant shipping was at risk but more especially those known to be carrying British cargoes, and the English-language newspapers told of ships being taken by gangs boarding as bona fide passengers and transferring entire cargoes at pre-arranged rendezvous to other gang-members, and of wealthy travellers being taken for ransom.

Soon after our arrival in Shanghai one or two men bought Chow dogs thus starting a spate of dog-buying so that every Tom, Dick and Harry — or every Jack, Jack and Jack — wanted a dog to take home and the situation was getting out of hand with Chows everywhere and resulting in an Order — "Owing to the changing climatic conditions in the near future it is not advisable to have dogs on board. — (Shades of the fate of poor old pussy!)

251

— They must be put ashore before the ship leaves Shanghai."

"Climatic conditions!" "Near future!" Both pairings had the rumour-mongers' tongues a-wagging in a trice and even more so when I posted the Steaming Orders "Full Watch below at 0900, Sat. March 2nd" on the Notice Board. It was only to raise steam to test all valves, joints and auxiliaries which had been refitted during routine maintenance but in less than no time at all the ship was half way round the world!

Swiftsure came up river on the 4th to take over as Guardship and secured alongside us. Her Chief came across and gave us tidings of some of the Age and Service Group men who had left the ship just before we sailed from Hong Kong — and after weeks of "Let's get away from this effing ship and station" had madly cheered as the motor-boat carried them over to the Depot-ship. He said, "They are still in Hong Kong. A couple of days after you sailed they were detailed to steam an Admiralty tug back to England but its engines failed when they were a few miles down the coast. They had to be towed back and are now refitting in the dockyard there."

CHAPTER 29

Hong Kong

We sailed from Shanghai at noon on March 6th, a cold and rough day, and after nigh on six-weeks of being roped between buoys in the Whangpoo river the movement came as a bit of a shock to many and there was a lot of sea-sickness, but as soon as the ship cleared Wusung we closed up Action and Damage Control Stations while we passed through possibly mined waters.

The Captain had the lower-deck cleared when we arrived in Hong Kong harbour at 9 a.m. on the 9th. He said it was in order to allay the doubts and stop the wild rumours about the ship's future. "We shall be making some trips to Japan and Singapore and be in Sydney in May or June, then probably a cruise to New Zealand before returning to the China coast. Then, and only then, will it be time to think about going home. At the moment we are the only ship on the Station to be in good running order."

His final remark was borne out by the fact that *Bermuda* should have joined us but had broken down and had been diverted to Singapore for repair; she came in on the 11th and as she dropped anchor our bugler sounded "Clear Lower deck. All hands muster on the quarterdeck". The timing was a surprise and the optimists said, "She's our relief. We're going home!" The pessimists said, "We're probably at war with Russia now!" The pragmatists said, "Another lecture on 'Behaviour ashore' coming up!" None were right. The Captain's message was, "Petty pilfering has been occurring in the ship for some time, starting in October while in Sydney when some £200 — the Wardroom Mess Fund — was taken from an officer's cabin. Many men have come before me to complain of money and personal gear being stolen from their lockers but *I* cannot do anything about that! It is up to you, the ship's company, to stamp it out. Some of you *must* have your suspicions and should report the matter. Now another £120 has gone missing from the Secretary's cabin in the past 24-hours so random searches of lockers will take place."

When a messmate suggested rats as the likely culprits I was reminded of another incident a few months earlier when a 'foul odour' pervaded one of the cabins. Seamen were called with a shipwright to remove panelling which revealed a nest of rats and the mouldering remains of food scavenged by the adult rodents from around the ship to feed their young (six of them) in the nest. Daddy-rat scarpered as the panel came away but the seamen killed the female — just as "Stand Easy" — the mid-morning break sounded, and they all went away to their messes for a cuppa and a smoke. Returning to the job 15-minutes later they were in time to see Daddy-rat scurrying off along the top of a cable to a safer home in the ship with the last of the litter firmly in his teeth!

(There was no record of the nest being lined with paper-money).

The Senior called me along to the Office when an Admiralty Order relating to "Reduction of Engine-room Personnel" arrived. He pointed to the paragraph which directed there should be only three Chiefs in the ship and the reduction should be made forthwith. He said, "Who can we spare?" Who? I suggested myself — "as I am due to be discharged to pension in September", — but his reply to that was, "I'm sorry, but we can't afford to let you go. Who's going to keep control? — Out of the question!" (I did not want to argue by reminding him that only a matter of a few weeks ago he proposed putting my name forward for promotion, and the certainty of having to leave the ship, so assumed he wanted me to be "happily settled"!)

We decided and I told the lucky chap to get his kit packed right away get across to *Ariadne* — "She sails tomorrow (the 12th)".

The *Duke of York* left on the 11th and *Euryalus* became the most senior ship remaining so we moved to the senior billet — and a vastly different aspect. We could now see the true expanse of the harbour and the huge amount of shipping it contained. From our previously regular berth we

253

had appeared to be lying in a narrow river with one or two other ships and a thousand sampans.

Our first 'emergency' as Senior Ship was to deal with a strike by dock- and power-workers and we had to send one Chief and 2-E.R.A's and a party of stokers ashore to take charge of the Power Station. They landed at 1 p.m. on Friday, March 15th. The strike was called off at 2.30 and they were back on board at 4 p.m. — but we remained at short notice over the week-end in case of any developments. There were none.

We went to sea on Monday morning for three days of exercises beginning with target practice against attacking aircraft. We went to "Action-Repel Aircraft-Stations" and waited for the planes to come. They didn't. They could not find us! We made smoke to attract their attention and carried on waiting, but they still did not appear. (Huns and Japs always seemed to find us even without smoke to help them!). Late in the afternoon we received a signal that one of the attacking planes had crashed into the sea, so it was our turn now to search and we steamed for hours — carrying on after dark with the aid of our searchlights until 8.30 p.m. when we became enveloped in thick fog which compelled us to anchor.

The fog only cleared at 9.30 a.m. when the sun's heat burnt through and the search resumed. At 3.30 p.m. a look-out spotted wreckage on a beach. A sea-boat's crew investigated and found it to be that of a Japanese fighter probably washed up from the sea.

Our search continued until dark (6.30) when we anchored as flashing-light signals appeared from shore. Two boat-loads of marines, seamen and stokers were sent in to the tiny village and even as they were on their way the rest of the ship's company were giving their version of the event. "A nest of pirates is 'holed up' near the village and our chaps are turfing them out!" "An R.A.F. Radio Station is beset by rebels and we're going to their relief."

The truth was that a Commando Unit on anti-piracy patrol had run short of provisions and asked for our help. We supplied a stock of dried potato and some meat — under armed guard!

The ship had to be guarded too as we became surrounded by scores of sampans which appeared almost from nowhere, all trying to come along-side. Many were filled with young girls and fire-hoses were hastily rigged — and used — to keep them away from the ship's side.

Our platoons returned during the night and we got under way at 0630 to continue our search for the missing airmen. Three hours later we received news that the air-crew had been picked up by a Sea-Otter of Air-Sea Rescue and flown to hospital at Hong Kong. We were thankful they had survived, especialy after our beefing at their inability to find us and so delaying our exercise, the next part of which was for us to locate the submarine *Tally-Ho*, hiding somewhere below the surface and then carry out a throw-off shoot at the destroyer *Finisterre* which was 'tendering' the sub.

On our return to harbour we received a 'Thank you' message from the R.A.F. "for your great effort in the search for our man". It appeared there was only one airman and he had started to send a distress signal but his radio ceased functioning before he could give his position and he had pancaked about a hundred-yards off-shore, launched his rubber dinghy and eventually reached a Chinese village.

There was another little incident during the long, hot day of our search. It was in the forenoon when a messmate coming into the machine-shop asked, "Did you see the junk which passed within a yard of us just now?" Of course, I hadn't, but he said, "Didn't you even *smell* it? We almost ran it down!"

A short time later another chap came in with the same sort of tale and added that the junk was now secured alongside — because the Captain thinks its people may know something about the airmen or the missing plane. So, being inquisitive I went on deck to see what was going on. The junk — smaller than a Medway barge, had been adrift for thirteen-days and had no fresh water so our pumps were busy filling her water-butts and some steel drums on her deck. I looked down on her and counted more than twenty Chinamen on her deck, and I am sure many more were below deck. Also on the deck were more than 50-pigs, lots of dogs and chickens, and dozens of baskets filled with eggs, and the smell was really terrible. The ship was constantly manoeuvring in an effort to keep the junk to leeward and it was 'a breath of fresh air' when she was cast off and we got moving again.

We went to sea on the 27th for more gunnery practice at sleeve-targets and anchored that evening at Tolo among a small group of barren, hilly islands not far from Hong Kong and were told we would remain at anchor the whole of the next day, and that picnic-parties would be landed — one party would go in the morning, taking their dinners and filled water-bottles with them and return at 1 p.m. when the second party would land until sunset. The Commander hoped that every one could be spared to take advantage of the opportunity to get some exercise but our (Engineering) department were in the middle of altering the layout of our workshop and re-positioning one of the big lathes, and as a Sunday-routine was being worked it was an ideal opportunity to get the job done — especially as our welder was willing to stay on board to help.

I think it must have been either a Hong Kong holiday or a Chinese one, but nobody seemed to know.

From our anchorage there were no signs of habitation on any of the islands but it was not long before the ship was surrounded with sampans almost by magic. Each about the size of a small rowing-boat and housing a

255

family comprising on average of parents and between six and ten children they remained close — too close at times! — to the ship the whole day.

Another source of aggravation to me and of discontent in the department was the inability — the impossibility — to maintain a steady and standing Watch Bill for steaming the ship. Practically every evening whether we were at sea or at anchor something was bound to break down or go wrong and need some alteration to the Bill. Maybe a dynamo — or the refrigerating plant — an air-compressor or some pump in one of the engine- or boiler-rooms — would decide to chuck its hand in and the man responsible for the care of that particular machine or plant had to be relieved from watch by another man who had been left off the 'bill' for some other specific job which was of less urgency. And Divisional Officers always wanted *their* man or men left off the Steaming Watch in order to overhaul some bit of machinery in *their* part of the ship, but the reduction in complement combined with the preponderance of junior, inexperienced ratings in the Department made it impossible to do their bidding. There *had* to be somebody to steam the ship!

On March 29th I again applied to see the Captain to ask for my relief to be sent for as my 22-years' Service would soon be completed and I would like to be at home before that, but the Commander (E) told me that he *had* applied and "When the Drafting Authorities start moving and send me some one *I* want — and I want some one to replace *you* — then we'll see about getting you home!" — which was very ego-boosting but not helpful.

We returned to "senior-ship's" berth in harbour with the Hong Kong waterfront about half-a-mile away on our port side and the Hospital-ship *Empire Clyde* about the same distance to starboard and the harbour stretching some three miles beyond her.

Astern of us on our starboard quarter a large merchant ship lay on her side on the sea-bed, and on our port quarter the funnel and masts of another ship poked out of the water. The American cruiser *Los Angeles* and two destroyers were anchored a little further off and a big oil-tanker rested on the bottom with her decks awash. The masts, funnel and bridge of yet another tanker were visible beyond *Empire Clyde* and at other points around the harbour could be seen the masts and funnels of many vessels which had been bombed and sunk by planes from our carriers in the final stages of war.

Ahead of us slightly to port lay the Chinese township of Kowloon with rows of piers lined with merchant-ships of all sizes, and included the *Aorangi*, an Australian liner which had been acting as Fleet Depot Ship but was now being prepared for return to her owners.

Argonaut arrived from a visit to Japan and anchored about a mile off our starboard bow and close to the harbour entrance, and *Bermuda* lay far astern alongside the Dockyard wall — refitting. To complete the picture several destroyers and a couple of sloops dotted the harbour at their anchorages and to make it more crowded scores of sampans and motorised junks weaved their ways between the anchored vessels and the numerous wrecks. And finally, to add to the busyness, steam ferry-boats fussily criss-crossed the harbour from the Victoria and Kowloon landing-stages to other islands in the group, belching thick smoke which enveloped everything to leeward in acrid, sulphurous gases. Yes, it was certainly a vastly different outlook to that of our previous billet, but there were hills all around us. Those of Hong Kong, Kowloon and Victoria had houses scattered about right to the tops; those of other islands were barren and rugged. Time wore slowly along.

April 1st — I had to tell three more messmates to "Pack your bags. Be ready to leave the ship tomorrow morning. You're off home!" — and not one query or thought of "April-fool-day"! They sailed on the P. & O. liner *Strathmore* and most of our ship's company were up on deck to watch her leave at 5 p.m. on April 3rd. As she passed from our sight I was called to the Office: "Have a full Steaming Watch below at once. Typhoon warning received!"

Luckily for us, the storm changed direction after a couple of hours and we were able to shut down in time to welcome the Ensa Concert Party scheduled to perform on board that evening.

The title of the show was "Chinese Crackers", music suppled by Jimmy Pickard and his Chinese Syncopators, a small band I had seen and listened-to in Bentalls Department Store at Kingston-upon-Thames shortly before I joined the ship.

The party consisted of a jolly good comedian, an out-of-the-ordinary magician, male and female vocalists, a young contortionist who would turn herself inside-out without spilling on the deck, a (very) scantily-dressed soubrette who sang and tap-danced on a bamboo mat laid on the quarterdeck — and when her foot dragged across the mat with a loud rasping sound a mateloe brought the house down by shouting, "Blimey! That's torn it!" and a Mystery Woman who was blind-folded and could answer any question posed by her partner/accomplice regarding articles he had borrowed from members of the audience but was unable to give a date when somebody at the back of the crowd called, "When's this two-funnelled b......d going to pay off?"

The show certainly boosted morale — at least for a few hours — after watching *Strathmore* go out and a hectic hour preparing for the onset of a typhoon.

I spent the next three days ashore in the Dockyard overseeing the making and fitting of a new spindle for the ship's capstan and running tests on the engine when it was back in the ship. "Variety is the spice of Life!"

The Commander-in-Chief, Admiral Lord Fraser, came aboard to say "Good-bye" to us on Saturday, April 13th and we sailed at 4 p.m. next day on a visit to —

CHAPTER 30

North Borneo and Saigon

It was a very hot and sticky voyage to Labuan, North Borneo, where we anchored on the 18th and found it to be a real scorcher. Labuan was just a small island of sand, jungle and coconut palms but with thousands of troops, Indians — including the Punjabi Regiment (with British troops attached), units of the R.A.F. and the R.A.F. Regiment, the Royal Australian Air Force, and Australian Army, housed in many camps, and almost before our anchor had touched bottom we received a challenge from the Indians to play them at football the following (Good Friday) afternoon.

We had no team but soon scraped a bunch of players together to play on a pitch of deep, white sand where every time the ball touched the ground it disappeared in a white cloud and could not be seen for most of the match, but there was such a vast 'gate' that it was obvious all the troops were happy to welcome some different faces to the island. The game ended in a 2 — nil victory for the ship and the immediate drifting-away of the crowd at 5.45 p.m. on that pleasant ideal-for-walking evening so, as our Notice Boards had advised "Every Camp has its Open-air cinema at which all crew members will be welcome" I walked along the road leading away from the sea. Quite tough on the legs walking the sandy road!

I had only gone a few hundred yards when — Bang! The sun set — and within a few minutes it was quite dark, with no street-lighting, just the occasionally-glimpsed dimly-lit Army huts amongst the trees and a complete silence except for the chirping of crickets.

Then I could see some distance ahead the luminous glow of a 'silver screen' above the trees, only to find when I eventually reached it that there was "No Show Tonight".

Back to the road I was just in time to be picked up by an RAF jeep the driver of which said, "Come along and see the film at *our* Camp".

I endured that most boring film for half-an-hour before making my way back to the Camp Gate — pitying the poor airmen who had had to remain in camp — and would have taken to the road back to the shore had it not been so dark and the distance (about six miles) so great.

The Corporal of the Guard thought there might be a Duty lorry passing later in the evening but did not know when, nor where it would be going, so I stayed talking to him and the two sentries until a truck belonging to their Marine section happened to stop at the gate and the sergeant-major sitting beside the driver offered me a lift down to his Base and then called away one of their launches to ferry me out to *Euryalus*.

Since landing at 2 p.m. it had been absolutely impossible to get a drink or anything to eat so I found it rather galling listening to the s/m during that journey, telling me about life on the island. "Food quite good, and plenty of beer — as much as we can drink!" — which directly contradicted what I was told as I sat alongside sergeants with glasses of beer standing on the arms of their chairs. They gratefully took my cigarettes saying "We're rationed to 70 fags and three bottles of beer a week so we've none to spare!"

That could have explained the lack of hospitality which was normally accorded by garrisons at these "Outposts of Empire" to visiting Navy ships. Who did I believe!

On that ride down to the R.A.F. Marine-section Base the truck's head-lights showed huge sign-boards beside the road at several points — boards with foot-high characters proclaiming at various intervals such observations as "SLEEVES", or "1800-HOURS — SLEEVES", or "SLEEVES AT DUSK", and then the 'revealing the answer' notice which announced "MALARIA PRECAUTIONS — 1800 TO 0600"! So — mosquitoes were the menace and although I was wearing short-sleeved tropical shirt I neither felt, heard nor saw any.

On the following evening came a surprise performance by the ship's newly-formed Concert Party consisting of a 6-piece Harmonica Band, vocalists, a violinist, and the 'Chorus' — the extras who played-out some Sketches, very creditable and well-received and two of which may bear recording here:-

Scene:- Naval Headquarters Hong Kong Office with Officer-in-Command seated at his desk and two Wren secretaries at their table. The officer picks up his phone, "Exchange — Get me Kowloon 1234" — then sits and waits — and waits. There is an indeterminate interval until one of the secs picks up the phone on the table — "Exchange — Long Distance — New York, please" — and within a few seconds is talking to her Yankee boyfriend.

The officer continues to wait, drumming his fingers on his desk. Wren No. 1 ends her conversation as No 2 finished powdering her nose and then takes over the receiver to ask Exchange for, "Long Distance — Sydney, please" and is soon chatting and laughing with an old friend in that city while the officer waits, impatiently tapping away until, in desperation he rattles his handset and says, "Exchange — Get London for me!" and in almost the same breath he is saying, "Hello, London. Will you get me 'China, Hong Kong, Kowloon 1234 please" followed by, "Is that the Kowloon Hotel? Will you save a table for me tonight, please. 8 o'clock — Thank you!" The curtain falls.

The 2nd Sketch was in two Acts, the first being "How *we* think film-makers of Hollywood think we go into Action".

Scene:- The Bridge. The Captain, all other officers and bridge personnel are dressed in immaculate white uniforms, saluting one another with greetings — "Topping weathah, what?" and such like.

An enemy battle-fleet is sighted. The Captain orders "Increase speed to 45-knots. Open fire when you see the white of their eyes! — Right — Fire number one torpedo! — Fire number two torpedo! — Fire number three torpedo! — Good huntin', chaps. We've sunk the lot. Jolly good show!" The curtain falls.

Act 2. Scene:- The Bridge — of the same cruiser but "How *we* think we go into Action".

The weather is filthy and the bridge appears to be manned by a bunch of ragamuffins as the look-out calls "Enemy battleship, port one-five, sir." The Captain asks the Navigator, "Have we enough speed to get away before she sees us? Ask Engines." They decide they haven't, so fire four torpedoes as they turn away. All miss and signal-lamps are seen flashing from the battleship.

The Captain asks, "What are they saying, Yeoman?"

"They're saying, sir, 'What the hell do you think you're doing?' It's the *Duke of York*, sir!"

Curtain — and a good laugh from the audience.

Next day — Easter Sunday, hot and sunny. I would let work have a rest and I would attend Church on the quarterdeck when along came the Senior Engineer to say there was a Sports meeting this afternoon and could I fashion a 'Shot — for the Putting of' event which it was hoped to stage.

I completed the job and decided to go ashore to watch, but when I stepped out onto the upper deck to thread my way through scores of prone and supine bodies of sun-bathers I could see a rain-storm speeding towards the ship so I stood back inside to watch the fun. The rain came so quickly and so hard in stinging stair-rods, surprising and shocking every one into life to grab for discarded shirts, singlets, books and cigarettes and rushing for cover, and the storm continued until dark. The rain was still pouring down when we got under way next morning and after 48-hours of very hot steaming and about 100-per cent humidity a pilot boarded the ship to take us 80-miles up the Saigon River to Saigon, the capital of French Indo-China.

Although the river was only half-a-mile wide we travelled at 20-knots through the low-lying swampy countryside of rough jungle almost to the water's edge, the pilot telling the ship's company they might be able to see quite a lot of wild-life along the way, mentioning tigers, huge snakes and crocodiles. I don't think any were seen!

As soon as we secured at the jetty I had to cross the road to the Fresh Water Terminal Office and make arrangements for a supply and measure the size of the supply-points and return on board to manufacture the necessary adapters — while the rain still rained!

Some French cruisers and two small aircraft-carriers lay at anchor in the river so we thought the city would be full, but most of the Mess went off ashore that evening only to return within two-hours saying — "There's nothing to do, and nothing to eat on shore!"

On the following day the local Sergeants' Mess invited Chiefs and Petty Officers to their Cabaret Evening — their lorries to collect from the ship at 6.30 — but I had already promised to support our football team against a French Army side and had a pleasant walk out to the ground at 4.30 on that sunny afternoon, through clean, wide, tree-lined streets of beautiful houses.

After the game — which was won by the ship two goals to one — I was walking leisurely back when two lorry-loads of chiefs and P.O's passed on their way to the Show, calling out as they went by 'was I coming along?'. I changed direction to walk out to the Army base if I could find it in the French-speaking city.

I arrived about half-an-hour behind the main crowd the majority of whom were already sprawled either side of long, wooden tables, knocking back beer, wines and spirits as though there was no tomorrow — trying to make up for months of lost 'drinking time'.

The 'singing' stage of intoxication was reached and beer and wine-glasses were soon rolling from the tables onto the floor as the noise got louder and the songs more bawdy and suggestive despite (or because of) the presence of several beautiful and smartly dressed French or Annamite ladies in the company of some of the sergeants. (Could they have been part of the Cabaret? I doubted there would be one!).

I surveyed the scene and remarked to a couple of messmates that things were getting out of hand and that I was going to walk back to the ship, — which I did, through the darkened streets in the cool, night air.

Night-leave expired at 11 p.m. and it seemed all who had been ashore had supped 'fighting' beer. There was fighting on the jetty — fights which halted as the participants came in-board only to start again as soon as they were clear of the gangway. One rating spent the night in cells after taking a swipe at the Commander as he came aboard, and a messmate who staggered into the Mess after having fallen into a open sewer was dragged to the bathroom and left to clean himself.

Another resented the fact that I walked off early from the Sergeants' Mess and took a swipe at me — a wild one by which he lost balance and cracked his head on a stool.

None had recollection of events by the morning but were apologetic when told.

The French Navy football team challenged ours that afternoon and I landed early in order to see more of the city. I took a different direction but found the same cleanliness and neatness everywhere, and lots of well-dressed French people. I assumed they were French because they were white and wore European-style clothes — suits and dresses — as opposed to the Annamite women, most of whom wore beautiful silks of marvellous colours — mainly white trousers beneath contrasting-coloured gowns of wonderful pastel shades, purple, green, blue, and some of gold brocade. It was indeed a brilliant scene until I approached the native Annamite quarter where things were slightly less elegant. Long lines of beggars severely deformed and covered with sores squatted beside the road, but unlike those of Shanghai these were silent. No pleading for alms, no moaning, no whining! They sat as though dead, but were alive.

The Annamite quarter itself was again as spotless as the other parts of the city I had seen, with more fine stores and shops, and then I was at the Football Field.

The match ended in a two – nil victory for the ship at 6 p.m. and I was almost back to the ship when I met the Chief E.A. with two of his staff on their first walk ashore. "Did I know where the Sergeants' Mess was?" It was a nice evening and, priding myself for having a sense of direction I would walk them there — it would be easier than explaining. At the Mess I stopped for one drink before heading back to the ship and had been walking for what seemed a number of miles along the well-lit road, with no passing traffic and no other pedestrians when I suddenly realised I was lost in "no-mans-land" but I walked on and presently came to a French Army barracks, passed through the gates and entered the Guard-house to enquire directions. None of the occupants could either speak or understand English so I mustered 'school-boy' French with, "L'centre du Ville?" — pointing the way I had been travelling, to which one replied, "Oui, m'sieur, du Cholon."!

So I had been walking away from Saigon and the ship. Neither they nor I were capable of giving or receiving explicit explanations of a route to be taken so I re-traced my steps until I came to the gates of a park I recollected walking through the previous night and followed a path leading to the far side — where once again I was 'lost in the wilds'! It was a 'select' district (fortunately) and the first knowledgeable-looking person I met was able to point me towards the jetty.

Back on board I called in at the Ship's Office lest any new orders or notices had been promulgated during my few hours ashore. There were two — the first being a "Warning to the ship's company that it is NOT safe for men to walk about in the dark unless there are three or four of you together." (I suppose I had been lucky on my lone walks on foreign soil but this new notice brought back the memory of the attempted mugging in Boston and of being told, after the event, to never walk alone through 'that part' of Halifax, N.S., both instances while serving in *Dragon*.)

My final run ashore in Saigon (April 27th) was to the large open-air Market for native-made sandals, shoes and silks to take home. The main stores and establishments closed between noon and 3.30 p.m. because of the extreme heat but lots of people remained on the streets of the city which had a large white (French) community amongst its majority Annamite, Indian and Chinese population, every one clean and well-dressed with the whole creating a really colourful scene.

I returned to the ship at 6.30 p.m. as an Identity Parade was being held on the road alongside. All seamen and stokers who were ashore the previous night had donned their shore-going uniform and were lined-up while two policemen and two civilians tried to recognize three ratings who had thrown a man into the river and whose body had been dragged out that morning.

No-one was identified that Saturday evening but a further Parade on Sunday morning to find three other ratings who, on Saturday night, beat-up and robbed a store-owner, two stokers and a Sick Berth steward were 'fingered' and placed under open-arrest as the ship sailed from Saigon at noon with the general consensus being that the crew were behaving like a crowd of gangsters both on and off the ship.

It was a blessing to be at sea and to have some fresher and cooler air blowing through the ship after lying some eighty-miles up a river. Two days later, at 10 p.m. I was called to supply a relief for a messmate who had been taken ill on watch in the engine-room. Most of the mess had already turned in so rather than disturb some one just to go below until midnight I did the stint myself, and during that short spell the Officer of the Watch told me that, being the Divisional Officer of two of the men under 'Open Arrest' he had spent the day in Court in the Captain's cabin reviewing the criminal charges levied against them, the Charge Sheet alleging that "They entered the shop shutting the door behind them and when the owner asked, "What is your pleasure?" they demanded his money. When he said he had none one of the 'sailors' hit him and the other 'sailor' (as opposed to the Sick Berth rating) hit the old man sitting behind the cash-box and stole about 1,000-piastres — between £40 and £50 — and the watches and wallets of the shopkeepers. As they ran from the shop their round hats fell off as the door shut and they could not open it again to recover them."

Both had admitted coming aboard hatless but said they had lost them while fighting in a restaurant.

When I had arrived in the engine-room that night I found it was even more as Tom had said:- "A cosmopolitan old tramp steamer trading among tropic islands!" The watch-keepers were sitting about while pumps ran at top speed, almost rattling themselves from their bed-plates, with steam blowing from joints and glands and making the place much hotter than need be. Water gushed from glands of circulators; match-sticks and cigarette-ends littered the plates. It was easy to see why we were having so many break-downs and so much work coming to the machine-shop.

After I had adjusted the speeds of the auxiliary machinery I had the watch-keepers off their backsides tightening glands and sweeping deck-plates so that even the O.o.W. noticed the improvement on his return from a visit to the boiler-rooms and other outside spaces. I spoke of the slovenliness and general indiscipline in the department — and the ship — and his comment was that "things would tighten-up when we were rid of the Age and Service groups, so we don't want to stir them up at this stage!" At that point we received orders to increase to 22-knots in order to arrive in Hong Kong next morning in time to discharge more Age and Service Groups to *Argonaut*, which would be leaving for the U.K. at noon. There were none going from our Mess this time but as soon as we anchored next morning (May 1st) those who *were* leaving were hurried across and an hour later our ship's company lined the rails to cheer *Argonaut* on her way out of the harbour; and even before she was through the gap a blanket of gloom and silence descended as the men's thoughts went with her. But — Fair's fair! She had been away from home for nigh on two years, but it was ever thus when "the other ship" was leaving a foreign station.

CHAPTER 31

Amenities at Hong Kong

We found part of the American 57th Task Force — two aircraft-carriers, a cruiser and several destroyers — moored in the harbour on our return and received a signal from Commodore Hong Kong asking us to do our best to entertain the crews. There was not much we could do to accommodate them as we had none of the facilities or amenities as were available to them in Shanghai. Our only asset was the China Fleet Club, and the main part of that was a shambles while attempts to arrange various sporting events elicited scant enthusiasm from either side — not even a cricket match.

As part of the operation I was called upon, at the request of a local Ten-pin Bowling Club, to make a set of skittles from hardwood and a pattern sent from shore as this was a popular American pastime and when made, polished and delivered it was explained to me that the Japs had taken the originals, either for souvenirs or to use as 'clubs' — although the Manager was inclined to the opinion his own countrymen were the culprits.

The local Press carried warning notices saying that nothing was safe from thieves — "They will take 'anything' from 'anywhere'" and every day there were dozens of reports of robberies and pickpocketings, half the victims being Chinese merchants travelling on the ferries from their homes in Kowloon to work in Victoria and 'lost' brief-cases and money-purses en route, and the other half were Servicemen on shore — who are very vulnerable. The reports added that the Chinese police are "sharp and catch a large number of the criminals who receive long terms in gaol, but that does not deter others".

Other warnings issued to all ships' companies were against drinking anything other than bottled beers even in the most reputable Bars and restaurants, these warnings coming after two American seamen died from wood-alcohol poisoning as a result of drinking Chinese "Scotch", distilled and bottled in the back streets and labelled as genuine Johnny Walker or Black & White and sold in the 'dives'.

The papers reported "Four more Americans are "seriously ill" and seventy others "very ill" in the local hospital."

There was also considerable risk in drinking mineral waters, tea and coffee because of the polluted water in the colony which resulted in a great deal of cholera and typhoid in the area.

I requested to see the Captain to jog his memory about my going to Pension in September. He said, "We shall be going down to Sydney for docking and refit at the end of the month and I'll see if you can leave from there, but if not I'll see if I can get you away as soon as we return to Hong Kong at the end of July."

I said I hoped to be at home by then so he conferred with his Secretary as to 'Normal procedures in these circumstances' and was told that it was usual in peacetime for men to spend their final year in Home Waters and in the normal course of events I would not have been sent to the ship, having less than two years to complete at that time.

The Captain then asked the Senior if I could be spared without relief to which he replied, "Only if it was for a very short time because he is very valuable here owing to the high percentage of junior ratings in the ship." The Captain said, "Well, there's your answer, chief. We'll do the best we can and I will send a letter to Chatham Barracks to hurry your relief." I felt I was making some progress, but later in the day felt rather sorry for the Captain and for causing him further harassment on top of his other worries. I was making out the Monthly Fuel Consumption Report when the Senior came for a talk and he had the same sympathetic feeling for the Skipper who he said had spent two whole days listening to the evidence and pleadings in the main case before him — that of the three men who had beaten and robbed the shop-owners in Saigon — and of other equally serious offences by other members of the crew, and adding "Stoker '— — — —' was brought aboard under escort at 10 o'clock this morning. Should have returned at 11.30 last night but was picked up 'drunk and disorderly' and fought the Shore Patrol. He is still cooling-off in the cells and I understand there are further charges pending. What fools these chaps are! The cases of those other three were referred to the C. in C. for sentence and each got 90-days Detention. A signal has gone to Admiralty to 'Stop Allotment of Pay' to the wife of the only married one of the trio, so it is his wife and family who will suffer too!"

And I had been pestering the Captain about going home!

On May 4th Chiefs and P.O's were invited aboard the American aircraft carrier *Antietum* for a movie show and when the film ended at 7.30 Fred Barratt and I were invited by some of the pilots to the Briefing-room — large and air-conditioned with big and comfortable easy-chairs, an automatic gramophone diffusing pleasant music.

Waiters brought giant ice-cream sodas and biscuits for us as we sat talking for an hour, and one of the comments by our host was, "It's a grand thing, and our fellers sure appreciate all that you British are doing for us here!"

It appeared that all Naval transport on shore had been assigned to take the Yanks sight-seeing round the islands during their stay and they had also been given the use of "the Amenities ship, *Amestheus*" our friend added, saying, "We're very impressed with the beer, the concerts, and the movies. They're just great!"

So — we *had* been able to entertain the Americans after all, but that was our first knowledge of the "Amenities ship" although we could see a 'stranger' lying in the harbour and had wondered who, and what, she was.

Fred and I joined the party invited to *Antietum*'s ENSA concert the next evening but when our boat arrived alongside the carrier at 7.30 we were told the show was cancelled. No reason was given and we returned to our own ship. Next morning the 57th Task Force steamed out of harbour and in the afternoon all their planes — about a hundred fighters and torpedo-bombers — flew over us in close formation as a Farewell salute. It was an impressive sight.

The Americans having departed we could now avail ourselves of the amenities although it was rumoured that *Amestheus* was about to be returned to her owners. She had been borrowed by the Admiralty and converted for her present usage and contracted until six-months after the end of the war, but the war ended just as she was ready to assume her role so the contract was extended to nine months — which accounted for her still being 'on station'.

For this first week *Euryalus* was allotted two 'benefit' evenings — Monday and Tuesday — with a maximum quota of 55-men per day, the numbers to be made up as 35-junior ratings, 15-Ch. and P.O's and 5-Officers, — the names of those wishing to go were to be handed-in to the Commander's Office by 1 p.m. on the day.

The allocation for our Mess was three but no names appeared on the list by dinner-time and when I asked if anyone wanted to go the reply was, "No, thank you!" I put my name on the list and both Fred and Tom added theirs. That was our quota anyway. Others then said, "If it's all right and worth going over they would go tomorrow."

There were just 35 of us in the boat when it was ready to leave at 6.30 — 20-junior ratings, 10-C. & P.O's and five officers — so the boat was held alongside while messengers were sent to all messes to see if more men wished to go — to complete our quota. No!

Amestheus was a lovely ship and we could quite understand the Yanks' enthusiasm. We three were entertained to a complete tour and found her appointments luxurious with lounges for all categories together with Reading- and Writing-rooms, restaurants, snack-bars and hot-and-cold buffets; the Information Desk, a Library, shops for the sale of clothing, toiletries, stationery, confectionery, and a Boot-repairer's workshop. There was a Church, and a Chapel, and on top deck a large and comfortable Cinema with the latest, most up-to-date film showing. *And* there was English beer on sale at nine-pence a pint, brewed on the ship and the very best we had tasted since leaving England.

The whole evening — the walk round the ship, the choice hot meal — the splendid film and the succulent beverage — all proved as good as a run-ashore as could have been enjoyed in any civilized place. She would have been a boon at Manus.

Next evening everybody in the Mess — every one in the ship — wanted to go to *Amestheus*! More than 300-names had to be put into hats or mess-kettles to be drawn and to satisfy the quota, and there was plenty of disappointment, annoyance, and even anger, among those who 'wished they had gone last night!'

And while placating the losers in my Mess — explaining that there were no strings I was able to pull which would get them a sample of 'amenities', — the chief Mechanician and the 1st Class Mechanician (the most senior two of the four we carried) asked me to sign their "Leaving-the-ship" chits — "We're going home on the *Venerable* — (a light aircraft-carrier) tomorrow." This was my first intimation of their leaving and on checking with the Senior he confirmed they would be going without reliefs — on compassionate grounds.

That meant an even higher percentage of juniors in the Department and also that they were the third and fourth Mechs to leave on the same 'grounds' since the start of the commission in June, 1944, in Glasgow; the first, as I handed him his Commissioning-card said, "Don't trouble about that, chief. I won't be here five minutes!' He wasn't.

The Chief now leaving had been 'made up' in the ship when we arrived in Sydney in February, 1945, to replace the then Chief who had been called home on our arrival.

Now the Release papers came for two more of the senior members of my Mess and as *Venerable* had been weather-bound for 24-hours they were able to rush about and pack their kits and sail with her and in their places we received — from some other ship in harbour — one 5th Class who was still under training!

The imbalance of staff and lack of training or experience showed itself to some effect as we sailed from Hong Kong at 9 a.m. on May 11th. I was at my regular station in one engine-room for manoeuvring when there was a panic in one boiler-room as one of the boilers could not hold its water-level. The Senior hurried to the scene and gave orders for it to be shut down and another boiler to be flashed-up in its place.

When the ship was clear of harbour I was called into conference in the Engineers' Office where the blue prints of the Automatic Boiler Feed Regulator — known as the 'Robot' — were spread out with half-a-dozen engineers poring over them. I was told the robot had been refitted just two days before and "Is it possible for it to be put back in such a way that it would not operate?"

"It *is* possible, but the mistake would soon be realised when the fitter came to test it by hand", which was normal routine because of that possibility. The Senior said he had already questioned the chap who did the work and had been assured that it functioned properly when hand-tested — "but the fact remains that it will not work now!"

We went below to open up the robot, the Commander (E) being the first on the scene in order not to miss a trick and as the boiler had only just been isolated it was very hot work, but as soon as the covers were removed it was obvious why it would not operate. A vital component had been replaced upside-down making it impossible for the testing lever to have even been moved, let alone used!

The fault was rectified and the boiler re-connected within a few hours while blame was apportioned between inexperienced staff and lack of supervision on the part of the chief boilermaker, although he for the past more-than-48-hours had been, and in fact still was, engaged in re-tubing another boiler because of negligence by a member of his staff during recent boiler-cleaning.

Of course, it could have been general malevolence as anything was possible at that time, but I recalled my experience of allowing an apprentice to box-up an underwater valve while I continued 'sighting' the tubes in a cleaned boiler aboard *Abdiel* in 1931 (Page 46) and what could have ensued for me.

We wondered whether other ships on the station were suffering.

Now we were on our way through the South China Sea, passing the Philippines and during succeeding days steaming through (if not the Seven Seas at least five of the smaller ones) the Sulu, Celebes, Molucca, Ceram and Banda seas — placid waters dotted with hundreds of tropical islands.

On Friday, May 17th we anchored off Darwin in Australia's Northern Territory and leave was piped from 4 p.m. until 10 p.m. but there were few takers because the Quartermaster had added, "There is no beer, and food is in very short supply!" I received confirmation of that when yet another 5th Class E.R.A. joined the Mess.

He had arrived in Darwin five days earlier aboard a small transport — *Ping Wo* (maximum speed 9-knots) — after a five-weeks voyage from Sydney, and she left port the previous day to continue her journey with reliefs for other ships still in Hong Kong where she was to be returned to her rightful owners.

Our new boy said there was absolutely nothing ashore as the entire population had been evacuated for the duration of the war and only just allowed back to their homes. "There is only one street, about fifty-yards long with two stores and one hotel — where I had to stay for the night, and the food is expensive at five shillings for each course. There is dust everywhere and it is a real scorcher!"

We sailed at 7 o'clock next morning and two hours later received an S.O.S. from *Ping Wo* saying she had an acute appendicitis case and required medical assistance.

269

Increasing to full speed we overhauled her at 2 p.m. and both ships hove to. We fired a line to her followed by a wire and then the patient was hauled across lashed to a wooden tray supported by a pulley on the wire. *Ping Wo*'s doctor and his attendent followed separately by bo'sun's chair to assist our doctor and his staff in the operation while both ships remained hove-to.

The operation was completed by 5 p.m. and the P W's doctor and aide returned home by chair and she turned to steam northward (so slowly!) as we continued our easterly course with the patient comfortable in the Sick Bay.

"The best laid schemes o' mice an' men . . ."

We had intended to carry out Fuel Consumption Trials en route 'Darwin to Sydney' by running on one boiler-room and one set of engines at a constant speed for a certain number of hours and then run at that same speed for the same length of time using both sets of engines and both boiler-rooms, and that sequence was to be followed by others at different revolutions but over the same periods. It was a pattern which would seriously disrupt a permanent Watch-bill so I had to devise a scheme which, while allowing the watchkeepers to switch from a 3-watch 'bill' when all boilers and engines were in use to a 4-watch 'bill' when only half the members were required below without anyone having to suffer at the change-over by working a double set of long, or night, watches. The system would have run smoothly and on Friday evening the Senior had said, "We'll leave harbour on both engine-rooms as normal in the morning and as soon as we are clear have them shut down one boiler-room and engine-room and start the trials."

The S.O.S. put paid to our plans and the minute the appendix was safely removed the rumours began to fly! "We're taking him back to Darwin" — "We're going at full speed to Brisbane" — or Cairns — or Cooktown — or "We've got to get him to Sydney" and "We arrive on Monday — Tuesday — or Wednesday — and will be staying a day — or two days" and "will" — or "won't" — arrive in Sydney before our 'due' date."

We steamed steadily eastwards crossing the Gulf of Carpentaria on Sunday in some of the worst weather experienced since leaving the U.K. It was worse than any typhoon and most of the crew went down with sea-sickness as the ship was battered by the mountainous waves — not a dry spot anywhere as we rolled continuously 35-degrees either way and most difficult to keep ones feet or to move about.

I ventured up to the bridge during the afternoon to see the turmoil of the waters, the tremendous waves crashing over the tops of the three forward turrets and the spray high above the mast-head. All bridge personnel were wearing oilskins and sou'westers — so different to the dress and conditions of past weeks. I had seen enough. Back down below no one wanted to talk

270

or even move. It was like a ghost-ship and the only sound was the thunderous crashing of the pounding waves. The best place to be was in one's hammock but there were watches to be kept — clinging tightly to valves and hand-rails as the ship lay on her beam-ends.

We thought — and spoke — of the patient in his cot and hoped he was comfortable, a somewhat forlorn hope in the existing conditions. It was easier on Monday after passing Thursday Island and turning southwards inside the Great Barrier Reef to anchor at 7 p.m. in Lloyd Bay, it being too hazardous to move in those restricted waters during the hours of darkness but the weather was still boisterous so that steam had to be kept on main engines until we moved again at 6 a.m. It became progressively calmer and cooler as we steamed southwards within the 'Reef'.

Then the "Phantom" struck again, with not a sampan in sight and no possible outside agency to take the blame this time!

We were carrying quite a number of passengers, mostly Australian Naval ratings on their way home from Hong Kong and one who was to be married when we arrived in Sydney had his suitcase stolen even as the ship steamed along. It held his personal papers, £50 cash and presents, but despite a search of lockers no trace of case or contents were found. The Captain broadcast over the Tannoy system asking everyone in the ship to be alert and try to catch the thief.

It was quite mysterious because throughout each night Damage Control Parties made hourly patrols to ensure all watertight doors and hatches were kept shut and secured at all times in case the Japanese had mined the coastal waters, and the only people who would be aware of the gifts and the money would have been his fellows and his messmates in the immediate vicinity of the 'open' mess. What kind of men are they who steal from comrades — people with whom they live and work every day?

The Defect List I began compiling in Hong Kong was now complete and I was making 'fair copies' ready to be forwarded to Cockatoo Island Dockyard when the Commander (E) came into the office with the draft of his covering letter to the Dockyard Engineer for me to type and we spoke about the extremely high number of defects on the List.

Then he said, "I don't know what we're going to do when you go, chief," but I did not take the bait and volunteer to remain with the ship until she returned home.

On the day before arriving at Sydney we carried out an abridged version of the Fuel Consumption Trials and it was most hectic trying to cram everything of our original programme into this shorter period. I doubted it gave a true reflection of what the 'powers that be' were seeking but we kept at it through the night until entering harbour on Saturday morning when all the paper-work had to be done. (An ambulance awaited our arrival and our patient was able to leave us).

271

Restricted shore-leave allowed me to fulfil a promise and deliver a personal letter and small parcel from an old *Ajax* (1942) messmate — Peter Henley, now serving in the sloop *Crane* in Hong Kong, — to his Australian wife at her North Sydney home.

Our leave was restricted as we were going to sea again at 6 o'clock next (Sunday) morning to carry out a pre-docking Full PowerTrial, during which the poor old gal could manage just 29-knots, almost shaking herself to pieces with the effort and throwing up lots more defects to be added to the list at the end of the day.

The ship moved to the Cockatoo Island Dock on May 29th and another very busy period, especially for the Engineering Department, began. All jobs had to be closed-up at the end of each day entailing late working on most evenings and thus restricting opportunities for shore-going as being an island it was necessary to rely on the liberty-boat and for many who worked late it was too much hassle to get cleaned and dressed.

I had another interesting experience when my Eastwood friend, Mr. Cragg the Chief Inspector of Signalling, N.S.W. State Railways, invited me on a tour of the Suburban network, travelling in great comfort in the special coach to meet the people manning the boxes at Strathfield, Ryde, Canterbury, Chilloon, and observing the intricacies of the controlling systems on the very busy tracks.

As I was going ashore that afternoon the Senior had said, "You might be going home about the 10th (June)" Was something happening at last? But it was only a 'maybe' — and no relief was apparent yet. Then, on the next day confirmation came — "Be ready to leave the ship at 0930 on Friday, June 7th!"

Now it was my turn to get Clearance chits signed, pack my kit and tools and also to turn all Mess Books and papers over to Fred.

My feelings were mixed. It would have been nice to have taken the ship home from a completed commission but I doubted the Service would have appreciated any sacrifice made although I still felt I was letting them down, — to get on as best they can!

While packing I received a chit from the Commander: "Could I attend the Ward-room at 6.30 p.m?" I thought it might be a hoax, but when I saw the Senior at 4 p.m. he said, "I hope you had not arranged to go ashore early this evening as there is a little Party in the Ward-room". Our three Warrant Engineers had also been invited and the Party ended as the Ward Room Officers filed in to dinner at 7.30. I did not go ashore!

CHAPTER 32

Finale

At 0900 on Friday, June 7th the ship's motor-boat returned from her first morning trip bringing my relief who had arrived from U.K. the night before aboard *Indefatigable* and I had the barest time to welcome and introduce him to Fred and Tom "who will give you all the help you need" before I was called to the gangway. There were hurried 'Good-byes' and 'Hope to see you all safely at home soon' for the mess-mates who came to the guard-rail as the boat's crew eased her away, and my time in *Euryalus* ended at 9.30 that morning.

Transport met me at Circular Quay and at the Naval Depot, *Golden Hind IV*, in the Domain, I was told to see my kit safely on board the aircraft-carrier and return to the Depot for my food and accommodation while she re-fuelled and re-victualled. I was then free to pay my final visit to Eastwood and say "Farewell" and thank Mr. And Mrs. Cragg for their kindness and hospitality, and at 10 a.m. on Sunday, 9th I boarded *Indefatigable* along with some 2,000 other 'passengers' — Navy, Army and R.A.F. and quite a large number of females (W.R.N.S. and nurses from all three Services) — all Homeward bound.

We sailed at 4.30 p.m. — a very happy crowd, but nothing like the festive atmosphere of that November, 1945 evening, — just a great feeling to know we were on our way home.

I was soon found employment in the main Machine-shop but work for the majority was impossible so their time was passed in sporting activities on the flight-deck, or in one of the hangars if wind and rain were too bad. All women were segregated and kept to their own part of the ship and at night were guarded by Royal Marine sentries; they even had their afternoon or evening film-shows in the lower hangar at different times to the rest of the company, and when the weather started to warm up and it was too hot to stay below decks the only restful entertainment was to listen to gramophone records on the flight-deck — where the females were still 'roped-off'. The authorities were certainly taking no chances nor giving opportunities for Romance.

We anchored off Fremantle on Friday afternoon to oil from a tanker and sailed again at 8 o'clock next morning, June 15th, only to turn back an hour later when a stowaway was found on board. The slight delay caused some annoyance as people thought it might put back our time of arrival in U.K. by even a few hours.

Passage across the Indian Ocean to Aden was fairly rough, causing some discomfort especially amongst those who had been shore-based in Australia.

Neptune was ignored when we crossed the Line at 0440 on Sunday (23rd) and the heat was quite gruesome when the ship anchored off Aden for a few hours on the 26th to take in more fuel; it was even hotter on passage through the Red Sea with not a cool spot anywhere in the ship but no one seemed to mind for they knew we were moving, and that every hour — every minute and every turn of the screws took them closer to home.

At Suez on the 29th the pilot boarded to take us through the Canal and, it being a Saturday most of the crew and practically all passengers spent the day on the flight-deck watching the Egyptians on the banks watching us steam past, and at Port Said the pilot was dropped off without the ship stopping. Then we were on our way through the Med towards Malta, getting much cooler now but not cool enough to quell the amorous (lecherous?) designs of some one who managed to breach strict security on Sunday night and assault three members of the W.R.N.S. in their cabin, so that during the forenoon of Monday, July 1st every man in the ship except those actually on watch had to muster for an identity-parade on the flight-deck and the three young ladies walked in front of us looking at faces and peering into the eyes of every one. I do not know whether they were successful but there must have been about 4,000 faces to scan.

At 4 p.m. *Indefatigable* entered Grand Harbour at Valetta, Malta, for just one hour — long enough to embark a few more passengers for Blighty, — and my thoughts went back to the peaceful days of 1930 and 1931, and the mad times of 1941 and 1942. How different!

Now a Sports' Day was organised for the morrow, with 'sprint' and 'relay' races on the flight-deck, and some 'jumping' and 'throwing' events but owing to the exuberance and the excitement being engendered by the approaching end of the voyage the whole thing was just a 'skylark'. At Gibraltar on July 4th a few more passengers joined us for the final leg and we took in more oil to roll our way across Biscay, entering Plymouth Sound during the afternoon of Sunday, July 7th where a tender met the ship to take off the West Country contingent, then at 9 p.m. we steamed out into the Channel for the final few miles of a long voyage and enter Portsmouth Harbour at 8 a.m. on Monday, 8th.

Customs Officers swarmed aboard immediately the ship had secured at South Railway Jetty in the Dockyard, checking all the goodies and collecting any Duty payable and at 5 p.m. the Chatham draft — approximately 150 men — marched in to *Victory* (barracks) to board the special train for our barracks (*Pembroke*) at Chatham.

The locomotive broke down near Wimbledon station about eight miles outside London leaving us marooned for more than an hour awaiting a relief. Men who lived — or had relatives or friends — in the London area wanted to drop onto the tracks and make their ways there with promises of "We'll report at the Barracks at eight in the morning!" but were ordered to stay with the train which eventually drew up at the Barrack Gate in Chatham Dockyard at 2 a.m. on Tuesday, July 9th.

It was a very weary party which straggled through the gates to be mustered in the Drill shed — (Nobody missing!) — before being allowed to proceed to their respective messes with the hopes of finding some place — chair — stool — mess-table or even billiards-table — anywhere to grab a little 'shut-eye'.

What a home-coming!

But at 8 a.m. all were running about doing a rapid Joining Routine followed by a speedy stowing of kits and hammocks into the Long Leave Store, then to the Cashier's Office for pay and the issue of Leave Passes — everyone hurrying here, there and everywhere and not a moan anywhere. The amount of leave granted depended on the length of time spent away from the U.K. and generally worked out at 14-days for each complete year plus one day for each month over. I went ashore for 28-days — a much better home-coming.

Returning on August 7th I was given charge of working-parties helping in the re-fit of the cruiser *Suffolk* — a sinecure — marching the party from the barracks to the ship at 9 o'clock each morning and allocating their jobs; checking and supervising and being on hand when any testing had to be done, and march them back into the Depot at 3.30 p.m. when I was then free to go ashore until 8 o'clock the next morning. It was my final job of work in the Royal Navy and on September 13th I was given 14-days Pension Leave from which I returned on Monday, September 30th, 1946 — my 40th birthday — to get my release into civilian life.

A Medical Examination to make sure no Hurt Certificate was needed — and therefore no Pension supplement — and get 'clearance' from various departments and the Mess President, then collect a "De-mob suit and Pork-pie hat" from the Clothing Store, and at noon I walked through the barrack Gate for the last time.

I had been lucky — with my ships and stations — throughout my time in the Royal Navy. Now I had to start a new career — in Civvy Street.

★   ★   ★

Gurr Crescent. Town of Ajax, Ontario, Canada. December 9th 1991.

APPENDIX A

The town of Ajax on the shores of Lake Ontario, Canada, was named in honour of our ship two years after the Battle of the River Plate. The town, now a small city of some 60,000 people, had previously been known as Pickering Township comprising a number of farms until in 1939 the Canadian government set up the biggest shell-filling plant in the British Empire. The town has adopted the Crest of *Ajax* as its official Badge, and all the new streets and thoroughfares bear the names of every member of the crews of *Ajax*, *Exeter*, and *Achilles*.

APPENDIX B

Volunteering (Pps 50, 51 and 107.)

In 1985 I met another of my *Fisgard* class-mates who told me he had been drafted "Advance Party" to *Cumberland* in July 1932, to meet her at Colombo and steam her back to Chatham for refit and then re-commission for further service in China. He too was a Fitter and Turner and this is his story:

"The 'trooping' trip was done by the old (1917) cruiser *Caradoc* of 4180-tons with a skeleton crew and was carrying relief half-crews for sloops attached to the East Indies squadron and for the destroyers of the China Fleet and for the numerous gunboats serving on the rivers of China, plus a considerable number for *Cumberland*, so the cruiser had many times the number of her normal complement. Every one had to be gainfully employed in working the ship and on general maintenance and it was purgatory living from suit-cases and kit-bags for weeks and taking meals at one of the several sittings required for each. Then there was the difficulty of finding somewhere to sleep in the over-crowded messes and gangways and coping with the heat, especially through the Red Sea and Indian Ocean. I tell you, we were most happy to be leaving her at Colombo and thankful not to be going all the way to Wei Hei Wei, her final destination. But it was worse for *Caradoc*'s steaming party who had to do the round trip. I dreaded the thought of ever doing another 'trooping' trip!"

That made me wonder. What if *I* had volunteered as my chums had suggested! Would that have been *me* and *my* story? Would our careers have been reversed and he have gone to *Dragon* and *Ajax*? And would — or *could* — I have survived the terrible experiences of the E.R.A. who went to Hong Kong with *Scout*? (Page 234).

Who knows?

And what if 'Bill' of Ajax had not 'volunteered himself to leave *Ajax* in my stead in October, 1938? Would *I* have been the one to lose a leg in 1940?

Who knows?

APPENDIX C

Re "JACK" — Page 77

A letter I wrote for publication in the October 1985 edition of *Navy News* asking if anyone knew the fate of the black Labrador which served in *Dragon* throughout our 1932 to 1935 commission elicited three (published) replies.

Two were from shipmates who quoted U.K. Quarantine regulations and the uncertainty of *Dragon*'s future and reported that Jack had been left in the Dockyard at Bermuda in the hope that another cruiser would adopt him.

The third letter, published in March, 1986, came from ex-Colour Sergeant R.W. Evans, R.M., who had served in *Dragon* during her following — and final — commission in the West Indies (1935 to 1937). He stated that Jack had rejoined the ship as soon as they reached Bermuda and had subsequently died on board while the ship was at Kingston, Jamaica. "He was given a real sailor's funeral, sewn up in canvas, weighted down, and 'buried at sea' in the middle of Kingston Harbour."

I am sure that other "Dragon's" — and others from "ships in company" — were happy to know of Jack's worthy end, and a considerate and fitting "Farewell" to a loyal and faithful animal.

APPENDIX D

Euryalus comes home.

On Monday, February 17th 1947 *Euryalus* arrived at Sheerness in the coldest weather experienced in the country for seven years. Snow had been falling and freezing and fuel supplies were drastically restricted. The ship came up river to Chatham on the 19th and I took time off from my position as Maintenance Engineer at Church House, Westminster, to go on board. Fred and Tom greeted me with a brief account of visits to New Zealand and Japan after leaving Sydney and said morale did not improve at all, and that one member of the Mess had nearly died after being stabbed while on shore in Tokyo. I had drinks in the Wardroom and attended at the Warrant Officers Farewell Party in their Mess the following evening. Every one I met was thankful that the Commission was behind them now and looked forward to Paying Off.

INDEX

284